Jewish Soldiers in Nazi Captivity

Jewish Soldiers in Nazi Captivity

American and British Prisoners of War during the Second World War

YORAI LINENBERG

Great Clarendon Street, Oxford, OX2 6DP,
United Kingdom

Oxford University Press is a department of the University of Oxford.
It furthers the University's objective of excellence in research, scholarship,
and education by publishing worldwide. Oxford is a registered trade mark of
Oxford University Press in the UK and in certain other countries

© Yorai Linenberg 2023

The moral rights of the author have been asserted

All rights reserved. No part of this publication may be reproduced, stored in
a retrieval system, or transmitted, in any form or by any means, without the
prior permission in writing of Oxford University Press, or as expressly permitted
by law, by licence or under terms agreed with the appropriate reprographics
rights organization. Enquiries concerning reproduction outside the scope of the
above should be sent to the Rights Department, Oxford University Press, at the
address above

You must not circulate this work in any other form
and you must impose this same condition on any acquirer

Published in the United States of America by Oxford University Press
198 Madison Avenue, New York, NY 10016, United States of America

British Library Cataloguing in Publication Data

Data available

Library of Congress Control Number: 2023942450

ISBN 978–0–19–889278–6

DOI: 10.1093/oso/9780198892786.001.0001

Printed and bound by
CPI Group (UK) Ltd, Croydon, CR0 4YY

Links to third party websites are provided by Oxford in good faith and
for information only. Oxford disclaims any responsibility for the materials
contained in any third party website referenced in this work.

To Milka, Omer, Inbar, and Daphni

Acknowledgements

This book is based on my doctoral dissertation which was submitted in 2021 to the London School of Economics and Political Science.

I am indebted to the scholars who engaged in this topic before me, and to two of them in particular: Yoav Gelber, whose early research on the captivity experience of Palestinian Jewish POWs was the first to deal with this topic in depth; and Rüdiger Overmans, whose research provided me with valuable insight into the German POW policies during the Second World War.

The research for this book took me to many archives around the world, and in all of them I was assisted by professional and friendly staff. Special mention is due however to Fabrizio Bensi, the archivist of the International Committee of the Red Cross archive in Geneva, who pointed me to the folder that held all the documents that dealt with Jewish POWs during the Second World War.

Special thanks are due to Yehuda Shefer and Yosef Shaked, who shared with me their research on the experience of their POW fathers, both of whom joined the British Army in Palestine and were held in Stalag VIII-B (Lamsdorf)—the POW card that appears on the front cover is of Shefer's father, Paul Fischer. Their contribution—especially by pointing me to the location of the Stalag's archive in Prague—has been enormously helpful. I would also like to thank Jens Binner, who shared with me the story of the Polish-Jewish POW Ignaz Hecht, which he presented at the conference 'Aspekte jüdischer Geschichte in Niedersachsen. Lager—Zwangsarbeit—Deportation 1938 bis 1945', 1 November 2012, Hannover.

Chapter 3 of this book incorporates a few sections that appeared previously in my article 'German Captors, Jewish POWs: Segregation of American and British Jewish POWs in German Captivity in the Second World War', which was published in the *Holocaust and Genocide Studies Journal*. I would like to thank the editors of the Journal for their permission to use this material.

The feedback I received from my external thesis examiners, Omer Bartov and Neville Wylie, was extremely helpful in turning my dissertation into this book and in identifying areas that required additional research and emphasis. Their own research—on the motivation of the German soldiers (Bartov) and on the British POW policy (Wylie)—also served me greatly in substantiating some of my conclusions.

In addition to pointing out errors in the original manuscript, the feedback and comments I had from the readers and editors of Oxford University Press have greatly benefited this book and helped in making it more clear and readable. Any remaining errors are, of course, my own responsibility.

And finally, my heartfelt thanks to my former PhD supervisors, Heather Jones and David Motadel, whose professional guidance, mentoring, and support over the past few years have been absolutely invaluable.

London,
March 2023

Contents

List of Acronyms	xi
List of Figures	xiii
Introduction	1
POWs in German Hands—the Numbers	3
Historiographic Review	7
Current Explanations for the Treatment of Jewish POWs	17
Primary Sources Review	22
The German POW Organization	27
Summary	36
1. American and British Jewish POWs in German POW Camps	39
Introduction	39
Capture and Transit	42
In the Camp	56
Outside the Camp	85
Conclusion	94
2. Being a Jewish Soldier in Nazi Captivity	102
Introduction	102
Capture	105
Palestinian Jewish Identity in German POW Camps	111
Segregation	115
Transnational Jewish Identity: The Encounter with Holocaust Victims	117
Religious and Cultural Activity	121
Funerals	127
Conclusion	135
3. Segregation of American and British Jewish POWs	139
Introduction	139
Segregation in the Geneva Convention and OKW Orders	141
POW Camps under the Wehrmacht: Initial Segregation Cases	146
POW Camps under Himmler: Segregations in 1945	157
Identifying Jewish POWs	168
International Reaction to Segregation	171
Conclusion	177
4. Why Were They Kept Alive? Explaining the Nazi Treatment of Jewish POWs	181
Introduction	181
The Commander-in-Chief: Hitler	185

The Oberkommando der Wehrmacht (OKW)   189
Interaction between the RSHA and the NSDAP and the Wehrmacht   195
The Kriegsgefangenenwesen (POW Office)   203
Explaining the Fate of Non-Soviet Jewish POWs   213
Conclusion   228

Conclusion   232

Appendix A: Sample of POW Commanders and Camp Commandants   243
Bibliography   251
Index   261

List of Acronyms

ACICR	International Committee of the Red Cross Archive
AFRHA	US Airforce Historical Research Agency
AFS	Swiss Federal Archives
AGSSt	Armee Gefangenen sammelstelle (Army Prisoner Collection Point)
ANZAC	Australian and New Zealand Army Corps
ARC	American Red Cross
AWA	Allgemeines Wehrmachtsamt (the OKW's General Office)
BA	Bundesarchiv
BA-MA	Bundesarchiv-Militärarchiv
BRC	British Red Cross
Btn	Battalion
CHAR	The Churchill Archive
COS	Chiefs of Staff
FRUS	Foreign Relations of the United States
HSSPF	Höherer SS- und Polizeiführer (Higher SS and Police Leaders)
ICRC	International Committee of the Red Cross
IDF	Israel Defence Force Archive
IMT	International Military Tribunal
IWM	Imperial War Museum Archive
JC	Jewish Chronicle
JISC	Joint Intelligence Sub Committee
JMM	Jewish Military Museum Archive
JTA	Jewish Telegraphic Agency
LMA	London Metropolitan Archive
Ln	Location
MOC	Man of Confidence
NARA	National Archives and Record Administration
NCO	Non-Commissioned Officer
NSDAP	Nationalsozialistische Deutsche Arbeiterpartei (the Nazi Party)
NSFO	Nationalsozialistischer Führungsoffizier (National Socialist Leadership Officers programme)
OKH	Oberkommando des Heeres (Army High Command)
OKW	Oberkommando der Wehrmacht (Armed Forces High Command)
OR	Other Ranks (i.e. not officers or NCOs)
PAAA	Politisches Archiv des Auswärtigen Amt
PMA	Prague Military Archive
POW	Prisoner of War
RAF	Royal Air Force

RSHA	Reichssicherheitshauptamt (Reich Security Main Office)
RSM	Regimental Sergeant Major
SA	Sturmabteilung (Storm Detachment)
SAO	Senior American Officer
SBO	Senior British Officer
SD	Sicherheitsdienst (Security Services)
SS	Schutzstaffel (Protection Squad)
TNA	The National Archives
USHMM	US Holocaust Memorial Museum Archive
WJC	World Jewish Congress
YVA	Yad Vashem Archive

List of Figures

1. Map of POW camps inside the Reich   30
2. Map of a typical POW camp   31
3. The Wehrmacht POW Organization structure 1939–January 1942   33
4. The Wehrmacht POW Organization structure January 1942–September 1944   34
5. The Wehrmacht POW Organization structure from October 1944   35

Introduction

> As I got nearer to the desks I could hear the questions being asked of the men in front of me...when it came to religion, lying seemed the safe thing to do. I hadn't heard [any other POW] admit to being Jewish. But I didn't care. In my mind I said, 'F**k you!' I was young, angry, and by any measure stupid. I answered, 'Jewish.'[1]

This is how Milton Feldman, a 19-year-old American infantry soldier who fought with the 106th division and was captured in December 1944 in the Ardennes, described his interrogation upon arrival in Stalag IV-B near Mühlberg in Germany. Since Nazi ideology considered Jews to be a separate 'race', which it defined as a group with heritable social and cultural characteristics that were 'innate, indelible, and unchangeable', and in view of what was already known by that stage of the war about Germany's murderous policies against Jews, Feldman's concern—although not his eventual reaction—was well founded.[2] Polish Jewish Prisoners of War (POWs) were segregated upon capture and mistreated; Yugoslavian Jewish POWs were in some cases shot after their surrender by their Croatian ex-brothers-in-arms; French Jewish POWs were segregated in POW camps from their non-Jewish comrades; and the Einsatzgruppen, with the Wehrmacht's cooperation, combed POW camps immediately after the invasion of

---

[1] Milton Feldman and Seth Bauer, *Captured, Frozen, Starved—and Lucky: How One Jewish American GI Survived a Nazi Stalag* (Kindle Edition: CreateSpace Independent Publishing Platform, 2018), ln. 588.

[2] George M. Fredrickson, *Racism: A Short History* (Princeton and Oxford: Princeton University Press, 2015), p. 5. Throughout this book, the term 'race' is used in the meaning attributed to it at the time by the Nazis, i.e. as a biological category. This 'theory' was disproved during the second half of the twentieth century, when the concept of race as a social, not scientific, construct became dominant. Judaism today is usually defined as an ethnic, cultural, and religious identity rather than a racial one (for a discussion regarding the components of the Jewish identity see Chapter 2 of this book). For discussions around the evolution of the concept of 'race' and racism throughout history see, for example, Charles Hirschman, 'The Origins and Demise of the Concept of Race', *Population and Development Review*, 30:3 (2004), pp. 385–415; and Fredrickson, *Racism: A Short History*. An example of the changes in the general attitude towards the term 'race' can also be found in the differences between the 1929 Geneva Convention relative to the Treatment of Prisoners of War and its newer version from 1949: while Article 9 of the 1929 Convention allowed—in fact, encouraged—the Detaining Power to segregate POWs according to their race, the 1949 Convention disallowed any discrimination based on 'race, nationality, religious belief or political opinions'. The question of race, it was explained, was left outside the Convention due to the 'derogatory implication' of that term (see Timothy L. Schroer, 'The Emergence and Early Demise of Codified Racial Segregation of Prisoners of War under the Geneva Conventions of 1929 and 1949', *Journal of the History of International Law*, 15:1 (2013), pp. 53–76, and esp. p. 74).

the Soviet Union in order to select and execute Soviet commissars and Jewish POWs.[3] In parallel, Germany's racial and POW policies had gone through a radicalization process throughout the war, and the Reich Security Main Office—the *Reichssicherheitshauptamt* (RSHA)—kept pressuring to extend the 'Special Treatment' ('*Sonderbehandlung*') of Soviet Jewish POWs to all Jewish POWs held by Germany.[4]

However, when it came to American and British Jewish POWs, this research will demonstrate that cases of their discrimination and mistreatment were not as common, and they were treated, with very few exceptions, according to the 1929 Geneva Convention relative to the Treatment of Prisoners of War (the Geneva Convention). To put this in context, this was the same country that had breached the Treaty of Versailles, violated the Munich Agreement, and flouted the Molotov-Ribbentrop Pact; that starved to death and murdered millions of Soviet POWs; and whose ingrained anti-Semitism and extreme racial policies eventually led to the Holocaust.[5] And yet, in the case of American and British Jewish POWs—in fact, in the case of most non-Soviet Jewish POWs—Germany had decided to stick to its international commitments and to treat them in most cases in the same way their non-Jewish brothers-in-arms had been treated. The significance of this conclusion is that it challenges the accepted perception of the Final Solution as Germany's indiscriminate attempt during the Second World War to murder 'every last Jew in Europe upon whom they could lay their hands'.[6] Among the reasons

---

[3] For Polish Jewish POWs, see Shmuel Krakowski, 'The Fate of Jewish Prisoners of War in the September 1939 Campaign', *Yad Vashem Studies*, 12 (1977), pp. 297–333, pp. 299–300; Jewish Telegraphic Agency (JTA), 17 November 1939, 27 October 1940, and 28 January 1941, https://www.jta.org/archive, accessed 8 May 2019. For Yugoslav and French Jewish POWs see ICRC to American Red Cross, 24 April 1941, ACICR BG 25/34, and JTA, 18 November 1941, https://www.jta.org/archive, accessed 8 May 2019; German Foreign Office representative in Belgrade to Berlin, 26 November 1941, PAAA R40960; Zvi Asaria-Helfgot, *We Are Witnesses* (Tel Aviv: Yavne, 1970), p. 32; Testimony of Vladimir Mautner, YVA O.3–6645 p. 19; Irit Keynan, *Memories from a Life I Have Not Lived* (Tel Aviv: Pardes, 2020), p. 431; Yves Durand, *La Captivité* (Paris: Fédération Nationale des Combattants Prisonniers de Guerre et Combattants d'Algérie, Tunisie, Maroc, 1980), p. 354; *Le Combattant Volontaire Juif 1939–1945* (Paris: Imprimerie Abexpress, 1971), pp. 44 and 64. For the RSHA actions in the Soviet Union see Richtlinien für die in die Stalags und Dulags abzustellenden Kommandos des Chefs der Sicherheitspolizei und des SD, 17 July 1941, BA R58/9016; Christian Streit, 'The German Army and the Policies of Genocide', in Gerhard Hirschfeld, ed., *The Policies of Genocide, Jews and Soviet Prisoners of War in Nazi Germany* (New York and Abingdon: Routledge, 2015), pp. 1–14, p. 4; and Raul Hilberg, *The Destruction of the European Jews*, vol. I (New Haven and London: Yale University Press, 2003), pp. 346–53. See also JTA, 9 February 1942, 28 September 1942, and 8 April 1943, https://www.jta.org/archive, accessed 8 May 2019.

[4] Letter from Theodor Krafft, 10 August 1951, BA-MA MSG 2/12656.

[5] The Nazi approach to its legal obligations was made clear by Goebbels in a press conference held on 5 April 1940, where he declared publicly that '...our apparent loyalty to legalistic concepts was simply a smokescreen' (quoted in Hans-Adolf Jacobsen, 'The Kommissarbefehl and Mass Execution of Soviet Russian Prisoners of War', in Martin Broszat, Hans Buchheim, Hans-Adolf Jacobsen, and Helmut Krausnick, eds, *Anatomy of the SS State* (Cambridge: Walker and Company, 1968), pp. 505–35, p. 507).

[6] Christopher Browning, 'The Nazi Decision to Commit Mass Murder: Three Interpretations', *German Studies Review*, 17:3 (1994), pp. 473–81, p. 473.

explaining this was the behaviour of the *Oberkommando der Wehrmacht*'s (OKW) POW Office, which, unlike other organizations in the Reich and despite the pressure exerted on it by the RSHA, refused to 'work towards the Führer' in anticipating his will and in implementing Nazi policies without receiving specific orders to do so.[7]

This book explores the story of American and British Jewish POWs from two points of view: first, it will look at the experiences that American and British Jewish POWs had in German POW camps throughout their captivity lifecycle, and investigate the reasons why their immediate captors—including commandants, camp guards, and civilians who worked with the POWs—treated them the way they did; it will then address the question of how American and British Jewish POWs dealt with their Jewish identity throughout their captivity period. The second point of view will look at the bodies above the POW camps: it will review the reasons the orders to segregate Jewish POWs in POW camps from their non-Jewish comrades were not always followed in the case of the American and British Jewish POWs; and will look at explanations for why these POWs (and in fact, Jewish POWs from all western armies) were treated, in most cases, according to the Geneva Convention, despite the German obsession with applying 'The Final Solution for the Jewish Question' to all Jews in occupied Europe.

POWs in German Hands—the Numbers

The Second World War broke out on 1 September 1939 with the German invasion of Poland. By the end of the Polish campaign, approximately 450,000 Polish officers and other ranks were taken into German captivity.[8] By June 1940, the German victories in Western Europe resulted an additional 2.2 million soldiers becoming POWs of Germany. The largest group among them was that of the French, which numbered approximately 1.9 million (of which about 980,000 remained in Germany by the end of the war as a result of repatriations and escapes).[9] Belgian POWs numbered 225,000, although the Flemish among them,

---

[7] Ian Kershaw defines 'Working towards the Führer'—a term coined in 1934 by Werner Willikens, German state secretary in the ministry of food—as 'anticipation of Hitler's presumed wishes and intentions as "guidelines for action" in the certainty of approval and confirmation for actions which accorded with those wishes and intentions' (see Ian Kershaw, '"Working Towards the Führer." Reflections on the Nature of the Hitler Dictatorship', *Contemporary European History*, 2:2 (1993), pp. 103–18, pp. 116–17). Christopher Browning described how 'rival Nazi chieftains constantly sought to expand their private empires and vied for Hitler's favour through anticipating and pursuing Hitler's desires' (see Christopher Browning, *Fateful Months* (New York and London: Holmes & Meier, 1991), p. 16); and General Franz Halder, the army's chief-of-staff until September 1942, described how Hitler's casual remarks could bring his subordinates to give a 'factual expression to the will of the Führer' (see Jacobsen, 'The Kommissarbefehl and Mass Execution of Soviet Russian Prisoners of War', p. 516).

[8] The estimates of the number Polish POWs vary. For a discussion about their numbers see Bob Moore, *Prisoners of War* (Oxford: Oxford University Press, 2022), p. 28 and especially n. 7.

[9] Moore, *Prisoners of War*, pp. 61 and 87.

about half of the total, along with most of the soldiers from Norway and the Netherlands were released in the weeks and months after the end of the campaign.[10] POWs from the British Expeditionary Force in France—most of which was evacuated through Dunkirk—numbered approximately 40,000.[11]

In April 1941, Germany invaded Yugoslavia and Greece in order to secure its southern flank ahead of its invasion of the Soviet Union and to bail Italy out of its disastrous campaign in Greece. 350,000 Yugoslavian soldiers became POWs; by the summer of 1942, 130,000 of them, mostly Serbs, remained in German captivity, and the rest were released.[12] The Greek army surrendered on 23 April 1941, and all of its soldiers—with the exception of those who fought in Crete, whom the Germans claimed had been involved in mistreatment of German POWs—were freed from captivity by the end of May 1941.[13] About 11,000 Allied soldiers who participated in the Greek campaign—mostly British but also soldiers from Australia, New Zealand, India, Cyprus, and Palestine—were also taken into German captivity.[14]

The German invasion of the Soviet Union, in June 1941, resulted in the largest number of POWs from any one country taken into captivity. Between 1941 and 1945, it is estimated that between 5.35 and 5.75 million Soviet soldiers had become POWs.[15] The brutal treatment of these POWs, who Germany claimed were not entitled to the protection of the Geneva Convention, resulted in the deaths, by the end of the war, from executions, starvation, diseases, and cold, of 2.5–3.3 million POWs.[16]

---

[10] For the number of Belgian POWs see ibid., pp. 100–2; for the release of the Flemish POWs see *War Journal of Franz Halder* (English ed.), Document N-16845-B, Library section, Fort Leavenworth, KS, 28 May 1940, vol. 4, p. 40; for Norwegian POWs see Hitler's decree, 9 May 1940, in Martin Moll, *Führer-Erlasse 1939–1945* (Hamburg: Nikol Verlag, 2011), pp. 118–19; for the Dutch POWs see Rüdiger Overmans, 'Die Kriegsgefangenenpolitik des Deutschen Reichs 1939 bis 1945', in Jörg Echternkamp, ed., *Das Deutsche Reich und der Zweite Weltkrieg*, Band 9/2 (Munich: Deutsche Verlags-Anstalt, 2005), pp. 729–875, p. 756, and Hitler's decree, 1 June 1940, Moll, *Führer-Erlasse 1939–1945*, p. 122.

[11] Simon MacKenzie, *The Colditz Myth* (New York: Oxford University Press, 2004), p. 66; and Hugh Sebag-Montefiore, *Dunkirk, Fight to the Last Man* (London: Penguin, 2007), p. 538. The total number quoted by Sebag-Montefiore, 41,338, comprises missing in action as well as POWs.

[12] Overmans, 'Die Kriegsgefangenenpolitik des Deutschen Reichs 1939 bis 1945', p. 782.

[13] Moore, *Prisoners of War*, p. 287.

[14] Ibid., p. 306. MacKenzie's estimate was 12,000 (see MacKenzie, *The Colditz Myth*, p. 77).

[15] Overmans, 'Die Kriegsgefangenenpolitik des Deutschen Reichs 1939 bis 1945', p. 820.

[16] Overmans estimated the number of Soviet POWs who died in German captivity to be between 2.55–3.45 million (Overmans, 'Die Kriegsgefangenenpolitik des Deutschen Reichs 1939 bis 1945', p. 820); Alfred Streim's estimate is 2.545 million (Alfred Streim, *Sowjetische Gefangene in Hitlers Vernichtungskrieg* (Heidelberg: C. F. Müller Juristische Verlag, 1982), p. 178); the estimates of Hans-Adolf Jacobsen and Christian Streit are 3.3 million deaths (see Jacobsen, 'The Kommissarbefehl and Mass Execution of Soviet Russian Prisoners of War', p. 531; Christian Streit, *Keine Kameraden* (Stuttgart: Deutsche Verlags-Anstalt, 1978), pp. 244–6). For an analysis of the causes of the mass deaths of Soviet POWs see Christian Hartmann, *Wehrmacht im Ostkrieg* (Munich: R. Oldenbourg Verlag, 2009), pp. 586–608.

The campaigns in the West between 1942 and the end of the war in 1945—the Strategic Air campaign and the campaigns in North Africa, Italy, and Normandy— resulted in approximately 150,000 British—bringing their total number to about 200,000—and 95,000 Americans falling into German hands.[17] These included Allied POWs held in Italian POW camps, which, after Italy's surrender to the Allies in September 1943, were transferred to German hands. Over 600,000 of Italy's own soldiers—those who refused to continue and fight on Germany's side—were also taken into German captivity; initially designated as 'Italian Military Internees' (IMI), and later as civilian workers, they were not considered POWs and did not come under the protection of the Geneva Convention.[18]

It is estimated that towards the end of the war, more than 2 million Allied soldiers were still being held as POWs by Germany. The largest group was that of the Soviet POWs; the stark contrast between their treatment and the treatment of non-Soviet POWs has been attributed mainly to the National Socialist racial policies which considered the Slavs to be an inferior race. Whereas the Geneva Convention was generally adhered to when it came to non-Soviet POWs, the war in the East was launched as a war of extermination ('*Vernichtungskrieg*'), which meant that both sides left their own POWs to their fate.[19]

In total, approximately 200,000 Jewish soldiers were captured by Germany and its European allies during the Second World War. The majority of them were Soviet (85,000), Polish (60,000–65,000) and French Jews (55,000); and although exact numbers are not available, it can be assumed that there were also several hundred Jewish POWs from Yugoslavia, The Netherlands, Belgium, and probably less from Canada, South Africa, Australia, and New Zealand.[20]

This research focuses mainly on the experience of Jewish POWs from the USA and Britain. The reasons for this specific focus are both the availability of primary and secondary sources that describe their experience, in comparison to Jewish POWs from other nationalities; and the reciprocity factor, which, since the USA and Britain (along with Canada) were the only western countries holding large numbers of German POWs, contributed to some extent to the treatment of their POWs in accordance with the Geneva Convention.

---

[17] Aryeh Kochavi, *Confronting Captivity* (Chapel Hill and London: University of North Carolina Press, 2005), p. 1.
[18] Overmans, 'Die Kriegsgefangenenpolitik des Deutschen Reichs 1939 bis 1945', pp. 829 and 835.
[19] Overmans, 'Die Kriegsgefangenenpolitik des Deutschen Reichs 1939 bis 1945', p. 871.
[20] Shmuel Krakowski, 'Jewish Prisoners of War', in Israel Gutman, ed., *Encyclopedia* of the *Holocaust* (Tel Aviv: Hakibutz HaMe'uchad, 1990), pp. 1180–1; Mark Spoerer, 'Die soziale Differenzierung der ausländischen Zivilarbeiter, Kriegsgefangenen und Häftlinge im Deutschen Reich', in Jörg Echternkamp, ed., *Das Deutsche Reich und der Zweite Weltkrieg*, Band 9/2 (Munich, 2005), pp. 485–576, p. 505. Many Jewish Polish POWs, along with other categories of Polish POWs, were released from captivity between October 1939 and March 1940 due to the overcrowding of the POW camps (the remaining POWs were converted to civilian labour); the release of the Jewish POWs sealed, in effect, their fate as most of them were sent later to the concentration camps (see Overmans, 'Die Kriegsgefangenenpolitik des Deutschen Reichs 1939 bis 1945', pp. 745–7).

The total number of Jews in the British army during the Second World War, including the Jewish volunteers from Palestine, was approximately 95,000, and they accounted for 1.6% of the total number of British servicemen and women.[21] The number of British Jewish POWs in German captivity is estimated at 2,200, of whom approximately 700 came from the different arms of the British armed forces.[22] The remainder, approximately 1,500, were Jews from mandate Palestine who volunteered for the British army and served mainly in the Royal Pioneer Corps, where they formed the majority in some of the companies that were captured by the Wehrmacht in Greece in April 1941. Interestingly, more than 1,000 of them were Jewish refugees who had immigrated—some of them illegally—to Palestine from Europe in the years before the war as a result of Nazi oppression.[23]

On the American side, statistics compiled by the United States National Jewish Welfare Board estimate that there were approximately 550,000 Jews in the different branches of the United States' armed forces (3.4% of the total) during the Second World War, and 3,700 of them became POWs.[24] Unlike the British statistics, no breakdown between the European and Pacific theatres is available for them; however, by applying the ratio between the number of American POWs in German captivity and the total number of American POWs (approximately 95,000 out of 143,000), it can be estimated that about 2,500 American Jews were held as POWs by Germany.[25]

Although the total number of approximately 4,700 American and British Jewish POWs, which constituted about 1.6% of the total number of American and British POWs in German captivity, is only an estimate, and the actual numbers are probably slightly different, it is still sufficiently accurate for the purpose of this study. The records and testimonies related to these Jewish POWs provide broad insights into the German Jewish POW policies, the experience and treatment of Jewish POWs in German captivity, the level of Nazification and anti-Semitism within the Wehrmacht and specifically in its POW organization, and the level of the Wehrmacht's compliance with the 1929 Geneva Convention.

---

[21] Henry Moriss and Martin Sugarman, *We Will Remember Them* (Portland, OR and London: Vallentine Mitchell, 2011), pp. 3–4.

[22] Ibid., pp. 340–53.

[23] Simon to Majerozik, 16 April 1943, CZA S-25\4720. The letter stated that only 400 (out of 1,500–1,600) Palestinian Jewish POWs had relatives in Palestine.

[24] Louis Dublin and Samuel Kohs, *American Jews in World War II*, vol. 2 (New York: The Dial Press, 1947), pp. 22 and 27. According to the US Department of Veterans Affairs, the total number of service members in the Second World War was 16.1 million (see Department of Veterans Affairs publication, November 2020, https://www.va.gov/opa/publications/factsheets/fs_americas_wars.pdf, accessed 1 April 2021).

[25] World War II prisoners of war data file, NARA, https://aad.archives.gov/aad/series-description.jsp?s=644&cat=GP24&bc=,sl, accessed 26 May 2023.

Historiographic Review

The literature covering POWs in German captivity in the Second World War is extensive; and the Nazi attempt to implement a 'Final Solution to the Jewish Question' and the resulting Holocaust form together a major field in the studies of twentieth-century history.[26] However, the converging point of these two fields—the research on Jewish POWs in German captivity during the Second World War—has not received the same level of attention. One reason for this gap might be that most studies of the POW experience were based on the nationality of the POWs, rather than their religion or ethnicity; another reason is that, with few exceptions, the treatment of Jewish POWs, whether on the Eastern or Western Fronts, was similar to the treatment given to their non-Jewish comrades: that is, leading to an almost certain death for Jewish POWs in the East, and mostly in line with the Geneva Convention in the West. The contradiction between the Nazi obsession with exterminating the Jews and, when it came to Jewish POWs from the western allies, their almost complete adherence to the Geneva Convention was in fact mirrored in the regulations issued by the POW Office: on one hand, an order that was issued towards the end of the war by the then-head of the POW Office, SS General Gottlob Berger, informed POW camp commandants that '...Jewish prisoners of war are to be treated like the other prisoners of war belonging to the respective armed forces'; and on the other, an order that was issued in 1942 and instructed camp commandants not to accept blood donations from POWs since 'it cannot be ruled out with certainty that even part-Jews [*jüdische Mischlinge*] among the prisoners of war will be used as blood donors'.[27]

The experience of Jewish POWs in German captivity has only been covered in very few studies and mostly comes to light in memoirs and collections of testimonies of individual POWs. This can be partly attributed to the fact that, on the Eastern Front, very few Jewish POWs survived the war, since their fate was determined by the Commissar Order; and in the West, to the fact that American POWs had to sign, after their release, an affidavit prohibiting them from discussing their experience.[28] Another contributing factor was that, with the exception of Palestinian Jews who fought as a group in the British army, Jews were fully

---

[26] It is not possible to list all the studies on the Holocaust; however, the important ones include Raul Hilberg's *The Destruction of the European Jews* (first published in 1961) and Saul Friedländer's *Nazi Germany and the Jews: The Years of Extermination: 1939–1945* (2007).

[27] Befehlsammlung 48, order 876, 15 December 1944, and Befehlsammlung 15, order 111, 10 August 1942, BA-MA RW 6/270.

[28] According to Raul Hilberg, only 6,000 Soviet Jewish soldiers came back from German captivity (Hilberg, *The Destruction of the European Jews*, vol. III, p. 1319n). For American Jewish POWs see Jeff Donaldson, *Men of Honor—American GIs in the Jewish Holocaust* (Central Point, OR: Hellgate Press, 2005), p. ix; and Gerald Daub, oral history, recorded 6 July 2000, Archive of the Museum of Jewish Heritage, New York.

integrated in the units they belonged to, whether on the battlefield or in POW camps, and did not always see their captivity experience as being very different to that of their non-Jewish comrades. The tendency of the belligerents during the first decade after the war to focus on their own suffering, which meant that Jewish war veterans and Holocaust survivors kept their experiences largely to themselves, can also explain the limited number of memoirs and testimonies.

The story of the Jews who fought in the Soviet and Polish armies—although outside the scope of this research—sheds light on the vast difference between their fate and the fate of those who fought for the western allies. Not many studies on this specific topic have been conducted: Raul Hilberg devoted eight pages to it in *The Destruction of the European Jews* (first published in 1961), describing how the Einsatzgruppen combed POW camps where Soviet POWs were held, throughout Europe and the occupied parts of the Soviet Union, looking for Bolsheviks and Jews, and then executed them.[29] Szymon Datner's early study of *Crimes against POWs—Responsibility of the Wehrmacht* (1964) which was published in Poland, is based mainly on the International Military Tribunal (IMT) protocols of the Nuremberg trials and includes a section that deals with Jewish POWs, describing the harsh treatment suffered by Polish and Soviet Jews.[30] The access to Soviet archives in the 1990s provided sources for further studies: Pavel Polian, in his article 'First Victims of the Holocaust: Soviet-Jewish Prisoners of War in German Captivity' (2005), used these sources to review the subject of Soviet POWs in general, before moving on to describe the specific fate of the Jews among them; and Aron Shneyer, in his book *Pariahs among Pariahs* (first published in 2005), describes in great detail the experience of Soviet Jewish soldiers in German captivity, beginning with an overview of Jews in the Russian—later Soviet—army and the anti-Semitism they had encountered. Given that very few Soviet Jewish soldiers managed to survive both the appalling conditions of German captivity and the extermination of the Soviet Jewish POWs, Shneyer's ability to find and interview those who survived, combined with his detailed research of primary sources, is impressive. Shmuel Krakowski's article 'The Fate of Jewish Prisoners of War in the September 1939 Campaign' (1977) is based mainly on personal testimonies and memoirs of Polish Jewish and non-Jewish POWs and describes the fate of Polish Jewish soldiers who fought in the Polish campaign in September 1939 and became POWs. Polish POWs were in general badly treated by the Germans, but the Jews among them—with the exception of the officers—suffered an even worse treatment, not least because of the anti-Semitism of the Polish POWs themselves. The number of Polish Jewish POWs who survived the war is difficult to estimate; most of those who were released in

---

[29] Hilberg, *The Destruction of the European Jews*, vol. I, pp. 346–53.
[30] Szymon Datner, *Crimes against POWs: Responsibility of the Wehrmacht* (Warsaw: Zachodnia Agencja Prasowa, 1964), pp. 98–109.

the months following the end of the Polish campaign were murdered later, together with their families, in the concentration and extermination camps.

Analysing this topic from the German side, *The Policies of Genocide: Jews and Soviet Prisoners of War in Nazi Germany*, edited by Gerhard Hirschfeld (1986), provides a collection of essays that links the treatment of Soviet POWs to the extermination of the Jews. In the first article in this collection, 'The German Army and the Policies of Genocide', Christian Streit argues that the turning point in the German policy against the Jews from a territorial solution to extermination came with the invasion of the Soviet Union. He describes how General Hermann Reinecke, the head of the OKW's General Office (*Allgemeines Wehrmachtsamt*, or AWA), allowed Reinhard Heydrich, the head of the RSHA, only a few days after the start of the invasion of the Soviet Union, to send his Einsatzgruppen units to select and execute Soviet Commissars and Jewish POWs.[31] This shift—from the execution of only political enemies (the commissars) to racial ones (Jewish POWs)—might indeed be considered as the watershed point; however, for reasons that will be discussed in Chapter 4 of this book, these orders were eventually not extended to non-Soviet Jewish POWs.

On the general subject of German treatment of Jewish POWs both in the West and in the East, Rüdiger Overmans's article, 'German Treatment of Jewish Prisoners of War in the Second World War' (2016), provides a high level overview of the experience of Jewish POWs from all Allied armies (including French, Yugoslav, Polish, etc.) in German captivity and highlights the differences in treatment between Soviet Jewish and non-Soviet Jewish POWs. Overmans explains that the almost-fair treatment received by the latter group can be attributed mainly to the principle of reciprocity—the German concern that mistreatment of western POWs would lead to reprisals against German POWs held by the western Allies.[32] However, this principle, which was used in multiple studies to explain the treatment of non-Soviet POW in general, has several inconsistencies and is discussed below in more detail.[33]

With regards to the specific topic of American and British Jewish POWs in German captivity, there are only a limited number of studies. One of these studies is of special relevance—Yoav Gelber's article 'Palestinian POWs in German

---

[31] Christian Streit, 'The German Army and the Policies of Genocide', in Gerhard Hirschfeld, ed., *The Policies of Genocide, Jews and Soviet Prisoners of War in Nazi Germany* (New York and Abingdon: Routledge, 2015).

[32] Rüdiger Overmans, 'German Treatment of Jewish Prisoners of War in the Second World War', in Anne-Marie Pathé and Fabien Théofilakis, eds, *Wartime Captivity in the 20th Century* (New York and Oxford: Berghahn, 2016), lns 1240–60.

[33] For other studies that suggested the reciprocity argument see Kochavi, *Confronting Captivity*, p. 195; Streit, *Keine Kameraden*, p. 70; Aron Shneyer, *Pariahs among Pariahs* (Jerusalem: Yad Vashem, 2016), p. 82; and David Killingray, 'Africans and African Americans in Enemy Hands', in Bob Moore and Kent Fedorowich, eds, *Prisoners of War and Their Captors in World War II* (Oxford: Berg, 1996), pp. 181–204, p. 199.

Captivity' (1981), which describes the experience of approximately 1,500 Palestinian Jews who volunteered to fight in the British army and were taken captive together in Greece in 1941. These POWs went mostly as one group through the same captivity lifecycle as their non-Jewish British brothers-in-arms. Gelber relied on British, German and Israeli archives, along with memoirs written by the Palestinian Jewish POWs, to construct a chronological account of events from their capture, through their experience during the captivity period, to the forced marches across Germany at the end of the war and their liberation in April and May 1945. Gelber's conclusion was that, in general, the Palestinian Jewish POWs were treated in a similar way to their non-Jewish comrades; however, the article does not provide an explanation as to why they were treated in that way. In addition, since the Palestinian Jewish POWs were mostly treated as a separate national group, similar to the way POWs from other British dominions were treated, their experience was different to that of individual American and British Jewish POWs. Both groups are dealt with separately in this book.

Bob Moore dedicates one chapter in his book *Prisoners of War—Europe: 1939–1956* (2022) to Jewish POWs, focusing on the experience of Jewish POWs from Poland, Yugoslavia, France, Belgium, and the Soviet Union. One section deals with the fate of Jewish POWs from Britain and the USA, and brings several examples of their treatment and their experience in POW camps; however, the chapter does not deal with the reasons for the different treatment of non-Soviet Jewish POWs and Soviet Jewish ones.

Other studies on the topic of American and British Jewish POWs include Martin Sugarman's article 'Two Notes on Jews on Active Service' (2004), which lists the Jewish POWs who passed through the POW camp at Colditz Castle—as well as those he had reason to believe were Jewish, but decided not to reveal their ethnicity—and provides a short description of the whereabouts of some of them; and one chapter in Russell Wallis's book *British POWs and the Holocaust: Witnessing the Nazi Atrocities* (2017), which describes the relationship between British Jewish and non-Jewish POWs. Wallis argues that even though the British POWs grew up in a liberal society and were not exposed to a totalitarian one, they were still able to recognize the German hierarchy of victims, in which the Jews came last; however, the treatment of the Jews evoked responses in the POWs that ranged from empathy and compassion on one hand all the way to indifference and anti-Semitism on the other. Other parts of Wallis's book provide detailed accounts of interactions between British (including Jewish) POWs and civilian Jews, victims of the Holocaust; a few of these interactions occurred in concentration camps, where some British POWs found themselves, usually when they were captured after taking part in a commando operation or after they were caught by the Gestapo following an escape attempt. For POWs, being incarcerated in a concentration camp was especially risky because it usually meant that they were no longer considered POWs and therefore were outside the protection of the Geneva Convention.

The story of the Berga slave labour camp, to where about eighty American Jewish and 270 non-Jewish POWs were sent from Stalag IX-B in Bad Orb, was actually an exception to the way most Jewish POWs from the West were treated. In his book *Soldiers and Slaves* (2006), Roger Cohen explains that Berga was selected to be the site of an underground jet-fuel production factory and the local SS authorities, who were in charge both of building the factory and, at this stage of the war, of POW camps, apparently decided to use American POWs in the construction work; however, no direct order to do so, or to specifically select Jewish POWs, has ever been found and many of the selected American cohort were also non-Jewish.[34] In addition to Cohen's book, the story is also described in Mitchell Bard's *Forgotten Victims* (1994) and in Flint Whitlock's *Given Up for Dead: American GI's in the Nazi Concentration Camp at Berga* (2005). These books describe the POWs' time in Bad Orb and the events in February 1945, when the Jewish POWs were segregated, in the face of loud protests led by the camp's Man of Confidence (MOC—the POWs' representative) and other POW leaders, from their non-Jewish colleagues, and sent a few weeks later (together with non-Jewish POWs, probably in order to fill a quota) to work in Berga.[35] There was no segregation in the Berga camp itself and all POWs were treated in the same way. The death rate in Berga—around 20%—was the highest of all European prison camps where British and American POWs were held.[36]

Both the Nazification process of the Wehrmacht and its interaction with various bodies of the German state are important in analysing the extent to which the Wehrmacht—from its senior generals down to its soldiers—was willing to adopt and implement Nazi policies and racial doctrines, and, in the case of POWs, apply them to the Jews among them. Wolfram Wette's *The Wehrmacht: History, Myth and Reality* (first published in 2002), Rolf-Dieter Müller's *Hitler's Wehrmacht* (2016) and Bryce Sait's *The Indoctrination of the Wehrmacht* (2019) describe how National Socialist ideology was adopted by the Wehrmacht, from its top level command, through areas such as its pastoring and justice systems, to the officer corps and its soldiers. Earlier works include Robert O'Neill's *The German Army and the Nazi Party* (1968) and Klaus-Jurgen Müller's books *Das Heer und Hitler* (1969) and *The Army, Politics and Society in Germany, 1933–1945: Studies in the Army's Relation to Nazism* (1987); these books provide an insight into the Nazification process, from the Wehrmacht's adoption in 1934 of the 'Aryan Clause', which prohibited Jews from serving in the Wehrmacht and Wehrmacht

---

[34] Roger Cohen, *Soldiers and Slaves* (New York: Anchor Books, 2005), pp. 9–10.
[35] Flint Whitlock, *Given Up for Dead* (New York: Basic Books, 2006), pp. 120–1. See also Cohen, *Soldiers and Slaves*, pp. 79–80.
[36] Mitchell Bard, *Forgotten Victims: The Abandonment of Americans in Hitler's Camps* (Boulder and Oxford: Westview Press, 1994), pp. 102–3.

personnel from shopping in Jewish-owned shops, through to General Walter von Brauchitsch, the Commander-in-Chief of the army, declaring in December 1938 that 'The Armed Forces and the National-Socialism are of the same spiritual stem'.[37] Hans-Adolf Jacobsen's article 'The Kommissarbefehl and Mass Execution of Soviet Russian Prisoners of War' (in *Anatomy of the SS State* (1968)), Manfred Messerschmidt, in *Die Wehrmacht im NS-Staat, Zeit der Indoktrination* (1969), and Jürgen Förster, in his article 'The German Army and the Ideological War against the Soviet Union' (first published in 1986) add another perspective to the analysis of this Nazification process by describing in great detail the Wehrmacht's work to convert Hitler's guidelines for a 'War of Extermination' in the East into specific military orders. Förster argued that the ideological and political consensus between Hitler and the Wehrmacht stood at the heart of the latter's acceptance and active implementation of these orders; Jacobsen presented a slightly different view by arguing that some of the Wehrmacht's generals expressed objections to them, and especially to the Commissar Order. However, he agreed that their objections were based mainly on their concern that the orders would harm military discipline and were not forceful enough to change the outcome.[38] The result of their eventual acceptance of the Commissar Order became apparent when the Einsatzgruppen were given free hand by the Wehrmacht to comb POW camps and to select for liquidation not only Soviet commissars but also other 'undesirables', such as Soviet Jewish POWs. This cooperation demonstrated that not only did the Wehrmacht follow orders even when they were in clear breach of international treaties and the accepted rules of warfare, but that it was also actively 'working towards the Führer' in implementing Nazi policies. It is therefore clear that had similar orders been given in the case of non-Soviet POWs—and specifically, of Jewish POWs—they would have been followed as well.

The question as to what extent the regular soldiers of the Wehrmacht adhered to National Socialist policies provides another important angle in understanding the Nazification process of the Wehrmacht and the will of its soldiers to follow this worldview even in cases when it contradicted military discipline. Specifically, such research could shed light on the motives of German soldiers when interacting with Jewish POWs. Omer Bartov's *Hitler's Army* (1992), which analyses the behaviour and motivation of the Wehrmacht's soldiers, challenged the accepted view at the time of the soldier being apolitical and emphasized the importance of military discipline as one of his main core values; Sönke Neitzel and Harald Welzer's *Soldaten* (2012), and Felix Römer's *Comrades, The Wehrmacht from*

---

[37] Quoted in Robert O'Neill, *The German Army and the Nazi Party* (London: Corgi Books, 1968), p. 103.
[38] Jürgen Förster, 'The German Army and the Ideological War against the Soviet Union', in Gerhard Hirschfeld, ed., *The Policies of Genocide, Jews and Soviet Prisoners of War in Nazi Germany* (New York and Abingdon: Routledge, 2015), pp. 15–29, p. 16; Jacobsen, 'The Kommissarbefehl and Mass Execution of Soviet Russian Prisoners of War', pp. 516 and 521.

Within (2019), both based on recordings of conversations of German POWs in Allied POW camps, reach the same conclusion regarding the importance of military discipline. However, these studies dealt mainly with frontline soldiers, whereas those who interacted with the Jewish POWs on a daily basis—the POW camp's chain of command and specifically the guard battalions—were not exposed, in general, to harsh fighting conditions and had very different age and health profiles, and as a result, their behaviour and motivation might have been different.[39] A more relevant explanation of the behaviour of POW camp personnel can be found in Christopher Browning's *Ordinary Men: Reserve Police Battalion 101 and the Final Solution in Poland* (first published in 1992), which analyses the behaviour of the members of the 101 Reserve Police Battalion who operated in Poland and participated in the murder of civilian Jews. Although the battalion's members were volunteers and therefore not necessarily 'Ordinary Men' as the book's title might have suggested, their age profile was closer to that of the POW camps' guards, which meant that unlike the Wehrmacht's conscripted frontline soldier, the majority of members of these groups did not spend their formative years being indoctrinated in the National Socialist worldview. Browning attributes the behaviour of the battalion members to situational factors, to conformity with the larger group and to the framework they were operating in, concluding that others would have behaved in a similar manner if placed in similar circumstances. These three factors can also be used to explain the behaviour of the guards in POW camps, albeit with a different outcome: any anti-Semitic beliefs they might have held were usually kept in check due to the fact that they had to conform with a group that was operating within the frameworks of both military discipline and the Geneva Convention.

The topic of the evolution of POW policies, internationally as well as in specific countries, is important as it describes the legal framework the belligerents had been operating in—or deviated from—in the treatment of POWs in general, and specifically of Jewish POWs. Simon MacKenzie analysed this topic in his important article on 'The treatment of prisoners of war in World War II' (1994), which provides a comparative analysis of the POW policies of Second World War belligerents and contributes interesting arguments for explaining some of the reasons behind them. MacKenzie argues that reciprocity was the main factor in Germany's adherence to the Geneva Convention in its treatment of POWs from western countries (although, as discussed below, he does not explain the generally fair treatment of POWs—and specifically, of Jewish POWs—from France, and in some cases from Yugoslavia, countries that did not hold any German POWs).[40]

---

[39] Rolf-Dieter Müller, *Hitler's Wehrmacht* (Lexington, KY: University Press of Kentucky, 2016), p. 112; Andrew Hasselbring, *American Prisoners of War in the Third Reich*, unpublished PhD thesis, Temple University (1991), p. 133.

[40] Although later in the war German POWs were held by Free French forces and Tito's partisans.

He also explains that Jewish POWs from western countries were not harmed simply because sending them to concentration camps could not be kept secret from the Protecting Power and the International Committee of the Red Cross (ICRC); and he argues that had Germany won the war, their days would have been numbered.[41]

Two years later, Bob Moore and Kent Fedorowich contributed to this field by editing *Prisoners of War and Their Captors in World War II* (1996), a collection of essays that deals with various aspects of the topic of Second World War POWs, including the POW policies angle; and *Prisoners in War* (2010), a collection of essays edited by Sibylle Scheipers, describes the evolution of the legal and ethical standards governing the treatment of POWs and how they were implemented in the Second World War as well as in irregular conflicts in the years following the war. Scheipers argues that while the 1929 Geneva convention was mostly adhered to when it came to non-Soviet POWs, it could not prevail against racism and the dehumanization of the enemy—as became evident in the Eastern and Pacific Fronts. As this research will show, however, adherence to the 1929 Convention was one of the reasons for the largely humane treatment of non-Soviet Jewish POWs, despite Jews being considered racial enemies of the Reich.

The research of POW policies of western countries was further enhanced in the following decade with Arieh Kochavi's *Confronting Captivity* (2005) and Neville Wylie's *Barbed Wire Diplomacy* (2010). Kochavi's book, based mainly on American and British sources, describes the evolution of prisoner of war policies in the USA and Britain and demonstrates how a combination of Nazi pragmatism and racial policy helped, to some extent, protect POWs from western countries from suffering the fate of their brothers-in-arms in the East (even though this protection was no longer taken for granted in the final year of the war).[42] One example of this pragmatism described by Kochavi is the exchanges of seriously injured POWs which began in 1943; these exchanges, which the Germans saw as a major goal, not only took place while German cities were being bombed on a daily basis but also included Palestinian Jewish POWs.[43] Neville Wylie provides a detailed analysis of the nuances behind British POW policy and, based on a wealth of primary sources from Britain, the USA, Australia, Switzerland, and Germany, explores the relationship between the British POW policy, the international POW framework, and German actions, in order to explain how the British government acted to protect its captive soldiers throughout the different stages of the war. Neither of these books, however, makes any reference to

---

[41] A Protecting Power is a third party that represents the interests of one country in another country, with which the former has no diplomatic relations; the USA represented British interests in Germany until it joined the war in December 1941, when Switzerland became Britain's Protecting Power. For MacKenzie's argument see Simon MacKenzie, 'The Treatment of Prisoners of War in World War II', *Journal of Modern History*, 66 (1994), pp. 487–520, p. 504.
[42] Kochavi, *Confronting Captivity*, p. 2; ibid., p. 5.   [43] Ibid., p. 125.

western governments' policies regarding their Jewish soldiers held as POWs by Germany.

Studies of German POW policies include Rüdiger Overmans's detailed overview of these policies in his chapter 'Die Kriegsgefangenenpolitik des Deutschen Reichs 1939 bis 1945' (2005), which also includes a few references to the treatment of Jewish POWs and the drivers behind it. Overmans argues that until 1941 the German treatment of POWs in general was based on their nation's position towards Germany during the First World War: POWs from nations which were either allies or neutral during that war were either not taken prisoner or released immediately. Later, when labour shortages became paramount, the treatment of POWs was based on a 'National Conservative' hierarchy of nations—which was not necessarily aligned with the Nazi racial hierarchy—where the US came first, followed by Britain and other western European nations.[44] However, as will be shown, Overmans's argument that the Wehrmacht's general non-discriminatory treatment of non-Soviet Jewish POWs was based only on its concern for reprisals against German POWs in Allied hands is too general in nature and does not provide a full explanation for this phenomenon.[45]

Vasilis Vourkoutiotis's study *Prisoners of War and the German High Command: the British and American Experience* (2003) provides an overview of the German POW regulations and policies using the command collections issued by the POW Office to the chain of command in the POW organization. The examples Vourkoutiotis uses of Hitler's direct involvement in POW matters demonstrate the influence he had on setting POW policies: in one example, during the last months of the war and when POW camps were being evacuated ahead of the advanced Allied armies, he went as far as instructing—in clear breach of the Geneva Convention—that POWs who were too ill to march should be evacuated as well.[46] Although Vourkoutiotis's study provides only minimal background regarding the drivers behind the German POW policies and does not place them in the context of the bigger picture of the war, the examples given, combined with a review of the original bulletins, help to better understand these drivers and the influence the Nazi leadership had on them.

The treatment of POWs from minority and political groups, such as French colonial soldiers, African American soldiers, and Spanish Republicans, fugitives from the Spanish Civil War who fought with the French army, is particularly relevant to this research. Comparing the treatment of POWs from groups who, similar to the Jews, were at the bottom of the Nazi racial and political hierarchies with the treatment of Jewish POWs can help shed additional light on German

---

[44] Overmans, 'Die Kriegsgefangenenpolitik des Deutschen Reichs 1939 bis 1945', pp. 869–70.
[45] Ibid., p. 872.
[46] Vasilis Vourkoutiotis, *Prisoners of War and the German High Command* (New York: Palgrave Macmillan, 2003), p. 73.

considerations in this matter. One example is Hitler's insistence on removing black French colonial POWs, but not Jewish ones, from German soil, probably to avoid 'racial defilement'; another is Germany's adherence to the Geneva Convention in giving military funerals to Jewish POWs who died in captivity (although in most cases the funerals did not include full military honours), but not to African ones.[47] Rafael Scheck's books *Hitler's African Victims* (2006) and *French Colonial Soldiers in German Captivity during World War II* (2014), which describe in great detail the captivity experience of these soldiers, mainly from Senegal and North Africa, provide testimonies of several instances where Black soldiers were massacred upon capture. Scheck argues that these massacres formed the missing link between the limited atrocities committed by the Wehrmacht in Poland to those committed later in the Balkans and the Soviet Union; and that although they were not part of an official policy, they were a result of the dehumanization of the Black soldiers and were permitted—even encouraged—by local commanders.[48] However, although Jews were also dehumanized by the German propaganda, Scheck does not explain why this dehumanization did not translate into cases of mass massacres of captured Jewish soldiers on the Western Front. Other sources dealing with treatment of POWs from minority groups include David Killingray's article 'African and African Americans in Enemy Hands' (1996) and one paragraphs in David Foy's *For You The War Is Over* (1984); citing several cases where African American soldiers were executed upon capture, both Killingray and Foy concluded that once in POW camps they were, in general, not discriminated against or mistreated. Michel Fabréguet, in his article 'Un Groupe de Réfugiés Politiques: Les Républicains Espagnols des Camps d'internement Français aux Camps de Concentration Nationaux-Socialistes (1939–1941)' (1986) chronicles the fate of the Spanish Republican refugees who fled to France after the loss of their side in the Spanish Civil War; after they became POWs of Germany and in clear breach of the Geneva Convention, most of them were deported to concentration camps where they were murdered. Fabréguet's research demonstrates the level of cooperation that existed between the Wehrmacht and the Gestapo when it came to POWs from western countries who were considered political enemies; however, it does not provide many details regarding the chain of events, or the individuals on the German side who were involved in them, that resulted in the Spanish Republicans being sent to concentration camps.

---

[47] On the segregation of French colonial soldiers see Raffael Scheck, *French Colonial Soldiers in German Captivity during World War II* (Cambridge: Cambridge University Press, 2014), p. 54; on military funerals see, for example, Shlomo Sela (Slodash), *Shackles of Captivity* (Tel Aviv: Mif'alei Tarbut ve-Chinuch, 1986), pp. 233–4; and Scheck, *French Colonial Soldiers in German Captivity*, p. 49.

[48] Raffael Scheck, *Hitler's African Victims* (Cambridge: Cambridge University Press, 2008), pp. 6–8 and 11.

Current Explanations for the Treatment of Jewish POWs

The explanations for the relatively fair treatment of non-Soviet Jewish POWs during the Second World War have been relatively few and have not been given the right level of attention in the literature. As mentioned earlier, the treatment of non-Soviet POWs in general can be attributed to the fact that Hitler's 'war of extermination' in the East was of course much different from the war in the west, which was for the most part a conventional war.[49] This was especially true during the first years of the war in the West and it also applied to the treatment of POWs from western armies, and by extension, to the Jewish POWs from these armies. However, as will be shown later, with the escalation in the German POW policies in the West during the war, and with army and SS units moving from the Eastern Front to the West during its last stages, the distinction between the fronts was no longer as clear-cut; cases such as the massacres of western POWs during the Normandy landings and during the Ardennes offensive demonstrate that East Front-type atrocities, although obviously not on the same scale, were no longer confined to the East. And as described in Chapter 4, the pressure exerted by the RSHA throughout the war to transfer all Jewish POWs to its control (which was fought back successfully by the OKW's POW Office) and Hitler's insistence on the abandonment of the Geneva Convention following the bombardment of Dresden (which his lieutenants eventually convinced him not to abandon) were not confined to Jewish POWs from a specific Front; in fact, since Germany argued that Soviet POWs were not protected by the Convention, Hitler's demand was meant to specifically influence the treatment of POWs from western armies.

In addition to the general explanation which links the treatment of POWs to the fronts they fought in, a more specific and widely used explanation for the treatment of non-Soviet POWs is the principle of reciprocity, which, despite several inconsistencies, was mentioned by Overmans, Mackenzie, and others, who also used it to explain the treatment of non-Soviet Jewish POWs.[50] The fact that this principle was used internally by Germany throughout the war might help to explain why it was quoted so often: Hitler himself issued an order in 1943 regarding the use of POWs in the German economy, stating that '[t]he treatment of enemy prisoners of war in German custody has an impact on German prisoners of war in enemy hands' (although his later orders stood in stark contrast to it).[51] The Wehrmacht made that point clear even before the Second World War broke out: in the service manuals issued by the OKW to Dulag (Dulag is short for Durchgangslager, a transit camp for POWs where they were interrogated and

---

[49] *War Journal of Franz Halder*, 30 March 1941, vol. 6, pp. 42–3.
[50] For the studies that suggested the reciprocity argument see Overmans, 'German Treatment of Jewish Prisoners of War in the Second World War', lns 1240–60, and n. 34.
[51] Moll, *Führer-Erlasse 1939–1945*, p. 340.

sorted before being sent to a permanent POW camp) and Stalag commandants early in 1939, commandants were reminded of the serious consequences any violations of the Geneva Convention might have on the treatment of German soldiers in enemy hands.[52] The manual went further and prohibited unauthorized reprisals even in cases when German POWs were known to be mistreated by the enemy; and it required all personnel responsible for not only the treatment of POWs but also for their administrative management to be thoroughly familiar with the Geneva Convention.[53] The concern about reciprocity might have saved the lives, at least initially, of Polish Jewish officer POWs (who, unlike most Polish Jewish POWs from other ranks who were released at the end of the Polish campaign, remained in captivity): demands to transfer them to concentration camps, together with demands to use the Polish officer POWs as slave labour, were rejected by the Wehrmacht on the ground of reciprocity as it would have resulted reprisals against German POWs held by the Allies.[54] In the same year, the POW Office even warned camp commandants not to be 'guided by personal attitude when dealing with English POWs, since repercussions against German POWs should be feared'.[55] And proposals to change the treatment of POWs which were brought up in meetings with the OKW were turned down when there was a risk they did not comply with the Geneva Convention, and therefore might impact the treatment of German POWs in enemy hands.[56]

However, there are several issues with the reciprocity argument which are not addressed by Overmans and the other scholars who used it in their studies. To begin with, while it might explain why American and British POWs were in general treated according to the Geneva Convention, it does not explain the treatment of POWs—and specifically, of Jewish POWs—who belonged to other countries such as France, Yugoslavia, and Poland. Jewish POWs from these countries were usually segregated in the same camp from their non-Jewish comrades, but otherwise (with the exception of Polish Jewish POWs) were in general not subjected to harsher treatment. This is despite the fact that none of these countries held any German POWs and therefore their mistreatment would not have posed any risk of reprisals (at least not until the second half of the war, when the Free French forces and Yugoslavian Partisans captured German soldiers). The

---

[52] Dienstanweisung für den Kommandanten eines 'Kriegsgefangenen Mannschafts Stammlagers', 16 February 1939, p. 8, BA-MA RH 1/612, and Dienstanweisung für den Kommandanten eines Kriegsgefangenen Durchgangslagers, 22 May 1939, p. 9, BA-MA RH 1/611.

[53] Dienstanweisung für den Kommandanten eines 'Kriegsgefangenen Mannschafts Stammlagers', 16 February 1939, pp. 7–8, BA-MA RH 1/612, and Dienstanweisung für den Kommandanten eines Kriegsgefangenen Durchgangslagers, 22 May 1939, p. 9, BA-MA RH 1/611.

[54] Overmans, 'Die Kriegsgefangenenpolitik des Deutschen Reichs 1939 bis 1945', p. 871.

[55] Meeting summary, 7488/41, 21 October 1941, point 18: 'bei der behandlung der Engländer nicht von persönlicher Einstellung leiten lassen, da Rückwirkungen auf deutsche Kriegsgefangene zu fürchten sind', PMA 31/1/5.

[56] Testimony of General Reinhard von Westrem, IMT, Trials of War Criminals, vol. XI—The High Command Case, The Hostage Case (Washington, DC, 1950), p. 50.

other argument, that POWs from countries that did not hold German POWs were treated according to the Convention because they were allies of the USA and Britain, who might retaliate against German POWs in their hands, is also lacking; this argument was refuted by none other than General Alfred Jodl, the OKW's Chief of Operations, who argued towards the end of the war against the abandonment of the Geneva Convention by telling Hitler that the USA and Britain would be 'indifferent' ('*gleichgultig*') to any mistreatment of French, Belgian, and Dutch POWs that this abandonment may result.[57] Jodl, of course, was correct: the harsh treatment of Soviet POWs, that of Italian POWs, whose POW status was removed after Italy switched sides in 1943, and that of Jewish POWs from Poland, whose invasion by Germany triggered its allies, Britain and France, to join the war in the first place, was not met by any reprisals against German POWs held by the Allies.[58]

The Allies' approach to reprisals after 1944 is another factor that weakens the reciprocity argument, as it fails to explain the treatment of the non-Soviet Jewish POWs after the murder of the fifty Royal Air Force (RAF) POWs who escaped from Stalag Luft III (Sagan), and after the lynching of Allied airmen during the same year became a major risk to downed airmen. Both events clearly demonstrated to Germany that the western Allies were limited in their ability—and will—to reciprocate against such atrocities by launching similar reprisals—or any reprisals, for that matter—against German POWs in their hands. Joseph Goebbels, the Reich's propaganda minister, remarked afterwards that 'our experience shows that the English are glad to avoid a fuss over prisoners'; and later that year, Hitler himself dismissed reprisal concerns by declaring that if a German soldier 'gives himself up as a prisoner, he cannot expect us to show consideration for American or British prisoners because of him'.[59] And yet, even then, the treatment of non-Soviet Jewish POWs remained the same and did not take any turn for the worse. The reciprocity factor can therefore partially explain the approach of the POW Office in treating non-Soviet POWs, as it was also responsible for the well-being of German POWs held by the Allies; however, it was not a major factor in the decisions related to POWs made by the levels above it—AWA, the OKW, and Hitler himself.

---

[57] Jodl to Hitler, 21 February 1945, Document 606-D, *IMT, Trial of the Major War Criminals*, vol. XXXV (Nuremberg, 1949), pp. 181–6.

[58] Hitler ordered the execution of Italian officers who refused to continue and fight on Germany's side after the Armistice (see "Treatment of Members of the Italian Army", 15 September 1943, Document NOKW-916, *IMT, Trials of War Criminals*, vol. XI, pp. 1081–3). The only potential exception to Allies' reprisals as a result of German mistreatment of POWs from countries who did not hold German POWs was the Allied declaration on 30 August 1944, following the Warsaw Uprising, that any mistreatment of captured Armia Krajova soldiers would trigger reprisals (see Overmans, 'Die Kriegsgefangenenpolitik des Deutschen Reichs 1939 bis 1945', p. 753).

[59] Goebbels is quoted in Neville Wylie, *Barbed Wire Diplomacy* (Oxford: Oxford University Press, 2010), p. 229. Hitler is quoted in ibid., p. 230.

The 'national conservative value system' of the Wehrmacht was another argument that has been suggested as an explanation for the generally fair treatment of non-Soviet POWs—and by extension, of non-Soviet Jewish POWs. Neville Wylie suggested this argument in his article 'Captured by the Nazis: "Reciprocity" and "National Conservatism" in German Policy towards British POWs' (2009); he went on to explain that the 'national conservative value system' stemmed from Germany's warrior code and was rooted in the German military tradition which dictated 'chivalric warfare' between honourable foes.[60] Overmans explains that Germany applied this value system according to a national hierarchy, at the top of which were American POWs, who were closely followed by the British, Dutch, Danes, and Norwegians; the second group included French, Belgians, Yugoslavs, Greeks, and Poles; and at the bottom were the Soviet POWs, who had no protection at all.[61] Wylie explained that since the national hierarchy, which was also suggested, among others, by Aryeh Kochavi, Christian Streit, and Simon MacKenzie, differentiated between Germany's enemies, it was not against it to treat western POWs differently than the Soviet ones.[62] Johanna Jacques, in her doctoral thesis *From Nomos to Hegung: War Captivity and International Order* (2013) and later in her article 'A "Most Astonishing" Circumstance: The Survival of Jewish POWs in German War Captivity during the Second World War' (2021), applied this argument to non-Soviet Jewish POWs; relying mainly on secondary sources and memoirs of Jewish POWs, Jacques explained that their general non-discriminatory treatment was a result of the Wehrmacht's 'honour-based rules'.[63]

However, although widely used, as was pointed out by Wylie himself, there is no clear definition of the scope and the contents of the national conservative value system as it pertains to the Second World War's Wehrmacht.[64] Overmans explained that national conservative values, which were paramount in defining the Nazi POW policy, 'were shaped in particular by the [behaviour of the belligerents in the] First World War' but did not elaborate on what these values were.[65] The other scholars mentioned above have also used this term without providing an exact definition. David Stahel gave a general description of the values of the German army by describing how the conservative Reichswehr officers saw it as 'a bastion of moral virtue imparting values such as devotion to the nation, sacrifice

---

[60] Neville Wylie, 'Captured by the Nazis: "Reciprocity" and "National Conservatism" in German Policy towards British POWs', in Claus-Christian W. Szejnmann, ed., *Rethinking History, Dictatorship and War* (London: Continuum, 2009), ln. 2331; ibid., lns 2655–80, and especially ln. 2672.

[61] Overmans, 'Die Kriegsgefangenenpolitik des Deutschen Reichs 1939 bis 1945', pp. 732 and 870.

[62] For National Hierarchy see Kochavi, *Confronting Captivity*, p. 221; Streit, *Keine Kameraden*, pp. 69–70; and MacKenzie, 'The Treatment of Prisoners of War in World War II', p. 504. For treating western POWs differently see Wylie, *Barbed Wire Diplomacy*, p. 271.

[63] Johanna Jacques, 'A "Most Astonishing" Circumstance: The Survival of Jewish POWs in German War Captivity During the Second World War', 30:3 (2021), p. 376.

[64] Wylie, 'Captured by the Nazis: "Reciprocity" and "National Conservatism" in German Policy towards British POWs', ln. 2331.

[65] Overmans, 'Die Kriegsgefangenenpolitik des Deutschen Reichs 1939 bis 1945', p. 871.

and comradeship'.⁶⁶ However, traditional national conservative values in general were not confined to the ones Stahel mentioned; in fact, the well documented anti-Semitism among the German Army's officer corps before and during the First World War, which resulted in Jews not being promoted to reserve officers and triggered the notorious '*Judenzählung*' ('Jew Count') of 1916, points towards a completely different interpretation of the concepts of 'moral virtue' and 'comradeship'.⁶⁷

Assuming that some of these national conservative values were reflected in international conventions such as the Hague and the Geneva ones, it was argued by Heather Jones that even so, during the First World War, the 'German army had been far more reluctant to accept [these humanitarian conventions] than the British or French'.⁶⁸ And the Wehrmacht itself, in a 1938 report which analysed the demands of modern war, concluded that 'necessity knows no law'.⁶⁹ Therefore, given the lack of consensus over the exact definition of 'national conservative values', for the purpose of this discussion the scope of this term should be confined only to 'chivalric warfare' between honourable foes, which includes the type of treatment given to such foes when they became POWs.

To that point, extrapolating the national hierarchy argument to apply to Jewish POWs belonging to the armies in this hierarchy would mean that American and British Jewish POWs were treated in the same way as their non-Jewish brothers-in-arms because they somehow 'inherited' the racial position of the army they belonged to, and any discrimination against them would be seen as discrimination against members of the American or British armies. Given the Nazi view of Jews as '*untermenschen*' regardless of the nation they fought for, and the German obsession with the extermination of the Jews, the combination of National Hierarchy and 'national conservative value system' still does not explain the relatively fair treatment of non-Soviet Jewish POWs. National conservative values might have been shared by some members of the OKW but in view of the Nazification process of the Wehrmacht—which, as described by Browning, 'accommodated itself to the systematic violation of international law'—it cannot be assumed that this value system was shared across all of its various bodies throughout all stages of the war.⁷⁰ In addition, regardless of the values they might have held, members of the OKW and the POW Office were still subordinated to the hierarchical structure of the Wehrmacht, whose Commander-in-Chief was

---

⁶⁶ David Stahel, 'The Wehrmacht and National Socialist Military Thinking', *War in History*, 24:3 (2017), pp. 336–61, p. 342.
⁶⁷ Werner T. Angress, 'Dokumentation. Das deutsche Militär und die Juden im Ersten Weltkrieg', *Militärgeschichtliche Mitteilungen*, 19:1 (1976), pp. 77–88, p. 77. Martin Kitchen described anti-Semitism as 'one of the fundamental creeds of the [Kaiser's] German Officer Corps' (see Martin Kitchen, *The German Officer Corps 1890–1914* (Oxford: Clarendon Press, 1968), p. 46).
⁶⁸ Heather Jones, *Violence against Prisoners of War in the First World War: Britain, France and Germany 1914–1920* (Cambridge: Cambridge University Press, 2011), p. 11.
⁶⁹ Quoted in Wylie, *Barbed Wire Diplomacy*, p. 64.   ⁷⁰ Browning, *Fateful Months*, p. 6.

Adolf Hitler. They could not disobey—in fact, they did not disobey—orders that breached the principles of 'chivalric warfare' in the West and were much broader in nature. These included the Commando Order, which ordered the murder of captured commando soldiers; the Kugel Erlass, which ordered the transfer of recaptured POW escapees to the Mauthausen concentration camp, instead of back to a POW camp; and the order to transfer a certain group of POWs—such as the Spanish Republicans who fought as part of the French army—to concentration camps. In some cases, the OKW seemed to have been the driving force in extending the scope of these orders, in complete disregard for any national conservative values it might have held.[71] As will be shown, the only body where the 'national conservative value system' might have played a role in was the POW organization, which could explain its general tendency throughout the war, and as long as there were no specific orders to the contrary, not to 'work towards the Führer' and not to take the initiative of implementing Nazi policies even without specific orders from above.

Primary Sources Review

When it comes to primary sources, the archival material that deals specifically with the categories of policies related to Jewish POWs, their treatment, and their experience during the Second World War, is sparse and is spread over multiple locations. A comprehensive picture that links and matches information from these three categories was devised mainly from documents in British, German, Israeli, American, Czech, and Swiss archives and from the transcripts of the Nuremberg trials.

The main source for analysing the German POW policies as they related to Jewish POWs is the set of orders that was issued by the OKW's POW Office throughout the war. The orders were sent to a wide list of recipients; the full set of these order compilations (with the exception of the last compilation, #50) is found in the Militärarchiv (BA-MA) in Freiburg, and its English translation (which includes compilation #50) is found in the National Archives and Records Administration (NARA) in Maryland. BA-MA also contains documents related to various POW policies and reports on POW camps; documents in this category are also found in the Bundesarchiv (BA) and in the Politisches Archiv des Auswärtigen Amts (PAAA) in Berlin.

---

[71] See, for example, Treatment of enemy terror flyer, Minutes of a Meeting, 6 June 1944, Document 735-PS, *IMT, Trials of War Criminals*, vol. XI, pp. 169–71; and Conduct of soldiers in cases where the civilian population takes matters in its own hands with regards to shot-down terror flyers, 11 December 1944, Document NOKW-3060, ibid., pp. 179–80.

The IMT in Nuremberg dealt specifically with POW policies and the treatment of POWs in the trials of war criminals, which took place between October 1946 and April 1949 and were recorded in the 'Green series' (specifically in volumes X and XI), as part of the 'war crimes and crimes against humanity' indictments. The transcripts of these trials (as well as those of the other Nuremberg trials which were recorded in the Blue and Red series) contain a wealth of information on German POW policies.[72] These include not only testimonies of witnesses who were directly involved in the POW organization, such as Reinhard von Westrem, who was the commander of POWs in military district XII (headquartered in Wiesbaden), or had first-hand knowledge of discussions related to it, such as Erwin Lahousen, who worked in the Abwehr under Admiral Canaris, but also various German documents that were submitted as evidence.[73] These documents, their various drafts, drafters, signers and recipients provide an insight into the level of involvement and influence that individuals in the OKW and in German state bodies such as the RSHA, the *Nationalsozialistische Deutsche Arbeiterpartei* (the Nazi Party—the NSDAP) and the SS had in setting and implementing POW policies. Additional documents related to war crimes investigations and transcripts of interrogations of suspects and witnesses are found in the National Archives of Britain (TNA) and the USA (NARA), and in the 'WWII Nuernberg [sic] Interrogation Records' section of the Fold3 online database.[74]

The archive of Stalag VIII-B (later renamed Stalag 344), near Lamsdorf in Silesia (today Łambinowice in Poland) is unique in that it was probably captured in its entirety by the Red Army, and as such it not only complements the documents found in BA-MA and in NARA, but also adds to them with more detailed and low-level orders that were issued by the commander of POWs in military district VIII (in the Breslau area) and by the various commandants of Stalag VIII-B. The Stalag's archive is kept in the Vojensky Archiv in Prague (PMA) and copies of it can also be found in the State Archives of the Russian Federation (GARF) and in Poland's State Archive in Opole. The archive includes multiple references to the Palestinian Jewish POWs, most of whom spent their captivity period in Stalag VIII-B and its labour detachments.

The main sources for information regarding international organizations that looked after the welfare of POWs are the archive of the ICRC in Geneva (ACICR) and the Swiss Federal Archive (AFS) in Bern. Article 86 of the 1929 Geneva Convention gives recognized organizations unlimited access to 'any place...where prisoners of war are interned.' In its role as the Protecting Power, the USA, and after it joined the war, Switzerland, along with the ICRC, conducted regular

---

[72] *IMT, Trials of War Criminals*, vol. X: *The High Command Case* (Washington, DC, 1951), and vol. XI.

[73] Testimonies of Reinhard von Westrem, *IMT, Trials of War Criminals*, vol. XI, pp. 56–7; and of Erwin Lahousen, *IMT, Trial of the Major War Criminals*, vol. II (Nuremberg, 1947), pp. 456–8.

[74] https://www.fold3.com/.

inspections of POW camps where American and British POWs were held and submitted their reports to the relevant governments.[75] These reports provide a set of objective, real-time observations of the conditions in the camp, the situation of the POWs, the behaviour of their captors, and of any issues they faced; they also offer a window into the relations between the POWs—including the Jewish ones—and the camp authorities and in some cases, usually in the labour detachments, with the civilians that interacted with the POWs. Most of these reports survived in various archives: while TNA and NARA contain reports that relate to POWs from Britain and the USA, since POW camps in some cases housed multiple nationalities, these reports were usually only sub-sets of the original ones, which referred to the POW population of the camp as a whole. The full reports are kept in the ICRC archive in Geneva (for ICRC visits) and the Swiss Federal Archive in Bern (for Protecting Power visits).

The reports followed a set format (there were slight variations between the ICRC reports and the Protecting Power ones), with seventeen sections beginning with general description, then describing specific categories such as the camp's washing and bathing facilities, food, medical and laundry conditions, and ending with the list of complaints made by the POWs and the general impression that the inspectors had from their visit. The complaints section was in effect the summary of the discussion held between the visiting delegates, the camp commandant, and the MOC, where issues from both sides—the POWs as well as the camp's authorities—were raised. When inspecting small labour detachments the reports usually deviated from this format and included only a short summary of the main points. Although very few of these reports specifically mentioned Jewish POWs or issues related to their ethnicity and religion, the information that they do contain still contributes to the understanding of their daily lives and their treatment by the German authorities.[76]

There are, however, a few important caveats to keep in mind when analysing the visit reports. The main one is the frequency of the visits: POW camps were usually visited once every three months, and, given the large number of labour detachments which belonged to each camp, these were visited even less frequently. For example, in its summary of activities for 1942, the ICRC delegation in Berlin, which consisted of a staff of eight delegates plus a secretary, listed fifty-seven Oflag (a POW camp for officers) visits, 117 Stalag visits, and 219 labour detachments visits; taking into account that some of these visits were to the same

---

[75] Article 86 of the 1929 Geneva Convention, https://ihl-databases.icrc.org/ihl/INTRO/305, accessed 4 February 2018.

[76] For example, the Protecting Power reports from March 1945 did not mention the segregation attempt of Jewish POWs in Stalag IX-A (Ziegenhain) nor the actual segregation in Stalag IX-B (Bad Orb), both of which had occurred in the month before their visit (see Swiss embassy report on Stalag IX-A (Ziegenhain), 22 March 1945, TNA 227/29, and Swiss embassy report on Stalag IX-B (Bad Orb), 23 March 1945, TNA 227/30).

camps provides an insight into the ICRC's true ability to cover all of those facilities, which, including labour detachments, numbered several thousands.[77] Another caveat is the limited ability of the ICRC and the Protecting Power to resolve POWs' complaints within a reasonable timeframe. A good example is the correspondence between the British Red Cross (BRC) and the ICRC regarding a complaint the BRC received in July 1944 regarding conditions in labour detachment E593 in Stalag VIII-B (Lamsdorf). The BRC asked the ICRC to arrange an urgent visit to E593; the ICRC responded a month later, explaining that the camp was visited in February 1944 and although they would try to arrange another visit they could not guarantee that it would happen immediately. Five months later, in January 1945, not getting a response and after receiving another complaint from the same labour detachment, the BRC asked again for a visit to be arranged.[78] By then the camps were about to be evacuated to the West and the situation in the Eastern Front probably meant that a visit would not have been possible anyway.

Additional issues that impacted the information presented in the reports includes the movement of camp commandants and guards, who were not always permanently stationed in a camp; movement of POWs, especially between labour detachments; and the fact that labour detachments were dismantled once the work on a specific project had been completed. The combination of these factors created a situation where the reports could not have fully reflected the situation in some of the camps, and more specifically, did not always cover cases of mistreatment and discrimination of American and British Jewish POWs.

Jewish organizations were understandably also concerned about the treatment of Jewish POWs and throughout the war had multiple interactions with the ICRC on that topic. One of these organizations was the World Jewish Congress (WJC); summaries of discussions and correspondence related to the issue of Jewish POWs are kept in its archives in the United States Holocaust Memorial Museum (USHMM) in Washington, DC. Another organization was the Jewish Agency for Palestine, which acted prior to the creation of the state of Israel as a the Jewish 'Government in waiting', and whose documents, which deal specifically with Palestinian Jewish POWs, are kept in the Central Zionist Archive (CZA) in Jerusalem. The British Foreign Office's POW department as well as Jewish organizations in Britain also initiated several queries related to British Jewish POWs; these are found in TNA and in the London Metropolitan Archives (LMA) in London.

First-hand testimonies regarding the experience of Jewish POWs in German POW camps were recorded in multiple ways by both Jewish and non-Jewish

---

[77] ICRC Berlin delegation to ICRC headquarters, 31 May 1943, ACICR BG 17 05/17. Bob Moore estimated the number of labour detachments to be 82,000 (Moore, *Prisoners of War*, p. 66).

[78] BRC to ICRC, 26 July 1944; ICRC to BRC, 9 August 1944; BRC to ICRC, 16 January 1945, ACICR BG 17 05/028.

POWs. These included, among others, testimonies given after the war to war crimes investigators, letters, diaries, and published and unpublished memoirs, both in oral and in written formats. Memoirs were also found in the archives of the Imperial War Museum (IWM) and the Jewish Military Museum (JMM), both of which are in London, as well as in the Israel Defence Forces (IDF) archive, the Yad Vashem archive (YVA) and the Central Zionist Archive in Jerusalem, which hold letters and personal testimonies of Palestinian Jewish POWs and Jewish POWs from other countries.

None of these categories provides a complete and objective view of the actual experience: letters were censored; diaries were hard to keep and the information in them was not always accurate, for fear that they might be found. Memoirs can be misleading too: having been written sometimes long after the event meant that the passage of time had impacted the way these events had been remembered and described.[79] This is a result of processes that impact the individual's original memory of the event (the 'memory trace'), such as its reinterpretation, interpolation, and retelling, as well as the result of consolidation of the individual memories into a collective one, 'the matrix of socially positioned individual [memories]'.[80] Collective memory, however, is not the same as historical knowledge, which is the historians' attempt to create a documentary record of events; collective memory incorporates the impact later knowledge about these events had on the individual's memory, and of how individuals—including historians—wanted to present such events to others.[81] For example, some of the testimonies mentioned in this research were given after the war, when the extent of the Final Solution became known; this was not the case during the war, when POWs—and, in fact, much of the world—were not yet aware of the scale of the mass murder that was taking place sometimes only miles away from their camp. In some cases, it is possible that this later knowledge was woven—sometimes inadvertently—into the original experience, in a process known as 'interpolated learning'.[82]

Other examples of the potential impact of the collective memory on the historical one include the memoirs of some of the Palestinian Jewish POWs who, in later years, went on to become prominent members of Israeli trade unions, parliament, and even governments; since they saw their struggle in the German POW camps as part of the bigger struggle of the Jews to achieve recognition as a people and independence as a nation, their memoirs, testimonies and media interviews incorporated, in some cases, aspects of the collective memory. This might have also been the case for non-Jewish POWs, who, after the war, wanted to show how

---

[79] See Mary Fulbruk and Ulinka Rublack, 'In Relation: The "Social Self" and Ego-Documents', *German History* 28:3 (2010), pp. 263–72 and esp. p. 267.
[80] Jay Winter and Emmanuel Sivan, *War and Remembrance in the Twentieth Century* (New York: Cambridge University Press, 2005), lns 340–403; ibid., ln. 594.
[81] Ibid., ln. 267.   [82] Ibid., ln. 374.

soldierly comradeship manifested itself not only on the battlefield but also in the POW camps, where non-Jewish POWs stood by their Jewish brothers-in-arms when the latter had been discriminated against. Such memoirs might have somewhat exaggerated the resistance of POWs in the face of their captors in order to present a more heroic version of events. Most, if not all, of the cases described in these memoirs did indeed occur; however it is possible that the writers chose to describe them in a way that would emphasize the bravery of the POWs rather than their helplessness. Nonetheless, after accounting for some of the issues described above and, where possible, cross-referencing memoirs and testimonies of the same events with other testimonies and with archival materials, the existing records can provide a powerful account of the experience of the Jewish POWs.

A point worth noting is that the testimonies and memoirs of American and British Jewish POWs are different to those of the Palestinian Jewish POWs in that they put less emphasis on their Jewish identity. The former had been in most cases fully integrated into their units and their identity usually did not play a role when they joined the army (although there were cases of German-Jewish immigrants who joined the British army in order to fight against the country that had discriminated against them).[83] Those who did write memoirs after the war—such as Cyril Rofe and Julius Green (the latter managed to hide his ethnicity for most of his time in captivity)—did not write them from the point of view of a Jewish POW, but from that of a British or American soldier who happened to be Jewish. Jewish POWs were mentioned in testimonies usually when cases of discrimination against Jews were described; in other cases, it was to emphasize a certain trait of an individual POW, such as his trading skills; or, it was to mention that the POW who told the story had never witnessed any discrimination against Jewish POWs.[84] Otherwise, the POW's religion or ethnicity was not mentioned simply because it was not considered relevant to the story that was being told.

The German POW Organization

Given the central role played by the POW Organization in the lives of the POWs, both Soviet and non-Soviet, it is important to provide a high level overview, before moving on to the main section of this book, of its structure, its responsibilities, and of how this organization evolved throughout the war.[85] A description

---

[83] Steven Kern, *Jewish Refugees from Germany and Austria in the British Army, 1939–45*, unpublished PhD thesis, University of Nottingham (2004), pp. 214–15.

[84] See, for example, Arthur Harvey, memoirs, http://www.pegasusarchive.org/pow/alan_harvey.htm, accessed 29 March 2018, and oral testimony of Alan Watchman, https://www.iwm.org.uk/collections/item/object/80010966, recorded 1989, accessed 1 February 2018, IWM catalogue number 11210.

[85] For a detailed description of the German POW organization and its evolution throughout the war, see Geoffrey P. Megargee, ed., *The United States Holocaust Memorial Museum Encyclopedia of Camps and Ghettos, 1933–1945*, vol. IV (Bloomington, IN: Indiana University Press, 2022), pp. 83–210.

of some of the personalities involved—e.g., the heads of the POW Office, POW camp commandants, etc.—their views and their actions is brought in the later chapters of this book.

Allied soldiers who were captured in battle were brought to improvised collection points, usually at the regimental level, before being sent to divisional- and corps-level collection points.[86] From these collection points they were sent, under guard, to the Army Prisoner Collection Point (*Armee Gefangenen sammelstelle—* AGSSt), which was the first dedicated organizational unit that dealt with POWs. The POWs' next stop was either straight to the permanent POW camp—a Stalag (short for *Stammlager*, or base camp, for enlisted personnel and NCOs), Oflag (short for *Offizierlager*, camp for officers), or Stalag Luft (for aircrews); or to an interim camp, a Dulag—the transit camp—for further interrogation, before being transferred to the permanent POW camp.[87] The POWs were transferred from the AGSSt by trains, usually in boxcars called 'forty and eight', meaning that they could carry either forty soldiers or eight horses—although in most cases the number of POWs per boxcar was much higher, making the sanitary situation in the carriages, which had no sanitary facilities, even more unbearable; in some cases, when transport was not available, POWs had to march for days in order to get to their final destination.[88] POWs were formally registered only when they arrived at the permanent camp; this meant that up until then there was no official acknowledgement by the Detaining Power of their capture and therefore cases of mistreatment or even murder of POWs at that stage could have gone unreported.[89]

POW camps in the Army operational area were called Frontstalags; together with the Dulags, they were mainly positioned in the occupied areas of the Soviet Union, held Soviet POWs and came under the jurisdiction of the OKH (*Oberkommando des Heeres*—the Army High Command). Stalags and Oflags within the area of the Reich (which included pre-war Germany, Austria, and the Protectorate of Bohemia and Moravia) were under the jurisdiction of the OKW (for inspection and professional supervision) and of the Replacement Army (*Ersatzheer*), through the POW commanders in the Reich's military districts.[90] This created a situation where although the POW Office was responsible for issuing to the various camps orders and general guidelines related to the treatment of POWs, it had no disciplinary authority over the POW commanders in the

---

[86] For description and examples of a POW's capture experience until he reached the POW camp see MacKenzie, *The Colditz Myth*, pp. 35–92.

[87] *The United States Holocaust Memorial Museum Encyclopedia of Camps and Ghettos, 1933–1945*, vol. IV, p. 149.

[88] For examples of the train transports and marches see MacKenzie, *The Colditz Myth*, pp. 81–2 and 66–7.

[89] *The United States Holocaust Memorial Museum Encyclopedia of Camps and Ghettos, 1933–1945*, vol. IV, p. 157.

[90] The Replacement Army was in charge of the military districts inside Germany, and for conscription, training, and replacement of personnel in the front.

military districts, who were in charge of the camp commandants and of the guard battalions.[91]

In total, there were 263 POW camps which were in use during different stages of the war: 254 Frontstalags, Stalags, and Oflags; seven Stalag Lufts, which came under the authority of the Airforce High Command (*Oberkommando des Luftwaffe*); and two Marinelagers (which were called *Marlags*) and came under the authority of the German Navy's high command (*Oberkommando der Marine*).[92] Frontstalags, Stalags, and Dulags in the Army operational area were usually given Arabic numerals, while those inside Germany were usually identified by Roman numerals—indicating the military district they were located in—followed by a Latin letter (A, B, C, etc.); for example, Stalag VIII-B (Lamsdorf) was located in military district VIII in Silesia. Stalag Lufts were given a roman numeral according to the air district the camp was located in (see Figure 1 for locations of POW camps in Germany).

The Stalag was usually divided into three main areas: the Commandant and camp administration's section, the guards' quarters, and the main camp, which contained the POWs' accommodations, infirmary, latrines, and kitchens (some camps also had their own hospital, the Lazaret). As can be seen in the map of Stalag I-B (Hohenstein) in Figure 2, the POWs section was secured by a double wire fence, while the 'German' camp, as it was known, laid outside the main camp and was enclosed by a single fence. Each camp was initially supposed to hold 10,000 POWs and administered by a staff of about 130 officers, NCOs, enlisted men and civilians, as well as two guard battalions with ~1,500 soldiers. As the war progressed and the number of POWs increased, the capacity of the camp grew to 30,000 POWs and the number of staff to more than 200.[93]

Since the Stalag's main task—other than to hold POWs—was to maximize the utilization of the POWs in the German economy, each Stalag usually served as the base camp for a network of sometimes hundreds of labour detachments (*Arbeitskommandos*), where the majority of POWs spent their captivity period.[94] Each labour detachment held anywhere between several POWs who might have worked on a farm and up to several hundred POWs who worked in factories, mines and construction. The Geneva Convention required POWs who were not officers to work for the Detaining Power, as long as the work was not directly

---

[91] Dienstanweisung für den Kommandanten eines 'Kriegsgefangenen Mannschafts Stammlagers', p. 7, BA-MA RH 1/612; and Overmans, 'Die Kriegsgefangenenpolitik des Deutschen Reichs 1939 bis 1945', p. 739. For the disciplinary authority of the POW Office see testimony of Reinhard von Westrem, *IMT, Trials of War Criminals*, vol. XI, p. 48.

[92] *The United States Holocaust Memorial Museum Encyclopedia of Camps and Ghettos, 1933–1945*, vol. IV, p. 160.

[93] Ibid., p. 163.

[94] For example, in March 1943, 67% of the POWs in Stalag VIII-B (Lamsdorf) (14,101 out of 20,952) were in labour detachments (see Swiss embassy report on Stalag VIII-B (Lamsdorf), 5 March 1943, p. 1, TNA 224/27).

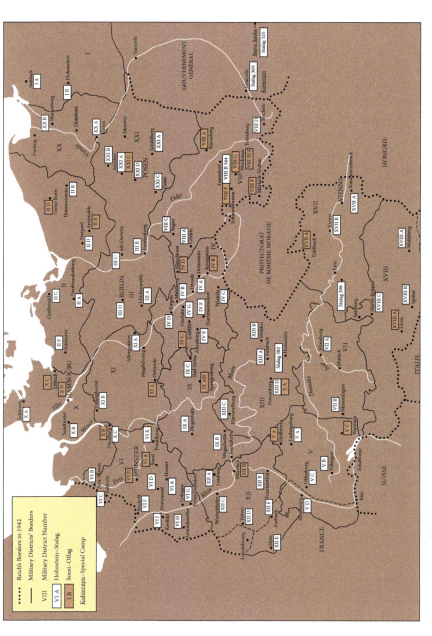

Figure 1 Map of POW camps inside the Reich
Durand, *La Captivité* (map attached at the end of the book).

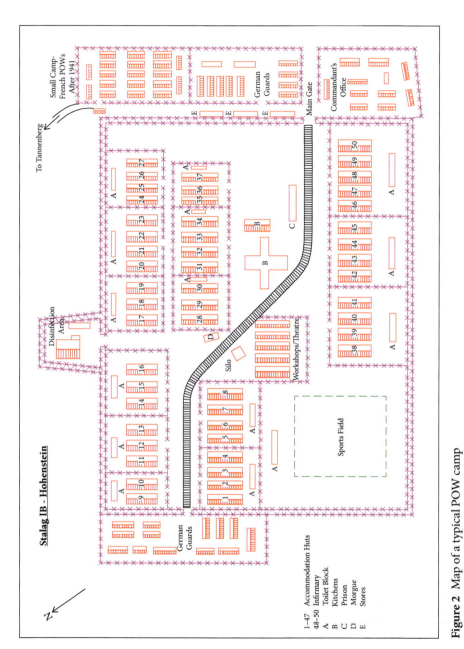

Figure 2 Map of a typical POW camp
https://www.pegasusarchive.org/pow/S1B/PicSt_1B_Plan.htm, accessed 1 December 2022.

connected to the war.⁹⁵ NCOs could choose whether to work or not; to overcome the boredom of daily life in the camp, some of them chose to do just that.⁹⁶ The nature of these labour detachments and the treatment they received differed greatly; being away from the base camp meant that the local commandants felt in some cases that they could run their own 'kingdoms' as they saw fit and did not have to adhere to the external rules.

The POW camp's organizational structure was headed by the camp commandant and his deputy. The main functions reporting into the commandant were that of the legal officer (*Gerichtsoffizier*), who was in charge of disciplinary matters; the camp leader (*Lagerführer*), responsible for the day-to-day running of the camp; the labour deployment group (*Gruppe Arbeitseinsatz*), which handled the deployment of the POWs according to the labour needs in the military district; the medical officer (*Sanitätsoffizier*); and the counterintelligence, or security, officer (*Abwehroffizier*), who was responsible for preventing escapes, sabotage, and espionage.⁹⁷ The camp commandant also had under his command one or more guard battalions which were initially assigned only guard duties, before being made responsible, in 1943, also for food provisioning and for medical care of the POWs.⁹⁸

The person who represented the POWs in front of the camp's authorities was the MOC, who was elected by the POWs but had to be approved by the OKW.⁹⁹ The MOC also took part in the meetings with the representatives of the Protecting Power and the ICRC when they visited the camp. In camps where POWs from different countries had been detained, each nationality usually had its own MOC.¹⁰⁰ Labour detachments also had their own MOC.

At the beginning of the war the responsibility for enemy POWs lied with the 'Wehrmacht casualties and POW administration' department (*Abteilung*) within AWA. The department, which was headed by Major Hans-Joachim Breyer, was also responsible for German POWs in enemy hands (see Figure 3).¹⁰¹ AWA, headed by Reinecke, reported to the chief of the OKW, Field Marshal Wilhelm Keitel, who was subordinated to the Commander-in-Chief of the Wehrmacht, Adolf Hitler.

---

⁹⁵ Articles 27 and 31 of the 1929 Geneva Convention, https://ihl-databases.icrc.org/ihl/INTRO/305, accessed 4 February 2018.
⁹⁶ Norman Rubenstein, *The Invisibly Wounded* (Hull: The Glenvil Group, 1989), p. 81; Rofe, *Against the Wind* (London: Hodder and Stoughton, 1956), p. 27.
⁹⁷ *The United States Holocaust Memorial Museum Encyclopedia of Camps and Ghettos, 1933–1945*, vol. IV, p. 162.
⁹⁸ Ibid., p. 102.
⁹⁹ Article 43 of the 1929 Geneva Convention, https://ihl-databases.icrc.org/ihl/INTRO/305, accessed 4 February 2018.
¹⁰⁰ Allgemeine Richtlinien für das Vertrauensmännerwesen, 15 September 1941, p. 1, PAAA R40954.
¹⁰¹ Figure 3 is based on the testimony of General Adolf Westhoff, BA-MA MSG 2/12656.

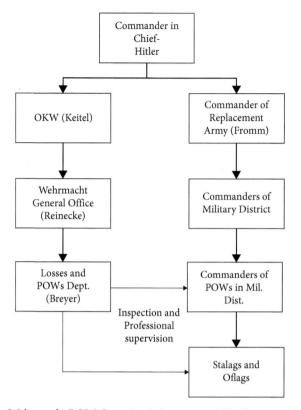

Figure 3 The Wehrmacht POW Organization structure 1939–January 1942

By January 1942, as the war progressed and the number of POWs grew, the unit became the POW Office (*Kriegsgefangenenwesen*), which by the end of the war had staff of approximately 4,000 (see Figure 4).[102] The POW Office consisted of two departments: one was the General Department, whose main roles were interacting with external bodies such as the ICRC and the Protecting Powers, arranging exchanges and releases, overseeing POWs' mail and parcel deliveries, and looking after the interests of German POWs in enemy hands. The other department was the Organization Department, which was responsible for providing statistics related to the POWs, distribution of POWs to the camps, overseeing POW camp personnel (commandants, guard battalions, etc.), and for the deployment of POWs in the German economy.[103]

In July 1944, following the assassination attempt on Hitler, Himmler replaced General Friedrich Fromm, who had been arrested as one of the plot's

---

[102] Overmans, 'Die Kriegsgefangenenpolitik des Deutschen Reichs 1939 bis 1945', p. 738 and Westhoff testimony, BA-MA MSG 2/12656.
[103] Stefan Geck, *Das deutsche Kriegsgefangenenwesen 1939–1945*, unpublished PhD thesis, Mainz University (1998), pp. 19–20.

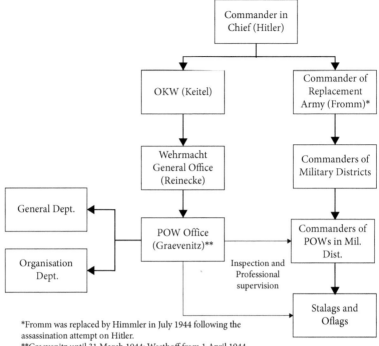

Figure 4 The Wehrmacht POW Organization structure January 1942–September 1944

co-conspirators, as Commander of the Replacement Army and took over the responsibility for all POW camps, including those of the Luftwaffe and the Navy. But it was not until October of that year that the POW Office itself was transferred from the OKW to Himmler and SS General Gottlob Berger was brought in to oversee it; the only responsibility the OKW was left with, through the Inspector of POWs (*Inspekteur Kriegsgefangene*), was for the relationship with external bodies such as the German Foreign Office, the NSDAP, the ICRC, and the Protecting Powers.[104] Berger had the Wehrmacht's POW commanders in the military districts report into a newly established position which he filled with Higher SS and Police Leaders—the HSSPF (see Figure 5).[105] However, this act seemed to have been an exception in terms of asserting SS influence over POW affairs; Berger did not replace any of the Wehrmacht personnel in that department and in general

---

[104] For the POW Office responsibilities see Geck, *Das deutsche Kriegsgefangenenwesen 1939–1945*, pp. 20–1. The role of Inspector of POWs was initially created in July 1943.

[105] Westhoff testimony, BA-MA MSG 2/12656; Jeremy Noakes and Geoffrey Pridham, eds, *Nazism 1919–1945*, vol. 3 (Liverpool: Liverpool University Press, 2014), p. 489.

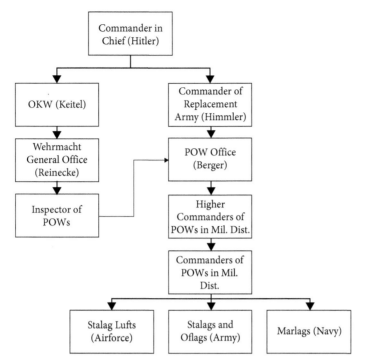

Figure 5 The Wehrmacht POW Organization structure from October 1944

continued with the implementation of the existing policies, although in some cases making them stricter.[106]

The rules for treating POWs in German POW camps were guided, in principle, by the 1929 Geneva Convention, of which Germany was one of the signatories and which was ratified by Germany in 1934, after Hitler came to power. The Convention, which attempted to combine the lessons of the First World War with previous conventions that dealt with the treatment of POWs, was the first international treaty that dealt specifically with the rights of POWs and the obligations of the Detaining Power. In previous conventions, such as the 1907 Hague Convention concerning the Laws and Customs of War on Land, POW policies were included only as a sub-set of the general military policies; the purpose of the 1929 Convention was not to replace these policies but to 'amplify and extend them, in the light of the experience of the [First] World War'.[107] Article 89 of the 1929 Geneva Convention stated that the Convention was complementary to

---

[106] In his trial, Berger explained that his decision not to replace OKW staff was done in order to ensure a 'smooth continuation of work' (see Berger interrogation, *IMT, Trial of War Criminals*, vol. XIII: *The Ministries Case* (Washington, DC, 1952), p. 62). A detailed analysis of Berger and his POW policies is discussed in Chapter 4.

[107] James Wilford Garner, 'Recent Conventions for the Regulations of War', *American Journal of International Law*, 26:4 (1932), pp. 807–11, p. 809.

Chapter 2 of the 1899 and 1907 Hague Conventions, which also dealt with POWs. The German interpretation, however, was that the Geneva Convention replaced ('*ersetzt*') Articles 4–20 in the 1907 Hague Convention and therefore German POW camp commandant manuals only referenced the 1929 Geneva Convention.[108]

The Convention's ninety-seven Articles—compared to the 1907 Hague Convention, which had seventeen Articles relating to POWs—covered areas such as the definition of a POW, the way they should be treated immediately after their capture, detailed aspects of their life in captivity (food, shelter, medical treatment, spiritual needs, work, post, etc.), and the role of international organizations and of the Protecting Power. The latter, together with the complete ban on reprisals against POWs, were the two main differences between the 1929 Convention and the preceding 1907 Hague one.[109] Another difference was Article 82, which stated that the Convention applied to both belligerents even if one of them had not been a signatory to it.[110] Germany's false argument, that since the Soviet Union did not ratify the Convention it did not have to comply with it, led directly to the death of millions of Soviet POWs.

Summary

The primary and secondary sources reviewed in this section deal with several aspects of the American and British Jewish POWs' experience, both on the macro and micro levels; however, this topic has not been addressed so far in a comprehensive, methodical manner. The conclusions of the limited number of studies that do deal specifically with the reasons behind the relatively non-discriminatory treatment of non-Soviet Jewish POWs are general in nature and do not take into account the intricacies of the Nazi hierarchy, the various German state organs and their differing interests, the radicalization in Germany's POW and Jewish policies, and the different stages of the war. In addition, the existing accounts of the general experience of American and British Jewish POWs in German captivity, of cases of discrimination against them, of their interaction with their German captors, and of other aspects specific to Jewish POWs, such as maintaining a Jewish identity in a Nazi POW camp, are only found in individual testimonies and

---

[108] See Alfons Waltzog, *Recht der Landkriegsführung* (Berlin: Franz Vahlen, 1942), p. 109; and Dienstanweisung für den Kommandanten eines 'Kriegsgefangenen Mannschafts Stammlagers', 16 February 1939, p. 7, BA-MA RH 1/612.

[109] For additional information regarding the 1929 Geneva Conventions and the differences with the 1907 Hague Convention see Neville Wylie, 'The 1929 Prisoner of War Convention and the Building of the Inter-War Prisoner of War Regime', in Sibylle Scheipers, ed., *Prisoners in War* (New York: Oxford University Press, 2010), pp. 91–110, pp. 94–101; and Garner, 'Recent Conventions for the Regulations of War', pp. 809–11.

[110] Article 82 of the 1929 Geneva Convention, https://ihl-databases.icrc.org/ihl/INTRO/305, accessed 14 September 2019.

memoirs and are anecdotal in nature. As a result, these topics have not been analysed in a way that will provide a complete end-to-end picture—from the individual American and British Jewish POW to the top of the Nazi hierarchy—of the experience of these POWs in German captivity. The purpose of this research is to address this gap.

The first part of this book looks at the lives of American and British Jewish POWs throughout their captivity lifecycle. Chapter 1 discusses the interaction that they had during their time in the POW camps and in the labour detachments with their captors—including camp commandants, interrogators, and camp guards—as well as with other groups they came in contact with, such as forced labour workers and German civilians. Interactions that occurred outside the camp, for example when a Jewish POW was brought in front of a military court, or was treated in a hospital, are also discussed. The chapter examines how Jewish POWs were treated by these different groups, and attempts to explain their treatment by assessing whether the National Socialist indoctrination and individual anti-Semitic beliefs of the German soldiers they encountered were strong enough to overcome specific orders to treat POWs according to the Geneva Convention.

Chapter 2 deals with the issue of being a Jew in a Nazi POW camp and maintaining the POW's Jewish identity, from the time of capture and the decision as to whether to declare one's ethnicity, through to the way captives displayed it as it relates to religious activities, cultural activities and funerals, to their interaction with their doomed civilian brethren. The chapter demonstrates how maintaining their Jewish identity not only helped the POWs to strengthen their spirit and resolve during their time in captivity, but was also used as an act of defiance against their captors.

The second part of the book takes a top-down approach and examines the OKW's POW policies as they related to Jewish POWs. Chapter 3 focuses on cases of segregation of American and British Jewish POWs from their non-Jewish comrades and uses them to assess to what extent orders related to Jewish POWs were actually implemented by commanders of POWs in the military districts and by their subordinates, the POW camp commandants. The chapter suggests explanations as to why camp commandants in most cases chose to ignore segregation orders, even after the POW Office was taken over in October 1944 by SS General Gottlob Berger, who was known as *'der allmächtige Gottlob'* ('the almighty Gottlob').[111]

Chapter 4 reviews the Wehrmacht's approach to Jewish POWs and describes the involvement that different levels in the Wehrmacht's chain of command, starting with its Commander-in-Chief, Adolf Hitler, through to the German High Command and the POW Office, had with setting POW policies, both in the East

---

[111] IMT, *Trials of War Criminals*, vol. XIII, p. 480. 'Almighty Gottlob' is obviously a play on 'Almighty God'.

and in the West. It also looks at the level of influence that state bodies such as the RSHA and the NSDAP had on these policies. The chapter analyses the way that POW policies were reflected in the orders issued by the POW Office which related to Jewish POWs, and suggests several explanations as to why these policies resulted in American and British Jewish POWs—and in fact, non-Soviet Jewish POWs in general—being treated in most cases in accordance with the Geneva Convention, despite the radicalization that took place throughout the war in Germany's anti-Semitic and POW policies.

This book tells the story of American and British Jewish POWs who were held captive by a regime determined to exterminate their people; yet, protected by the POW Office and by the Geneva Convention, almost all of them emerged alive from their captivity. The analysis of the reasons for this outcome, together with the description of the experience of these POWs in captivity, will help reshape our understanding of the Holocaust and of Nazi Germany.

1
American and British Jewish POWs in German POW Camps

Introduction

> ... [W]e had hunger, we had bombing by our own planes; fleas now were in command, and rats were everywhere .... And with it all, there was the ever present horror of being a Jew in prison in Germany, and it all added up to a hopeless situation.[1]

This is how Leonard Winograd, an American Jewish navigator with the 376th Bomb Group who was captured in the winter of 1945 after his plane was shot down over Yugoslavia, described the feeling of being a Jewish POW in a German POW camp.[2] Initial reports on the mass murder of Jews in Europe began appearing in the American and British press in late 1941; these reports became more prominent in mid-1942 especially in the British press, while the American press usually relegated them to the inner pages.[3] As a result, although POWs' knowledge of the systematic nature of the Final Solution was in most cases, much like that of the rest of the world at the time, still vague, Jewish POWs knew enough about Germany's anti-Semitic policies for it to add another dimension to the long list of sufferings and uncertainties every POW faced in captivity.

This chapter will describe the experience of American and British Jewish POWs who were held in German POW camps and analyse the behaviour of those who interacted directly with them, namely the camp commandants, guards, and civilians. The chapter will address the following three questions: first, whether there were cases of mistreatment and discrimination against them because of their religion and race; second, if there were such cases, whether they were a result of an official policy or the local initiatives of anti-Semitic camp commandants, guards, or German civilians; and third, whether the Wehrmacht's military discipline, which, in POW camps where non-Soviet POWs were incarcerated, required adherence to the Geneva Convention, was strong enough to curb the

---

[1] Leonard Winograd, 'Double Jeopardy: What an American Army Officer, a Jew, Remembers of Prison Life in Germany', *American Jewish Archives Journal*, 1 (1976), pp. 3–17, p. 15.
[2] Ibid., p. 4.
[3] Deborah Lipstadt, *Beyond Belief* (New York: The Free Press, 1986), pp. 141 and 153–5.

presumed anti-Semitism of the individual Wehrmacht soldiers and officers when they interacted with American and British Jewish POWs. The following sections will demonstrate that in general, during the Second World War, despite its ingrained anti-Semitism, its extreme racial policies and its obsession with applying the 'Final Solution' to all Jews in Nazi-occupied Europe, Germany treated American and British Jewish POWs, with very few exceptions, according to the 1929 Geneva Convention.

Many aspects of POW camps would support Erving Goffman's definition of a 'Total Institution', where inmates' activities were conducted in one place, were tightly scheduled and were controlled and dictated by a single authority. However, there were a few aspects that did not follow this definition: first, POW camps did not serve as a 'barrier to social intercourse with the outside'.[4] Most POWs were interned in labour detachments and in most cases interacted closely with civilians and forced labourers, working side by side with them in mines, factories, and farms; the endless number of directives issued by the Wehrmacht prohibiting interaction between POWs and German women was only one attestation to that.

Second and more importantly, in the case of Jewish POWs, the barrier to interaction with the outside world worked also in the opposite direction, and in addition to 'protect[ing] the community against what are felt to be intentional dangers to it', the camp also shielded non-Soviet Jewish POWs from the radicalization that was going on outside its walls.[5] Processes of radicalization in POW policies in the West—such as the October 1942 'Kommando Befehl', the March 1944 'Kugel [bullet] Erlass', or the official endorsement and encouragement of lynching of downed Allies' air-crews by civilians (all of which are described in detail in Chapter 4)—did not result in a similar deterioration in the treatment of non-Soviet Jewish POWs inside POW camps, even after their control was transferred to SS General Gottlob Berger in October 1944.

In addition to the policies, the general anti-Semitic atmosphere in Germany could have been expected to influence the conduct of POW camp staff towards Jewish POWs; however, as mentioned in the Introduction to this book, historical research analysing the anti-Semitic behaviour and motivation of German soldiers has dealt mainly with front-line soldiers (e.g. Neitzel, Welzer, Römer, and Bartov), whereas those who interacted with POWs on a daily basis have been neglected—the POW camp chain of command and specifically the guard battalions. Although some of them were former front-line soldiers who were transferred to the guard battalions after they were injured in battle, the majority of these men were usually of different age and health profiles to combatant soldiers and possibly with different motivations as well, and therefore the two groups cannot be easily

---

[4] Erving Goffman, *Asylums* (New York and London: Taylor & Francis, 2017), p. 6; ibid., p. 4.
[5] Ibid., pp. 4–5.

compared.⁶ A more relevant comparison to the behaviour of POW camp personnel can be found in Browning's analysis of the behaviour of the 101 Reserve Police Battalion who operated in Poland and participated in the murder of civilian Jews; although they were volunteers, operated closer to the front line and in different situational conditions, the age profile of the battalion's members was closer to that of the POW camp guards, which meant that unlike the Wehrmacht's conscripted front-line soldier, the majority of the members of these groups did not spend their formative years being indoctrinated in the National Socialist worldview.⁷ This difference was recognized by Jewish POWs themselves—Cyril Rofe, a British Jewish pilot who at the beginning of 1944 was held in one of Stalag VIII-B's (Lamsdorf) labour detachments, compared the behaviour of one of the middle-aged guards there to that of a younger one, who was 'brought up on Goebbels and Hitler Youth [and] very anti-Semitic'.⁸

Camp staff, front-line soldiers, and reserve policemen did share, however, the same set of military values, first among them the adherence to military discipline: this was strictly enforced during the Second World War, as demonstrated by the figures for capital punishment in the German army in comparison to the First World War, 15,000 vs. only forty-eight; and this disciplinary context must have contributed to the camp personnel's almost full compliance with the Geneva Convention.⁹ Another possible reason for the protection provided by the POW camp is related to the American and British Jewish POWs being front-line soldiers and part of armies of nations considered racially closer to the Germans: as one of the German guards explained to a Palestinian Jewish POW, they had nothing against Jewish soldiers who fought bravely against them; their war was only against 'the Rothschilds and the Jewish capital'.¹⁰ Therefore, the fact that a specific order to treat Jewish POWs in the same way as non-Jewish POWs 'belonging to the respective armies' was only issued in the last months of the war only formalized a de facto situation—American and British Jewish POWs were also protected probably because they belonged to the American and British armies and despite their racial status.¹¹

---

⁶ Sönke Neitzel and Harald Welzer, *Soldaten* (London: Simon and Schuster, 2012); Felix Römer, *Comrades, The Wehrmacht from Within* (Oxford: Oxford University Press, 2019); Omer Bartov, *Hitler's Army* (New York: Oxford University Press, 1992). On the age and health profile of the guards see Müller, *Hitler's Wehrmacht*, p. 112; Hasselbring, *American Prisoners of War in the Third Reich*, p. 133.

⁷ Christopher Browning, *Ordinary Men: Reserve Police Battalion 101 and the Final Solution in Poland* (New York and London: Harper Perennial, 2017).

⁸ Rofe, *Against the Wind*, p. 175. Complaints to inspecting officers ensured that the latter type of guards did not last long in their roles (ibid., p. 176).

⁹ Neitzel and Welzer, *Soldaten*, pp. 238–44; Bartov explains that this increase was attributed mainly to several categories of offenses being redefined as political ones and punishable by death (see Omer Bartov, 'Soldiers, Nazis and the War in the Third Reich', *Journal of Modern History*, 63 (1991), p. 51).

¹⁰ Fritz Yordan, *My Escape from Captivity* (Ain Harod: HaKibutz HaMe'uchad, 1945), p. 75.

¹¹ Befehlsammlung 48, order 876, 15 December 1944, BA-MA RW 6/270.

This chapter examines the interaction between the approximately 4,700 American and British Jewish POWs and their German captors throughout their captivity lifecycle.[12] It is divided into three sections: the first describes their experience from the moment of capture, through the transfer from the front to the transit camp, until they reached the permanent POW camp; and the second describes their experience in the POW camps and labour detachments. Each section is further divided into two sub-sections: one deals with individual Jewish POWs in the American and British armies, interned in different POW camps and fully integrated with their non-Jewish comrades; and the other with the Palestinian Jewish POWs, who volunteered for the British army, were captured in Greece in April 1941, and then spent the majority of their captivity period together in Jewish-only groups. The third section of this chapter describes the interaction Jewish POWs had with their captors when they found themselves, for various reasons, outside the walls the POW camps—the Total Institution that was protecting them. Cases of Jewish POWs who were brought before military courts, of their medical treatment in hospitals, and of their escapes, will be reviewed. The chapter also describes the attempts by various bodies, such as governments, the ICRC and Jewish organizations, to obtain information regarding the condition and treatment of the Jewish POWs.

Capture and Transit

The immediate hours and days after a soldier became a POW were arguably the most dangerous period of his captivity. Article 2 of the 1929 Geneva Convention stipulated that POWs were the responsibility of the Detaining Power from the moment of capture; however, the Convention did not contain a clear definition of that specific event. Therefore, from the moment he raised his arms (or a white flag) to indicate surrender, until he reached a POW camp where he could be formally registered by delegates of the ICRC, a POW's fate was, in practice, still uncertain. Enemy soldiers, still in a battle state of mind and sometimes wanting to avenge fallen or injured comrades, might not hesitate before shooting a surrendering soldier, an act described by historian Oliver Wilkinson referring to such incidents in the First World War as 'kneejerk reactions made in hot blood'.[13] If anyone challenged a captor for such shooting—which was rarely the case—they could easily justify it as a case of self-defence or preventing an escape.[14] And later,

---

[12] For the calculation of the number of American and British Jewish POWs see the Introduction to this book.
[13] Oliver Wilkinson, *British Prisoners of War in First World War Germany* (Cambridge: Cambridge University Press, 2017), p. 25.
[14] For examples of the risks associated with the period immediately following capture, see Memorandum to the British War Cabinet on The Committing of Acts of Violence towards British Prisoners of War, 18 October 1944, TNA CAB 66/56/4; MacKenzie, *The Colditz Myth*, pp. 35–41; and Neitzel and Welzer, *Soldaten*, pp. 331–3.

while the POW was being transferred from the improvised collection points at the regimental, divisional and corps level to the rear, cases of beating or even shooting could be even more difficult to prevent since discipline during the journey was usually not as strict as in the front line.

The Capture Experience of American and British Jewish Soldiers

For individual Jewish soldiers who fought as part of the American and British armies the danger during capture was, in most cases, not any different to the one facing their non-Jewish comrades. However, in addition to the feelings of disempowerment and humiliation associated with being captured, given what was already known about the German treatment of Jews, Jewish soldiers also faced the fear of being singled out.[15] Norman Rubenstein, a British Jewish soldier who was captured in Calais in 1940, described his feelings when the realization of imminent captivity dawned upon him: 'It was impossible to shut out the thoughts about being a Jew, about to become a prisoner of war in Nazi Germany'.[16] In fact, in an intelligence briefing given in the 446th American Bomb Group in 1943, the intelligence officer explained that since so far they had not encountered any Jewish escapees from POW camps, their assumption was that Jewish airmen were being treated differently; and therefore, they should hide their identification discs (also known as 'dog tags') when captured.[17] The identification discs were the fastest way for the Germans to identify captured Jewish soldiers: in the United States army, Jewish soldiers had the letter H, for Hebrew, inscribed on their discs, while those in the British army had the letter J (their religion was also recorded in their army paybook).[18] There were also cases where the concern for becoming a POW led some Jewish soldiers, when joining the army, to identify as non-Jews in order to ensure that the mark on their identification discs would be different.[19]

The concern regarding the treatment of Jewish POWs was in fact first raised by the French government with the ICRC even before the end of the campaign in France. On 10 June 1940, Carl Burckhardt, then a member of the ICRC and later its president, responded to a letter sent by M. G. Vermeil, from the French Ministry of Information, and explained to him that although there was no specific agreement concerning French Jewish or part-Jewish POWs, the ICRC believed it would be inappropriate to bring up this topic with the Germans. In any case, Burckhardt added, POWs belonged to the German army, and not to civilian or party organizations; and the case of reciprocity (which apparently had been

---

[15] Wilkinson, *British Prisoners of War in First World War Germany*, p. 38.
[16] Rubenstein, *The Invisibly Wounded*, p. 25.
[17] Bruce Wolk, *Jewish Aviators in World War II* (Jefferson, NC: McFarland & company, 2016), p. 96.
[18] For more details regarding the methods used by the Germans to identify captured Jewish soldiers see the Identifying Jewish POWs section in Chapter 3.
[19] For a discussion regarding the issue of declaring a different religion see Chapter 2 of this book.

raised by Vermeil in his original letter, which was not found) was not relevant because there were no Jewish soldiers in the German army.[20] The last comment provides a disturbing insight into the frame of mind that existed at the time—and perhaps even later—within the ICRC: French Jewish POWs (and therefore French Jewish soldiers in general, and perhaps even Jewish soldiers in other armies as well) were not considered by the ICRC to be French POWs, but a separate group; and therefore if reprisals were to occur as a result of their mistreatment, they would be applied only to German Jewish POWs—of which, since Jews were not allowed to serve in the Wehrmacht, there were none—and not to German POWs in general. Vermeil's letter, however, demonstrates that even at such an early stage—and perhaps based on reports regarding the treatment of Polish Jewish POWs in the previous year—there was already a real concern regarding the possible mistreatment of Jewish POWs in the hands of the Germans.[21]

The experience that Leonard Winograd—the American Jewish navigator mentioned earlier in this chapter—had in a prison in Zagreb after he was captured is an example of why these concerns were not unfounded; at the same time, it demonstrates the conflict between the German attempt to follow correct military procedure and discipline on the one hand and an individual soldier's personal anti-Semitic beliefs on the other. Upon arrival, a German Non-Commissioned Officer (NCO) slapped Winograd because he refused to tell him his religion; the NCO was then ordered by his commander to apologize for hitting an officer but refused on the grounds that Winograd was a Jew.[22] Winograd was later transferred to a Dulag in Oberusel, the Luftwaffe interrogation centre near Frankfurt, where the interrogator told him that although he had nothing against Jews he would have to pass him on to the Gestapo unless he answered his questions; and that the Gestapo would not be as considerate as he had been. This turned out to be an empty threat, and Winograd was eventually sent to a POW camp without having any interaction with the Gestapo.[23] The mention of the Gestapo was a standard practice in these interrogations; it carried additional weight since the POW had not yet, at this stage, been formally registered as a POW, and therefore could have been kept hidden or even murdered with hardly a trace being left. And, if the captured Jewish POW had relatives in Germany, the interrogator could use that to exert even greater pressure on him to talk.[24] In the final stages of the war Winograd was transferred to Stalag VII-A near Moosburg; the British POW who recorded his arrival told him it was better not to register as a Jew,

---

[20] Burckhardt to Vermeil, 10 June 1940, ACICR BG 25/34.
[21] Datner, *Crimes against POWs*, pp. 99–107; Krakowski, 'The Fate of Jewish Prisoners of War in the September 1939 Campaign', p. 305.
[22] Winograd, 'Double Jeopardy', p. 7.   [23] Ibid., p. 11.
[24] Arthur Durand, *Stalag Luft III* (London: Simon and Schuster, 1989), p. 66.

because during his own five years of captivity he had seen too many Jews disappear. Winograd refused.[25]

The captors were not always interested in the POW's religion. Second Lieutenant Hyman Fine, an American Jewish navigator of a B-24 bomber, was captured in September 1944. Although he had kept his identification discs, the Germans did not check them when he was brought to the interrogation centre in Oberusel, and when asked for his religion, he simply did not answer; apparently, this saved him a few months later from the segregation of Jewish POWs in Stalag Luft I (Barth).[26] Second Lieutenant Irwin Stovroff, a Jewish bombardier with the 44th Bomb Group who was captured in France in August 1944, had a strange encounter with the officer who interrogated him before he was sent to Stalag Luft I (Barth). It turned out that prior to the war this officer had lived in the same neighbourhood as Stovroff in Buffalo, New York and was even in the same class in school as his older sister. The officer promised to help him and had apparently done so by putting a question mark on the form next to Stovroff's religion.[27] When 19-year-old Sonny Fox surrendered during the Ardennes offensive in December 1944, he was not thinking about his ethnicity; he described his feelings as a combination of 'relief at being alive, fear of what was about to befall us, but also a keen curiosity about…new experience'.[28] Later, when he arrived at Stalag IX-B (Bad Orb) he insisted that the registration clerk, an American POW, list him as Jewish; the clerk ignored him and recorded his religion as Protestant. Fox recalled how the clerk 'could not be bothered to spend any more time [arguing] with the putz who did not appreciate the gift he was just given'.[29] Although he kept his identification discs which identified him as a Jew, the clerk's insistence saved Fox a few weeks later when a group of 350 POWs, which included all the American Jewish POWs in the camp as well as non-Jewish POWs, was sent from Stalag IX-B (Bad Orb) to the Berga slave labour camp.[30]

While some of the capture experiences of Jewish POWs ended, at worst, with a slap on the face, there were also testimonies that point to different outcomes, where the captors' anti-Semitic beliefs took priority over military discipline and adherence to the Geneva Convention. One such case was Norman Rubenstein's, who destroyed his identification discs when he was captured but decided to give his real name, which identified him as a Jew.[31] While being marched to the rear he managed to escape but was caught a few days later by an SS unit. One of the soldiers identified him as Jewish and started to beat him, only to be stopped by

---

[25] Winograd, 'Double Jeopardy', p. 17.
[26] Hal LaCroix, *Journey Out of Darkness* (Westport and London: Praeger, 2007), pp. 168–9.
[27] Irwin Stovroff, https://www.vetshelpingheroes.org/about-irwin-stovroff/, accessed 1 August 2019.
[28] Sonny Fox, *But You Made the Front Page!* (Kindle Edition: Argos Navis Author Services, 2012), ln. 840.
[29] Ibid., ln. 241.   [30] Ibid., ln. 255.
[31] Rubenstein, *The Invisibly Wounded*, p. 26.

his officer who told him that as a POW he should not be mistreated. Later on the same soldier announced to him that he would be executed the following day, because 'we are the SS...[a]nd we kill all Jews'.[32] The soldier was then stopped by one of his colleagues who said 'Jew or no Jew, that is a man'.[33] Even indoctrinated SS members, on rare occasions, seemed to have followed their own moral principles rather than Nazi values.

However, other testimonies given after the war as part of war crimes investigations showed that not all Jewish POWs caught by the SS were that lucky: after the Normandy landings, near the village of Montmartin-en-Graignes, SS stabscharführer (NCO) Erwin Schienkiewicz withdrew two Jewish members of a captured American unit and shot them; and an SS Colonel testified that two American doctors who had been captured during the Battle of the Bulge in December 1944 and were put to work in a German field hospital were later shot by an SS officer on their way to the POW camp because they were Jewish.[34] Similarly, during the same battle, there were cases of American POWs who were marched to the rear by the SS being ordered to expose their identification discs; some of them were taken aside and shot. Suspecting that the religion named on their discs was the reason for these murders, 'Mexicans and Indians began swapping their tags with the Jews in the columns [and] Catholics and Protestants began passing them their Bibles'.[35] When other American POWs arrived in Stalag XIII-C near Hammelburg, the Jews among them were ordered by the guards to step forward. According to Curtis Whiteway, who fought with the 99th Infantry Division and collected these testimonies, those who came forward were never seen again.[36] Corporal Harold Gattung, an American soldier with the 361st Infantry Division, was captured in Italy on 28 July 1944; when arriving at the Dulag near Mantova he testified that the Germans had looked for Jewish soldiers; they had found three and took them away. Gattung said he never saw them again.[37]

These types of testimonies about Jewish soldiers being murdered after capture were not, however, common. In any case, those given forty to fifty years after the events took place are more difficult to corroborate. It is possible that witnesses incorporated their later knowledge of the Holocaust into their stories.[38] However, it is not a coincidence that the murders that were investigated by the American Judge Advocate General's war crimes units immediately after the war involved the SS, since for them military discipline was completely aligned with their National Socialist beliefs, first and foremost with their anti-Semitism. Such behaviour

---

[32] Ibid.   [33] Ibid., pp. 31–3.
[34] Noel Story, 'Recommendation for Closing Case', 13 February 1947, NARA RG 549, box 174, 290/59/22/5.
[35] The Checkerboard (99th Infantry Division Association), September 1990, p. 5.
[36] Ibid., March 1989, p. 8.
[37] Harry Spiller, *Prisoners of Nazis: Accounts by American POWs in World War II* (Jefferson, NC and London: McFarland and Company, 1998), pp. 27–8.
[38] Winter and Sivan, *War and Remembrance*, ln. 374.

mirrored the behaviour of SS units in the East—and some of these units were likely to have taken part in both campaigns. Nevertheless, the fact that more testimonies have not surfaced supports the conclusion that such events were not widespread and in cases where they did occur, they were not the result of a general policy but probably a decision by low-ranking unit commanders in the field of battle. Although there were cases of mass executions of POWs in the West immediately after capture—for example, of British POWs during the French campaign and American POWs during the Battle of the Bulge—these were not linked to their religion or ethnicity.[39] A more relevant comparison can be made with the several German massacres during the French campaign of 1940 of hundreds of Black French colonial troops, who, like Jews, belonged to a racial group which was considered inferior by the Nazis, and with the deportation of Spanish Republican POWs, who also fought with the French army, from POW camps to concentration camps, where most of them perished. However, there were no similar massacres of captured Jewish soldiers on the Western Front, either in 1940–1 or in 1944–5; nor were there cases of non-Soviet Jewish POWs being sent to concentration camps because of their ethnicity.[40] Although it is not likely that Jewish POWs were aware of the treatment of Black French colonial troops, the fact that they thought they might be targeted for killing and in some cases tried to hide their Jewish identity provides an insight into their state of mind and the feelings of uncertainty and vulnerability they felt when captured.

The POW's religion was one piece of information that was required to be filled in on the POW registration card; in some cases the Germans made an effort to obtain this information, and in other cases they did not. There were cases where Jewish soldiers were singled out and murdered upon capture, most notably by SS soldiers; cases where the soldier's Jewish identity was used to pressure him during interrogation or to mistreat him; and other cases where the soldier's Jewish religion was ignored altogether. These examples therefore support the conclusion that other than the segregation policy, which instructed camp commandants to separate Jewish and non-Jewish soldiers in the POW camps, which is described in Chapter 3, there was no policy dictated from above to treat non-Soviet Jewish POWs differently from their non-Jewish comrades.

---

[39] MacKenzie, *The Colditz Myth*, p. 40.
[40] For cases of massacres of West African soldiers see Scheck, *Hitler's African Victims*, pp. 33–41; for the treatment of Spanish Republican POWs ('Rotspanien'), see Michel Fabréguet, 'Un Groupe de Réfugiés Politiques: les Républicains Espagnols des Camps d'internement Français aux Camps de Concentration Nationaux-Socialistes (1939–1941)', *Revue d'histoire de la Deuxième Guerre mondiale et des conflits contemporains*, 36:144 (1986), pp. 19–38. There are testimonies about Yugoslavian Jewish POWs who were executed upon capture by the Croatian Ustaša, who collaborated with the Germans (see Keynan, *Memories from a Life I Have Not Lived*, p. 431).

The Capture Experience of Palestinian Jewish Soldiers

The case of the Palestinian Jews who volunteered for the British army and were organized in Palestinian-only companies (some of which also included Palestinian Arabs) within the Royal Pioneer Corps provides a different angle for analysing the treatment of Jewish POWs during capture. Unlike the individual Jewish POWs who in most cases could choose whether to hide their religion or not, the Palestinian Jews could not—in fact would not—hide it; their commanders had made a conscious decision to go into captivity as Jews. The vast majority of the soldiers followed; the only exceptions were those who managed to escape, and a small number who committed suicide.[41] These Palestinian Jews, who had volunteered to fight for Britain, were among the 10,000 British soldiers who waited to be evacuated in the Greek port of Kalamata, only to eventually surrender on 29 April 1941 to the advancing German army. When the British soldiers received the order to surrender, Colonel Renton, the commanding officer of the Pioneer companies, advised them to try and disappear in small groups into the surrounding hills.[42] The Jewish soldiers turned down his advice: the concern of one of their officers, Shimon Hacohen, was that if they followed it and were subsequently captured, as Jews, they could be executed on the spot.[43] The captured Palestinian Jewish soldiers then destroyed their arms, shaved, fixed their appearance and marched into captivity.[44]

The Germans—even at the highest command level, as an entry in the diary of the chief-of-staff of the army, General Halder, indicated—were aware that a large Jewish contingent had fallen into their hands but no specific orders were issued as to how to deal with them.[45] An unexpected encounter occurred when one of the Jewish POWs, a refugee from Austria, met a Wehrmacht soldier who had been

---

[41] Yosef Almogi (Karlenboim), *With Head Held High* (Tel Aviv: Ministry of Defence Publishing, 1989), p. 31. See also Alexander Glantz, *Struggle in Captivity* (Tel Aviv: Eshel, 1966), p. 46.

[42] When they realized that they were about to become POWs, most British officers who led the Palestinian companies left them and joined 'pure' British units; their conduct was later questioned in the British Parliament (see Sela, *Shackles of Captivity*, p. 50; and Wedgwood to Margesson, minutes of the House of Commons, 11 November 1941, https://hansard.parliament.uk/commons/, accessed 17 June 2022).

[43] Almogi, *With Head Held High*, p. 31. Later in the war, one of Hacohen's—which means 'the priest' in Hebrew—fellow POWs in Oflag IV-C (Colditz) said of him jokingly that 'a more unpriestly character you could not have found if you searched for years' (see Julius Green, *From Colditz in Code* (London: Robert Hale & Company, 1971), p. 131).

[44] Ibid., p. 32. See also Yohanan Yaacovi, *The Road to Captivity*, unpublished MA Thesis, Tel Aviv University (1976), p. 103; Yitschak Ben-Aharon, 'In Nazi Captivity', in Zeev Shefer and Yitshak Lamdan, eds, *The Volunteering Book* (Jerusalem: Mosad Bialik, 1949), p. 650.

[45] *War Journal of Franz Halder*, 2 May 1941, vol. 6, p. 95; German intelligence report, 30 April 1941, BA-MA RH 20–12/208; and interview with Alfred Jädtke of the 5th Panzer Division, in Yaacovi, *The Road to Captivity*, p. 104. General Halder, the chief-of-staff of the German army noted in his diary on 2 May 1941 the capture in Greece of '1,350 Jews and Arabs'.

his former classmate.⁴⁶ Although there was an initial attempt to segregate the POWs according to nationality—English, Scottish, Indian, Palestinian, and so on—it was not especially decisive and given the objections of the POWs the Germans did not attempt to rigorously enforce it.⁴⁷ In fact, a British Sergeant-Major tried to enforce his own method of segregation when the hungry POWs stood in line for tea—the first hot drink they received since being captured. He arranged the approximately 9,000 POWs in three lines—the British, Australians, and New-Zealanders in one, the Palestinians and Cypriots in another, and the Indians in the third—and made sure the first group were served ahead of the rest.⁴⁸ When one of the Palestinian POWs complained, the German guard moved the Palestinian POWs to the front of the queue and ordered the British Sergeant-Major to serve them first.⁴⁹

A few days after they were captured, on 2 May 1941, the Palestinian Jewish POWs were transferred, together with their non-Jewish comrades, to a newly erected POW camp in Korinth.⁵⁰ The meagre food rations forced some of the POWs to trade their valuables with their German captors: one of the Palestinian Jews, originally from Vienna, traded a valuable diamond ring for some bread, and was surprised when, on the following day, the guard returned the ring telling him that he could not sleep at night with the thought of how he acquired the ring from a starving prisoner.⁵¹ 'So much for Adolf's 1000 year Reich and the indoctrination of Nazi Germany's Hitler Youth', commented Paul Weiner, one of the Palestinian Jewish POWs, when he recounted the story in his memoirs.⁵²

The concern for the Palestinian Jewish POWs must have been the trigger behind the letter that was sent on 29 May 1941, a month after they had been captured, by the British Foreign Office to the Protecting Power, raising the issue of potential discrimination against 'non-Aryans'.⁵³ In its response, the USA—the Protecting Power at the time—confirmed that it was not aware of any such discrimination, but that it would continue to 'keep watch'; furthermore, it advised that it would be 'impolite' to draw the attention of the German government to this category of POWs.⁵⁴ The use of the word 'impolite' in this context—instead of, perhaps, 'unwise'—is not clear; after all, it was the role of the Protecting Power to look after the interests of the British POWs, and not to be concerned about hurting the feelings of the Detaining Power. Regardless, this letter is arguably the

---

⁴⁶ Sela, *Shackles of Captivity*, p. 56. See also Yosef Karlenboim, 'The Captivity', *The Volunteering Book*, p. 628; test in German captivity, July 1945, p. 61, IDF 182/1867/1998. A similar case occurred in Oflag XIII-B (Nürnberg-Langwasser), where a Yugoslav Jewish officer POW met a German officer with whom he fought shoulder to shoulder in the First World War (see Ženi Lebl, *Jewish Soldiers from Yugoslavia as POWs in Nazi Germany* (Tel Aviv: The Association of WWII Veterans in Israel—the Yugoslav section, 1995), p. 33).
⁴⁷ Yaacovi, *The Road to Captivity*, p. 103; see also Glantz, *Struggle in Captivity*, p. 74.
⁴⁸ Yordan, *My Escape From Captivity*, p. 70.   ⁴⁹ Ibid.
⁵⁰ Almogi, *With Head Held High*, p. 33.
⁵¹ Hans Paul Weiner, unpublished memoirs, pp. 34–5, JMM WW2 files.
⁵² Ibid., p. 35.   ⁵³ Butler, 28 July 1941, TNA CO 323/1868/8.   ⁵⁴ Ibid.

first official acknowledgement by the British Government of their concern that Germany's racial policies might take precedence over its Geneva Convention obligations. In parallel, Jewish organizations attempting to clarify the situation of the Palestinian Jewish POWs with the ICRC received reassurances from the organization which were probably unfounded: while the ICRC told the WJC that the Palestinian Jewish POWs were not being treated differently, an ICRC delegate who visited their camp on 20 May 1941 reported that while British, Australian, and New Zealand POWs were housed in barracks, the rest, including Palestinians and Indians, had to dig trenches in the sand and sleep in the open.[55]

Even though both the ICRC and the WJC were aware of this possible discrimination, this issue reached the British Government only at the beginning of July 1941, and does not seem to have caused it to spring into action: the High Commissioner for Palestine, Sir Harold MacMichael, informed Walter Guinness (Lord Moyne), the Secretary of State for the Colonies, that based on a telegram from the Jewish Agency being held by the British censor, Palestinian Jews and Indian POWs in Greece were not provided with accommodation—unlike their British and Australian comrades.[56] Guinness relayed this information to the Foreign Office, with a specific request that it should be put in front of the Foreign Secretary, Anthony Eden.[57] The Foreign Office responded somewhat evasively on 28 July, stating that according to the information received from the US embassy in Berlin on 9 July all POWs from Greece were on their way to Germany; and that the USA had assured them even earlier that they were not aware of any discrimination. Eden asked to await a report from John Winant, the American ambassador to the UK, before discussing this topic further.[58] A few weeks later, responding to a question raised in Parliament regarding the treatment of the Palestinian Jewish POWs, David Margesson, the Secretary of State for War, reconfirmed that 'There is no evidence of any discrimination against any particular category of prisoner.'[59]

The British Government was not the only British body that kept watch on the situation of the British—and Palestinian—Jewish POWs. On 24 June 1941, Sydney Jeannetta Warner, the Director of the Dominion and Foreign Relations Department at the BRC, wrote to M. Barbey of the ICRC and asked him to find

---

[55] Minutes from the meeting between the WJC and ICRC, 11 June 1941, USHMM RG-68.045M Acc. 2004.507, reel 55, document 419; ICRC report on Korinth camp, 20 May 1941, PAAA R40741; see also Pilloud to London, 13 June 1941, ACICR BG 17 05/146. A German report confirmed this but argued that this was because they did not have sufficient accommodation (see report on visit to the Korinth camp, 17 May 1941, BA-MA RH 20–12/208).

[56] MacMichael to Guiness, 8 July 1941, TNA CO 323/1868/8. See also letter from Shertok of the Jewish Agency to Vaucher of the ICRC, apparently bypassing the British censor, 15 July 1941, CZA S-25\4753.

[57] Parkinson to Butler, 18 July 1941, TNA CO 323/1868/8.

[58] Butler to Parkinson, 28 July 1941, ibid. Winant's son, an American pilot, became a POW himself later in the war (Green, *From Colditz in Code*, p. 136).

[59] Margesson to Wedgwood, 10 September 1941, https://hansard.parliament.uk/Commons/1941-0 9-10#undefined, accessed 2 February 2022.

out discretely whether all those fighting with British uniforms, including 'those who are obviously not of British ancestry... Jews etc.', were treated as POWs in the same manner.[60] Jacques Cheneviere of the ICRC responded several weeks later, assuring her that based on the ICRC's information and experience, POWs 'of foreign origin' who fought with the British army were treated in the same way as British soldiers.[61] Without making specific references, he mentioned cases where lists of POWs which included names that were clearly non-British were sent to the ICRC, ensuring that the ICRC had a record of them and would be able to keep track of them in the future.[62]

The use of the term 'of foreign origin' demonstrated once again (as the case of the French Jewish POWs mentioned earlier in this chapter has shown) that the ICRC viewed Jewish soldiers (and perhaps Jews in general) not as an integral part of the nation for whom they fought, but as a separate group.[63] In any case, this response stood in contrast to the ICRC's own findings from just a few weeks earlier: based on visits to POW camps as well as letters from POWs' families, the ICRC concluded that Jewish POWs were sometimes separated from their non-Jewish comrades, and that Jewish medical personnel were not allowed to provide care to other prisoners.[64] Although these cases probably referred to French Jewish POWs and not to British ones, the ICRC response to Warner, although inaccurate, seemed to have been another attempt to reassure the BRC, along with the relatives of British Jewish POWs, that British Jewish POWs were not being mistreated.

Soon after arriving in Korinth, the Germans began interrogating the POWs. After his escape, one of the Palestinian POWs—who emigrated from Germany to Palestine before the war—recalled how a few POWs, who told their interrogators that they had joined the British army because they had been unemployed and needed a job, were beaten; while to his surprise, the response he gave—that he joined because he hated Germany—was praised by the interrogating officer.[65] This behaviour can probably be attributed to the fact that the motivations of unemployment and money fitted well with the Nazi anti-Semitic stereotypes of the 'lazy' Jew, while the 'honourable' warrior decision to volunteer to fight an enemy did not.

The Germans discovered at quite an early stage that the Palestinian contingent included a large number of German and Austrian Jewish immigrants who had volunteered to fight against what used to be their homeland.[66] They did not take this lightly: while the POWs were in Korinth, the legal advisor to the German

---

[60] Warner to Barbey, 24 June 1941, ACICR BG 17 05/006.
[61] Cheneviere to Warner, 16 July 1941, ibid.   [62] Ibid.
[63] Burckhardt to Vermeil, 10 June 1940, ACICR BG 25/34.
[64] Notes from a meeting with OKW representatives, 12 June 1941, ibid.
[65] Aufbau, 15 October 1943, p. 1, https://archive.org/details/aufbau, accessed 30 June 2019.
[66] Plack to the German Foreign Office, 7 May 1941, PAAA R40718.

12th Army had tried to find a legal loophole that would allow the Germans to remove POW status from German-born Palestinian POWs, whom they considered to be traitors.[67] However, since the POWs claimed that they had been granted Palestinian citizenship and were no longer German citizens, and since British documents only specified the parents' nationality, the advisor had to withdraw the treason claim as 'their claim to have acquired a Palestinian citizenship cannot be refuted'.[68] He then tried to prove that some POWs had left Germany in the middle of legal proceedings against them; these POWs were segregated from their comrades but eventually were sent to the permanent POW camp in Germany without any additional action taken against them.[69] According to another legal argument, supposedly uncovered by the Geneva correspondent of an American Jewish newspaper, since Palestine was under an international mandate any entry of Palestinians into the British army was illegal; however, since the report of the legal adviser of the 12th Army did not mention this claim the argument of the Geneva correspondent could not be verified.[70] Nevertheless, the article was forwarded on 4 July 1941 by Lewis Namier of the Jewish Agency for Palestine to Sir Cosmo Parkinson, Permanent Under-Secretary of State for the Colonies.[71] Parkinson's response on the following day simply asked Namier to keep him updated in case he received any additional information.[72]

Interestingly, the German legal advisor was not far off the mark: two years earlier, in January 1939, a German-Jewish lawyer—Dr Moshe Smoira, who emigrated to Palestine in 1921 and who, after Israel gained its independence, became the first president of the Israeli Supreme Court—had written a legal opinion that

---

[67] A few weeks later, an order issued by the 12th Infantry Division during the invasion of the Soviet Union was even more specific: Reichsdeutsche (soldiers of German ancestry) fighting against Germany should be identified and shot while in the POW camps (quoted in Bartov, *Hitler's Army*, p. 69, BA-MA RH26-12/236, 21 June 1941). There was a similar attempt to charge with treason Czech pilots who fought with the RAF and became POWs (see Protecting Power report on Oflag IV-C (Colditz), 7 October 1944, TNA WO 224/69).

[68] The Legal Advisor (*Oberstkriegsgerichtsrat*) of the 12th Army to OKH (the army high command), 19 May 1941, BA-MA RH 20-12/208. Interestingly, in 1943 the Germans revoked the POW status of French Jewish POWs from Alsace-Lorraine by stripping them of their French citizenship (Judisal to Marti, 27 January 1943, ACICR BG 25/34). Arabs and Jews living in Palestine were granted Palestinian citizenship by the British authorities; they were considered 'British Protected Persons', but not British citizens (see Norman Bentwich, 'Palestine Nationality and the Mandate', *Journal of Comparative Legislation and International Law*, 21:4 (1939), pp. 230–2, p. 232). However, German Jews who immigrated to Palestine and did not receive Palestinian citizenship before the outbreak of the war were considered German citizens until their citizenship was revoked by Germany in November 1941. See Smoira to Senator, 12 January 1939, CZA S-25\4720; and Lange to the editor of the *Palestine Post*, 16 April 1941, CZA S-25\4720.

[69] Yordan, *My Escape From Captivity*, p. 88. See also Aufbau, 15 October 1943, p. 1, https://archive.org/details/aufbau, accessed 30 June 2019; Yoav Gelber, 'Palestinian POWs in German Captivity', *Yad Vashem Studies*, 14 (1981), pp. 89–137, p. 101.

[70] Letter from 'a Geneva correspondent', 2 July 1941, TNA CO 323/1868/8.

[71] Namier to Parkinson, 4 July 1941, ibid. The British-Jewish historian Lewis Namier was at the time on secondment to the Jewish Agency from the university of Manchester, where he was Chair of Modern History.

[72] Parkinson to Namier, 5 July 1941, ibid.

predicted the exact same situation. In a letter to the Jewish Agency, Dr Smoira explained that German Jews who volunteered for the British Army would not be protected if they became POWs unless they became Palestinian citizens before the outbreak of a war.[73] Then, on 16 April 1941, less than two weeks before the Palestinian Jewish volunteers became POWs, another Palestinian Jewish lawyer, Dr Walter Lange—who, judging by his name, was probably also a German immigrant—wrote a letter to the *Palestine Post* newspaper arguing that putting on a British uniform did not turn a soldier into a British subject; he would still keep his former citizenship and would not be protected by international law.[74] Although this issue was not addressed in the Geneva Convention, Wehrmacht regulations stated that POWs had to be treated according to the uniform they were wearing when captured, and not according to their original citizenship; but these regulations may have not taken into account cases of German ex-patriates fighting against Germany.[75] This specific case was addressed in 1942 by Alfons Waltzog, a senior Luftwaffe field court judge, whose book about international POW conventions was distributed to all POW camps and labour detachments. Waltzog essentially confirmed the legal opinion of the two Palestinian Jewish lawyers and argued that, if captured, German citizens who fought against Germany would not be entitled to a POW status unless they had dual citizenship.[76]

The situation of German Jews who had fled Germany and joined Allied armies was somewhat improved by an addition to the Reich's citizenship Law of November 1941, which revoked the German citizenship of Jews who had emigrated from Germany; however, this did not apply to the Palestinian Jewish POWs, who were captured before that.[77] Eventually, the British Chief Recruitment Officer in Palestine issued an instruction on 5 July 1941 to all recruitment offices in Palestine to change the documents carried by Jewish volunteers to designate them only as Palestinians, without any mention of nationality or place of birth.[78]

This issue, which applied not only to the Palestinian Jewish POWs, but also to German and Austrian refugees who had immigrated to Britain and joined the British army, was also raised in 1941 by British and South African Jewish organizations; nevertheless, it was only addressed several years later, in June 1944, when the question of giving these immigrants British citizenship in order to

---

[73] Smoira to Senator, 12 January 1939, CZA S-25\4720.
[74] Lange to the Editor of the *Palestine Post*, 16 April 1941, ibid.
[75] Sammelmitteilungen 1, Kr. Gef. Fremder Volkszugehörigkeit in feindlichen Heeren, 16 June 1941, BA-MA RW 6/270.
[76] Waltzog, *Recht der Landkriegsführung*, p. 114. Waltzog's book was officially endorsed by the OKW and distributed to all POW camps (see Befehlsammlung 11, order 22, 11 March 1942, BA-MA RW 6/270).
[77] Viscount Cranborne in the House of Lords, 16 March 1943, https://hansard.parliament.uk, accessed 17 June 2019.
[78] Major Davidson, 5 July 1941, CZA S-25\4720.

protect them in case they became POWs was raised in the British parliament.[79] The British Home Secretary, Herbert Morrison, argued that the protection afforded by the Geneva Convention 'applies to any member of the Armed Forces whatever may be his nationality' and granting such citizenship would only aggravate the situation of the POWs in the eyes of the enemy.[80] Morrison did not explain why Jewish refugees who volunteered to fight and even die for Britain were not entitled to British citizenship and its protection, especially at a stage in the war when the mass murder of Jews by the Germans was known; nor was he able to explain why, unlike Britain, alien refugees were granted almost automatic citizenship when joining the American and British Dominion armies.[81]

Although the German legal advisor ended up adhering to the regulations that were in place at the time, his overzealous attempts to find legal justifications for the removal of POW status from German-born Palestinian POWs were a clear discrimination against them. After all, the Wehrmacht did not make a similar attempt to find recent German immigrants among the non-Jewish British POWs who were captured in Greece, nor to apply the same process to British POWs in general. However, even though the SS Einsatzgruppen were operating at the time in Greece behind the front lines with specific instructions to identify and arrest communists and Greek Jews, it is more likely that this specific case was a local initiative by the legal advisor, rather than an execution of a well-thought out policy dictated from above; a similar attempt at the end of 1941 to put two escaping German-born Palestinian POWs on trial for treason also ended with them being returned to the POW camp without being tried.[82] The Germans, after all, did not know in advance the size of the Palestinian contingent in the British army; and in any case, they were not prepared for the capture of such a large number of Jewish POWs all at once, and therefore no guidelines were available for dealing with such a situation.[83] This conclusion is also supported by the fact that the 120 Palestinian POWs captured in Crete and detained in the POW camp in Galatas were not interrogated at all.[84]

While the POWs were in Korinth, given the different nationalities of the British POWs, the German Foreign Office was making its own suggestions as to where their final destination should be. On 11 June 1941 it sent a letter to the POW

---

[79] South African Jewish Board of Deputies to Board of Deputies of British Jews, 21 February 1941 and its response, 19 April 1941; and Jewish Refugees Committee to Brotman, 16 April 1941, LMA ACC/3121/E/003/065/3.
[80] Morrison to Bartlett, 8 June 1944, https://hansard.parliament.uk, accessed 1 May 2020.
[81] Morrison to Rathbone, 15 February 1945, https://hansard.parliament.uk, accessed 1 May 2020.
[82] Robert Gerwarth, *Hitler's Hangman, The Life of Heydrich* (New Haven, CT and London: Yale University Press, 2012), p. 186; testimony of Mosche Grüner, YVA O.3-1602.
[83] Yaacovi, *The Road to Captivity*, p. 104.
[84] Gelber, 'Palestinian POWs in German Captivity', p. 105. See also MacKenzie, *The Colditz Myth*, p. 49: it seems that after Crete the Germans felt that their victory in Greece was assured, and they did not bother with additional interrogations.

Office where it recommended that while the British, Australians, and New Zealanders should be sent to POW camps in Germany, the Cypriots, for 'climatic reasons', should remain in the Balkan Peninsula.[85] It then recommended that the Jewish POWs should not be sent to Germany, but remain in the Balkans as well and be used for military-related work.[86] The Foreign Office also recommended that for political reasons, Arab—who were also part of the Palestinian contingency—and Indian POWs should be treated better than the rest.[87] It was not clear from the letter whether the Foreign Office's intention was to send all Jewish POW to the Balkans, or only the Palestinian ones; given that Cypriots, Arabs, and Indians were also mentioned in the letter, it is more likely that the intention was to send only the Palestinian Jewish POWs to the Balkans, and not all Jewish POWs. It should be noted that the person who drafted the letter, Dr Erich Albrecht, the deputy head—and later head—of the legal division in the German Foreign Office, was before Hitler's ascension to power a member of Far-Right associations and also of the German National People's Party (the DNVP); however, the applications he submitted to become a member of the Nazi Party had been refused.[88]

It is unlikely that Albrecht was unaware that such a suggestion was in breach of Article 31 of the 1929 Geneva Convention, which specifically prohibited the employment of POWs in work directly connected to the operations of the war; but given that formal guidelines related to the treatment of Jewish POWs had still not been issued at this stage of the war, it is possible that the German Foreign Office decided to step into the gap. A year earlier, after the conclusion of the French campaign, Hitler had issued an order that due to the impact that the German weather had on 'prisoners of colour'—French colonial troops—who were kept in POW camps in Germany, they should be transferred back to

---

[85] Dr Albrecht to Major Stacke of the OKW POW Office, 11 June 1941, PAAA R40741.
[86] Ibid.   [87] Ibid.
[88] Hans Jürgen Döscher, *Das Auswärtige Amt in Dritten Reich* (Berlin: Siedler, 1987), pp. 43 and 194. Although the legal division had one of the lowest numbers of NSDAP members among the German Foreign Office divisions (see Eckart Conze, Norbert Frei, Peter Hayes, Moshe Zimmermann, *Das Amt und die Vergangenheit—Deutsche Diplomaten im Dritten Reich und in der Bundesrepublik* (Munich: Pantheon, 2010), p. 159), and Friedrich Gaus, Albrecht's predecessor as head of the division, was also not a member (probably because his wife was considered half Jewish—see Döscher, *Das Auswärtige Amt in Dritten Reich*, p. 195 n. 15), there are several examples that demonstrate how Albrecht used his position to provide legal advice that supported Nazi policies: in December 1941 he proposed ways to bypass international treaties in order to instate Germany's Jewish policies in other European countries (document NG 4669, 31 December 1941, *IMT, Trial of War Criminals*, vol. XIII, pp. 205-7); in 1942 he wrote a document providing guidance on how to prevent Sweden, as Netherlands' Protecting Power, from finding out about the fate of Dutch Jews who died in concentration camps (document NG 2633, 31 July 1942, ibid., pp. 241-2); and in 1945 Albrecht drafted a legal opinion that justified the intention not to inform the Protecting Power about the murder of the French General Mesny, who was shot 'while trying to escape' (Sebastian Weitkamp, 'Kooperativtäter—die Beteiligung des Auswärtigen Amts an der NS-Gewaltpolitik jenseits der "Endlösung"', in Johannes Hurter and Thomas Raithel, eds, *Das Auswärtige Amt in der NS-Diktatur* (Berlin: De Gruyter Oldenbourg, 2014), pp. 197-218, p. 207).

France.⁸⁹ The real reason was probably more related to Nazi ideology: Hitler was concerned about potential 'racial defilement' as a result of relations between African POWs and German women.⁹⁰ It is therefore possible that the German Foreign Office simply proposed to extend Hitler's 'prisoners of colour' policy, without specifically referring to it, to Jewish POWs.

The German Foreign Office proposal is the first non-Wehrmacht record found in this research which specifically referenced Jewish POWs and proposed to treat them differently from their non-Jewish comrades. The POW Office, for its part, perhaps considering the Geneva Convention and the potential reprisals against German POWs in the event that adopted the Foreign Office's suggestion, did not accept it and at the end of June 1941 the whole British contingent, including the Palestinian Jewish POWs, began their long journey to the permanent POW camps in Germany.

Their first stop along the way was Salonika (today Thessaloniki), where they spent three weeks. Given that a few of the Palestinian Jewish POWs originally came from this city, the Germans did not want to risk them escaping and did not allow some of the Jewish POWs to go outside the camp on work details.⁹¹ However, some of them did manage to escape and went back to their families, only to be deported two years later to Auschwitz, together with the rest of Greece's Jewish population.⁹²

Continuing their journey to the permanent POW camps in Germany, the British POWs were accommodated along the way for several weeks in two POW camps, Stalag XVIII-A (Wolfsberg in Austria) and Stalag XVIII-D (Maribur, then Marburg an der Drau); their treatment in these camps is detailed in Chapter 3 of this book. Finally, at the end of July 1941, the POWs were put on a train and sent to their final destination—Stalag VIII-B near Lamsdorf in Silesia.⁹³

In the Camp

Overview

Once a POW arrived at a permanent camp some of the uncertainties and risks to which he had been exposed prior to his arrival were lessened. From then on, he was, in theory at least, inside a 'Total Institution', its primary objective being to protect the community surrounding it from him; together with thousands of other prisoners, he was to conduct all his activities inside the camp, adhere to a

---

⁸⁹ Scheck, *French Colonial Soldiers in German Captivity*, pp. 54–5.   ⁹⁰ Ibid., p. 54.
⁹¹ Sela, *Shackles of Captivity*, p. 70; see also Glantz, *Struggle in Captivity*, p. 76.
⁹² Sela, *Shackles of Captivity*, p. 184; Almogi, *With Head Held High*, p. 40.
⁹³ Glantz, *Struggle in Captivity*, p. 90.

strict set of rules, and be controlled by a single authority.[94] POW camps, however, did not completely conform to the concept of a Total Institution: although it can be argued that the Stalag, as the base camp, was in most cases secluded from the environment surrounding it, and therefore did achieve the objective of protecting the community around it from those inside, the majority of POWs spent their captivity period in labour detachments which by their very definition allowed for almost daily interaction with the population surrounding them. As such, with these dozens—sometimes hundreds—of labour detachments, the boundaries of this 'Total Institution' were not only flexible; as the testimonies in this section will show, at times they even became porous: POWs in labour detachments worked side by side with, or under the supervision of, civilians; when the labour detachment did not have a canteen, they shopped in village stores; and when military doctors or dentists were not available to treat them, they visited civilian ones. More importantly, the protection that POW camps were supposed to provide to the communities around them from the camp's inmates worked, especially for Jewish POWs, also in the opposite direction and shielded the POWs from the radicalization that was taking place outside the camps' fences.

As mentioned earlier, policies against Jewish civilians in Europe escalated throughout the war from segregation to deportation to extermination, culminating in the Holocaust, and policies against non-Soviet POWs went through their own radicalization process, with Reichsführer-SS Heinrich Himmler eventually taking over responsibility for POWs from the OKW.[95] However, with the exception of the evacuation of POW camps during the last months of the war, which resulted in hundreds of thousands POWs being forced to march for weeks in poor conditions, the impact of the orders and policies described above and the absorption of the POW organization into Himmler's fiefdom on POWs inside the camps was quite limited. The radicalization process mainly affected POWs who were caught outside the POW camp, either because they had not yet arrived at a camp and registered as POWs, or in the last year of the war, because they had escaped from it. Despite an SS General being in charge of the POW Office, demands by the RSHA to hand over Jewish POWs and complaints by local Party functionaries that POWs in general were being treated too well, the 'Total Institution' provided an unintended reverse-protection for POWs inside the camps from external events.[96]

The protection was achieved through two sets of externally imposed rules: the Geneva Convention rules and the POW Office's ones. The prominence of the

---

[94] Goffman, *Asylums*, pp. 4–6.
[95] For a discussion related to the radicalization of the German POW policies see Chapter 4 of this book.
[96] For RSHA and Party functionaries pressure on camp commandants see *IMT, Trials of War Criminals*, vol. XI, p. 56; Adolf Westhoff, 15 January 1966, BA-MA MSG 2/12655; Krafft, 10 August 1951, BA-MA MSG 2/12656; and Chapter 4 of this book.

former was made clear by the OKW even before the war, when it emphasized on the first page of its POW camp commandant's manual that POWs should be treated in accordance with the Convention in a 'strict but fair' manner.[97] The importance the Germans assigned to the Geneva Convention can also be seen from their treatment of their own personnel: for example, the commandant of Stalag IV-F's (Hartmannsdorf) labour detachment C114 was replaced on the spot when it was found that he had told the American POWs in the detachment that the Geneva Convention was no longer in use.[98]

POWs who had been captured together ended up in most cases in the same POW camp. Jewish soldiers in the American and British armies, who served across all army, navy, and air force units, found themselves in various camps; as mentioned, most of the Palestinian Jewish POWs were sent to Stalag VIII-B (Lamsdorf) and its labour detachments (the number of these detachments changed continuously; for example, in December 1941, 16 out of 234 labour detachments in Stalag VIII-B (Lamsdorf) consisted only of Palestinian Jews).[99] Their incarceration together in several mostly Jewish groups allows for a relatively detailed analysis to be conducted of the interaction between these Jewish POWs and their German captors. This section is therefore divided into two parts: the first describes the camp experience of American and British Jewish POWs, and the second the experience of Palestinian Jewish POWs.

American and British Jewish POWs

Testimonies of the experience of individual American and British Jewish POWs are usually found in memoirs of Jewish and non-Jewish POWs, and are different in nature to the memoirs of Palestinian Jewish POWs, who spent their captivity mostly in one camp and its affiliated labour detachments in Jewish-only groups. Most of these testimonies focused on the general POW experience, and the ethnicity and religion of the POW played only a small part, if any, in them.[100] In addition, unlike the Protecting Power and ICRC reports on Stalag VIII-B (Lamsdorf), which made specific references to Palestinian Jewish POWs, only a few of the reports on other camps holding American and British POWs were found to specifically reference Jewish POWs: one example is the ICRC report regarding a British Jewish medic in Stalag XVIII-A (Wolfsberg) who was not

---

[97] Dienstanweisung für den Kommandanten eines 'Kriegsgefangenen Mannschafts Stammlagers', 16 February 1939, p. 7, BA-MA RH 1/612.
[98] Swiss embassy report on Stalag IV-F (Hartmannsdorf), 18–21 March 1945, NARA RG 389, box 2148, 290/34/19/3.
[99] ICRC report on Stalag VIII-B (Lamsdorf), 11 December 1941, p. 1, TNA WO 224/27.
[100] See, for example, Green, *From Colditz in Code*, and David Westheimer, *Sitting It Out* (Houston: Rice University Press, 1992).

recognized as Protected Personnel and was sent to work at a labour detachment (the report did not mention the camp commandant's explanation, nor any action taken to correct the situation); another example is the ICRC report on Stalag VII-A (Moosburg) which described a case of segregation of Jewish POWs.[101] A reference to the treatment of Jewish POWs was also made in September 1941 in correspondence between the ICRC and the German Foreign Office: in response to an ICRC letter from 3 July 1941, which apparently highlighted a case of mistreatment of Jewish POWs (their nationality was not mentioned) by a German NCO, the German Foreign Office wrote that 'Jewish camp inmates receive the same treatment as the other prisoners. If, in individual cases, violations have occurred against this rule, then action has always been taken. The...action of the NCO mentioned in the report is, of course, completely unacceptable and he has been reprimanded accordingly'.[102]

In Stalag Luft III in Sagan, even though the German authorities were clearly anti-Semitic and the guards were allowed to incite non-Jewish POWs against the Jewish ones, these were individual cases and in general, adherence to the Geneva Convention took precedence: in a conversation with Colonel Spivey, the Senior American Officer (SAO) of the centre compound, the commandant stated that for him, a Jew was just another POW.[103] In general, the Germans did not bother with the Jews in the camp and according to testimonies, they were treated exactly as their colleagues.[104] There were, however, a few cases where the Germans in Stalag Luft III (Sagan) refused to deal with Jewish POWs: for example, when they found that one of the POWs who acted as a cook was Jewish, they insisted that he should be replaced.[105]

Unlike the officers held in Stalag Luft III (Sagan), NCOs held in Stalag Luft IV, near Gross Tychow, Pomerania (today Tychowo, Poland), described a different experience, where individual guards, clearly anti-Semitic and backed by their commandant, Oberstleutnant Aribert Bombach, a member of the Nazi Party who was described as a 'staunch Nazi', ignored the basic requirements of the Geneva Convention; a Protecting Power report from October 1944 described the

---

[101] ICRC report on Stalag XVIII-A (Wolfsberg), 24 October 1941, p. 4, TNA WO 224/45; ICRC report on Stalag VII-A (Moosburg), 27 January 1945, p. 4, TNA WO 224/24. According to Article 9 of the 1929 Geneva Convention for the Amelioration of the Condition of the Wounded and Sick in Armies in the Field, medical staff and chaplains came under the definition of 'Protected Personnel' that should be respected, protected, and not be treated as POWs.

[102] German Foreign Office to ICRC, 16 September 1941, ACICR BG 17 05/006.

[103] Delmar Spivey, oral history, US Airforce Historical Research Agency (AFRHA), Irisnum 01015417, reel 31,923.

[104] Durand, *Stalag Luft III*, p. 209; oral testimony of Jack Lyon, https://www.iwm.org.uk/collections/item/object/80025667, recorded 2 October 2005, accessed 1 February 2018, IWM catalogue number 28532.

[105] David Foy, *For You the War Is Over* (New York: Stein and Day, 1984), p. 130.

commandant as 'not in the least interested in the welfare of the prisoners'.[106] Although most POWs in that camp suffered constant mistreatment by their captors, Jews were especially singled out: in a deposition given to war crimes Investigators after the war, staff sergeant Bill Krebs described how the head of security in the camp, Oberfeldwebel Reinhard Fahnert, 'was always after anyone of Jewish extraction'; in another deposition, Private Raymond Allaby testified how mistreatment by guards, sometimes using dogs, was a common practice and described one case where a guard named Sergeant Schmidt (who was also known as 'Big Stoop') had severely beaten one of the POWs after he found out that he was Jewish.[107]

Alec Jay, a British Jewish Territorial Army soldier with the Queen Victoria's Rifles who threw away his identification discs when he was captured in Calais in 1940, was interned in Stalag VIII-B's (Lamsdorf) E173 labour detachment near Setzdorf (today Vápenná in Poland). In 1942 an anti-Semitic British POW exposed him to the Germans as a Jew; at first they dismissed it, saying 'he cannot possibly be a Jew—he is such a good fellow!', while the POW who informed on him was punched 'to a jelly' by Jay's comrades.[108] However, sometime later the deputy commandant appeared in the camp together with an SS officer in order to take Jay away. His comrades formed a protective ring around him and a British Sergeant threatened the Germans that if Jay was taken away, they would either have to take everyone else away with him or shoot them all.[109] The Germans gave way and Jay remained in the camp; however, in order to humiliate him, the camp commandant, for whom Jay had acted as the interpreter until then, forced him to wear a white turban whenever he was outside his barracks. He did, however, remain the commandant's interpreter.[110] The 'turban' order was withdrawn a few months later, when a new deputy commandant arrived; a veteran of the First World War, he had different ideas about the treatment of POWs, including the Jewish ones.[111] A similar case of a Jewish POW in Stalag VIII-B (Lamsdorf) who

---

[106] John Nichol, Tony Rennell, *The Last Escape: The Untold Story of Allied Prisoners of War in Germany 1944–1945* (New York and London: Penguin Books, 2003), ln. 2261; Swiss embassy report on Stalag Luft IV (Gross Tychow), 10 October 1944, TNA WO 244/64. The commandant's Nazi convictions were praised in his appraisal from 1942; this is worth mentioning since the 'National Socialist convictions' category was only added to the evaluation form as a mandatory evaluation criterion in the following year, and therefore mentions of officers' Nazi convictions were quite rare before 1943 (see evaluation, 27 March 1942, Bombach Wehrmacht personnel file, BA-MA PERS 6/12131. His NSDAP membership card is in BA R/9361-VIII).

[107] Testimony of William Krebs to the American Judge Advocate War Crimes Investigation, 10 June 1947, https://b24.net/powStalag4.htm, accessed 30 April 2018; testimony of Raymond Allaby, 21 September 1945, NARA RG 549, box 174, 290/59/22/5; Murray Adler, oral history, https://stalagluft4.org/naratives.html, accessed 1 August 2021. Additional testimonies of mistreatment of Jewish POWs in Stalag Luft IV (Gross Tychow) are found in Laura Caplan, 'The Captain Leslie Caplan Story', https://stalagluft4.org/pdf/CaptainCaplan.pdf, accessed 1 August 2022.

[108] John Jay, *Facing Fearful Odds* (Barnsley: Pen and Sword, 2014), ln. 3871.

[109] Ibid., ln. 3914.

[110] Ibid., ln. 3928. A photo of Jay wearing the turban is found in ibid., ln. 6207.

[111] Ibid., ln. 4060.

was exposed as a Jew by a non-Jewish POW after the two had an altercation had resulted in the Jewish POW being beaten by the German guards; he was later taken to the guards' compound and the POW who recounted the story in his memoirs claimed that he never saw him again.[112]

Wilfred Ofstein, a British POW who was captured in North Africa in June 1942, was initially held by the Italians who did not show any interest in his religion. When Italy surrendered in 1943 and he was sent to a POW camp in Germany, he expected the worst.[113] In 1945, when he was segregated with other Jewish POWs from the commonwealth in Stalag IV-A's (Hohnstein) labour detachment 234 near Dresden—which he described as 'the most comfortable of all' the POWs camps he had been to—the Jewish POWs were even allowed to use the nearby football pitch, despite the fact that it belonged to the Hitler Youth organization.[114] When the local Hitler Youth leader told their guard that he suspected the POWs were Jewish, the guard simply told him 'they are British prisoners'. Ofstein described being 'on good terms' with the German civilians who worked in the same factories where the POWs were employed, as well as with their families; the factory manager was 'particularly helpful and friendly'.[115] The Geneva Convention and military discipline can explain the behaviour of the guard in protecting 'his' prisoners; and although the behaviour of the German civilians can be attributed to simple moral values, after considering how slave labour was treated during that period and the fact that the POWs were Jewish, it is more likely that given the late stage of the war, it was a result of their fear of retribution in the hands of the Allies.

Palestinian Jewish POWs in Stalag VIII-B (Lamsdorf)

'[The Palestinian POWs] spent their time [in Stalag VIII-B (Lamsdorf)] refusing to work, going on hunger strike over bad food, committing sabotage, escaping, black marketing, spreading pro-British propaganda...and generally causing the Hun far more trouble than they could possibly have done as a mere fighting unit'.[116] This is how Cyril Rofe, the British Jewish RAF pilot who spent part of his captivity in Stalag VIII-B (Lamsdorf) during the same period as the Palestinian Jewish POWs, described them in his memoirs. And although the picture he painted might have been slightly exaggerated and neglected to mention their share of hardships, it does demonstrate the general impression they had on the Stalag's other occupants throughout their captivity period.

The Palestinian Jewish POWs arrived at their permanent camp in Lamsdorf at the beginning of August 1941. As it happens, this coincided with the beginning of

---

[112] W. A. Harding, IWM 82/27/1, pp. 25–7.   [113] Testimony of Wilfred Ofstein, YVA O.3–8111.
[114] Ibid.   [115] Ibid.   [116] Rofe, *Against the Wind*, p. 31.

the mass murder phase of the Holocaust: Germany's anti-Semitic policies had gone into the next stage of radicalization and the Einsatzgruppen in the East had begun mass killings of Jews only a few weeks earlier. As can be seen, however, this radicalization, with few exceptions, did not filter into the POW camps where American and British Jewish POWs were held. As discussed in Chapter 4, Germany continued to adhere to the Geneva Convention almost until the end of the war, and non-Soviet Jewish POWs were, in general, protected from the events which took place outside the fences of the POW camps.

In his memoirs, first published immediately after the war, Shlomo Sela (Slodash), one of the Palestinian Jews who volunteered for the British army, described how upon arrival at the camp a German officer informed them that from then on they had become the responsibility of the Wehrmacht; that they would be treated as British POWs; and that they would have the same rights and duties as them.[117] Despite this declaration, British POWs who worked in the camp's offices told them that the German authorities were uncertain as to how to treat them: as Jews in Germany they had no rights; as British Jewish POWs they should be treated as the other British POWs; but the authorities had no precedent for the treatment of Palestinian Jewish POWs.[118] This confusion, which seemed to have followed the Palestinian POWs from the day they were captured, also manifested itself the first time Red Cross parcels were handed out after their arrival. The Germans informed them that since the parcels were sent from Britain and were intended for British POWs, not for Palestinian Jews, they would not receive any. In response, Regimental Sergeant Major (RSM) Sydney Sherriff, the camp's MOC, told the commandant that the British army was not subject to the Nuremberg laws and that all British POWs would refuse to accept the parcels until this order was retracted.[119] Sherriff served in the Royal Welsh Fusiliers and was captured in Dunkirk; his performance as the MOC in Stalag VIII-B (Lamsdorf) during his five years of captivity, looking after the administration, welfare and discipline of 40,000 POWs, was described by a POW who was incarcerated with him as 'one of the finest examples of character and leadership shown by any prisoner throughout the war'.[120] As a result of his insistence, the commandant had to contact his superiors and was then told to reverse the order.[121] In a letter sent by one of the Palestinian Jewish POWs several days after this incident, he mentioned receiving the Red Cross parcels and compared life in the camp to a 'recruiting depot without leave granted'.[122]

---

[117] Sela, *Shackles of Captivity*, p. 87.   [118] Ibid.

[119] Test in German captivity, July 1945, p. 39, IDF 182/1867/1998; Sela, *Shackles of Captivity*, p. 89; Almogi, *With Head Held High*, p. 54.

[120] Jack Pringle, *Colditz Last Stop* (London: William Kimber, 1988), p. 130; see also James Badcock, IWM 99/47/1.

[121] Sela, *Shackles of Captivity*, p. 89. See also Almogi, *With Head Held High*, p. 54; Aufbau, 4 February 1944, p. 32, https://archive.org/details/aufbau, accessed 30 June 2019.

[122] POW letter, 11 August 1941, CZA S-25\4753.

The Palestinian prisoners' arrival was mentioned a few weeks later by the American embassy delegates who visited the camp in their role as the Protecting Power. The report from their visit listed about 13,000 British prisoners and 7,000 French, Belgian, Polish, and Yugoslav ones; among the British, it made specific mention of 293 Indians and 1,160 Palestinians.[123] The meeting between the American delegates, the camp commandant and the Stalag's MOCs was the first one to be attended by the MOC of the newly arrived Palestinian Jewish POWs, Sergeant Major Assir Schustermann, and he used it to clarify the conditions that the Jewish POWs should expect. Specifically, Schustermann wanted to know whether Palestinian NCOs would still keep the right, accorded to them by the Geneva Convention, to decide whether to work or not; whether the Palestinian troops would receive clothes; and most importantly, whether they would 'receive treatment equal to that of the British prisoners'.[124] In the discussion that followed, complete agreement was reached between Schustermann, the embassy delegates, the camp commandant, and the British MOC, Sherriff, that 'Palestinian troops would receive treatment absolutely equal to that of other British troops'. It was also clarified that the Palestinian troops would receive their share of Red Cross parcels, and that Palestinian NCOs could choose whether to work or not.[125] It is interesting to note that the Red Cross parcels incident which occurred a few weeks earlier was not mentioned in the report; however, this was one example out of many of ICRC and Protecting Power visit reports not necessarily reflecting actual events, either due to the timing of the visit, or because the visiting delegates did not want to trigger a cycle of reprisals caused by an issue that had already been resolved. The American representative further confirmed that the Palestinian POWs' accommodation was 'exactly as those of the British'.[126] It seems that the German authorities in Lamsdorf did not have an issue dealing with a Jewish MOC; this was not always the case. Although the general guidelines issued by the OKW regarding the selection and the responsibilities of an MOC did not make any reference to cases of Jewish MOCs, when Norman Rubenstein was appointed as an MOC only two months earlier—in June 1941—by the commandant of a labour detachment in Stalag XXI-B (Thure, today Tur, Poland), the OKW refused to approve the appointment, arguing that Jews cannot be trusted in this role.[127] Similarly, in July 1944, after a year in the MOC role, the Germans discovered that Private Harry Galler, the MOC of Stalag II-B (Hammerstein) in Pomerania, was Jewish, and insisted on him being replaced.[128]

---

[123] American embassy report on Stalag VIII-B (Lamsdorf), August 1941, p. 1, TNA WO 224/27.
[124] Ibid., p. 5.   [125] Ibid.   [126] Ibid., p. 7.
[127] Allgemeine Richtlinien für das Vertrauensmännerwesen, 15 September 1941, PAAA R40954; Rubenstein, *The Invisibly Wounded*, p. 58.
[128] American Prisoners of War in Germany, prepared by Military Intelligence Service, War Department, 1 November 1945, https://catalog.archives.gov/id/893506, accessed 30 April 2018; see also Foy, *For You the War Is Over*, p. 130.

Most of the Palestinian Jewish POWs remained in the camp and in its dependent labour detachments over the next 3.5 years, until its evacuation at the beginning of 1945 ahead of the advancing Red Army.[129] As the following examples will show, their treatment during this period in the camp—but not during the camp's evacuation in the last months of the war—was in general in line with the Geneva Convention. Where discrimination and mistreatment due to anti-Semitism did occur, it was in most cases either the result of the interaction of POWs in labour detachments with German civilians, who attempted to treat the POWs in the same way that Jewish civilians had been treated; or the fault of individual commandants and guards who held anti-Semitic views. In fact, this was also the impression of the Palestinian POWs themselves: Tibor Weinstein, a Hungarian-born Jew who immigrated to Palestine in 1939 and volunteered for the British army, testified after the war that although 'there have been a few cases where individual Germans cursed the Palestinian POWs and called them 'damn Jews', [and] there were even a few blows given here and there', in general 'this was an individual initiative and not policy dictated from above'.[130] Cyril Rofe had the same experience: according to him, although some individual guards were anti-Semitic, in general the Wehrmacht treated the Palestinian Jewish POWs the same as British POWs.[131]

One of the first visits of the ICRC to Stalag VIII-B's (Lamsdorf) labour detachments after the arrival of the Palestinian Jewish POWs was conducted on 13 December 1941 by Dr Jean-Maurice Rubli. The construction of the first extermination camps, Belzec and Chelmno, had begun two months earlier; mass murder of Jews had been taking place in the East since Germany's invasion of the Soviet Union in June of that year; and the visit itself happened to coincide almost to the day with the intensification of this process with Hitler's declaration in front of senior Nazi officials that the extermination of the Jews was now the necessary consequence of the World War.[132] However, Rubli's report on his visit to E287 in Neukirch (today Polska Cerekiew, in Poland) did not reflect any of that. The report indicated that the camp consisted of twenty Palestinian Jewish POWs who were employed in a sugar beet factory where they had daily access to hot shower facilities; that the camp had a German civilian doctor, assisted by a British medical orderly; and since there was no canteen, the prisoners were allowed to buy supplies in the nearby village.[133] According to the report, the Jewish prisoners had no complaints and testified that they were treated like the other POWs, and that the German civilians were 'very correct in their treatment of them'. They added that according to their information, the same applied to their Jewish

---

[129] Gelber, 'Palestinian POWs in German Captivity', p. 133.
[130] Testimony of Tibor Weinstein, YVA O.3-2417.   [131] Rofe, *Against the Wind*, p. 45.
[132] Browning, *Fateful Months*, p. 30; Gerwarth, *Hitler's Hangman*, pp. 208-9.
[133] ICRC report on labour detachments E253 and E287, 13 December 1941, p. 2, TNA WO 224/27.

comrades in other labour detachments.[134] The Jewish POWs mentioned a case of one of their colleagues who had been hospitalized in the Lazaret at Kosel (today Koźle, in Poland), separated from his British comrades and put in a ward with Russian POWs, where the treatment and food had been markedly worse.[135] The report did not mention any actions taken to address this issue; however, other than the hospital incident, it was clear that the Jewish POWs had regular contact with German civilians, in the factory, in the surrounding villages when buying supplies, and obviously with the German civilian doctor; and that they did not feel any discrimination in their interaction with camp personnel or the civilian population.

As it happens, the commandant of Stalag VIII-B (Lamsdorf) around the same period was Oberst Luger, who had been appointed as a temporary commandant for a period of several weeks until a permanent commandant arrived. During these weeks, Oberst Luger became known for his harsh treatment of British POWs and in particular of Palestinian Jewish POWs, in some cases instructing guards to drive them out to work using rifle butts.[136] However, although the ICRC report might not have reflected the actual situation, during the short period of his appointment this behaviour was apparently not adopted throughout the camp and its labour detachments. Unlike the case described above of Stalag Luft IV (Gross Tychow), where the commandant's Nazi worldview was reflected in the behaviour of the guards towards POWs in general and towards Jewish POWs in particular, it seems that Oberst Luger did not remain in his position long enough to make the same impact. It is, however, quite possible that had he become the permanent commandant of Stalag VIII-B (Lamsdorf), the experience of the Palestinian Jewish POWs—and perhaps of all Jewish POWs in the camp—would have been quite different.

Five months later, at the beginning of May 1942, the Swiss embassy delegates (Switzerland replaced the USA as the Protecting Power after America entered the war in December 1941) visited eighteen of the Stalag's labour detachments, two of which consisted of Palestinian Jewish POWs—E207 in Ehrenforst and E366 in Neudorf-Walsbrücke. Their report summarized the main complaints of the POWs in all of those detachments, most of which were about health, overcrowding and insufficient number of blankets.[137] However, the report can also serve as an example of the limited ability of the bodies entrusted with the protection of POWs to obtain a clear view of actual events that occurred in the POW camps and labour detachments, or at least to report on them. The events which are described below, which occurred in labour detachment E207, also demonstrated the protection a POW camp provided to the Jewish POWs from anti-Semitic civilians and *Sturmabteilung* (SA) personnel with whom they had contact outside the camp.

[134] Ibid. [135] Ibid.
[136] Testimony of Captain Webster to JAG, undated, TNA WO 309/2178.
[137] Swiss embassy report on Stalag VIII-B (Lamsdorf), 5 May 1942, TNA WO 224/27.

E207 consisted of 184 Palestinian Jewish POWs, all employed in construction work and in the building of a canal. The MOC was Haim Glovinsky, one of the Jewish prisoners (in later years he served as the head of Israel's Olympic Committee).[138] During their first months in this camp the POWs had reached an agreement with the German captors that as long as they delivered their daily quota of work, they would be allowed to manage their own affairs. This agreement resulted in the work on the canal being completed after eighteen months, instead of the planned six, but was beneficial to both parties: the POWs wanted to extend their stay in what they considered a relatively comfortable camp, while the Germans were concerned about potentially being sent to the Eastern Front once the project had been completed.[139] The POWs also conducted regular Friday religious ceremonies and on the eve of the Jewish New Year in September 1941, the commandant even came to wish them 'Happy New Year'.[140] During their visit, the inspectors noted that the prisoners were well dressed and that there had been an adequate supply of books (mainly in German) and of sport equipment. There were a couple of minor complaints about lack of letters from Palestine (although the prisoners did receive parcels) and a shortage of toothpaste in the camp's canteen. The inspectors summarized the situation in the camp by stating that 'the camp is a good one, and the prisoners here are treated in exactly the same way as prisoners in other camps'.[141] The inspectors then moved to labour detachment E366 in Neudorf-Walsbruecke, which consisted of forty-four Palestinian Jewish POWs employed in the same construction work as their comrades in E207. The conditions, too, were similar, and the inspectors concluded that 'the camp is quite good and there are no real complaints'. The MOC, Isac Zmudziak, asked them to pass a message to his father in Tel Aviv, letting him know that he and two of his brothers were POWs, while a fourth brother had managed to escape in Greece.[142]

E207's peaceful appearance and the relative minor issues raised by the POWs were, however, somewhat deceptive. A few months earlier several clashes had occurred with the civilians, most of whom were Polish of German origin ('*Volksdeutsche*'), who were working with the Jewish POWs on the construction of the canal. The civilians repeatedly told the Jewish POWs '[we] will teach you how to work, lazy Jews' and some of the incidents had become violent and required the intervention of the Wehrmacht guards.[143] Eventually, in a meeting between the commandant of E207, the civilian manager, and the MOC, Glovinsky, it was agreed that going forward the civilian workers would be prohibited from using derogatory terms with the POWs and could only address them as

---

[138] Ibid., p. 9.
[139] Yoav Gelber, *The History of Volunteering*, vol. 4 (Jerusalem: Yad Ben Tzvi, 1984), pp. 168–9.
[140] Glantz, *Struggle in Captivity*, pp. 111–12.
[141] Swiss embassy report on Stalag VIII-B (Lamsdorf), 5 May 1942, p. 9, TNA WO 224/27.
[142] Ibid., pp. 16–17.   [143] Sela, *Shackles of Captivity*, pp. 99–100.

'Palestinian POWs'.[144] Another outcome of the meeting was that the commandant, who was probably considered 'soft' for protecting the POWs, was replaced by a stricter one. The new commandant did not wait long before accusing the MOC of being responsible for the reduction in the daily output of the POWs. The investigation that was launched led to the new commandant himself being replaced, this time by a 50-year-old German officer who made sure that the rules of the Geneva Convention were strictly adhered to.[145]

Other incidents in E207 were triggered by the presence of the SA representatives, who were assigned to the civilian companies involved in the projects the POWs were working on, and who used their role as controllers of the food rations to decide what and how much the POWs would receive.[146] Their decision—which was in clear breach of the Geneva Convention—that Palestinian Jewish POWs should be treated like civilian Jews and receive food accordingly, led to multiple incidents.[147] When the MOC, Sergeant Glovinsky, accused the SA person of stealing food from the POWs rations, the SA person promised revenge; he would not allow a 'damn Jew' to talk to him like that.[148] Eventually, after investigation, the food rations were increased back to their original size.[149] A similar case occurred in labour detachment E433 in Alt Rothwasser (today Stará Červená Voda in the Czech Republic), where food ration decisions were also made by local Nazi Party officials. The small group of Palestinian Jewish POWs who had been working in the stone quarry there went on a hunger strike until they received their full food rations.[150]

None of these incidents were mentioned in the Protecting Power report; it is possible that the POWs told the delegates about them but they might have decided, since they had already been resolved, to omit them from the written report in order not to trigger a reprisal cycle. Alternatively, although less likely, they were not aware of these incidents at all since the POWs may have not mentioned them in their meetings with the delegates. The incidents, however, demonstrate the clear boundaries that existed between the POW camp and the external world—while the POWs interacted with people outside the camp, they were still governed—and protected—by the camp's rules; the radicalization in the

---

[144] Ibid., pp. 100–1. Beatings of POWs by German civilians were not rare incidents; see, for example, Swiss embassy report to the German Foreign Office on Stalag XX-B (Willenberg, today Wielbark in Poland), 8 July 1942, PAAA R40985.

[145] Sela, *Shackles of Captivity*, pp. 101–2.

[146] Rofe, *Against the Wind*, p. 45. Rofe, a British Jewish RAF pilot, joined the labour detachment in order to escape by switching identities with Simon Kacenelenbeigen, a Palestinian Jewish POW, who was transferred to Stalag Luft III (Sagan) in his place (ibid., p. 39). Exchanging identities with POWs in labour detachments in order to facilitate escape attempts was not rare but not always successful; see letter from Stalag VIII-B (Teschen) to Stalag 344 (Lamsdorf), 27 July 1944, PMA 191/2/45; Sela, *Shackles of Captivity*, pp. 226–7; testimony of Moshe Zigelbaum, YVA O.3-2967.

[147] Rofe, *Against the Wind*, p. 45.   [148] Sela, *Shackles of Captivity*, pp. 103–4.

[149] Ibid.   [150] Rofe, *Against the Wind*, pp. 45–8.

treatment of Jews that was taking place outside the fences, which the civilian workers had attempted to apply to the Jewish POWs, met with resistance not only from the POWs themselves but also from their guards and the camp's commandant. Glovinsky himself, the MOC of E207, testified after the war that throughout his time in E207 there was hardly an incident where a Jewish POW was hit or punished by the guards; the military discipline and adherence to the Geneva Convention took priority over the personal ideologies, whatever they were, of the individual soldiers and officers who were overseeing the Jewish POWs.[151]

Interestingly, an ICRC report from the same period, while highlighting a general improvement in working conditions in labour detachments, also mentioned that in nearby labour detachments during the previous year, eight British POWs had been killed and four wounded because they went too close to the camp's fence.[152] Sela in his memoirs described visits to a nearby labour detachment which consisted of about 1,000 British POWs who were also being treated in a harsh manner: in one case, a British POW was killed because he refused to carry the suitcase of a German soldier.[153] In another camp, to which 150 POWs from E207 were later transferred, Sela described a German factory manager who used to threaten the Jewish POWs that he would take the British uniforms off them and make them dress in civilian clothes 'like all the other bloody Jews'.[154] This, however, seemed to be a local incident; in one of the coal mines the POWs were moved to sometime later, Sela described the conditions as being similar to that of the British POWs who worked there.[155]

In August 1942, as a reprisal for the mistreatment earlier that month of German POWs in the Latrun POW camp in Palestine by their Polish guards (the ICRC report stated that the guards were Jewish but this was probably wrong) the Germans moved 149 NCOs from Stalag VIII-B (Lamsdorf) to a newly erected British barracks in Stalag 319, near Cholm.[156] In an obvious act of discrimination against the Palestinian Jewish POWs, perhaps because the mistreatment of the German POWs had occurred in Palestine, eight-two of the 149 NCOs were Palestinian Jewish POWs.[157] In addition, in an order that resulted a complaint by the MOC to the Protecting Power, the camp commandant instructed that beds in the barracks would be occupied alternately by British and Palestinian Jewish POWs.[158]

---

[151] Test in German captivity, July 1945, p. 42, IDF 182/1867/1998.
[152] Summary of ICRC visit, 17 May 1942, ACICR BG 17 05/11; this was in all probability a reference to the deaths of British POWs in Stalag XX-B (Willenberg) which were mentioned in the ICRC visit report from 1 May 1942, p. 9, TNA WO 224/49.
[153] Sela, *Shackles of Captivity*, p. 118.   [154] Ibid., p. 150.   [155] Ibid., p. 181.
[156] Wylie, *Barbed Wire Diplomacy*, p. 78; ICRC report on Stalag 319 (Cholm), 12 February 1943, p. 1, TNA WO 224/27.
[157] Ibid.
[158] Swiss embassy report on to Stalag 319 (Cholm), 9 January 1943, p. 2, TNA WO 224/52.

The ICRC visited the camp, which mainly held Soviet POWs, on 12 February 1943, and their report was not a positive one. The POWs had several complaints about the transfer—their blankets and Red Cross parcels had been confiscated when they left Lamsdorf six months earlier, and they had not received them back yet.[159] The report stated that 'No brutality has been reported' and the treatment of the Jewish POWs, although bad, was not different from that of their British comrades who were incarcerated with them.[160] The ICRC delegates summarized their report on Stalag 319 (Cholm) by saying that 'it was installed particularly as a reprisal [and] it cannot be compared to an ordinary camp... the relations between the prisoners and the guards is [sic] not particularly good'.[161]

The incident was resolved in April 1943: after the German POWs were transferred from Latrun to Egypt, all 149 British NCOs (including the eighty-two Palestinian Jewish NCOs) were sent back to Stalag VIII-B (Lamsdorf).[162] A few months later, about one hundred Palestinian Jewish NCO POWs, which included most, if not all, of those who returned from Stalag 319 (Cholm), were transferred to Stalag 383, an NCO POW camp in Hohenfels near Nuremberg, which had better conditions; their transfer was a result of a complaint by the ICRC, who demanded that the German authorities explain why there were hardly any Jewish POWs among the camp's 5,000 POWs.[163]

Although the number of Jewish POWs which were sent to Stalag 319 (Cholm) was obviously disproportionate, the incident demonstrated again that the treatment—this time mistreatment—of Jewish POWs was not different to that of non-Jewish ones; and even when initial discrimination had occurred with the number of Jewish NCOs sent to Stalag 383 (Hohenfels), this was corrected following the intervention of the ICRC. The Protecting Power and ICRC, other than reporting on the figures, did not file a formal complaint regarding this discrimination nor did they raise it as an issue in any of their reports. The ICRC's intervention, however, shows that their opinion carried some weight with the Germans.

However, this was not always the case: during the Shackling Crisis, 1838 POWs in Stalag VIII-B (Lamsdorf) were handcuffed, 101 of whom were Palestinian Jews—5.5% of the total, much higher than their 3.5% share of the camp's population.[164] The same 'miscalculation' occurred during the Shackling Crisis in

---

[159] ICRC report on Stalag 319 (Cholm), 12 February 1943, p. 1, TNA WO 224/27.
[160] Ibid., p. 6; ICRC to the Jewish Agency in Jerusalem, 9 March 1943, CZA S-25\4720.
[161] ICRC report on Stalag 319 (Cholm), 12 February 1943, p. 7, TNA WO 224/27.
[162] Marti to Meylan, 20 April 1943, ACICR BG 17 05/18.
[163] Gelber, 'Palestinian POWs in German Captivity', p. 116; test in German captivity, July 1945, p. 57, IDF 182/1867/1998. The number of Palestinian Jewish POWs in Stalag 383 (Hohenfels) went up from 2 (ICRC report on Stalag 383, 11 March 1943, p. 1, TNA WO 224/55A) to 101 (Swiss embassy report on Stalag 383, 6 November 1943, p. 1, ibid.).
[164] Swiss embassy report on Stalag VIII-B (Lamsdorf), 5 March 1943, p. 1, TNA WO 224/27. The Shackling Crisis was triggered by the German discovery of British orders to shackle German POWs during the August 1942 Dieppe raid. The crisis led to year-long reprisals where thousands of POWs

the Oflag where the Palestinian Jewish officers were held—the commandant insisted on including all Jewish officers in the group of the shackled POWs, even though the British officers were selected at random.[165] These cases of discrimination against Jewish POWs, as well as a case in 1944 where a German civilian doctor changed the health status of several Palestinian Jewish POWs in order to remove them from a list of exchanged POWs, demonstrated that the German authorities were not completely objective when it came to dealing with Jewish POWs; and when they thought they could stretch the interpretation of the Convention without being caught, they did just that.[166]

Several incidents that occurred in the following year—1943—provide additional insight into the ongoing conflict between the Wehrmacht soldiers' and officers' personal Nazi beliefs and their duty to comply with military discipline and the Geneva Convention. As can be seen, in some cases the soldier's anti-Semitic beliefs took precedence, and in others, his duty to follow orders overcame these beliefs. The first incident occurred at the beginning of 1943 in Stalag VIII-B's (Lamsdorf) labour detachment E456 near Kalkau (today Kałków, Poland). At the time, the number of Palestinian POWs in Stalag VIII-B was 1,231: 243 in the main camp (out of total of 6,851) and 988 in ten (out of 307) Palestinian-only labour detachments; labour detachment E456 consisted of thirty-six Palestinian Jews.[167] The Swiss embassy's report found the living quarters there to be sufficient, but insisted on notifying the German High Command about the lack of washing and bathing facilities, a problem that had not been resolved since the camp's construction two years earlier. The Jewish POWs were allowed to visit the nearby village, either to see the civilian doctor, or, since there was no canteen, to shop there (although they testified that it was almost impossible to find anything in the shops).[168]

The main complaint of the POWs was, however, about their treatment several weeks earlier. Their then-MOC, Sergeant Biegun, had complained several times about not receiving the correct food rations; since his requests to meet the commander of the guards company to discuss the issues had not been answered, on 30 January 1943 the POWs announced a strike and refused to go to work. The labour detachment's commandant immediately reported the issue to the guards' company commander; the commander arrived with six guards, had a row with the MOC and ended up beating him and a few of the POWs. He then assembled

---

on both sides were shackled. For a detailed description of the Shackling crisis see Kochavi, *Confronting Captivity*, pp. 40–54; Wylie, *Barbed Wire Diplomacy*, pp. 136–62.

[165] Yitschak Ben-Aharon, *Pages from the Calendar 1906-1993* (Tel Aviv: HaKibutz HaMe'uchad, 1994), p. 79.

[166] Sela, *Shackles of Captivity*, pp. 228–9.

[167] Swiss embassy report on Stalag VIII-B (Lamsdorf), 5 March 1943, p. 1, TNA WO 224/27; Swiss embassy report on Stalag VIII-B's (Lamsdorf) labour detachments, 6 March 1943, p. 3, ibid.

[168] Ibid., p. 4.

the detachment and insulted them 'as being Jews'.[169] Interestingly, this strike triggered the POW Office to issue an order two weeks later specifically referencing a hunger strike by British Jewish POWs. The order, which was not included in the periodical collection of commands that was issued by the POW Office, instructed the disciplinary supervisors to immediately report on such cases because they 'undermine military discipline' ('*Manneszucht*').[170] The POW Office's sudden interest in this event was probably caused by the fact that there were no specific regulations in the Convention against hunger strikes; it was a loophole that POWs could use in order to become weaker and, as a result, to avoid work.[171]

It is also likely that the strike caused the camp authorities to launch an immediate investigation, since only a few days after the incident took place, on 2 February, the guards battalion's adjutant, Hauptman Kiethe, arrived to investigate the case on the orders of the battalion's commander, Major Mielke. According to his report, he spoke to several POWs and tried to persuade the sergeant in charge, without success, to get his men back to work. He also identified two of the POWs, Feingold and Goldberg, as the main culprits; without making specific reference to their Jewish identity, the inspecting officer stated that 'of course, for well-known racial reasons [*aus bekannten rassischen Gründen*]...it is not easy for them to maintain good order'.[172] Kiethe also mentioned in his report the hitting of the POWs and the withholding of Red Cross parcels as punishment.[173]

Eventually, Kapitan zur See (Naval Captain) Gylek, the commandant of Stalag VIII-B, arrived and relieved the MOC, along with one of the guards, of their duties. The Swiss delegates were told that since then, the food had greatly improved and the POWs had no more complaints.[174] It is interesting to note that, as mentioned above, the inspectors insisted on escalating the lack of washing and bathing facilities to the German High Command, but not this incident, which appeared only in their visit report; it is possible that since the issue had been resolved internally to the satisfaction of all parties, they decided, rightly or wrongly, not to file a formal complaint.

In this case three different types of behaviour could be observed: the guards' company commander, who hit and insulted the Jewish POWs, clearly allowed his anti-Semitism to dictate his behaviour. The battalion adjutant, however, who, judging by his comments—which were included in his official report—was no less anti-Semitic, was nonetheless correct in his approach and did not let his personal beliefs impact his investigation: he did not try to hide any of the events, handled the POWs' complaints in a serious manner, and went as far as putting the

---

[169] Ibid., pp. 4–5.
[170] Maßnahmen bei Hungerstreik von Kgf. im Arbeitseinsatz, 25 March 1943, PMA 194/1/47.
[171] Rofe, *Against the Wind*, p. 46.
[172] Report to Battalion (Btn) 565, 4 February 1943, PMA 190/1/43.   [173] Ibid.
[174] Swiss embassy report on Stalag VIII-B's (Lamsdorf) labour detachments, 6 March 1943, p. 5, TNA WO 224/27.

blame for the POWs' poor work performance on the labour detachment's commandant himself.[175] As for the commandant of Stalag VIII-B (Lamsdorf), although there was no mention of his personal beliefs, the report of the Protecting Power indicated that he had acted quickly and ensured that the situation had been resolved.[176]

The incident in E456 described above was in all likelihood the trigger for the Stalag-wide investigation that took place a few weeks later and dealt with a case of mistreatment of a British Jewish POW. A letter sent on 15 March 1943 by the commander of the POWs in military district VIII (who was in charge of all POW camps in that military district, around Breslau in Silesia) to Stalag VIII-B (Lamsdorf) referenced an incident in which a British Jewish POW in Stalag VIII-B had been beaten and refused Red Cross parcels.[177] The investigation that was launched as a result of this letter is described below; it can serve as an interesting case study for the way that the POW organization responded in general to complaints made by the Protecting Power and for its adherence to internal processes. More specifically, it shows the way it handled matters even when the subject of the investigation was none other than a Jewish POW, a fact that was made clear in all correspondence related to this case, which used the same subject line, 'Treatment of British POW of Jewish ethnicity [*Volkstums*]'.[178] The term 'Jewish ethnicity', and not 'Jewish race', was probably used in order to assist in the identification of the POW and referred to the fact that he was a Palestinian Jew, and not a British Jew.

The complaint was initially reported by the British embassy in Berne to the Swiss embassy in Berlin, which forwarded it to the OKW. The urgency of this matter was made clear by the military district's POW commander, who demanded a response by 30 March 1943—fifteen days after he sent his first letter—and emphasized the need to include all of Stalag VIII-B's (Lamsdorf) labour detachments, totalling almost three hundred, in the investigation.[179] The Stalag's headquarters sent a letter three days later to all five guard battalions in charge of the labour detachments—battalions 337, 398, 515, 559, and 565—and demanded that they investigate and report back by 26 March 1943, hence giving them only eight days to complete their investigations.[180]

The reports began arriving back a few days later. On 24 March, battalions 398 and 559 reported that they had completed their investigations and concluded that no such incident had occurred in the labour detachments under their control;

---

[175] Report to Btn 565, 4 February 1943, PMA 190/1/43.
[176] Swiss embassy report on Stalag VIII-B's (Lamsdorf) labour detachments, 6 March 1943, p. 5, TNA WO 224/27.
[177] Wehrkreis VIII to Stalag VIII-B (Lamsdorf), 15 March 1943, PMA 190/1/43. [178] Ibid.
[179] Ibid. [180] Stalag VIII-B (Lamsdorf) to battalions, 18 March 1943, ibid.

Battalion 337 reported similar findings four days later.[181] The reports included depositions from company commanders and deputy commanders who testified to that effect; for example, the commander of the 6th company of Battalion 398 reported to the battalion's headquarters that he reached this conclusion after questioning all commanders in his company, with the exception of those who were in the hospital or those who were no longer with the company.[182]

Battalion 565 reported the incident (already described above) that occurred in labour detachment E456 on 30 January 1943, describing it as a case of a rebellious POW who was hit with a rifle butt in order to force him to work. Red Cross parcels were also denied (the report did not make it clear whether the whole detachment had been denied them, or only that POW), however the order was lifted shortly afterwards.[183] The report also included as an attachment the original report of the incident, sent on 4 February 1943 and signed by the battalion commander, Major Mielke.[184]

The last battalion to send its report back was 515. The battalion commander reported that he had completed his investigation; although the report concluded that none of the battalion's guards had been involved in a beating of British Jewish POWs, it suggested that the incident in question might in fact be related to a case of Polish civilian workers, who beat a British Jewish POW from labour detachment E562 in Johannagrube in Libiaz after claiming that he had made homosexual advances towards them. The battalion commander argued that the MOC had deliberately misreported the incident to the ICRC by claiming that the POW was beaten because his supervisors were not satisfied with his work performance.[185]

On 28 March 1943, two days before the deadline, the commandant of Stalag VIII-B (Lamsdorf) sent his interim report to his superior, the commander of POWs in military district VIII. Summarizing the findings, the commandant reported that with the exception of the incidents reported by battalions 515 and 565, there were no findings that could justify the complaint made by the Swiss legation.[186] In parallel, he also sent a letter to the commander of Battalion 515, explaining that since the report would eventually be submitted to the Protecting Power and to the British government, he expected a detailed account of the incident to be produced, including the names of the Polish civilians and the British POW who were involved.[187]

4th Company of Battalion 515, which was in charge of E562, sent its report to the battalion headquarters on 27 April 1943. In the report, the company

---

[181] Btn 398 and 559 to Stalag VIII-B (Lamsdorf), 24 March 1943, PMA 190/1/43; Btn 337 to Stalag VIII-B (Lamsdorf), 28 March 1943, ibid.
[182] 6/398 to Btn 398, 23 March 1943, ibid.
[183] Btn 565 to Stalag VIII-B (Lamsdorf), 23 March 1943, ibid.
[184] Report to Btn 565, 4 February 1943, ibid.
[185] Btn 515 to Stalag VIII-B (Lamsdorf), 25 March 1943, ibid.
[186] Stalag VIII-B (Lamsdorf) to Wehrkreis VIII, 28 March 1943, ibid.
[187] Stalag VIII-B (Lamsdorf) to Btn 515, 3 April 1943, ibid.

commander explained that the incident occurred on 12 March 1943 and had already been reported to Stalag VIII-B and to the ICRC. It added that the British Jewish POW was beaten by the Polish workers while working underground but the reasons for the beating were not clear: the MOC, Joseph Luxenburg, a Polish-born Palestinian Jew, reported to the ICRC that the POW was beaten because he was slow in carrying a heavy load, while the commandant of E562 repeated his accusation that it happened because the POW made homosexual advances towards one of the workers. The commander added that the Polish supervisors who reported the incident did not see it with their own eyes and he was not able to identify the workers involved; therefore, a detailed report was not possible.[188]

The date the incident had reportedly occurred, 12 March 1943, suggested that it was clearly not the one that triggered the initial demand for investigation, as it occurred only three days before the first letter was sent by military district VIII to Stalag VIII-B—not enough time for the complaint to go through the formal channels. Regardless, the report of 4th Company had clearly annoyed the battalion commander. In his response two days later he told the company commander that his report was insufficient and that he should find the witnesses that could support these claims. In any case, continued the battalion commander, both Polish supervisors should be interviewed by the police to make sure they did not make up the reasons for the beating. Apparently unable to hide his own opinion on this matter, he concluded his letter by explaining to the company commander that 'it would be very important to tell the Protecting Power that the Jew has been beaten by Polish civilians because he is a swine [*Schwein*]'.[189] The battalion commander then informed Stalag VIII-B in Lamsdorf that his report would be delayed because he was waiting for two witnesses to be interviewed by the police.[190]

Five Polish workers were interviewed by the police on 14 May 1943. Two of them, Gonschorek and Kulas, testified that the POW was hit by Kulas in self-defence after he attacked them; Kulas also claimed that he did not remember calling the POW 'a damn Jew'.[191] The testimony of the other three, regarding homosexual advances made by the POW towards them, did not seem to be relevant to the case and were probably given only to smear the POW's character.[192] The investigation into the E562 case was finally brought to an end on 21 May 1943, slightly over two months after the initial investigation had been launched, when the testimonies of the Polish workers were sent to military district VIII.[193] Although there was still an attempt to charge the Jewish POW with indecent

---

[188] 4/515 to Btn 515, 27 April 1943, ibid. [189] Btn 515 to 4/515, 29 April 1943, ibid.
[190] Btn 515 to Stalag VIII-B (Lamsdorf), 29 April 1943, ibid.
[191] Gonschorek stated that Mallach's POW number was 169, and not 6666. The reason for this is not clear.
[192] Testimonies of Gonschorek, Kulas, Lichota, Baran, and Lelito in front of the Chief of Police, 14 May 1943, PMA 190/1/43.
[193] Stalag VIII-B (Lamsdorf) to military district VIII, 21 May 1943, ibid.

behaviour based on section 175 of the German law, the legal officer of Stalag VIII-B argued that the case should be dropped since the Poles' testimony could not be relied on due to their poor knowledge of German, and since the action itself did not meet the legal threshold of achieving 'satisfaction of one's own or another's sexual desire'.[194]

The reasons for the effort invested by the different levels of military district VIII's chain of command to investigate a case of maltreatment of a Jewish POW are not immediately clear. After all, worse cases were recorded during the same period, such as the beating, mentioned above, that took place on 30 January 1943 in E456. Two potential reasons can be offered: the first is the pressure from the POW commander in military district VIII to respond to the Protecting Power inquiry and to demonstrate that all possible investigation paths had been exhausted. The second reason might be that this was an attempt by the commander of Battalion 515 to prove that the battalion's conduct was in order by trying to pin the blame for the event on the POW himself.

In any case, the reports described above provide an interesting insight into the way commands were passed on and followed in the Wehrmacht. Of course, an army is a hierarchical institution and cannot survive without a clear chain of command and the following of orders; however, the army is also a bureaucratic institution and as such it will try to protect its own members and defend itself against external accusations that not only may impact its credibility and reputation, but may also result in the punishment of those found guilty. In this case, however—aside from the unsuccessful attempt by the commander of Battalion 515 to pin the blame on the Jewish POW himself—the investigation was more open and transparent than would have been expected in these situations. Although it may not be completely accurate to draw conclusions regarding the general behaviour of the POW organization based on one example, this case still demonstrates that at least when dealing with complaints from external bodies, the organizational culture was such that the different levels within the chain of command did not attempt to hide cases of mistreatment, even when the case being investigated was of a Jewish POW; military discipline was stronger than Nazi ideology.

A month before the investigation described above began, in February 1943, a more serious incident occurred in Stalag VIII-B's labour detachment E561 near Jaworzno, where 365 Palestinian Jewish POWs were employed in a coal mine. The details of this incident are another example of the relations between the POWs and the civilians with whom they worked outside the camp. In general, the living conditions in the detachment were described by the visiting Swiss embassy delegates as satisfactory; since there was no canteen, the prisoners were allowed

---

[194] Dept. IIIa to Dept. Ic, Stalag VIII-B (Lamsdorf), 1 June 1943, ibid.

to shop at the nearby town. Medical treatment was provided by a civilian doctor and a civilian dentist; their behaviour towards their POW patients had been specifically praised.[195]

The situation in the mine, however, was not as smooth. The manager complained that in the first few weeks the Palestinian Jewish POWs did not work properly and even damaged the pits; the POWs, on the other hand, complained that they had been treated badly by the civilian guards 'as being Jews'.[196] More serious, however, was the fact that two Palestinian Jewish POWs, Sapper Ezra Nasser (on 13 February 1943) and Signalman Isaak Zassler (on 23 February) were killed by the civilian workers. These incidents were reported at the time in letters sent by the POWs back to Palestine; they managed to bypass the German censors by using Hebrew words written in English letters, addressing one letter to '*c/o Hargoo 2 Meitanu Bemichrot Pecham* [they killed two of us in the coal mines]'.[197]

Based on testimonies given by fellow POWs after the war to the British Judge Advocate General investigating German breaches of the Geneva convention, it was established that Nasser was killed by the foreman of the mine, Rempe, a *Volksdeutsche*, who was also the Gestapo agent for the district; Zassler, who had just been released from hospital where he had been treated for rheumatism, was shot by one of the mine's foremen—a *Volksdeutsche* as well—after he refused to work in the damp mine (according to another version, Zassler was clubbed on the head by two guards and was then shot by a German soldier as he laid dying in order to cover up the incident).[198] In response, on the following day (24 February 1943) the Palestinian POWs went on a strike; they agreed to go back to work only after they were promised that the murders would be investigated. Later that day a committee made up of German officers showed up and began an investigation; ICRC representatives came a week later to conduct their own.[199] The German investigation regarding one of the POWs, Zassler, which was completed several months later, concluded that his death was a case of self-defence, claiming that the foreman was forced to shoot him after he was attacked by Zassler.[200]

The Swiss embassy delegates who visited E561 a couple of weeks after the incidents had occurred emphasized to the mine's civilian manager, as well as to the detachment's German commandant, that the Jewish POWs were British soldiers

---

[195] Swiss embassy report on Stalag VIII-B's (Lamsdorf) labour detachments, 9 March 1943, pp. 9–10, TNA WO 224/27.
[196] Ibid., p. 10.
[197] Letter to the Chief Secretary of the Government Offices in Jerusalem, 4 June 1943, CZA S-25\4720. This method of bypassing the German censor was first pointed out by Yoav Gelber.
[198] Testimony of Friedland, 26 June 1945, and Afgan (undated), TNA WO 309/22; and Rofe, *Against the Wind*, p. 95. The second version was reported by Sela (see Sela, *Shackles of Captivity*, pp. 175–6). Cyril Rofe described how all foremen were *Volksdeutsche*, carried guns and were hated by the POWs (Rofe, *Against the Wind*, p. 95).
[199] Sela, *Shackles of Captivity*, p. 176.
[200] Letter from the Chief Secretary's Office, the Government of Palestine, 29 September 1943, D/34/43, CZA S-25\4720.

and should be treated exactly the same as any other British soldiers.[201] Other than this comment, no other record was found suggesting that any action was taken against the civilians. However, when a similar case occurred later in a different mine, where the mine's foreman used a gun to try and force one of the Palestinian Jewish POWs back into the mine after the shift had ended, his friends, who were aware of the murders, surrounded the foreman and threatened to kill him. The German commandant of the labour detachment was then called and reprimanded the civilian foreman for treating the POWs in that way; their guard was also reprimanded for losing control over the situation and allowing it to deteriorate.[202]

Around the same time period another incident in which Palestinian Jewish POWs were involved occurred in Stalag VIII-B's labour detachment E479 in Tarnowitz (today Tarnowskie Góry, Poland), where 254 Palestinian Jewish POWs were employed in loading and unloading of railway wagons and in building a railway line. The details of this incident demonstrate the complexity of the captor-captive relationship, which could not be viewed as being simply hierarchical in nature, but also required cooperation between the parties most of the time. The incident also highlights the role played by those who became leaders of POWs not through rank, but through personal authority, the issues they sometimes encountered in enforcing their authority on their fellow POWs, and how this authority was recognized and used by the Germans.

The Swiss embassy delegates visited E479 in March 1943 and noted the lack of ventilation during the night in the POWs' accommodation. The camp's doctor insisted that there was no scientific need for it; he also claimed that for 'technical reasons' it was impossible to obtain sheets for the infirmary's beds, and that a special diet could only be provided in the Lazaret, and not in the infirmary (a claim that was found to be untrue). The delegates escalated the medical issues to the commander of the military district.[203] The main issue, however, was the food, which was cooked outside the camp by the '*Arbeitsfront*', the Nazi labour organization. Since this was a Nazi Party organ, the Jewish MOC, Sergeant Simon Kaplan, who prior to the war had been a policeman in Palestine, was not allowed in the kitchen and could not check the food rations. The German officer who accompanied the legation explained that the MOC was allowed in the kitchen only with a German guard; to solve the issue, he proposed that the prisoners have their own kitchen inside the camp.[204] In addition to the kitchen issue, the MOC complained that a few of the guards, along with their commander, often insulted the prisoners 'as being Jews' and sometimes even beat them. The inspectors

---

[201] Swiss embassy report on Stalag VIII-B's (Lamsdorf) labour detachments, 9 March 1943, p. 11, TNA WO 224/27.
[202] Testimony of Moshe Zigelbaum, YVA O.3–2967.
[203] Swiss embassy report on Stalag VIII-B's (Lamsdorf) labour detachments, 10 March 1943, p. 16, TNA WO 224/27.
[204] Ibid., p. 15.

escalated this issue to the POW commander in the military district, and asked him to see that the Jewish POWs were treated 'exactly like the others'.[205]

The Swiss legation reports from March 1943, however, only tell part of the story regarding the situation in E479. In letters sent to POWs' families a few months earlier, in November 1942, the POWs used Hungarian and Hebrew words written in English letters to describe their treatment: one POW wrote home and asked to pass his regards to 'Mr. *Makim Otanu* [Hebrew for "they are beating us"]...Mr. *Yachas Ra* [bad treatment]...Mr. *Aroumim* [naked] and Mr. *Bakor* [in the cold]'.[206] Interestingly, the use of the Hebrew language in letters sent by the Palestinian POWs was not prohibited during that period; however, since Hebrew-proficient censors were relatively scarce, resulting in delays of up to six months in the delivery of the letters, the commandant advised the POWs to write letters in other languages.[207] Letters sent to the POWs in Hebrew were only prohibited in 1944; until then, they were allowed into the camps presumably without any checks.[208]

The situation in E479 had apparently improved before the visit of the Protecting Power, when Sergeant Kaplan became the MOC there.[209] Kaplan used to 'bully the Germans around as though dealing with a crowd of schoolchildren[;] there was never any doubt who was in charge [of labour detachment E479]'.[210] When he was accused by the camp commandant of covering up the escape of two POWs for almost a week (which he did), Kaplan refused to work with the commandant anymore. A few days of chaos ensued, after which the commandant came back begging him to be 'friends as before'.[211] Although the specifics of this event were included in a memoir which was written after the war and therefore might have contained details intended to exaggerate the resistance of the POWs, it seems that the fact that the POWs were Jewish played a minor role in this situation; the commandant was more concerned with meeting his work quota than in dealing with racial issues.

Not surprisingly, the Germans were not satisfied with the way the Tarnowitz labour detachment was being run and wanted to replace Kaplan. The agreements

---

[205] Ibid., pp. 16–17.
[206] POW letter, 8 November 1942, CZA S-25\4720. The POWs had to be creative in the use of Hebrew words: dozens of letters containing such words which had raised the German censor's suspicion were returned (see Sela, *Shackles of Captivity*, p. 132). In some cases the censors tried to investigate the meaning of the words; for example, in March 1944, the word '*Mizpah*' (in Hebrew: a watchtower) in one of the (non-Palestinian) POW's letters raised the suspicion of a censor in military district VIII, and he sent it for further analysis to Stalag Luft III in Sagan. The censor there explained that this word was not meant as anti-German propaganda, but rather as a reference from the book of Genesis which meant that God is watching over the POW and his wife even when they are apart (Stalag Luft III to military district VIII, 31 March 1944, PMA 191/1/44).
[207] ICRC report on Stalag VIII-B (Lamsdorf), 12 February 1943, ACICR G25 Carton 618.
[208] Verwendung der hebräischen Sprache auf Arb. Kdos. und im Briefverkehr, 19 July 1944, PMA 195/1/47.
[209] Rofe, *Against the Wind*, p. 85.   [210] Ibid.   [211] Ibid., p. 87.

he reached with the camp commandant, for example regarding work quotas (which allowed the POWs—and their guards—to work only half days), and the ongoing black market activities between the POWs and the civilian population, meant that the camp was not operating in an efficient manner.[212] As a result, in March 1943 a German officer was sent from the main camp in Lamsdorf to labour detachment E549 in Jakobswalde, where around 250 Palestinian Jewish POWs were employed, and asked the MOC there, Sergeant Yosef Karlenboim, to take over the leadership of the camp in Tarnowitz. When Karlenboim refused, the officer explained bluntly that if the problem was not addressed, the Germans might resort to 'radical solutions...the Germans had already killed many Jews, and if your comrades can be saved, I see it as my duty to do so'.[213] Assuming Karlenboim's recollection of the conversation was accurate, this astounding statement—a German officer telling a Jewish POW that he sees it as his duty to save Jewish POWs—is not only a testimony for the extent of the knowledge of the Holocaust within the POW organization; but also an example for how POW status protected non-Soviet Jewish POWs from the ongoing radicalization that was taking place outside the walls of the camp, and how those who were part of the POW camp chain of command chose to follow the Geneva Convention rules—and their own national conservative values—rather than Nazi ideology.

After confirming that the 'request' was approved by Sherriff, Stalag VIII-B's (Lamsdorf) MOC, Karlenboim agreed to the move. Karlenboim, who in later years changed his name to Almogi and served as a member of the Israeli parliament, the Knesset, and as a minister in several Israeli governments, was known throughout the district around Jakobswalde as 'The Gauleiter of Oberschlesien' (Upper Silesia).[214] In his memoirs, Captain Julius Green, a British Jewish POW, described a visit he made to labour detachment E549 as part of his duties as Stalag VIII-B's (Lamsdorf) dental officer. According to him, the camp was run as a communal farm, and all proceeds from the camp's 'commercial'—black market—activities went into a common pool. Apparently, Karlenboim—who was a commander in the Haganah, the Jewish paramilitary organization, before he joined the British army—had struck a deal with the German authorities, according to which, in return for leaving the POWs to run their own affairs and delivering the required daily quotas, the Germans would receive regular 'donations' of soap, tea, chocolate and cigarettes from the POWs' Red Cross parcels.[215]

Karlenboim's position was such that when Green, accompanied by his German guard, was ready to make his way back to the camp in Lamsdorf on foot, Karlenboim would not hear of it. He arranged for him to be taken by a

---

[212] In the following year, the OKW issued a specific order instructing the suppression 'by all available means' of black market trade between POWs and civilians. See Befehlsammlung 33, order 542, 15 January 1944, BA-MA RW 6/270.
[213] Almogi, *With Head Held High*, pp. 73–4.   [214] Green, *From Colditz in Code*, p. 105.
[215] Ibid.

horse-drawn carriage and forced the guard to sit next to the coachman instead of in the back, demanding to know 'what makes you think you are entitled to sit beside an officer?'.[216] Karlenboim was described as a firm disciplinarian with a strong personality and had a large following among the Palestinian Jewish POWs; however, the fact that he forbade escapes, which he probably thought of as a waste of time, together with the order he imposed, resulted in several POWs accusing him of being 'disgustingly servile to the Germans'.[217] This might have been the reason the Germans had approached him in the first place.

Karlenboim moved to E479—Tarnowitz—at the end of March 1943 and became the MOC there. Soon after his arrival and against strong objections from the majority of the POWs, who did not like the new restrictions he imposed, the situation in the camp began to change: gambling was forbidden, one of the huts was converted into a club, and social and cultural activities began to take place. Within a few weeks the situation was defused.[218] It should be noted that Karlenboim's authority—in E479 as well as in other POW camps and labour detachments—was not always accepted by everyone; POWs who outranked him, and those who saw him as an 'establishment' figure, sometimes resented his interference and opposed his attempts to introduce order and discipline. The issues Karlenboim faced were reflected in a letter sent by one of the repatriated POWs (who was among almost 4,000 sick and wounded Allied POWs, including sixty Palestinian Jews, who were exchanged in October 1943) to the Jewish Agency, suggesting that they help Karlenboim by sending a letter to Sherriff, Stalag VIII-B's MOC, formally appointing Karlenboim as the representative of the Palestinian Jewish POWs.[219]

A summary of the incidents that occurred in Stalag VIII-B's (Lamsdorf) labour detachments at the beginning of 1943 was sent by the Swiss legation to the British Foreign Office in April 1943. Out of the seven major incidents they chose to highlight, three—in labour detachments E456, E479, and E561—related to ill-treatment of Palestinian Jewish POWs due to their ethnicity.[220] It is worth mentioning that during the same period there was a lot of tension in other labour detachments in the area, and over a period of six weeks, seven Australian and four British POWs were killed in several incidents; three British POWs died in accidents in the mines; and around forty British POWs were injured or killed after an escape attempt.[221] In January 1943, John Allman, a British (non-Jewish) POW who was held in Stalag VIII-B's labour detachment E8 in Krappitz, wrote to

---

[216] Ibid., p. 106.   [217] Rofe, *Against the Wind*, pp. 171–2.
[218] Almogi, *With Head Held High*, pp. 84–5.
[219] Kochavi, *Confronting Captivity*, p. 125; Pinnes to Golda Meirson (the future Prime Minister of Israel), 6 August 1944, CZA J-10/122.
[220] Berne to Norton, 9 April 1943; and Berne to Norton, 24 April 1943, TNA WO 224/27.
[221] Sela, *Shackles of Captivity*, p. 177. See also Jack Elworthy about his experience in E72, memoirs, http://www.pegasusarchive.org/pow/jack_elworthy.htm, accessed 29 March 2018. For examples of killings of POWs see MacKenzie, *The Colditz Myth*, pp. 232–5.

his family that 'now the civilian people are allowed to beat us if we do not work all day and every day'.[222]

An incident that occurred in June 1943 in labour detachment E593 in Schomberg (today Chełmsko Śląskie in Poland), which consisted of 455 Palestinian Jewish POWs, demonstrated that the report mentioned above that was sent by the Swiss legation two months earlier summarizing the incidents in Stalag VIII-B (Lamsdorf) had clearly reflected the situation that existed at the time in the camp and its labour detachments.[223] Upon their arrival in the camp, the local SA area commander—the SA was responsible for assimilating, organizing the work and indoctrinating the local *Volksdeutsche* population—warned the Palestinian Jewish POWs that he intended to turn the camp into a concentration camp for Palestinian Jewish POWs, in the same way that Auschwitz was a concentration camp for civilian Jews.[224] The MOC complained to the ICRC, which, in turn, told the commandant that 'the relations with the POWs should be different'; an indication that the ICRC seemed to have had, by 1943, some knowledge of the conditions in Auschwitz, and at the very least, it knew that the conditions there were not suitable for POWs.[225]

In any case, this incident was not mentioned in the letter sent by the Swiss embassy delegates to the British Foreign Office, summarizing their visit in October 1943. This time, only two out of the fourteen labour detachments mentioned in the letter were Palestinian ones; however, unlike the previous summary letter sent in April of that year and mentioned above, the issues escalated this time related mostly to overcrowding and general conditions in these camps, and not to mistreatment of Palestinian Jews.[226] It seems that the ICRC either did not update the Swiss embassy about the June incident in E593; or, since the incident was considered closed, the Swiss embassy delegates did not think it should have been mentioned in their letter. This is despite the fact that by that stage, the ICRC had additional information, through letters sent by Palestinian Jewish POWs directly to Geneva, regarding the conditions in Stalag VIII-B's (Lamsdorf) labour detachments: two postcards sent in June and July 1943 by POWs in E479 included hidden Hebrew words, such as '*Makot*' (beatings) and '*Minharot Ded*' (dead in the tunnels, a reference to the mines).[227]

---

[222] BRC to ICRC Geneva, 3 March 1943, ACICR BG 17 05/018.

[223] They were joined in October 1943 by a group of South African Jewish POWs who had been separated from their non-Jewish comrades (see Sela, *Shackles of Captivity*, p. 190).

[224] Bruce Campbell, 'The SA after the Rohm Purge', *Journal of Contemporary History*, 28:4 (1993), pp. 659–74, p. 668; from the beginning of 1944, the SA also participated in the guarding of POWs (see affidavit of Walter Schellenberg, document 3232-PS, *IMT, Nazi Conspiracy and Aggression*, vol. V (Washington, DC, 1946), p. 937. Sela, *Shackles of Captivity*, p. 187).

[225] Sela, *Shackles of Captivity*, p. 187.

[226] Letter from Berne to Norton in the British Foreign Office, 15 November 1943, marked 5449, TNA WO 224/27.

[227] Postcards from POWs Shalit (7 June 1943) and Savicky (17 July 1943), ACICR BG 17 05/019.

Internally, the ICRC took these letters as examples of mistreatment of Jewish POWs, which was contrary to the external statements they were consistently making about their equal treatment. After discussing them within its headquarters, a letter was sent on 27 October 1943 to the ICRC's Berlin delegation, asking them whether they believed this case represented an isolated incident or indicated an overall different approach to Jewish POWs.[228] The discussion within the ICRC clearly points towards the inefficient coordination that existed at the time between it and the Swiss Protecting Power, which only six months earlier had reported about such cases of mistreatment of Palestinian Jewish POWs. Although no follow-up correspondence was found in the ICRC files it is obvious that despite the consistent message it was presenting outwardly regarding the non-discriminatory treatment of Jewish POWs, it did have sufficient evidence to know that this was not always the case; whether it had done enough to challenge the German authorities by using this evidence, as well as the evidence it had at that stage of the fate of Europe's Jewish population, is debateable.

The ICRC's involvement did not bring to an end the issues in labour detachment E593. In May 1944 a new camp commandant arrived: Oberfeldwebel Fritz Pantke, who was a member of both the SA and the Nazi Party.[229] A devoted Nazi, he did not hesitate to put his personal anti-Semitic beliefs above military policies and the need to adhere to the Geneva Convention: from the moment he arrived he kept reminding the POWs about his intention to make sure all Jewish POWs ended up in Auschwitz.[230] He had the first opportunity to demonstrate his intention when three Palestinian Jewish POWs escaped from the camp shortly after his arrival. Two of them, Eliyahu Krauze and Dov Eisenberg, were caught the following morning by one of the guards and marched back to the camp, together with a group of POWs who had just returned from a night shift. Pantke and his deputy, Unteroffizier Kanzler, stopped the group and pulled the escapees out; that was the last time they were seen alive by their comrades.[231]

Based on testimonies given after the war by fellow POWs, it was established that Pantke had ordered the POWs to show him where they had hidden during the night. He then ordered them to start running, and he and his deputy pulled their pistols and shot them in the back.[232] Both POWs were injured; Krause died of his wounds after a few hours, while Eisenberg was brought to a German

---

[228] Schwarzenberg to Meylan, 15 October 1943, ACICR BG 17 05/019; Schwarzenberg to Berlin, 27 October 1943, ACICR BG 25/36.

[229] Deposition of Fritz Pantke, 4 February 1947, TNA WO 309/22; see also Rofe, *Against the Wind*, p. 201. Although Sela dated Pantke's arrival to the end of 1943 (Sela, *Shackles of Captivity*, p. 191), he was probably mistaken.

[230] Almogi, *With Head Held High*, p. 135.

[231] Testimony of Read, 4 April 1946, TNA WO 309/22.

[232] Ibid. and Rofe, *Against the Wind*, p. 203. The OKW reported that their death was a result of 'insubordination', and not of an escape attempt (see report on shot American and British POWs, 25 September 1944, PAAA R40999).

military hospital in Laurahotte, where he died six weeks later. During this period he was kept alone in a room and was not allowed visits from his fellow POWs. In a smuggled statement he wrote that he was being treated badly and asked to be moved to a hospital with British medical staff. The events described in his statement were confirmed afterwards by two POWs who stayed in the same ward. He was buried with a military funeral in the civilian cemetery in Schomberg.[233]

When rumours about the shootings and of Pantke's anti-Semitic behaviour reached Stalag VIII-B (Lamsdorf), Sergeant Karlenboim, who had been transferred back to the Stalag from labour detachment E578 in Peiskretchem several months earlier, went to see the commandant, Kapitan zur See Gylek, together with Sherriff, the camp's MOC. After explaining the situation to the commandant, he asked to be transferred to Schomberg to try and deal with it. The commandant, apparently aware that a formal investigation might not achieve the required result quick enough and perhaps trying to prevent additional incidents, approved the request; when parting, he said to Karlenboim 'may God be with you'.[234]

Karlenboim's approach was to confront Pantke head on. He instructed the POWs to sing Hebrew songs as loud and as frequently as they could and to refuse to work when it was raining. He also informed the civilian management of the mine where the POWs were working that due to Pantke's treatment, they would no longer be able to deliver the agreed quota. This of course resulted in the mine's management complaining about Pantke to the German authorities.[235] Pantke was getting irritated; he told his soldiers (who disliked him as well) that if it were not for the investigation being conducted for the murder of the two escapees, he would have shot Karlenboim, but did not want to give 'the damn Jews' the satisfaction of seeing him transferred.[236] Eventually, an investigating party from Stalag VIII-B arrived and heard both Karlenboim's complaints and Pantke's explanations. That evening the POWs were informed of the outcome by three drunken German guards who yelled 'he's gone! He's gone!'.[237] Apparently, the investigating officers did not let Pantke's—and perhaps even their own—anti-Semitism stand in the way of military procedure: the minute they completed their inspection, they instructed him to pack his belongings and leave the camp.[238]

Pantke was still able to exact some revenge during the POWs' forced marches at the end of the war, when POWs were evacuated ahead of the advancing Allied armies. At that stage he was in charge of a column of Soviet POWs; whenever he recognized a Palestinian Jewish POW marching by, he made sure the POW was transferred to his column, where the conditions and treatment were much

---

[233] Testimonies of Gibian, 27 March 1945, Szego, 14 April 1945, and Read, 4 April 1946, TNA WO 309/22.
[234] Almogi, *With Head Held High*, p. 136.   [235] Ibid., pp. 139–40.
[236] Rofe, *Against the Wind*, p. 201; Almogi, *With Head Held High*, p. 140.
[237] Ibid., p. 142.   [238] Ibid.

worse.²³⁹ Pantke was tried after the war for the murder of the escaped POWs but was acquitted; by then it was difficult to trace and bring key witnesses back to clarify a few minor inconsistencies in the testimonies.²⁴⁰ Although shooting of escaping POWs was not uncommon in the days shortly after the escape from Stalag Luft III, in this case Pantke's anti-Semitic beliefs seemed to have been the driver behind the murder of the POWs.²⁴¹ His removal probably improved to some extent the situation in E593; however, a letter of complaint which was received by the BRC in July 1944 from one of the POWs there indicated that the conditions there were far from satisfying.²⁴² The BRC asked the ICRC to investigate the situation but when the ICRC visited E593 again in September of that year, the MOC did not raise any complaints and its report stated that it had found the conditions in the labour detachment to be in order.²⁴³ The Protecting Power, who visited the camp in January 1945, had similar findings.²⁴⁴

To complete the review of the experience of the Palestinian Jewish POWs, it is necessary to mention the experience of the Palestinian officers who were captured with them in Greece in April 1941. Available testimonies—given that there were only three Palestinian Jewish officers, there are not as many as those of the soldiers—indicate that their treatment was in most cases in line with the treatment of their non-Jewish comrades. Yitschak Ben-Aharon was one of three Palestinian Jewish officers who became POWs and spent the next four years in several Oflags. Ben-Aharon—as mentioned earlier, after Israel's independence he became a member of the Knesset and served as the general secretary of Israel's biggest labour union and as transport minister—was surprised to find that throughout his period of captivity the Germans treated him in the same way that they treated the other British officer POWs.²⁴⁵ The only exception occurred during the Shackling Crisis, when, as mentioned earlier, the Germans insisted on including all Jewish officers in the group of the shackled POWs, even though the British officers were selected at random.²⁴⁶

Although some of the events described above provide a grim picture regarding the treatment of Jewish POWs, the example of Paul Weiner, an Austrian-born Palestinian Jewish POW who immigrated to Palestine from Czechoslovakia in 1940 and volunteered for the British army, gives a somewhat different angle to

---

²³⁹ Sela, *Shackles of Captivity*, p. 250.
²⁴⁰ Cleaver to HQ Intelligence Division, BAOR, 15 September 1947, TNA 309/22; Armstrong to the Military Department in JAG Office, 10 May 1947, TNA 309/22.
²⁴¹ Almogi, *With Head Held High*, p. 136. The escape from Stalag Luft III in Sagan (known as 'The Great Escape' after the movie that was made about it) occurred in March 1944. Seventy-three of the seventy-six escapees were caught, and fifty of them were murdered by the Gestapo following a direct order of Hitler.
²⁴² BRC to ICRC, 28 July 1944, ACIRC BG 17 05/28. Similar POW letters regarding conditions in Stalag VIII-B's (Lamsdorf) E152 and E724 were received during the same period (ibid.).
²⁴³ ICRC report on Stalag VIII-B (Lamsdorf), 30 September 1944, PMA 191/2/45.
²⁴⁴ Swiss embassy report on Stalag VIII-B (Lamsdorf), 18 January 1945, AFS, E2001/02#1000/114#195.
²⁴⁵ Ben-Aharon, *Pages from the Calendar*, p. 79.   ²⁴⁶ Ibid.

this complex situation. As a reward for one of the Palestinian Jewish POWs—who was originally from Germany—completing building work to the satisfaction of the German officers in Stalag VIII-B (Lamsdorf), a group of German-speaking Jewish POWs, which included Weiner, was sent to work on a farm near Lubowitz.[247] One day the owner of the farm appeared, and after sending the guards away, demanded to know why the POWs did not inform him that they were Jewish. Without waiting for an answer, he told them that he was from Vienna, where his best friend, a Jewish Lawyer, was made to scrub the streets with a toothbrush before being kicked to death. He then told the confused POWs that from then on he would take care of all their needs.[248] In his memoirs, Weiner described the three years that followed mostly as an uneventful, almost pleasant period: the POWs had sufficient food, were usually treated with respect by their guards, and developed close—sometimes amorous—relations with the women from the nearby village.[249] The several unavoidable pregnancies that had resulted from these relations were always blamed on a 'soldier on leave', who was later reported killed in action.[250] In some cases these relations caused jealous villagers—usually older and those exempt from army service for various reasons—to take action against the POWs: in one such incident, the local blacksmith (who was also a member of the Nazi Party) fired shots at a couple after he found out that the girl, who was the subject of his affection, was meeting with a POW. The guards were enraged—not at the Jewish POW, but at the blacksmith who dared fire at one of their charges; the blacksmith's exemption from military service was immediately revoked and he was sent to the Eastern Front.[251]

Outside the Camp

There were several aspects of POWs' lives that took place outside the camp. These included cases where POWs were brought in front of military courts, since staff within the camps could only deal with disciplinary issues; cases where POWs were sent for medical treatment in military, and sometimes civilian, hospitals; and cases of POWs who escaped. In general, these cases point towards the same conclusion that was reached earlier: when it came to American and British Jewish POWs, the Geneva Convention in most cases took precedence over Nazi racial policies, and Jewish POWs were treated in the same manner as their non-Jewish comrades even when they were on the other side of the camp's fences.

---

[247] Hans Paul Weiner, unpublished memoirs, p. 51, JMM WW2 files.   [248] Ibid., pp. 53–4.
[249] Ibid., pp. 57–8 and 61–3.   [250] Ibid., p. 63.   [251] Ibid., p. 72.

Judicial Proceedings

Article 45 of the 1929 Geneva Convention stated that POWs were subjected to the military law of the Detaining Power and established the supremacy of this law over the civilian one—which, in Germany's case, included the Nuremberg Laws. Furthermore, the Detaining Power was prohibited from subjecting POWs to punishments which were 'less favourable than that prescribed, as regards the same punishment, for similar ranks in the armed forces of the detaining Power'.[252] The Convention also distinguished between disciplinary punishment, which was exercised inside the POW camp and was limited to a maximum of thirty days imprisonment, and judicial proceedings, which had the death penalty as its most severe punishment. For example, a POW escapee who was recaptured was only liable for a disciplinary punishment—which probably contributed to the large number of escapes, at least until the Kugel Erlass (which ordered that captured POW escapees would be sent to concentration camps, and not returned to the POW camp from which they had escaped) was issued.[253]

In theory, judicial trials had been another area where discrimination against Jewish POWs could have been expected, since the German authorities had the ability to produce charges and evidence at will in order to secure a conviction. However, this does not seem to have been the case. Anecdotal evidence related to trials involving Jewish POWs indicates that in general, there was no discrimination against them and their ethnicity was not mentioned by the judges or the prosecution in any of the court documents reviewed.

In his unpublished memoirs, RSM Frederick Read, the MOC of Stalag VIII-B after it was moved from Lamsdorf to Teschen in October 1943, told the story of a Jewish corporal who had become romantically involved with a German housewife, who happened to be the wife of the local Nazi Party Gauleiter.[254] After the woman had bribed one of the guards, the Jewish POW was able to slip almost every night from Stalag VIII-B's labour detachment E535 near Sosnovitch and visit her; eventually he was caught by her husband, who returned home unexpectedly early one day.[255] At that time, according to the Nuremberg laws, having sexual relations between Aryans and Jews was a criminal offence; forced labourers who were caught faced the death penalty. However, since the Jewish POW was protected by the Geneva Convention, he received 'only' two years in prison, which seemed to have been in line with the Wehrmacht's guidelines for these cases; harsher punishments for this offence were reserved for Polish POWs, who,

---

[252] Articles 45 and 46 of the 1929 Geneva Convention, https://ihl-databases.icrc.org/ihl/INTRO/305, accessed 4 February 2018.

[253] Article 50, ibid.

[254] RSM Read was described as 'thoroughly able and competent man' (see Rofe, *Against the Wind*, p. 188).

[255] Frederick Read, *A War Fought Behind the Wire* (Kindle Edition: F. C. Read, 2013), p. 104.

according to the Wehrmacht, were not protected by the Convention since Poland was no longer considered a state.[256] As Read remarked in his memoirs, the POW had explained to him that the sentence was worth it: after all, he had just had a whole year of active sex life, something none of his comrades could have claimed to have had. In contrast, the woman's sentence for fraternizing with the enemy was to sweep the streets of Sosnovitch for five years.[257] In comparison, a Polish POW who was sent to prison by a military court for having sexual relations with a German woman was later handed to the Gestapo and executed.[258] Even in Nazi Germany, a POW's uniform—either American or British—was more important than his ethnicity and protected him from discrimination.

In another case, the Palestinian Jewish POWs Jack Glesner and Otto Schweiger were sentenced to forty-two days and nine months' imprisonment, respectively, for intimate relations with German women.[259] The judge mentioned the defendants' immediate confession, as well as their youth, as mitigating factors for the punishment. In the Court documents it was also mentioned that both held British citizenship, even though this was probably not the case since Palestinian residents, although considered 'British Protected Persons', held Palestinian citizenship and not a British one.[260] In his affidavit, the defendant Glesner had found it necessary to state that only his father was Jewish, but not his mother; however, other than this statement, the defendants' ethnicity was not mentioned anywhere else in the court documents.

In less colourful cases, Two Palestinian Jewish POWs from Stalag VIII-B's labour detachment in Jaworzno were put on trial for bribing guards. They were appointed a defence lawyer and were acquitted of the charges.[261] In another case, Samuel Lorbeerbaum, a Palestinian Jewish POW in Stalag IX-C (Bad Sulza), was put on trial, along with two British POWs, for making contact with German women.[262] In his report to the Protecting Power, the German lawyer who was assigned to the defendants did not make any reference to the fact that one of the defendants was Jewish; Lorbeerbaum and one of his comrades were sentenced to 1.5 months imprisonment, while the third POW was sentenced to nine months imprisonment. The judge added that the punishment could have been much milder had the defendants confessed to their crime at an earlier stage.

---

[256] See, for example, Befehlsammlung 20, order 240, 11 January 1943, BA-MA RW 6/270; and Reinecike's interrogation, 22 October 1945, https://www.fold3.com/image/231935826, accessed 1 October 2019, pp. 23–4.
[257] Fredrick Read, *A War Fought Behind the Wire*, (Kindle Edition: F. C. Read, 2013), p. 104.
[258] Nicolas Stargardt, *The German War* (New York: Penguin, 2015), p. 141.
[259] Field judgement, 3 August 1942, Israel State Archives M 109/39.
[260] The German court had no way of establishing the citizenship of the POWs and therefore had to rely on their declarations (see n. 68 above for more details).
[261] Letter from Dalgleish to Joseph, 26 October 1943, CZA S-25\4720.
[262] Solicitor Office to Swiss Legation in Germany, 6 May 1943, Israel State Archives M 109/40.

There were, however, court cases of Jewish POWs which demonstrate that the German military judicial system was not always impartial. Alexander Glantz, a Palestinian Jewish POW, was put on trial for what he thought was his recent escape and assuming a false identity. Together with him were thirteen other POWs, five of whom were Jews. The Germans explained to them that according to the Geneva Convention, they were entitled to be represented by a lawyer, either a German one or one from the Protecting Power, Switzerland. Glantz, who assumed that he would be found guilty in any case, wanted to save money and opted for the German lawyer, whose costs were paid by the Germans; he also believed—wrongly, as it turned out—that a German lawyer would have a better standing in court than a foreign one.[263]

The POWs were charged with several counts, including destruction of property, refusal to work, bad-mouthing Hitler and fraternizing with German women (they were not, however, charged with escaping—which, as explained earlier, was a disciplinary matter and not a judicial one).[264] The German lawyer who represented Glantz and several of the other POWs argued that even though the POWs were of a different faith—he did not specify which faith—since they fought under the British flag they deserved to be treated with respect, and not to be mocked by their captors; but when he continued and argued that the defendants acted in the way they did because of the way they were treated by their captors, the judge warned him that this line of defence may cost him his life.[265] As a result, the lawyer withdrew and the Swiss lawyer—who represented the other defendants—took over the defence of all of the POWs. Glantz was among those who received the lightest sentence—eighteen months imprisonment.[266]

When he arrived in prison, the wardens were surprised to learn that some of their new charges were Jews; it seemed that they were certain that by that stage of the war there were no more Jews left in Europe. Their main concern was regarding their own fate, in case the SS would find that Jews were being held in the prison. Fortunately, the officer in charge had some knowledge of the rules and explained to them that unlike civilian Jews, these prisoners were considered British soldiers and were under the protection of the Wehrmacht and the Geneva Convention.[267]

There were also cases where the appointed lawyer did not act with their client's best interests in mind: Tibor Weinstein, a Hungarian-born Palestinian Jewish POW, was put on trial after he was caught during his sixth escape attempt (he finally succeeded in his eighth attempt). Since he had been on the run for more than six months, according to the Geneva Convention he was no longer considered a POW, and he was therefore tried as a partisan. The court-appointed German lawyer was more interested in obtaining information from him about the

---

[263] Glantz, *Struggle in Captivity*, pp. 220–1.   [264] Ibid., p. 223.
[265] Ibid., p. 225.   [266] Ibid., pp. 225–6.   [267] Ibid., pp. 230–1.

Jewish contacts he had in Hungary than in properly defending him. His death sentenced was later commuted to life imprisonment.[268]

The two last example seems, however, to have been the exception, rather than the rule; and one possible explanation for the mostly non-discriminatory treatment of American and British Jewish POWs in the German military courts is the transparency of their proceedings. Not only were lawyers from the Protecting Power assigned to some of these cases, but the Geneva Convention also required the Detaining Power to send all court documents to the Protecting Power, which, in turn, forwarded them to the defendants' country. This meant that any type of discrimination could have been exposed, resulting in retaliatory measures. However, had they wanted, it was still possible for the German authorities to fabricate evidence against Jewish POWs to ensure their conviction; based on the cases reviewed in this research, this was not the case.

Medical Treatment

Article 1 of the 1929 'Convention for the Amelioration of the Condition of the Wounded and Sick in Armies in the Field'—which, together with the 1929 Geneva Convention Relative to the Treatment of Prisoners of War, was ratified by Germany in 1934, when Hitler was already in power—stated that wounded and sick soldiers 'shall be treated with humanity and cared for medically, without distinction of nationality, by the belligerent in whose power they may be'.[269] Article 2 of this Convention established that international law—which later meant the 1929 Geneva POW Convention—would apply in the case of sick and wounded POWs; it added that belligerents would be free to treat them 'beyond the limits of the existing obligations'.[270] More specifically, Article 14 of the Geneva Convention dictated that each POW camp should have an infirmary, where sick POWs could be treated; the more serious cases were sent to the Lazaret, the POW camp's hospital.[271] This was therefore the framework according to which sick and wounded POWs were supposed to be treated.

Not all POWs were treated in the camp's infirmary or hospital. There were also cases where injured soldiers who were taken prisoner, or POW escapees who were injured during their escape, were brought to Wehrmacht or even SS military hospitals. In these cases, unlike the transparency that existed with trials of POWs in military courts, the treatment of Jewish POWs in such hospitals could have led

---

[268] Testimony of Tibor Weinstein, YVA O.3-2417, p. 67.
[269] Article 1 of the 1929 Geneva Convention for the Amelioration of the Condition of the Wounded and Sick in Armies in the Field, https://ihl-databases.icrc.org/ihl/INTRO/300, accessed 4 June 2022.
[270] Article 2, ibid.
[271] Article 14 of the 1929 Geneva Convention, https://ihl-databases.icrc.org/ihl/INTRO/305, accessed 4 June 2022.

to more fatal outcomes: Jewish patients could have easily been left to die on the operating table—if they reached it at all—or provided with the wrong treatment, and reported as 'died of his wounds', without anyone knowing. And although it is quite possible that such cases existed, testimonies of Jewish POWs who were treated by German doctors and survived suggest that this might not have necessarily been the case.

When Cyril Rofe was captured in 1941 and broke his arm while bailing out of his plane, he was hospitalized in a Luftwaffe hospital in Amsterdam before being sent to Stalag VIII-B in Lamsdorf. He described the treatment he received there as 'the best medical attention possible'.[272] His treatment was not affected even by the fact that he was quite vocal about his ethnicity and got into constant arguments with Nazi Party members who were hospitalized with him.[273] George Saunders, a German Jew who immigrated to Britain in 1933, had described a similar experience: Saunders fought with 10 Commando and was captured in June 1944, a day after D-Day. The Germans knew that he was Jewish but not that he was a German refugee; regardless, they did not treat him differently. Due to the parachute wings on his uniform he was hospitalized in a Luftwaffe hospital outside Paris where, according to his testimony, he was treated extremely well.[274]

During the evacuation and the forced march from Stalag 344 (Lamsdorf, previously Stalag VIII-B) at the end of the war ahead of the advancing Soviet army, Yosef Karlenboim, the Palestinian Jewish POW, suffered from a punctured appendix and was brought to a hospital in Bautzen, near Dresden. Karlenboim described how the face of the young doctor who treated him turned white when he heard that Karlenboim was in fact a Jew from Palestine; the hospital he was brought to turned out to be a Waffen SS one. When a senior doctor came to examine him, the young doctor, knowing full well that Karlenboim spoke German (which indicated that in all probability he was Jewish), translated the conversation into English in order to conceal the fact that the POW was a Jew. The treatment he received, however, was excellent.[275] In a similar case, a wounded British Jewish POW who was treated in a German hospital overheard the German doctors, who were aware of his ethnicity, discussing his case. One doctor insisted that he should be left to die; his colleague countered that he should be treated properly because 'he is a soldier [and] it is our job to treat him!'.[276]

There are also examples, however, that when it came to Jewish POWs, the Hippocratic oath did not always take precedence over the doctor's personal ideology; this might indicate that there had been cases where Jewish POW patients were not treated as they should have been and perhaps did not survive. Mosche

---

[272] Rofe, *Against the Wind*, p. 18. [273] Ibid., pp. 15–16.
[274] Oral testimony of George Saunders, https://www.iwm.org.uk/collections/item/object/80013267, recorded 11 November 1993, accessed 1 February 2018, IWM catalogue number 13358.
[275] Almogi, *With Head Held High*, pp. 178–9. [276] Rubenstein, *The Invisibly Wounded*, p. 84.

Grüner, a Palestinian Jewish POW, arrived at Stalag XVIII-A (Wolfsberg in Austria) suffering from a stomach problem, and was sent to the hospital. When the senior doctor, who was German, heard that he was Jewish, he refused to treat him and sent him back to the Stalag.[277] A few months later, in Stalag VIII-B (Lamsdorf), he had a similar experience: when he complained about a pain in his gull bladder, the senior German doctor refused to believe him and although he sent him to the regional hospital, he wrote in his file that Grüner was consistently faking his illnesses.[278] He then told Grüner that 'even 15 Jewish lawyers will not be able to release [you] from work'. Grüner was eventually diagnosed and operated on by a British surgeon and returned to the Stalag; he said that in the hospital itself there was no discrimination between Jewish and non-Jewish patients.[279]

Escapes

The risks associated with escaping from a POW camp—being shot by the guards while still in the area of the camp, or by the police, who could always claim that the POW was 'killed while trying to escape'—presumably were even higher for Jewish POWs who were caught outside the POW camps. The responsibility for capturing escapees was in the hands of the German police, which was controlled by Himmler, and in the hands of the local police forces in each of the occupied countries; in August 1943 the Wehrmacht was ordered to coordinate searches for escaping POWs with the SS, which should have increased further the risk to Jewish POWs escapees.[280] Therefore, when an escaping POW was caught and until his identity was confirmed and contact made with the POW camp from which he had escaped, his fate was in the hands of his captors who in some cases were not familiar, or did not bother with, the rules of the Geneva Convention. Anti-Semitism played a role too: in some countries the local population was not always sympathetic to Jews.

Despite these unfavourable conditions, the POW status seemed to have protected the escapees even outside the camp. In his memoirs, Rofe, who was captured in June 1943 after his second escape attempt from Stalag VIII-B's labour detachment E561 in Jaworzno, described how he was interrogated by the Kriminalpolizei chief and an SS person. He told them that he was a Jew from Palestine who volunteered to fight the Nazis (this was the identity he assumed after swapping his own with a Palestinian Jewish POW—since pilots, like officers, did not work, they had limited opportunities for escaping; some of them overcame this by exchanging identities with regular soldiers so that they could be placed in labour detachments, from where it was, in theory, easier to escape).

---

[277] Testimony of Mosche Grüner, YVA O.3 1602.   [278] Ibid.   [279] Ibid.
[280] Vourkoutiotis, *Prisoners of War and the German High Command*, pp. 104–5.

The SS man told the prison warden that he was bringing him 'another Jew'; to which the police chief responded 'no, not Jew; a POW', a distinction which was apparently understood even by those outside the camps.[281] Later, when Rofe was being transferred back to Stalag VIII-B in Lamsdorf he was stopped along the way and interrogated by a Wehrmacht officer who kept insisting that he was being deceived by a Jew and threatened to send Rofe to prison. The threats only stopped when Rofe told the German that he was protected by the Geneva Convention and threatened to report him to the ICRC.[282]

Palestinian Jewish POWs, many of them refugees from Europe, were sought after as escape partners. Their knowledge of the local language, including German, Polish, and Hungarian, and sometimes even of the local area, was considered a big advantage. Moshe Zigelbaum was asked to be an escape partner by an American pilot named Howard Long, who exchanged identities with another Palestinian Jewish POW so that he could be placed in a labour detachment.[283] Tibor Weinstein, the Hungarian-born Palestinian Jewish POW mentioned earlier who spent most of his captivity years in repeated escape attempts, explained that he did it because he realized that recaptured POW escapees were only punished with seven days in the 'bunker' and therefore decided that it was a worthwhile risk (as mentioned earlier, escape was considered a disciplinary matter for which the maximum punishment was limited to thirty days).[284] After he was caught following his fourth escape attempt, the camp's escape committee asked him to help a British colonel escape and make sure he reached Hungary safely.[285] Weinstein brought the colonel to Budapest, where they stayed with Weinstein's aunt until he managed to make contact with British Intelligence.[286]

Aharon Yerushalmi, a Palestinian Jewish POW, was captured in Greece in 1941. He escaped with two of his comrades, was caught seven months later and was accused of being a spy; he did not hide the fact that he was Jewish. Yerushalmi was placed in a civilian prison and was badly treated. However, after being interrogated by a German army NCO who reminded him that as a Jew he should be very careful in how he behaved, Yerushalmi countered that as a British solider he could not be threatened since he was under the protection of the Geneva Convention. A few days later he was transferred to a POW camp.[287]

One of Alexander Glantz's (mentioned earlier in this chapter) escapes from a labour detachment of Stalag VIII-B (probably Gleiwitz, E494) occurred in the spring of 1942. He happened to reach Prague in the days after the assassination attempt of Reinhard Heydrich, and decided to turn himself in to the local police fearing he would be caught by the Gestapo in the aftermath of the event. The

---

[281] Rofe, *Against the Wind*, p. 146.   [282] Ibid., pp. 150–3.
[283] Testimony of Moshe Zigelbaum, YVA O.3-2967.
[284] Testimony of Tibor Weinstein, YVA O.3-2417.   [285] Ibid.   [286] Ibid.
[287] Aharon Yerushalmi, *Three Who Escaped* (Tel Aviv: Ayanot, 1957), pp. 115–20.

police sent him to a Gestapo prison where he was placed with Czech civilians, suffered beatings and was made to watch some of them being executed. The Gestapo was well aware of the fact that he was Jewish but his POW status protected him: after two weeks he gained the courage to complain to one of the Gestapo officers and in the following day he was taken away by two Wehrmacht soldiers.[288] He was held in a local barracks for another week while the Germans made inquiries along his escape route to find out whether he had committed any crimes that might result him being punished; unable to find any, Glantz was then returned to Stalag VIII-B (Lamsdorf).[289]

In March 1945, Norman Rubenstein, the British Jewish POW mentioned earlier in this chapter, escaped with a few of his comrades from Stalag 344 (formerly VIII-B) in Lamsdorf while it was being evacuated. He was caught a few days later and was handed over to the SS, who recognized him as Jewish and took him and his non-Jewish comrade to the Theresienstadt concentration camp. He was mistreated throughout the journey and severely beaten when he arrived at the camp. During the first night there, Rubenstein was separated from his comrade and placed in a cell; but apparently his British uniform protected him from being another victim of the 'Kugel Erlass' and the following morning he was returned to the POW compound. Rubenstein himself attributed his release to the efforts of a young SS Private whose sister was interned in the UK at the time. After twelve days in 'hell', as he described it, and in all likelihood following clashes between the Wehrmacht and the SS unit regarding who 'owned' them, the POWs were sent to a POW camp.[290] It seems that even at such a late stage in the war, when German state institutions were crumbling, the Geneva Convention was still being adhered to in some cases: although these recaptured POWs did not have the POW camp's Total Institution walls to protect them, when the National Socialist and anti-Semitic beliefs of the SS clashed with the Wehrmacht's military discipline that demanded adherence to the rules, in this case the latter took precedence.

The treatment of Jewish POWs inside the camp, described earlier in this chapter, demonstrated the difference in attitude between camp personnel who, despite any personal opinion they might have held, in general followed military discipline, which dictated adherence to the Geneva Convention and proper treatment of POWs; and those whose behaviour and treatment of these POWs was dictated by Nazi ideology. The same conflict—between the professional duty of doctors, prison wardens, and even judges and their personal beliefs—surely existed in the interaction with Jewish POWs outside POW camps. However, the cases reviewed in this section—of American and British Jewish POWs being tried in military

---

[288] Glantz, *Struggle in Captivity*, pp. 169–73.   [289] Ibid., pp. 182–3.
[290] Rubenstein, *The Invisibly Wounded*, pp. 192–6. See also oral testimony of Leonard Camplin, https://www.iwm.org.uk/collections/item/object/80010487, recorded 12 July 1989, accessed 20 June 2018, IWM catalogue number 10710.

94　JEWISH SOLDIERS IN NAZI CAPTIVITY

courts, undergoing medical treatment in military hospitals and being handled after attempted escapes—point towards the conclusion that in general, duty took precedence and demonstrate that the Geneva Convention was in general recognized and adhered to outside the camp as well. Although it is possible that there had been cases where Jewish POWs had not been given proper medical treatment and perhaps even left to die, and where recaptured Jewish POW escapees had been mistreated and ended up in concentration camps or even shot, such cases, by their definition, could not have been verified.

Conclusion

The cases described above regarding the experience of approximately 4,700 Jewish POWs—2,500 American, 1,500 Palestinian, and 700 British—who were held in German POW camps during the Second World War were taken from the visiting reports of the Protecting Power and the ICRC, depositions given after the war to the Allies' war crimes investigators, and various memoirs and letters by POWs, both Jewish and non-Jewish. By their nature these tend to highlight the exceptions and provide less focus on the day-to-day life, which, in POW camps, consisted mainly of long periods of mundane, repeated activities. What they describe are incidents where German soldiers, mostly from SS divisions, signalled out captured Jewish soldiers and shot them; civilians who exploited the power handed to them to mistreat defenceless prisoners, and in some cases shoot them (as in Stalag VIII-B's (Lamsdorf) labour detachments E207, E561, and E562); SA personnel, clearly anti-Semitic and outside the control of the Wehrmacht and its rules, attempting to treat Jewish POWs in the same way that civilian Jews were being treated (in E207 and E578); and cases of individual guards and camp commandants acting of their own accord and treating Jewish POWs according to their anti-Semitic world views (in E456 and E593 and in Stalag Luft IV (Gross Tychow)). In the latter cases, the individuals responsible were usually dealt with by their superiors, who ensured that both the Wehrmacht's POW regulations and the Geneva Convention rules were adhered to: the commandant of Stalag VIII-B (Lamsdorf) personally intervened and relieved a guard in E456 of his duties after it was found that he mistreated Jewish POWs; and when the clearly anti-Semitic commandant of Stalag VIII-B's E593 in Schomberg murdered two escaping Jewish POWs after they were caught, an internal investigation resulted in the commandant being relieved of his role. The examples also describe the treatment of Jewish POWs who, for various reasons, were outside the POW camp; as with the cases inside the camp, their POW status protected them and although they were, in some cases, mistreated, their treatment was not worse than that of their non-Jewish comrades.

American and British Jewish POWs were held across most, if not all, the POW camps where American and British POWs were held. The number of POW camps and labour detachments where this study has found any type of mistreatment is insignificant in comparison. Although it was established that not all cases of mistreatment of American and British Jewish POWs were reported to or by the ICRC and the Protecting Power, it seems that the rate of the reported incidents was not higher than those that emerged for non-Jewish prisoners. Some indication of this can be found in an analysis of the ICRC and Protecting Power visit reports: throughout the war, out of twenty-five reports mentioning shooting or serious harassment of American and British POWs by guards and civilian employers, only one mentioned Jewish POWs.[291] Since each report combined multiple incidents from the same visit this is not necessarily an accurate analysis; however, the 4% ratio (one out of twenty-five reports), even though higher than the 1.6% ratio of American and British Jewish POWs out of the total number of American and British POW (roughly 4,700 out of approximately 300,000), still does not point to institutionalized mistreatment of the Jewish POWs. Instead, when analysing each individual example, it is evident that the vast majority of cases of mistreatment and discrimination were a result of individuals acting of their own accord. American and British Jewish POWs were indeed mistreated in some cases, but in general, and without diminishing from the severity of these cases, they were not treated any worse—or better—than their non-Jewish comrades; cases of mistreatment, as a whole, were not the result of an official policy to discriminate against and mistreat Jewish POWs.[292] In fact, the lack of such policy created confusion in the lower ranks of the POW organization and allowed individuals that were holding even minor positions of power to implement the same anti-Semitic policies that were in force outside the POW camp; these individuals were 'working towards the Führer' in anticipating his will, in the same way many organizations in the Reich were. However, these cases were rare, and the treatment of American and British Jewish POWs by German captors throughout the captivity lifecycle was mostly in line with the Geneva Convention. This conclusion has also been mentioned in other studies.[293]

---

[291] Five of the reports—none of which referenced Jewish POWs—dealt with serious violations of the Geneva Convention, including the murder of the fifty escapees from Stalag Luft III (Sagan); see Vourkoutiotis, *Prisoners of War and the German High Command*, p. 180 n. 28 and pp. 180–2. The report that mentioned harassment of Jewish POW was the March 1943 report on the incidents in E456 and E561, mentioned earlier (see Swiss embassy report on Stalag VIII-B's (Lamsdorf) labour detachments, 6 March 1943, pp. 4–5 and p. 11, TNA WO 224/27).

[292] For examples of general mistreatment of POWs see Swiss embassy report on Stalag II-B's (Hammerstein) labour detachments, 17 May 1944, NARA RG 389, box 2148, 290/34/19/3; and Anna Wickiewicz, *Captivity in British Uniform* (Opole: Centralne Muzeum Jeńców Wojennych, 2018), pp. 84–6.

[293] See, for example, MacKenzie 'The Treatment of Prisoners of War in World War II', p. 504; Overmans, 'German Treatment of Jewish Prisoners of War', ln. 1146; Foy, *For You the War Is Over*, p. 129; and Gelber, 'Palestinian POWs in German Captivity', p. 136.

The reasons for the non-existence of an official policy to treat American and British Jewish POWs differently, while at the same time outside POW camps German policies towards Jewish civilians and POWs in general went through a clear radicalization process, are discussed in Chapter 4 of this book. However, given that a specific order not to discriminate against Jewish POWs was only issued by the POW Office in December 1944, after SS General Gottlob Berger took over the POW Office, it is likely that the Wehrmacht's military discipline had resulted in, at least until then, almost full compliance in POW camps with the 1929 Geneva Convention and prevented most cases of mistreatment of Jewish POWs by lower-level personnel, such as commandants of labour detachments and guards. Berger might have issued the order in anticipation of the collapse of the German state and as a result, the collapse of the discipline within the Wehrmacht; until that stage, however, military discipline kept in check anti-Semitic policies that were in effect towards civilian Jews outside the camps, as well as any anti-Semitic beliefs which were held by some, if not all, of those serving in POW camps, from spilling over into them.

Several studies which addressed the role played by ideology in the behaviour and motivation of the Wehrmacht soldier can be used in order to understand the reasons for the attitude of POW camp staff towards American and British Jewish POWs. Shils and Janovitz analysed the Wehrmacht soldiers' motivation to continue to fight effectively almost until the very end of the war: they argued that the main factor was not ideology but the cohesion of the Primary Group—the soldier's squad—and its ability to meet the individual soldier's basic needs such as esteem, affection and adequacy; according to their study, the bond of the Primary Group only broke in the final months of the war.[294] Their study, however, was based on German soldiers who fought on the western front, where Primary Group cohesion was mostly maintained until the end of the war. Omer Bartov, who based his study mainly on the *Ostheer*, countered that the Primary Group was, for all practical purposes, destroyed during the first months of the war in the East due to the high casualty rate (even though the Wehrmacht replacement system was designed to rebuild the Primary Group by withdrawing the whole division from the front and allowing the new joiners to assimilate with the group); and therefore, the reason the German soldier continued to maintain his fighting spirit was the attachment not to a real primary group but to an abstract one, a product of 'ideological internalization' that brought together a certain category of people who shared the view that 'humanity is divided into opposing groups of "us" and "them"'.[295] Bartov argues that '[Wehrmacht] soldiers were more...likely than the civilians to belong to those categories supportive of the regime, its ideology,

---

[294] Edward A. Shils and Morris Janowitz, 'Cohesion and Disintegration in the Wehrmacht in World War II', *Public Opinion Quarterly*, 12:2 (1948), pp. 280–315, p. 281; ibid., p. 289.

[295] Ibid., pp. 287–8; Bartov, 'Soldiers, Nazis and the War in the Third Reich', pp. 49–50.

and its policies' even though 'differences of age, social background and education, political tradition and religion all played a part in each individual's actions'.²⁹⁶ Therefore, soldiers saw the Wehrmacht's mission as not only to accomplish military objectives, but also to accomplish the regime's ideological ones. This view was evident in a communication sent by a Corps chief-of-staff, who reported to his commanders that 'The attitude of the German soldier towards the Jews is by no means in question. Down to the last man, the standpoint has been taken that it is impossible to mix with this race and that it must be completely disposed of in the German living space one day'.²⁹⁷

Sönke Neitzel and Harald Welzer downplay the role of ideology in a soldier's actions: based on analysis of thousands of recorded conversations between German POWs held in the Britain and in the USA, they conclude that the military value system was the prime motivator behind his decisions; and within this system, discipline and obedience were ranked at the top.²⁹⁸ Felix Römer, who based his analysis on similar sources, reached the same conclusion and argued that ideology had played only a minor role in the actions of Wehrmacht soldiers while nationalism, militarism, and loyalty to Hitler were part of the basic beliefs of most soldiers, and were more internalized than vague, superficial ideological opinions.²⁹⁹ Alex J. Kay and David Stahel also concurred and defined the *Manneszucht* (military discipline) as 'the most important edict of German military life'.³⁰⁰

These studies, however, dealt mainly with German fighting troops, and not with those in non-fighting roles, such as commanders and guards in POW camps. Although conscription ensured that the Wehrmacht was in many aspects a mirror image of German society, the profile of the guards in POW camps was not necessarily so. The 240,000 guards, assisted by 420,000 auxiliary personnel, were responsible for guarding approximately 250 POW camps and several thousand labour detachments; and although they also included front-line soldiers who were injured in battle, the vast majority were older, infirm soldiers who were unfit for front-line duties.³⁰¹ The argument of a 'Primary Group' that held Wehrmacht

---

²⁹⁶ Ibid., p. 60.
²⁹⁷ Alex J. Kay and David Stahel, 'Crimes of the Wehrmacht: A Re-evaluation', *Journal of Perpetrator Research*, 3:1 (2020), pp. 95–127, p. 120; the Corps chief-of-staff is quoted in Jürgen Förster, 'Complicity or Entanglement? Wehrmacht, War and Holocaust', in Michael Berenbaum and Abraham Peck, eds, *The Holocaust and History* (Bloomington: Indiana University Press, 2002), p. 272.
²⁹⁸ Neitzel and Welzer, *Soldaten*, p. 238.
²⁹⁹ Römer, *Comrades, The Wehrmacht from Within*, pp. 50–3.
³⁰⁰ Kay and Stahel, 'Crimes of the Wehrmacht: a Re-evaluation', p. 100.
³⁰¹ See, for example, Rofe, *Against the Wind*, p. 175; Tom Guttridge, *Behind the Wire, Everyday Life as a POW* (Stroud: Amberley Publishing, 2017), ln. 767; testimony of Westhoff, BA-MA MSG 2/1656; Müller, *Hitler's Wehrmacht*, p. 112; Hasselbring, *American Prisoners of War in the Third Reich*, p. 133; Datner, *Crimes against POWs*, p. 9. One POW described how, while being transported, the guards were 'so old they got tired of holding their rifles' so the POWs carried the rifles for them (Deborah Moore, *GI Jews* (Cambridge, MA: The Belknap Press, 2006), p. 181); another POW described how an

soldiers together in battle, and of being motivated by ideology and 'moral outrage' against the enemy even when the original 'Primary Group' no longer existed, did not necessarily apply in the case of these older, less-motivated, less-trained soldiers.[302] Although studies of this specific group of soldiers are not available, it is possible to draw conclusions from Christopher Browning's study of Police Battalion 101's actions in Poland: the policemen, most of them reservists and older than the average front-line soldier, were of the same age group as the POW camps' guards; like them, they did not go through the indoctrination system which was put in place after Hitler came to power in 1933. Browning argued that their participation in the murder of Jews was therefore not driven by anti-Semitic ideology but was mainly a result of the frame of reference in which they were operating as part of a unit operating behind the front lines and exposed to an escalating process of brutalization. Responding to the authority of their superiors and to the need for conformity with the larger group, the majority of men declined the option not to participate in the executions.[303]

POW camp guards, who were of the same age as the members of the police battalions, were obviously operating in a completely different situational framework to that of the policemen; however, it was the type of framework that eventually dictated their behaviour. Although it can be assumed that, similar to other soldiers in the Wehrmacht, they were subjected to Nazi indoctrination throughout their service with written and spoken propaganda, by education officers and later in the war by the NSFO (*Nationalsozialistischer Führungsoffizier*—National Socialist Leadership Officers) programme—with the Wehrmacht's equivalent of the Soviet commissars—the behaviour of most of them did not reflect that.[304] POW camp guards—even the small number of younger soldiers who were assigned to guard duties after they were injured in the front—demonstrated a behaviour which was more aligned with the conclusions of Neitzel/Welzer, Römer, and Browning: their frames of reference were both the Wehrmacht, where discipline was a key value that was shared by fighting as well as non-fighting troops; and the POW camp for non-Soviet POWs, where the Geneva Convention dictated most aspects of the staff's behaviour.[305] The combined effect of discipline

older German guard brought food—which he smuggled in his coat—to a sick POW (Fox, *But You Made the Front Page!*, ln. 928).

[302] Omer Bartov, 'The Conduct of War: Soldiers and the Barbarization of Warfare', *Journal of Modern History*, 64 (1992), Supplement: Resistance against the Third Reich, pp. S32–S45, p. S40.

[303] Browning, *Ordinary Men*, p. 175.

[304] Stephen G. Fritz, '"We Are Trying...to Change the Face of the World"—Ideology and Motivation in the Wehrmacht on the Eastern Front: The View from Below', *Journal of Military History*, 60:4 (1996), pp. 683–710, p. 695. For a study of the NSFO see Robert Quinnett, *Hitler's Political Officers: The National Socialist Leadership Officers*, unpublished PhD Thesis, University of Oklahoma, 1973.

[305] Explaining the behaviour of the younger soldiers, Cyril Rofe wrote that '[since they were b]rought up on Goebbels and the Hitler Youth [their] antipathy was natural'; but that 'as long as our guards kept their opinions to themselves and behaved properly, we put up with them'. Rofe, *Against the Wind*, pp. 175–6.

and respect for authority resulted in conformity to the larger group: in the case of the police battalions, this conformity led to their participation in the murder of Jewish civilians; in the case of POW camp personnel, the conformity meant that cases of mistreatment of American and British Jewish POWs—in fact, of most non-Soviet POWs—were not common, regardless of how anti-Semitic a guard might have been. The fact that a guard who disobeyed orders by mistreating POWs might be punished and even sent to the Eastern Front must have also contributed to his motivation to follow the rules. There were of course exceptions: some commandants and guards did indeed let their anti-Semitic ideology dictate their behaviour towards POWs, and some guards disobeyed orders by trading items from Red Cross parcels with POWs. However, even though the latter was also against the rules, the fact that it benefited both parties—in comparison to mistreatment that could have been reported—probably made it a more acceptable activity despite the risk.

A few additional observations can be made based on the findings of this chapter. The first one (which was mentioned briefly in the Introduction to this book) relates to POW camp visits by the Protecting Power and the ICRC. Since these organizations only visited the camps every three months (and in the case of labour detachments, even less frequently), the timing of the visit was of great significance. As was shown, incidents, even serious ones, that had occurred prior to the visit but had already been resolved, were usually not mentioned in reports. The delegates may have decided that since they had already been resolved, mentioning them might trigger unnecessary reaction or even reprisal by the POWs' home country; alternatively, they might not have been made aware of these incidents in the first place. Incidents which were not included in the reports often came to light only in POWs' memoirs and in investigations of war crimes conducted after the war; it is highly probable, therefore, that many incidents in other camps or labour detachments went unreported.

The second observation relates to the way that Jewish POWs reacted to cases of discrimination and mistreatment. The Palestinian Jews, interned in groups and with Jewish MOCs representing them, did not let such cases go unanswered and, despite the imbalance of power, used any means possible—including complaints and in some cases strikes—to make a stand against their German captors. This, along with the occasional intervention of the ICRC and the Protecting Power, was probably the reason for the decline from 1943 onwards in the number of complaints by Palestinian Jewish POWs related to their treatment. The American and British Jewish POWs, on the other hand, sometimes encountering anti-Semitism from within their own ranks, had to rely on the support of their non-Jewish comrades—who in some cases stood by them and caused the Germans to back down. Racial ideology had its limits too: camp authorities, for their part, did not hesitate to cooperate with Jewish POWs' leaders when they found it to be to their benefit, as demonstrated in Karlenboim's involvement in the incidents in E479 and E593.

The third observation relates to interaction with people outside the camp. As described above, a Second World War German POW camp or labour detachment did not necessarily follow the definition of a Total Institution as an entity which is mostly detached and secluded from its environment. However, while Goffman's definition might be relevant to the main POW camp, the Stalag, it did not necessarily apply to the labour detachments that usually surrounded it: the boundaries of the POW camp entity, which included the labour detachments under its control, were not fixed and were not hermetically closed. In addition to the cases where Jewish POWs found themselves outside the camp as a result of judicial proceedings, hospital treatment, or escape, there were cases where incarcerated Jewish POWs visited nearby villages and towns on a regular basis to shop or for medical treatment; and, of course, while working in mines, factories, and farms, they had daily interaction with civilians as well as representatives of organizations such as the SA. There were cases where the POWs struck deals with civilians and even SA members outside the camp; clearly, in such cases pragmatism took precedence over racial ideologies. Given the relatively small number of testimonies and reports that mention incidents related to these interactions, it seems that despite the POWs being Jewish, they were treated in most cases in a correct manner. In view of the above, Goffman's definition of the POW camp as a 'Total Institution' should perhaps be re-visited in order to reflect the reality of the POW camp as an entity with flexible, sometimes porous boundaries.

The fourth and final observation relates to the role played by the POW camp in protecting American and British Jewish POWs. The ongoing radicalization throughout the war in Germany's POW policies in the West—as reflected, for example, in the Kommando Befehl and the Kugel Erlass—and in parallel, the radicalization in its anti-Semitic policies, with millions of civilian Jews being worked to death and murdered, did not cross the boundaries of the POW camps and labour detachments where American and British Jewish POWs—in fact, where non-Soviet Jewish POWs in general—were interned. Although there were cases where individual commandants, guards, and civilians attempted to treat Jewish POWs in the same way that civilian Jews were treated, these were the exceptions, rather than the rule; and overall, the 1929 Geneva Convention and the concern of potential reprisals against German POWs took precedence over the anti-Semitic policies that were being implemented outside the camps. Inside the camp, the racial beliefs and National Socialist indoctrination of the individual commandants and guards were, with few exceptions, either not strong enough to compel them to act according to these beliefs, or were not strong enough to make them break military discipline and act against strict Wehrmacht orders relating to compliance with the Geneva Convention.[306]

---

[306] The protection provided by the POW camp is evident also from cases of POWs who refused to be released from captivity, knowing what their fate would be once their POW status would be removed, as happened to Yugoslavian Jewish officers released from Oflag VI-C (Osnabrück-Eversheide) (see Asaria-Helfgot, *We Are Witnesses*, p. 63, and Pilloud to WJC, 3 November 1954,

The brutalization process which the Wehrmacht had undergone during the Polish campaign meant that when it invaded the Soviet Union in 1941 it was ready to fight a war of extermination, and was equipped with a set of orders that were not aligned with traditional army discipline and values. As Omer Bartov explained, 'the Wehrmacht's legal system adapted itself to the so-called Nazi *Weltanschauung* [worldview], with all its social Darwinist, nihilist, anti-Bolshevik and racist attributes'.[307] This worldview was evident in the way the Wehrmacht treated Soviet POWs; however, despite the radicalization of Germany's POW policies in the West and the harsher treatment meted on captured commando soldiers, air crews, and escapees from western armies, this worldview did not manifest itself when it came to American and British Jewish POWs—for them, the Nazi *Weltanschauung* stopped at the gates of the Stalag. The 'dehumanized image of the enemy', which Germany applied to Soviet Jewish POWs and civilian Jews and which excluded them from the 'norms of behaviour and morals of human society', was not applied to American and British Jewish POWs; in fact, during the Second World War, it was not applied to non-Soviet Jewish POWs in general.[308]

USHMM RG-68.045M Acc. 2004.507, reel 54, document 416); testimony of Vladimir Mautner, YVA O.3-6645, p. 16; and Rofe, *Against the Wind*, p. 188. Yugoslavian Jewish POWs were kept continuously informed about the fate of their families by neighbours and other family members who sent them letters, telling them about orders to deport Jews from certain cities or regarding the death of family members in work camps. Some of the letters warned the POWs not to make any effort to return home because of the fate that awaited them (see Asaria-Helfgot, *We Are Witnesses*, pp. 43 and 61). Hundreds of Polish Jewish POWs who were released in 1942 were murdered while they were being marched back (see testimony of Menachem Rozentzweig, YVA O.3-12,021, pp. 13-15).

[307] Bartov, *Hitler's Army*, p. 70.
[308] Bartov, 'The Conduct of War', p. S41; Overmans, 'Die Kriegsgefangenenpolitik des Deutschen Reichs 1939 bis 1945', p. 870.

2
Being a Jewish Soldier in Nazi Captivity

Introduction

'A moral crisis for a nineteen-year-old[;] do I remain mute, or do I say, take me?' this was the dilemma facing Sonny Fox, a young American Jewish POW, when the Germans ordered the segregation of Jewish POWs in Stalag IX-B in Bad Orb in January 1945 (he eventually decided not to identify himself as Jewish).[1] Roger Berg, a French Jewish POW who faced the same dilemma, explained his decision not to reveal his Jewish identity in that he 'was not a Jewish prisoner, but a French non-commissioned officer [prisoner]. Nothing more. Nothing less' (Berg's Jewish identity was eventually exposed and he was segregated in the '*Judenbaracken*' inside Stalag XVIII-C (in Markt Pongau in Austria)).[2] The decision both Fox and Berg, as well as many other Jewish POWs, had to make forced them to consider, under immense pressure and in trying circumstances, questions that prior to that moment were almost philosophical in nature.

The previous chapter dealt with the day-to-day interaction between the American and British Jewish POWs and their immediate captors, and with the reasons for the way they were treated. This chapter will address the question of how individual American and British Jewish POWs in German captivity dealt with their Jewish identity and with their situation as Jewish soldiers incarcerated in Nazi POW camps.

Throughout history the Jewish identity had always been only one among many identities by which Jewish people defined themselves. As part of their study of Jewish life in suburban America, Sklare and Greenblum defined this identity along three sometimes overlapping models: religious, nationalistic (or ethnic), and cultural.[3] The religious element relates mainly to faith and ritual observance, two components that were not necessarily linked; the latter had to do more with tradition than with faith, and was practiced with different levels of adherence by different Jewish communities during different periods in history. The national

---

[1] Cohen, *Soldiers and Slaves*, ln. 1424. In the years following the war, Irwin 'Sonny' Fox became a famous television host and broadcaster in the US.
[2] *Le Combattant Volontaire Juif 1939–1945*, p. 59.
[3] Marshall Sklare and Joseph Greenblum, *Jewish Identity on the Suburban Frontier* (Chicago: University of Chicago Press, 1979), pp. 323–7.

element—or ethnic, which is more appropriate to the era before the creation of the state of Israel—is the transnational identity and the sense of kinship to the Jewish people as a whole; and the cultural element consists of components with custom, historical, intellectual, linguistic, and other cultural characteristics.[4]

The Jewish identity was however only one component in the identity of American and British Jewish soldiers; and its relative importance among the multiple components that made up an individual's identity was not constant and changed over time. Jewish soldiers in general did not necessarily consider their Jewish identity to be the main characteristic by which they defined themselves; since most Second World War soldiers—volunteers as well as conscripted—joined the army in order to defend, fight and sometimes die for their country, they tended in most cases to view their nationality—or their profession as soldiers—as their primary identity, above their Jewish one, which was more transnational in nature.[5] As Norman Rubenstein, a British Jewish soldier, described it: 'When I signed up... it was more out of a desire to defend the British way of life than my hatred for... the anti-Semitic Nazis'.[6]

In the First World War the primacy of national identity and mass conscription meant that Jewish soldiers found themselves fighting on opposite sides as part of several armies, including the British, Russian, German, Austro-Hungarian, and French ones. However, although in most cases the national identity of Jewish soldiers, even first- or second-generation immigrants, was that of their adoptive country, there were still a few exceptions in the Second World War: Jewish refugees who had recently arrived from continental Europe and joined the American and British armies did not necessarily identify themselves yet as American or British nationals; Martin Goldenberg, a Jewish refugee from Austria who immigrated to Britain explained that even after he had joined the British army he still identified himself as an 'Austrian Jew with no religion'.[7]

Another exception were the Palestinian Jewish soldiers—Jewish residents of Palestine, which was under British rule since the end of the First World War, who

---

[4] Arnold Dashefsky, 'Being Jewish: An Approach to Conceptualization and Operationalization', in Isidore D. Passow and Samuel T. Lachs, eds, *Gratz College Anniversary Volume, 1895–1970* (Philadelphia, PA: Gratz College 1971), pp. 35–46, p. 38. Milton Steinberg discusses these three components (he uses the term 'peoplehood' instead of 'ethnic') in more detail in *a Partisan Guide to the Jewish Problem* (Indianapolis and New York: Charter Books, 1963), pp. 145–53. Benedict Anderson argued that the national element is, in fact, a cultural artefact of a particular kind; and therefore the nation is nothing but 'an imagined political community' (see Benedict Anderson, *Imagined Communities* (London and New York: Verso, 2016), pp. 4 and 6).

[5] Research suggests that only 5% of American soldiers fought in the Second World War for ideological reasons (see Moore, *GI Jews*, p. 26). Armies of empires which consisted of several nations tended to build the soldier's identity and motivation around the empire's dynasty or religion (see Alfred Rieber, 'Nationalizing Imperial Armies: A Comparative and Transnational Study of Three Empires', in Stefan Berger and Alexei Miller, eds, *Nationalising Empires* (New York and Budapest: CEU Press, 2005), pp. 593–628, p. 627).

[6] Rubenstein, *The Invisibly Wounded*, p. 15.

[7] Kern, *Jewish refugees from Germany and Austria in the British Army, 1939–45*, p. 214.

volunteered for the British Army. Most of them did not join the British army out of loyalty to the British crown, and although some joined out of economic necessity, others—especially Jewish refugees from Europe—saw it as a way to both fight the Nazis and to protect the Jewish population in Palestine. Some of the volunteers were also members of Jewish underground movements that fought the British in Palestine with the aim of establishing an independent Jewish state there.[8] Despite the fact that such a state did not exist at the time, the ethnic and national identities of these soldiers, and especially of those who served together in the same units, had merged in this case into one.

For Jewish soldiers in general, religion was usually a private matter; it was carved on the soldier's identification discs along with his name and serial number, so that the appropriate burial services could be given in case of death. Soldiers also took part from time to time in religious ceremonies organized by the army chaplains—Rabbis, in the case of Jews. However, Jewish communities in the USA and Britain had gone through a process of secularization between the wars, and as a result the majority of the Jewish soldiers—and POWs—in the American and British armies in the Second World War were either secular or not deeply religious; being Jewish for them was more a matter of the ethnicity and culture they were born into, rather than a matter of religion.[9] Jewish soldiers might have celebrated Jewish Holy days and special events by going to the synagogue or having a family meal where some of the Jewish prayers were said; but in most cases this had more to do with a tradition to commemorate events in the history of the Jewish people, rather than a demonstration of a belief in God and in the Old Testament. Armies in general do not differentiate their soldiers based on religion: in order to build cohesive, functioning units, all differences must be eliminated. As William Shapiro, an American Jewish medic with the 28th Division, had put it: 'I wasn't a Jew when I went to war; I was an American soldier.'[10]

---

[8] Yoav Gelber, *The History of Volunteering*, vol. 1 (Jerusalem: Yad Ben Tzvi, 1979), p. 192; ibid., pp. 214–15. Some of them also joined out of economic necessity.

[9] Research conducted in the 1930s in New York City found that more than 70% of Jewish youth (aged 16–24) did not visit a synagogue in the year before the study took place; and more than 90% did not visit one in the week prior to it (see Nettie McGill, 'Some Characteristics of Jewish Youth in New York City', *Jewish Social Service Quarterly*, 14 (1937), pp. 251–72, p. 253). A 1910 study found that more that 75% of New York's Jewish children did not receive any Jewish education (see Jonathan Sarna, *American Judaism* (New Haven, CT and London: Yale University Press, 2019), p. 175). Additional references to the decline in the religiousness of Jews in American can also be found in ibid., pp. 161–4 and pp. 224–5; and in Jeffrey Gurock, 'Twentieth-Century American Orthodoxy's Era of Non-Observance, 1900–1960', *Torah U-Madda Journal*, 9 (2000), pp. 87–107, pp. 87–91. A similar decline in Jewish religious observance occurred during the same period in Britain—see Elaine Smith, 'Class, Ethnicity and Politics in the Jewish East End, 1918–1939', *Jewish Historical Studies*, 32 (1990-2), pp. 355–69, p. 357; and Vivian Lipman, *Social History of the Jews in England, 1850–1950* (London: Watts & Co, 1954), pp. 182–3. The Union of Orthodox Hebrew Congregations in the UK estimated in the Second World War that the total number of ultra-orthodox Jews who would join the army would be no more than fifty per year (see Orthodox Jewish militiamen, undated memo, LMA ACC/3121/E/003/065).

[10] Cohen, *Soldiers and Slaves*, ln. 366.

Maintaining their identities in captivity gave all POWs not only a sense of belonging to a bigger group, a feeling that contributed to their morale during their time in captivity, but also played a role in the power struggle with their captors. Any act that displayed even one element of this identity, such as a celebration of national, ethnic, or religious event, or conducting a funeral where symbols of the POW's religious and national identities could be displayed, helped the POW feel that despite the existing circumstances he was still able to maintain—and even boast in—his identity. The German attitude towards Jews forced Jewish soldiers to reconsider the way that they thought about their own identity: as Jewish POWs, their ethnicity, and to the non-secular ones, their religion, now had the same importance as their nationality; whether they managed to hide these components or not, this chapter will show that it became an important part of their identity as POWs in German captivity.

Several aspects of the Jewish identity are reviewed in this chapter: the Jewish POW's ethnicity, which manifested itself when the POW was faced with the dilemma of whether to expose himself as a Jew when captured, or later, when the issue of segregation of Jewish POWs in the POW camps was raised; his religion and culture, when it came to commemorating Jewish Holy days and with regards to funerals of Jewish POWs who died in captivity; and for the Palestinian Jewish POWs, their nationality—which had been defined for them by the Germans, who treated them as a separate people within the British Empire. The chapter also looks at the transnational nature of the Jewish identity, which manifested itself when Jewish POWs encountered Jewish victims of the Final Solution.

This chapter argues that the hardships of captivity, together with what they knew about the treatment of civilian Jews by the Germans, strengthened the spirit and resolve of American and British Jewish POWs—even those who concealed their Jewish identity—during their time in captivity; for most of them, Jewish identity no longer manifested itself only through the letters which were carved on their identification discs.

Capture

> I had gone to [synagogue] occasionally for a wedding, bar mitzvah or funeral[;] I'm not a religious person but I was brought up as a Jew, so there's an H on the dog tags. The purpose is so they can give the proper burial....I thought, if I leave it on and fall into the hands of the Gestapo, I'm not a POW, I'm a KIA Killed In Action.[11] But if I rip

---

[11] Even though there were no known cases of American or British Jewish soldiers being murdered by the Gestapo during interrogations, Loevsky's concern was understandable. It is also important to note that since these testimonies were given after the war, when the extent of the Final Solution and

them off and throw them away, I'm not a POW, I'm a spy. Without dog tags you risk being killed as a spy. So, I left them on.[12]

This is how Second Lieutenant Louis Loevsky, an American Jewish B-24 navigator with the 466th Bomb Group who was shot down over Berlin in March 1944, described the dilemma that many Jewish soldiers had when the realization of becoming a POW of the Germans had dawned on them—should they keep their identification discs or throw them away? Should they expose themselves to their captors as Jews? This dilemma became even more pressing as the war progressed and reports about the extent of the murder of Jews by the Germans became more frequent. Julius Karp, an American Jewish Flight engineer who flew with the 2nd Bomb Group and was shot down in August 1944, addressed this issue much earlier: Karp 'heard rumours that the Germans were killing Jews' so he 'smashed the H with pliers before [going] overseas'; when asked for his religion after he was captured, he told his interrogator that he was Protestant.[13]

Upon joining the army, American and British soldiers were required to state their religion, which was then imprinted, along with other information such as name and serial number, on their identification discs. Marking a soldier's religion was not considered a controversial issue, merely a way to ensure that the appropriate services, such as reading last rites and funerals, were given in case of death. However, for British Jews, this changed a few months before the war in the West broke out: aware of the way that Germany was treating its Jewish citizens, British Jewish soldiers began considering the option of registering under a different religion when enlisting.[14] Reports in the Jewish press in Britain about the issue of listing a soldier's religion on his identification disc appeared as early as November 1939; in January 1940 it was reported that Jews were hiding their religion when enlisting, 'fearing mistreatment if captured'.[15] The issue was even raised in the British Parliament in November 1939 by John Morris, a Member of Parliament, who asked the Ministry of War's Financial Secretary Victor Warrender whether religion could be omitted from the identification discs. Warrender responded that the issue had been considered and that a decision was made not to change the existing practice.[16]

---

the roles played by the Gestapo and the SS became evident, the POWs might have added arguments that perhaps were not part of their original experience—a process known as 'interpolated learning' (see Winter and Sivan, *War and Remembrance in the Twentieth Century*, ln. 374).

[12] Testimony of Louis Loevsky, the American Air Museum in Britain, http://www.americanairmuseum.com/person/150458, accessed 20 March 2018.

[13] The Julius Karp Story, unpublished memoir, https://stalagluft4.org/pdf/JuliusKarp.pdf, accessed 1 August 2022.

[14] See Jews serving in H.M. Forces, unsigned memo, 27 July 1940, LMA C3121/015/003/014.

[15] JTA, 12 November 1939, https://www.jta.org/archive, accessed 8 May 2019; and the JC, 17 November 1939, p. 8, https://www.thejc.com/archive, accessed 16 June 2019; JTA, 3 January 1940, https://www.jta.org/archive, accessed 8 May 2019.

[16] Morris to Warrender, 23 November 1939, https://hansard.parliament.uk/Commons/, accessed 17 June 2019.

Jewish leaders, for their part, who were in all likelihood also worried that under-counting the actual number of Jewish soldiers who served in the British army would stoke anti-Semitism, appealed against the actions of some of the enlisted Jewish soldiers and declared that 'We cannot...believe[,] and this opinion is shared by military circles[,] that the powerful military tradition of Germany will make them disregard the respect due [to] His Majesty's uniform irrespective of the race or creed of the person by who it is worn'.[17] A Jewish chaplain went as far as arguing, in December 1939, that British Jews should not fear enlistment as Jews since Hitler's concern for reprisals, which explained the restraint he had shown by not bombing civilian towns, would also apply in the case of Jewish POWs.[18]

These statements were rebuked on the other side of the Atlantic; an article that appeared in the American-Jewish press argued that given the recent atrocities against Jewish POWs in Poland, it would be naïve to expect the Nazis to maintain the soldier's tradition of Old Germany, and therefore religion should be removed from the soldier's identification disc in order to protect him.[19] When America entered the war two years later, American Jewish soldiers encountered the same issue, and some chose to omit their religion from their identification discs, although doing so did not mean that they renounced their identity: coming from different backgrounds, Jewish identity united secular and religious Jews in the army 'across denomination, class and ideology'.[20] German and Austrian Jewish refugees who joined the American and British armies preferred in most cases, rather than to enlist as non-Jews, to change their names in order not to be charged with treason if they became POWs; this also helped them to better integrate with their non-Jewish comrades.[21] Others, on the other hand, decided to keep their names as the one remaining part of their identity that the Nazis could not take; they saw it as an act of defiance and a way to commemorate their families, some of whom had been left behind in German-controlled areas.[22]

The decision to hide one's Jewish ethnicity or change a name when enlisting might not have been a simple one for the individual soldier, but at that early stage its consequences were negligible. For those who decided to register their real

---

[17] See Jews in the B.E.F., undated memo regarding a Reuters article from 28 December 1939 mentioning the number of Jewish soldiers in France, LMA ACC/3121/E/03/065/2; correspondence between Robert Cohen (the president of United Synagogue) and Reuters, 9, 12, and 17 January 1940; and correspondence between Robert Cohen and G. W. Lambert of the War Office, 27 and 29 January 1940, LMA ACC/3121/E/03/065/3. For the declaration of the Jewish leaders see JC, 22 December 1939, p. 20, https://www.thejc.com/archive, accessed 16 June 2019.

[18] JC, 29 December 1939, p. 9, https://www.thejc.com/archive, accessed 1 May 2020. The Chaplain was, of course, proven wrong in the following year.

[19] Aufbau, 12 January 1940, p. 3, https://archive.org/details/aufbau, accessed 30 June 2019.

[20] New York Times, 22 June 1994, p. A20, https://timesmachine.nytimes.com/timesmachine/1994/06/22/470333.html?pageNumber=20, accessed 21 August 2020; Moore, GI Jews, pp. 73–4.

[21] Anne Schenderlein, Germany on Their Mind (New York: Berghahn, 2020), p. 88; Kern, Jewish Refugees from Germany and Austria in the British Army, 1939–45, p. 192.

[22] Ibid., p. 190.

ethnicity, the realization that the marking on their identification discs might mean more than just a way to receive the appropriate burial dawned together with the realization that they were about to be taken prisoners by an enemy which viewed them as a race of '*Untermenschen*'. At that stage they were forced to make a quick decision: whether to discard their identification discs and army paybook (which also confirmed their rank), or keep them. An issue which most Jewish soldiers had only previously considered as a theoretical risk now had to be decided in a very short timeframe and amid conditions of extreme confusion and uncertainty. Discarding identification discs not only delayed a soldier's family from receiving information regarding his destiny and allowed the enemy to treat him as a spy; given the importance that the soon-to-be POWs perceived their captors to assign to it, their ethnicity and religion suddenly became the most important part of their identity. Therefore, discarding identification discs meant also discarding parts of the soldier's heritage—his culture, his religion (if he defined himself as religious), and his family's and people's history, to name a few of the issues this moment raised. On top of this there was also the fear of what his comrades, Jewish soldiers who did not hide their ethnicity, would think of him; and what his non-Jewish comrades would think or even do: was it possible that one of them would reveal his true identity to the German captors?

Those who chose when enlisting to record their religion as non-Jewish had already been through this thought process and must have felt vindicated when captured; others made a quick decision and decided to keep their discs and face the consequences—as Lieutenant Bernie Levine, a bombardier with the 100th Bomb Group he was shot down on 4 February 1944, had put it: 'There were a lot of fellows who took the H off, but I figured hell, as long as I'm gonna [sic] be a martyr, I'll be a martyr all the way.'[23] However, there were also American and British Jewish soldiers who decided to discard their identification discs when captured. Some of them said afterwards that the decision to do so and to hide their identity made them feel guilty; others just mentioned it in their memoirs without delving into the dilemma that must have accompanied it: Bernard Sakol, a driver with the British 51st Highland Division, threw away his tags when he was taken prisoner in France in 1940 and spent the rest of the war in a POW camp as a 'devout member of the Church of Scotland'.[24] Captain Julius Green, a Jewish officer who served as a dentist with the same Division, did the same when captured and 'underwent probably the most rapid conversion on record' by declaring himself a member of the Presbyterian Church.[25] His true religion was almost exposed a few years later when one of his relatives mentioned in a letter which was read by the German censor that she had visited a synagogue and was going away for Passover. A German doctor was called to check whether Green was

---

[23] Aaron Elson, *Prisoners of War: An Oral History* (New Britain, CT: Chi Chi Press, 2023), p. 155.
[24] Green, *From Colditz in Code*, pp. 47–8.   [25] Ibid., p. 127.

circumcised, but a British medical officer intervened and convinced his German counterpart to close the issue.[26]

The Palestinian Jewish soldiers who were captured in April 1941 in Greece did not face the same dilemma the American and British Jewish soldiers were facing of whether to hide their Jewish identity or not simply because they did not have that choice. As mentioned, the approximately 1,500 soldiers, part of the British Pioneer Corps, were among the 10,000 British soldiers who waited to be evacuated in the Greek port of Kalamata, only to eventually surrender on 29 April 1941 to the advancing German army.[27] Although the mass murder phase of the Holocaust had not yet begun, the soon-to-become POWs were deeply concerned regarding their fate in the hands of the Germans to the extent that some of them committed suicide.[28] Their officers, however, made efforts to ensure that the loss of liberty would not be accompanied by the loss of Jewish and soldierly dignity. They ordered the soldiers to fix their appearance and marched into captivity singing 'Hatikvah' (Hebrew for 'The Hope', which after Israel had gained its independence became the state's national anthem).[29] As shall be seen, this attitude of defiance characterized the behaviour of the Palestinian Jewish POWs throughout their captivity; nevertheless, the first days of captivity, already fraught with confusion and despair, became even more tense for them. Eventually, the POWs' leaders decided on a few principles that would guide the Palestinian Jewish POWs throughout their captivity period; first among them was to stick to their identity as Palestinian and Jewish—their national and ethnic identity—and not to hide it.[30]

There are more testimonies of American Jewish soldiers discarding their identification discs when captured or hiding their Jewish identity than there are British ones, probably because the former were taken prisoner during the later stages of the war and therefore were more exposed to reports regarding the fate of their Jewish civilian brethren. Gerald Daub, an American Jewish soldier with the 100th Infantry Division, hid his identification discs in his boots when he was captured in France in January 1945. He then decided against taking the risk of spending his captivity period as a Jew and told his interrogator that he was a member of the Lutheran Church. 'I didn't feel too good about denying the fact that I was Jewish, but there was just this compelling feeling of wanting to survive', he said later.[31] Harold Radish, who fought with the 90th Infantry Division, also disposed of his identification discs when he was captured with his unit; in solidarity, many of his comrades threw away theirs as well.[32] When technical Sergeant Aben

---

[26] Ibid.   [27] Sela, *Shackles of Captivity*, pp. 52-3.
[28] Glantz, *Struggle in Captivity*, p. 46.   [29] Almogi, *With Head Held High*, p. 32.
[30] Sela, *Shackles of Captivity*, p. 57.
[31] Donaldson, *Men of Honor*, p. 82; and Gerald Daub, oral history, recorded 6 July 2000, archive of the Museum of Jewish Heritage, New York.
[32] Moore, *GI Jews*, p. 181.

Caplan, who was captured in January 1945, was about to hide his Jewish identity by throwing away his Jewish prayer book, he recalled how he 'just recently called upon God for the saving of [his] life', and decided that 'come what may that prayer book would stay'.[33] On the other hand, David Schenk, an American Jewish POW, encountered such a dilemma only later, when he was already in a POW camp. Schenk kept his identification discs throughout his captivity and his captors never bothered checking them, but when he was asked one day by a German officer in Stalag XII-A (Limburg an der Lahn) whether he was Jewish, he said that he was Catholic. As a combat soldier, his 'cowardly reply', as he described it, and his fear of exposing his Jewish identity to the officer bothered him afterwards; he later borrowed a Jewish prayer book and, standing among and protected by his POW comrades, began a routine of saying a daily prayer, which restored his confidence as an American soldier and a Jew.[34]

Leonard Winograd (who was mentioned earlier in this book) does not seem to have had that dilemma. The American Jewish navigator with the 376th Bomb Group who was captured in the winter of 1945 when his plane was shot down over Bosnia (after the war he became a Rabbi in McKeesport, Pennsylvania) was asked by his interrogators for his religion; he answered 'Jewish' and remembered that 'all mouths were wide open'.[35] His German captors then insisted on taking his clothes away to be dried, and fed him soup which he described as 'the best I ever ate in my life'.[36] Second Lieutenant Aaron Kuptsow, a Jewish radar navigator with the 398th Bomb Group, had a different experience: he was forced to bail out after his plane was shot down in November 1944. The first thing he did after he landed was to throw away his identification tags.[37] Unfortunately, the German farmer in whose farm he landed found the tags, and since Kuptsow was the only one of the crew without them he was singled out and punched in the face by the farmer. However, when he was later interrogated in the Dulag in Oberusel, the Luftwaffe's main interrogation centre near Frankfurt, his religion was never mentioned.[38]

Jewish soldiers reacted differently to the realization that their Jewish identity might mean, at the very least, being treated differently as POWs than their non-Jewish comrades. One letter on these discs forced some of them to re-evaluate, under extreme conditions, questions such as their primary identity, the consequences of hiding their Jewish one, and in general, the meaning of this identity to them. Different soldiers dealt with these questions in different ways: some planned ahead and either did not register themselves as Jews when enlisting or

---

[33] Memoirs of Aben Caplan, http://memory.loc.gov/diglib/vhp/story/loc.natlib.afc2001001.05190/, accessed 21 August 2020.
[34] Moore, *GI Jews*, p. 184.
[35] The American Ex-Prisoners of War Organization, http://www.axpow.org/roster.html#, accessed 22 March 2018; Winograd, 'Double Jeopardy', p. 6.
[36] Ibid.
[37] Aaron Kuptsow, http://www.merkki.com/kuptsowaaron.htm#ak, accessed 1 August 2022.
[38] Ibid. For additional capture testimonies see Donaldson, *Men of Honor*, pp. 103–4 and 136.

changed their names to hide any links they might have had with their former home country; others, faced with the dilemma at the time of capture, threw away or hid their identification discs and paybook; and yet there were still those who decided to stick to their Jewish identity regardless of the consequences. However, when reviewing the act of hiding a soldier's Jewish identity, whether when he enlisted in the army or when it became clear to him that he was about to become a POW, the external circumstances should be taken into account: even before the scale of the Holocaust was known, given the way Jewish civilians throughout Europe were being treated by the Germans and what was known about the treatment of Polish Jewish POWs, these soldiers made what they considered to be a logical decision by removing one uncertainty from the long list of uncertainties that awaited them if they became POWs of the Germans. Hiding a soldier's Jewish identity meant hiding the external expressions of this identity; and even though, in general, Jewish soldiers did not feel comfortable doing that, this did not mean that they ceased to be Jewish. Yet, there were also those who decided to stick to their Jewish identity and for them a feeling of uncertainty and fear, no doubt, accompanied them throughout their time in captivity. However, since eventually the Wehrmacht did not discriminate, in general, against American and British Jewish POWs, most of them must have felt vindicated once they realized that their decision generally did not have any severe consequences.

Palestinian Jewish Identity in German POW Camps

For the approximately 1,500 Palestinian Jewish POWs mentioned above the question of identity requires a separate mention as it was more complex than the one faced by American and British Jewish POWs. Even though they volunteered for the British army, they did not consider their nationality to be British; rather, Jewish nationalism was 'the very essence of their creed'.[39] When they became captives they could not—would not—hide their identity as Jews; nevertheless, the Palestinian POWs were far from being a homogeneous group. Many of them were new immigrants that came—some of them illegally—from a large number of countries, including Germany, Austria, Hungary, Poland, and even Yemen, and most of them did not have any relatives in Palestine.[40]

In addition, the POWs were also divided according to their reason for joining the British army: about 15% of the POWs, most of them part of the Jewish

---

[39] As described by Leonard Montefiore (president of the Anglo-Jewish Association), who visited Palestinian Jewish units in 1944 (see welfare visit to the Mediterranean, 8 June 1944, LMA ACC/3121/E/002/021).

[40] Sela, *Shackles of Captivity*, p. 58; test in German captivity, July 1945, p. 41, IDF 182/1867/1998; Simon to Majerozik, 16 April 1943, CZA S-25\4720. The letter stated that only 400 (out of 1,500–1,600) Palestinian Jewish POWs had relatives in Palestine.

establishment in Palestine, volunteered for the British army for ideological reasons, viewing Germany as theirs as well as Britain's enemy, despite the fact that before the war some of them had participated in the struggle for independence from Britain.[41] Members of this group, also known as '*Sochnutnicks*', a reference to their links to the Jewish Agency, '*Sochnut*' in Hebrew, had a strong nationalistic, Zionist identity; most of them were either born in Palestine or immigrated there when they were still young and their main, sometimes only language, was Hebrew.[42] The second group, which formed the majority of the Palestinian POWs, was that of the new immigrants: many of them originally from Europe, they joined the army for a combination of ideological—to fight the Germans—and financial reasons: arriving in Palestine with very little knowledge of Hebrew and encountering difficulties in finding a job, they were not always fond of the establishment which the '*Sochnutnicks*' represented.[43] The third group, about 15–20% in total, included Palestinian Jews who had joined the British army solely for financial reasons: the economy in Palestine at the time was not doing well and the British army was to them simply a place that provided job security.[44]

As a result, at the start of their captivity period there was no mutual identity that all of the Palestinian Jewish POWs could gather around; most of them were not religious and the differences between these groups in terms of countries of origin, language, and the reason for joining the British Army in the first place led to multiple clashes, sometimes even involving violence.[45] Unlike their American and British comrades, the Palestinian Jewish POWs did not have a military tradition to fall back on nor a flag to gather around; they only served together for less than a year and since their officers were held captive separately, the NCOs and the soldiers had to establish their own rules by themselves.[46] The resulting clashes occurred in most cases when members of the first group, the '*Sochnutnicks*', who viewed the Palestinian POWs as 'ambassadors' for the Jewish people as a whole, became concerned about maintaining the cohesion and reputation of the group and attempted to reign in cases of asocial behaviour on the part of the third group. The '*Sochnutnicks*' insisted on maintaining the highest standards of cleanliness and order in the labour detachments they were assigned to and were not afraid to enter into arguments with the German authorities and to file complaints with the ICRC or Protecting Power when they felt they were being mistreated or discriminated against.

---

[41] Test in German captivity, July 1945, p. 69, IDF 182/1867/1998.
[42] Rofe, *Against the Wind*, p. 95.
[43] Test in German captivity, July 1945, p. 71, IDF 182/1867/1998.
[44] Almogi, *With Head Held High*, p. 36.
[45] Test in German captivity, July 1945, p. 72, IDF 182/1867/1998.
[46] A manual titled 'What to Expect in German Captivity (for Other Ranks)' (CZA S-25\4720) was only issued in 1944. It is quite accurate in its description and was probably based on testimonies of escapees.

Interestingly, the nationality component of the identity of the Palestinian Jewish POWs—their Zionism—was in some ways defined and strengthened for them by their German captors. The Palestinian Jewish soldiers clearly did not join the British army because they were British patriots; and despite their differences they did, after all, share the same ethnicity and religion. The Germans viewed Jews as a separate race; for them, this was a heredity characteristic that did not depend on a person's nationality nor did it change if a person had converted to another religion.[47] Although the ethnicity of the Palestinian Jewish POWs was obviously the main reason for housing them together as a separate group, nationality mattered too: the fact that the Germans did not house non-Palestinian Jews with them points to the conclusion that the Germans treated them primarily as a separate national group, in the same way that they treated other nationalities belonging to other dominions of the British Empire. In several German documents they were referred to as 'British POW[s] of Jewish ethnicity [*volkstums*]' and in Stalag VIII-B (Lamsdorf), where most of them spent their captivity period, they had their own MOC, in the same way that other British dominions did and in line with the Wehrmacht regulations regarding MOCs.[48]

Another aspect that strengthened the mutual identity of the Palestinian Jewish POWs was their shared concern for their relatives. An American POW must have known that the family he had left behind was in most cases healthy and secure and was supported by the social and family circles around it; British POWs, while obviously worried about the bombing of British cities, in most cases must have shared that feeling. Most of the Palestinian Jewish POWs, on the other hand, were concerned about the fate of the families they left behind when they immigrated to Palestine from Europe before the war; and those who left families in Palestine were most likely concerned about their fate had Rommel's army been able to break through in North Africa and reach Palestine.[49] American and British POWs knew that there was a sovereign, independent country supporting them and looking after their interests; even if this country lost the war, this still would not trigger a complete annihilation of the state and its people. Most of these POWs—but not all, as there were immigrants among them as well—had a shared history, shared culture, and shared language to gather around; this was not the

---

[47] Although according to Germany's racial laws a Jew did not have to belong to the Jewish religion, he was defined as such if two or more of his grandparents had belonged to it (see Hilberg, *The Destruction of the European Jews*, vol. I, p. 68).

[48] Allgemeine Richtlinien für das Vertrauensmännerwesen, 15 September 1941, p. 1, PAAA R40954. For reference to Palestinian Jews as a nationality see, for example, Wehrkreis VIII to Stalag VIII-B (Lamsdorf), 15 March 1943, PMA 190/1/43.

[49] The concern for their families that were left behind was shared by Jewish POWs of all nationalities; for example, for French Jewish POWs see Delphine Richard, 'La captivité en Allemagne des soldats juifs de France pendant la Seconde Guerre mondiale: l'ébauche d'un phénomène diasporique éphémère?', *Diasporas*, 31 (2018), pp. 65–81, p. 72; for Yugoslavian Jewish POWs see, for example, Asaria-Helfgot, *We Are Witnesses*, p. 38.

case for the different groups of the Palestinian Jewish POWs, who came from different countries, with different cultures and languages and had only their Jewish ethnicity to bind them together.

The Palestinian Jewish POWs' national identity as Palestinian of Jewish ethnicity was demonstrated in cultural events where each POW group was required to represent its country of origin; at such events, the Palestinian POWs represented Palestine and appeared under a flag with the Star of David on it. For example, when Stalag 383 (Hohenfels)—a Stalag for NCOs—celebrated ANZAC Day, the Palestinian NCOs, who like other nationalities in the Stalag established their own club, marched to the tune of a Hebrew song, which they taught the sixty-piece British orchestra to play; and their sports team, which represented Palestine, competed in the Empire Day sports events which were held in the Stalag.[50] In the parade that was held as part of the 'Empire' carnival in Stalag VIII-B (Lamsdorf), the Palestinian Jewish POWs, all wearing uniforms with the Star of David on them, won a prize with their 'Land of Israel—Old and New' exhibition, which included a man-made camel and cow.[51] And even though most of the Palestinian POWs were not religious, in some of Stalag VIII-B's (Lamsdorf) labour detachments their leaders established an 'Oneg Shabat' (the pleasure of the Sabbath) ceremony every Friday. This event was not meant as a religious one, but was intended as an occasion for the POWs to get together, listen to recent news and to a lecture, and discuss various issues.[52]

The efforts the Palestinian Jewish POWs made to present to their captors a group with a unified identity sometimes led to confusing situations: despite the fact that many of the Palestinian Jewish POWs spoke fluent German, they decided early on that interaction with the Germans would be handled only through an interpreter; this led to the German-speaking POWs, who spoke very little Hebrew, asking their colleagues to translate the translator's instructions for them from Hebrew back into German.[53] A similar situation occurred when the POWs received their first pay checks: only a small number of them could read and write Hebrew but since the POWs' leaders insisted on signing for these payments in Hebrew, some of the POWs had to be taught to sign their own names in a language they could barely understand.[54]

---

[50] Stephen Wynn, *Stalag 383 Bavaria* (Barnsley: Pen & Sword, 2021), p. 52; test in German captivity, July 1945, p. 59, IDF 182/1867/1998; *Sunday Post*, 8 August 1943, p. 13.

[51] Test in German captivity, July 1945, pp. 116–18, IDF 182/1867/1998; Sela, *Shackles of Captivity*, pp. 231–2.

[52] Test in German captivity, July 1945, p. 77, IDF 182/1867/1998.

[53] Ibid., p. 44; Hans Paul Weiner, unpublished memoirs, p. 56, JMM WW2 files. The issue of English language knowledge of the Palestinian Jewish soldiers was even raised in the British Parliament in June 1941, when a suggestion was made to provide them with English teachers (see Jones to Margesson, written answers, 10 June 1941, https://hansard.parliament.uk/Commons/, accessed 17 October 2020).

[54] Test in German captivity, July 1945, p. 45, IDF 182/1867/1998.

The Palestinian Jewish POWs were, in effect, the only group in German captivity that was held as a separate Jewish group as a result of being recognized as a separate national and ethnic group, and not as happened on several other occasions, as a result of forced segregation only due to 'race'. American and British Jewish POWs were always an integral part of their national groups and saw nationality as the main component in their identity; captivity, however, and the activities that took place throughout it, helped most of the Palestinian Jewish POWs, who came from different countries, spoke different languages and joined the British army for different reasons, to strengthen parts of their Jewish identity—ethnic, religious and cultural—and to combine them into one.

Segregation

Nowhere was the issue of maintaining the Jewish identity of an American or British Jewish POW more fundamental than during cases of their segregation from their non-Jewish comrades. As described in Chapter 3 of this book, although the OKW had issued orders in 1941 and 1942 to house Jewish POWs in separate barracks within POW camps, it was not until the order was reiterated in December 1944 that the majority of segregation cases of American and British Jewish POWs took place.[55] Since Palestinian Jewish POWs were considered a separate nationality within the British Empire, they had already been housed in separate barracks and labour detachments, in the same way that Australian, New Zealander, and South African POWs had been housed; but the segregation attempts placed American and British Jewish POWs who until that stage had managed to keep their Jewish identity a secret in a difficult situation. The Germans, for their part, were well aware that some Jewish POWs would not be forthcoming in revealing their identity and in some POW camps instructed commandants and guards to report suspicious cases to the camp's security officer.[56]

Registering one's religion as non-Jewish when enrolling in the armed forces or later, just before being captured, throwing away the identification discs which specified the soldier's religion, were precautionary acts performed before the soldier became a POW; hiding one's religion in the POW camp after a specific order had been given for Jewish POWs to identify themselves carried a much greater risk. Despite efforts to hide their Jewish identity, there were several ways a POW could still be identified as Jewish: these included being circumcised, having a Jewish-sounding name, which the POW had to keep in order to stay in contact

---

[55] Sammelmitteilungen 1, order 7, 16 June 1941; Befehlsammlung 11, order 5, 11 March 1942; and Befehlsammlung 48, order 876, 15 December 1944, BA-MA RW 6/270.

[56] See, for example, Stalag III-A's (Luckenwalde) Sammelheft für den Kommandoführer, March 1943, p. 39, BA-MA RH 49/33.

with his family, or, in some cases, having knowledge of the German language, which, as it was not dissimilar to Yiddish, often meant that even Jewish POWs who were not originally from Germany or Austria had a good understanding of it if they understood Yiddish.[57] In addition, the POW's letters were regularly read by the camp's censors, and his family, sometimes unaware of the dangers he was facing, could inadvertently reveal his identity; and of course, there was always the risk of being exposed as a Jew by an overzealous guard or an anti-Semitic POW.[58] But this risk was only one issue the POW was facing; the other one, perhaps even more daunting, was the fact that by hiding his Jewish identity, the POW also often faced an inner moral crisis which involved issues of identity, dignity, and self-betrayal. 'What we did was to deny our mothers and fathers', was how one American Jewish POW described his decision not to reveal himself when the Germans ordered the Jewish POWs to step forward: 'It was a terrible mental thing.'[59] As the French Jewish POW—and philosopher—Emmanuel Levinas described it, 'hiding under a false identity, the Jewish prisoner suddenly regained his Jewish identity'.[60]

For Fred Weiner, a Jewish staff sergeant and B24 gunner with the 44th Bomb Group who was held in Stalag Luft I (Barth), the decision not to identify himself when, in January 1945, a German sergeant ordered the Jewish POWs in his barracks to take a step forward, was simple—he thought that exposing himself would lead to a certain death.[61] Although he still had his identification discs with the letter 'H' on him, he decided not to do that; but when the German repeated the order and followed it with a threat to open fire on all the POWs in the barracks, he decided there was no point in hiding: 'if I'm going to get it, there's no sense in everyone getting it'—and took the step forward.[62] Weiner's initial decision was understandable; and so was his decision to eventually take the step forward, which was a result of a quick evaluation of the possible outcome: if his destiny was doomed, there was no point in dragging all his comrades with him. Fortunately for him, his comrades—without planning it in advance—all took a step forward with him; the angry Sergeant had to leave the room empty-handed.[63]

The segregation in Stalag IX-B in Bad Orb, which led to the eighty segregated Jewish POWs, together with 270 of their non-Jewish comrades, being sent to the Berga slave labour camp, was one of the documented examples of this inner

---

[57] The Germans were well aware of the fact that some Jewish POWs spoke good German. See Gylek to POW Commander of military district VIII, 15 March 1944, PMA 191/1/44.
[58] See, for example, testimony of Raymond Allaby, 21 September 1945, NARA RG 549, box 174, 290/59/22/5; W. A. Harding, IWM 82/27/1 pp. 25–7; and Jay, *Facing Fearful Odds*, ln. 3871.
[59] Sam Kimbarow, http://www.jewishsightseeing.com/usa/california/san_diego/veterans_administration/19990423-world_war_ii_pows.htm, accessed 21 August 2020.
[60] Emmanuel Levinas, *Carnets de captivité et autres inédits* (Paris: Bernard Grasset, 2017), p. 205.
[61] Fred Weiner, memoirs, https://stalagluft4.org/pdf/weinernew.pdf, accessed 15 August 2022.
[62] Ibid.   [63] Ibid.

struggle. Edwin Cornell, who fought with the 28th Division and decided not to reveal his ethnicity when the segregation order was given in Bad Orb, described the feeling that followed the decision as a 'period of guilt' which made him feel 'sick to my stomach...these [were] my brothers really'.[64] The feeling of guilt had made Ernst Kinoy, an American POW from the 106th Division also held in Bad Orb, reveal his identity after initially hiding it. Kinoy described how he 'decided that [he] really could not live with [himself] pretending otherwise', and explained his decision to give himself in as 'an ethical decision [involving] all kind of subtle things...as to what your identity is or is not'.[65] Jack Goldstein of the 28th Division, who declared his religion to be Pennsylvania Dutch when captured, did not hide his real religion when the segregation order came. His fellow POWs knew that he was Jewish and he did not want to appear as a coward in their eyes.[66] David Barlow's fear of the Germans was apparently greater than his fear of what his comrades in Bad Orb might think of him, and he decided to hide his identity, counting on them not to reveal it and figuring that without a Jewish-sounding name and identification tags—which he hid in his boots—the Germans would have a hard time proving that he was Jewish.[67] As he recounted after the war, 'I cannot tell you whether this was straight fear or an intellectual exercise. A little of both perhaps, but mostly fear.'[68]

Judging by these testimonies, it is obvious that the dilemma Jewish POWs faced during segregation was much more tasking than the one that they faced when they had to decide whether to state their religion or record their real name when enlisting; it was also a more trying event than the one they faced having to decide whether to throw away their identification discs just before they were taken captive. Combining issues such as Jewish identity, self-respect and self-betrayal, soldierly dignity and fear, together with what POWs already knew about the German treatment of Jews, placed American and British Jewish POWs in an intolerable situation. In the POW's mind, segregation was clearly the first step in taking away his POW status which had so far protected him; to him, the question of whether to reveal his Jewish identity or not became a question of life or death.

Transnational Jewish Identity: The Encounter with Holocaust Victims

Nowhere was the transnational nature of Jewish identity more apparent than in the encounters that American and British Jewish POWs had with their oppressed European brethren. Part of the empathy they felt in these encounters towards the

---

[64] Cohen, *Soldiers and Slaves*, ln. 1438. [65] Ibid., ln. 1481.
[66] Ibid., ln. 1488. [67] Ibid. [68] Ibid., ln. 1489.

emaciated civilian Jews was the natural compassion towards the suffering of fellow human beings, regardless of who they were and where they came from; but part of it was also the result of their shared Jewish heritage. Being better treated and better fed (although food was always scarce), in uniform and under the protection of the Wehrmacht and the Geneva Convention, the American and British Jewish POWs often felt it was their responsibility to help their brethren in their hour of need.

At first, and similar to the reaction of the rest of the world, Jewish POWs refused to believe the news about the extermination of Europe's Jews. Wilfred Ofstein, a British Jewish POWs, testified that even when they had heard, towards the end of the war, about the mass murder of the European Jews they found it 'so utterly impossible…that [we] didn't believe it'.[69] Moshe Zigelbaum, a Palestinian POW, had the same reaction a few years earlier, when he was working in a labour detachment not far from Auschwitz. When the Polish civilians told him that Jews were being murdered in gas chambers there he refused to believe it and attributed the rumour to the naivety of the locals, who would believe anything they were told.[70] Mosche Grüner, another Palestinian POW, had a similar reaction, and so did Cyril Rofe.[71] When he was in Stalag VIII-B's labour detachment E479 near Auschwitz, a Pole told him about the gas chambers there; in his memoirs, Rofe said that 'most of us flatly refused to believe him. [Even] knowing the Germans as we did, we still found the story too horrible to believe.'[72]

The encounters with Jewish slave labour provided the Jewish POWs with a glimpse into the reality of these rumours; it also made some of them realize what their fate might have been had they (or their families) stayed in Europe instead of emigrating to other countries. Their level of empathy towards these victims was probably dependent on their own level of misery at that time: Sam Palter, an American Jewish POW who encountered Jewish inmates from Dachau while working on the repair of railroad tracks, described them as 'skeletal men in striped shirts with Stars of David stitched on their arms and "*Juden*" marked across their back'. The Dachau inmates were treated much worse than the POWs and Palter felt both guilty and fortunate at the same time for not having to be marked with the Star of David.[73] David Westheimer, an American Jewish POW, had different feelings: when he passed through an Austrian town on the way to Stalag VII-A (Moosburg), he saw a group of Jews with Star of David armbands cleaning the street under guard. He said he could not identify with them because at that point his identity 'was the boxcar'.[74]

---

[69] Testimony of Wilfred Ofstein, YVA O.3–8111.
[70] Testimony of Moshe Zigelbaum, YVA O.3–2967.
[71] Testimony of Mosche Grüner, YVA O.3–1602.
[72] Rofe, *Against the Wind*, pp. 90–1.
[73] LaCroix, *Journey Out of Darkness*, p. 117.
[74] Westheimer, *Sitting It Out*, p. 148.

Witnessing the terrible conditions to which their Jewish brethren were subjected, Jewish POWs tried where possible to assist them by sharing their food and giving them the contents of their Red Cross parcels.[75] One such situation was recounted by Paul Weiner, the Austrian-born Palestinian Jewish POW who immigrated to Palestine so that he could volunteer for the British army to fight the Nazis. When working in one of Stalag VIII-B's (Lamsdorf) labour detachments he was sent one day to bring coal from a coal mine near Auschwitz. While loading the truck with his fellow POWs he noticed a group of inmates, whom he described as looking like 'walking skeletons', standing around the truck. All of them wore striped clothes with a yellow star attached. The POWs tried to speak to them in several languages but the frightened inmates, seeing the uniforms of the POWs, refused to respond. It was only when one POW began to cite a Jewish prayer—the words of which every Jew, religious or not, is familiar with—that they realized that the POWs were Jewish as well and they all started to cry. The POWs gave them all the food they had with them.[76] A similar encounter occurred in the Blechhammer forced-labour camp (a sub-camp of Auschwitz), where Palestinian Jewish POWs saw a group of Jewish boys, probably not older than 14 years of age, some of whom were wearing rags instead of shoes, carrying heavy sacks of cement. The POWs testified that the young boys seemed to have been more encouraged by the mere exchange of glances between the groups than from the food and clothing items the POWs had given them; the looks on the children's tortured faces remained burnt into the memories of the POWs for years to come.[77]

In another case, Palestinian Jewish POWs who were employed in the distribution of food parcels to Nazi Party members in the town of Gleiwitz, encountered Jewish women—recognized by the '*Judenstern*' they were wearing—clearing snow from the streets; an elderly Jew who was passing by had his briefcase discretely filled with foodstuffs by the POWs.[78] On another occasion, while driving through Gleiwitz, one of the Palestinian Jewish POWs, a refugee from Germany, recognized his mother and younger sister on the street; unable to control himself, he yelled '*mammeh*' (mummy in Yiddish) and had to be held back from jumping off the truck by his comrades, who feared that being in contact with enemy POWs would put the mother and sister at risk.[79] In the following weeks, the son arranged—through a Polish person and in return for a large 'commission'—for food to be sent to his family; eventually he received a note from his mother, asking him to stop sending any more parcels since their secret had been exposed.[80]

The same group of Palestinian Jewish POWs also witnessed the moment when a large group of Jewish men, who were transported with their families from the area of Krakow, realized that they were being separated from their wives and

[75] Test in German captivity, July 1945, pp. 53–4, IDF 182/1867/1998.
[76] Hans Paul Weiner, unpublished memoirs, p. 72, JMM WW2 files.
[77] Sela, *Shackles of Captivity*, pp. 143–4.   [78] Ibid., p. 135.
[79] Ibid., pp. 135–6.   [80] Ibid., p. 136.

children. The families were ordered off the train and the POWs could see that they were all properly dressed; the women and children, however, were then driven back to opposite ends of the train, leaving the men behind holding their suitcases.[81] Only when locomotives were attached to either side of the train and two separate trains began moving in opposite directions did the men, who believed they were about to board the empty carriages in the middle, realize what had happened and started to cry.[82] The deceit did not end there: the men were then told that since there was not enough room on the train, they should load their suitcases onto waiting trucks; they themselves climbed back to the remaining carriages of the train. The Palestinian Jewish POWs then witnessed how the train made its way to the nearby Blechhammer forced labour camp, while the trucks, which remained behind, were quickly emptied of the suitcases.[83]

Encounters with concentration camp inmates and slave labour sometimes caused frictions with their guards: in mid-1943 in Stalag VIII-B's labour detachment E578 in Peiskretchem several Palestinian Jewish POWs found themselves working side by side with Jewish inmates from a nearby concentration camp. When they tried to pass them food, an SA guard started to hit one of the Jewish inmates with his rifle. In response, a Palestinian Jewish POW intervened and pushed the SA guard away, causing the rest of the SA guards to pull out their weapons. The Wehrmacht guard who was overseeing the POWs then stepped in, warned the SA men not to touch 'his' POWs, and told them to direct any complaints to the camp commandant.[84]

When the group reported the incident to their MOC, Yosef Karlenboim, he went to discuss it with the commandant, who seemed himself quite shook up by it and told Karlenboim that SA people were 'professional murderers'.[85] Karlenboim, however, proposed that the commandant reach an agreement with the local SA commander, according to which in return for generous 'donations' from the POWs of coffee, chocolate, and English cigarettes, the incident would be silenced; in addition, thirty Jewish inmates would be allowed into the POW camp every day to be properly fed and medically examined, and thirty POWs would take their place laying railway tracks.[86] The POWs then arranged for the whole camp to provide the inmates with daily donations of food, soap, and cigarettes from their own daily quota. The Jewish slave labourers were in such a bad physical shape that a few days after the arrangement had begun the British doctor treating them asked Karlenboim for his opinion regarding mercy killing; Karlenboim flatly rejected it. The arrangement ended after a few weeks when the Jewish concentration camp inmates disappeared; in all likelihood, they were sent to the

---

[81] Ibid., pp. 138–9.   [82] Ibid., p. 139.   [83] Ibid.
[84] Almogi, *With Head Held High*, p. 96; testimony of Mosche Zigelbaum, YVA O.3-2967.
[85] Almogi, *With Head Held High*, p. 97.
[86] Ibid.; such an 'arrangement' with Jewish inmates also took place in another of Stalag VIII-B's (Lamsdorf) labour detachments near Beuthen (see testimony of Mosche Grüner, YVA O.3-1602).

extermination camps.[87] Their status was not, after all, that of POWs; they were not protected by the Geneva Convention. Some of the Palestinian POWs, who only a few years earlier had emigrated from the same countries from which their slave labour brethren came, must have felt fortunate: in not so different circumstances, it could have been them.

It should be noted that witnessing the conditions and eventual fate of the Jewish population in Poland was not limited to the Palestinian Jewish POWs. Many of those supposedly secluded behind barbed wire were aware of it as well to the extent that they began to draw conclusions regarding their own fate. Reporting on their visits to POW camps in the General Gouvernement, the ICRC delegation in Berlin wrote to ICRC headquarters in Geneva on 21 September 1943 that 'The sincere and great concern of all MOCs in the General Gouvernement is the question of what would happen to them if political turmoil broke out[.] In many cases POWs have become eyewitnesses to the measures taken against the Jews'.[88] However, it seems that racial doctrines and Nazi ideologies had their limits and when it came to meeting work quotas or accepting 'donations' from POWs, even SA members—and SS members as well, in a similar case that occurred in Stalag VIII-B's labour detachment E207 (Ehrenforst)—were willing to cooperate with the Jewish '*Untermenschen*'.[89]

The protection accorded to the Jewish POWs by the Geneva Convention and, despite their 'race', by being members of nations which were considered racially closer to the Germans, was made even more clear by these encounters. It was also clear to some of the POWs, as Captain Julius Green, a British Jewish POW, commented in his memoirs, that 'under other circumstances, [this] would have been our lot'.[90] Jewish POWs could not ignore the transnational nature of their identity and their potential mutual fate; their Jewish heritage united them with their Jewish brethren across different nationalities, places of birth, and social classes and compelled them to provide them with as much help as they could.[91]

Religious and Cultural Activity

Article 16 of the 1929 Geneva Convention stated that 'Prisoners of war shall be permitted complete freedom in the performance of their religious duties,

---

[87] Almogi, *With Head Held High*, p. 100; for a similar case in Stalag VIII-B's E479 see Rofe, *Against the Wind*, p. 81. In July 1944 the POW Office forbade POWs and concentration camp inmates from working together in the same place due to the negative impact it had on the productivity of the POWs (see Befehlsammlung 39, order 743, 15 July 1944, BA-MA RW 6/270).

[88] Bubb to ICRC, 21 September 1943, ACICR BG 17 05/017.

[89] Glantz, *Struggle in Captivity*, pp. 119–20.   [90] Green, *From Colditz in Code*, p. 99.

[91] Many Jews were raised on the tradition of Jewish philanthropy both at home and abroad, especially to Eastern European Jews. See, for example, Zosa Szajkowski, 'Private and Organized American Jewish Overseas Relief (1914–1938)', *American Jewish Historical Quarterly*, 57:1 (1967), pp. 52–3, 55–106; and Derek Penslar, *Shylock's Children: Economics and Jewish Identity in Modern Europe* (London: University of California Press, 2001), especially lns 2433–564.

including attendance at the services of their faith'. The Wehrmacht's manual for Stalag commandants elaborated on this, recognizing that POWs in particular have religious needs, and therefore 'From a purely human point of view and in the interest of peace and order', their wishes should, as far as possible, be accommodated.[92] The manual, which was issued by the OKW before the start of the Second World War, did not mention any specific religion and there was no reference in it to the religious needs of Jewish POWs.

More detailed instructions were issued by the OKW as the war progressed: guidelines issued just before the invasion of the Soviet Union stated that it was the camp commandant's responsibility to provide the POWs with their religious needs and to assign a clergyman from the POWs to each religion or denomination.[93] Although the guidelines did not mention Jews, it made a general reference to non-Christian POWs, allowing them to conduct acts of worship only if a cleric was present but permitting individual POWs to pray privately.[94] Since there were very few specific mentions of Christianity in this document, and none mentioning non-Christian faiths such as Islam, Hinduism, Sikhism, or Judaism, faiths from which there were already POWs in German captivity by that time, it can be assumed that its stipulations referred to all religions in general. Where OKW guidelines on religion did make references to non-Christian religions, such as Islam or Hinduism, it was usually in the context of gaining POWs' support against their own countries—the Soviet Union in the case of Soviet Muslim POWs and Britain in the case of Indian POWs.[95]

Regardless of their nationality and given the German treatment of civilian Jews, Jewish POWs saw the celebration of Jewish Holy days—which was sometimes preformed in secrecy—as another component in the ongoing power struggle between captors and captives. These celebrations served not only to strengthen the Jewish part of their identity, but also helped them, in their minds, to share these moments with their families back home; as Aben Caplan, an American Jewish POW held in Stalag VII-A (Moosburg) commented in his memoirs, the celebration of Passover made 'all hearts and eyes [feel] far away with wonderful memories of the past and thoughts of the future'.[96]

Most of the detailed testimonies regarding the celebration of religious events came, however, from the Palestinian POWs; this is despite the fact that one of their leaders, Yosef Karlenboim, stated after the war that 'I have never been a

---

[92] Dienstanweisung für den Kommandanten eines 'Kriegsgefangenen Mannschafts Stammlagers', p. 25, BA-MA RH 1/612.
[93] Religionsausübung der Kriegsgefangene, 12 May 1941, pp. 2–3, PMA 202/1/47.   [94] Ibid.
[95] See, for example, the extension of guidelines for animal slaughter according to Islam from Muslim units in the Wehrmacht to Muslim POWs, Befehlsammlung 36, order 659, 1 June 1944, BA-MA RW 6/270.
[96] Memoirs of Aben Caplan, http://memory.loc.gov/diglib/vhp/story/loc.natlib.afc2001001.05190/, accessed 21 August 2020. More about POWs' fantasies about home are described in Clare Makepeace, *Captives of War* (Cambridge: Cambridge University Press, 2017), pp. 137–8.

religious person, but in captivity I was sorry for that...the English [POWs] had priests, who led them in prayer and gave encouraging sermons; we did not'.[97] As for the rest, evidence suggests that American Jewish POWs made more efforts to organize and participate in such events than the British ones. Unlike POWs of other religions, who in most cases had chaplains from their own religion with them in captivity, American and British Jewish POWs had none; when it came to organizing religious sermons (such as for funerals), they had to improvise and rely on whatever texts they were able to memorize.

The approach of American and British Jewish POWs to religion and to the marking of religious events varied. The Palestinian Jews saw this as an opportunity to demonstrate their Palestinian-Jewish national identity. Their celebration of religious Holy days was more along the lines of commemorating events of historical significance to the Jewish people, such as the exodus from Egypt (celebrated in Passover) or the destruction of the Temple in Jerusalem, and they used these events to renew and strengthen the connection between themselves and their ancient homeland. For the American and British Jewish POWs—those who kept their Jewish identity in the POW camp—marking these dates had to do with keeping with the tradition back home, when Jewish families celebrated together over a meal or, for some of them, in the synagogue. Since most Jewish POWs did not know the Jewish prayers associated with these events, the commemoration of the act itself was sufficient to make them feel connected to their Jewish roots.

The first record of a commemoration of a religious event by American or British Jewish POWs was that of the Jewish Memorial Day ('*Tish'a Be'Av*') for the destructions of the First and Second Temples, which occurred at the beginning of August 1941, just a few days after the arrival of the Palestinian Jewish POWs in Stalag VIII-B (Lamsdorf). Yosef Karlenboim managed to persuade one of the German guards, a devout Catholic, that the Jews had the same right to hold public prayers as the Christian POWs; this was, in fact, in line with the Geneva Convention as well as the OKW regulations mentioned earlier.[98] A surreal event ensued: the Jewish POWs stood in a U-shaped formation, under the German flag and in the middle of a German POW camp, and listened to Karlenboim's speech about the importance of that day. The event left a strong impression not only on those who participated in it but also on the other POWs, including some of the Jews among them who, until then, had hidden their religion but now felt confident enough to reveal it.[99]

Another Jewish Holy day, the Jewish New Year, occurred a few weeks later, on 21 September 1941. The German authorities again allowed the Palestinian Jewish POWs to celebrate the event and even arranged for the dining room to be

---

[97] Test in German captivity, July 1945, pp. 75–6, IDF 182/1867/1998.
[98] Ibid., p. 67.
[99] Almogi, *With Head Held High*, pp. 59–60; Glantz, *Struggle in Captivity*, p. 94.

available for them to pray in.¹⁰⁰ The Star of David they had hung publicly there caused some confusion among the Germans; after the POWs refused to take it down, the same Catholic guard intervened and explained to his officer that according to the Geneva Convention, the Jews should be allowed to celebrate their Holy days according to their religion and customs, just like any other religion. The officer relented.¹⁰¹ In the following years the celebration of Jewish Holy days became a regular event in Stalag VIII-B (Lamsdorf) and was attended by hundreds of POWs, both Jewish and non-Jewish; the British camp leadership was invited to take part in some of them.¹⁰² In another Holy day, in December 1942, at the height of the Shackling Crisis, the Palestinian Jewish POWs in Stalag VIII-B asked for permission—through the ICRC—to celebrate Hanukah, a Jewish Holy day commemorating the victory of the Jewish rebels over the Greek Empire around 160 BC. The permission was granted and after releasing some of the POWs from their shackles—some with the permission of the guards, who received a large 'donation' of cigarettes for their help, and some, after the guards had left, without their permission—the POWs prepared a big ceremony, where they lit the ceremonial candles and performed a Jewish-themed theatre show in front of hundreds of POWs, Jews and non-Jews alike. At some stage several German officers and guards also joined the audience.¹⁰³

This relatively tolerant approach in Stalag VIII-B (Lamsdorf) towards the celebration of Jewish Holy days might be attributed to the large number of Jewish—Palestinian Jewish—POWs there, and was not necessarily repeated in other POW camps. Although, with the exception of Soviet POWs, the official German policy allowed POWs to exercise their religion, when it came to Jewish POWs, different commandants seemed to have implemented different policies.¹⁰⁴ For example, Yugoslav Jewish officers in Oflag XIII-B (Nürnberg-Langwasser) initially held Sabbath and religious ceremonies and prayers; however, they were later forbidden from doing so and in 1941 had to conduct the Jewish New Year service in secrecy. But when the Jewish POWs in that camp held the traditional Yom Kippur (the Day of Atonement) fast a few days later, the Germans, who came to investigate suspecting a hunger strike was taking place, left after hearing the explanation.¹⁰⁵

---

¹⁰⁰ Ibid., p. 96; postcard from a POW, 21 September 1941, CZA S-25\4720.
¹⁰¹ Sela, *Shackles of Captivity*, p. 110. In fact, the right of Jews in Germany to do so was enshrined in Article 4 of the Law for the Protection of German Blood and German Honor (the Nuremberg Laws), see https://www.ushmm.org/wlc/en/article.php?ModuleId=10007903, accessed 30 April 2018.
¹⁰² Test in German captivity, July 1945, p. 111, IDF 182/1867/1998. Evidence of these celebrations can also be found in photos taken by the Palestinian Jewish POWs—see, for example, photos of Hannukah celebration in POW Camp 383 (Hohenfels) in 1943 and Jewish New Year celebration in Stalag VIII-B's labour detachment E475 (Weidengut) in 1944 (https://www.jewishpioneers.com/copy-of-1, accessed 20 September 2020).
¹⁰³ Glantz, *Struggle in Captivity*, pp. 212–17.
¹⁰⁴ Military district VIII, Merkblatt für Führer von Arbeitskommandos und Wachmannchaften, p. 11, 1 November, 1942, PMA 129/1/36.
¹⁰⁵ Asaria-Helfgot, *We Are Witnesses*, pp. 32–5.

On the other hand, and despite the concern of some of them, the 400 Yugoslav Jewish officers held in Oflag VI-C (Osnabrück-Eversheide) held their religious ceremonies in public, and were even given a few prayer books by the ICRC; they later moved the daily prayer back inside the barracks.[106] These public ceremonies took place throughout their captivity period and even after they were moved between several POW camps; the Germans did not prohibit them.[107] In another case, Jewish POWs who were brought to Stalag IV-B (Mühlberg) from Italian POW camps after Italy's capitulation, continued to hold Jewish services in their new camp. In November 1943 one of the German guards warned them that they might be shot by the SS if they continued to do so.[108]

Since there were no Jewish chaplains—Rabbis—in German POW camps, the Christian clergy present stepped in in some cases and offered their help to the Jewish POWs in conducting services such as the Jewish New Year and Yom Kippur; finding it quite unusual, Norman Rubenstein, who witnessed one such situation, commented that 'surely this was one of the few places in what remained of Hitler's Germany where such services were held'.[109] And in a visit by the Protecting Power to Stalag VIII-B (Lamsdorf) at the beginning of 1943, the Christian padres obtained the agreement of the camp authorities to visit 'Jews of Christian faith [sic]' in the labour detachments and for the padres to officiate at Jewish funerals there.[110] In Stalag Luft I (Barth), the British Catholic chaplain, Father Michael Charlton, allowed Jewish POWs to attend his religious sermons; the Jewish POWs in that camp also held Friday services and on Saturdays they used to replace the cross in the camp's chapel with the Star of David and hold religious services. Judging by the letter he sent to his wife, the American Jewish POW who organized these sermons was clearly not religious: he said he had found it 'Odd... I never thought I had it in me'.[111] The German authorities allowed this practice despite the fact that the Jewish POWs were segregated at the time in separate barracks; according to the testimony of a Jewish airman, attendance was high, mainly as an act of defiance and in order to annoy the Germans.[112]

In the last month of the war, as Allied armies were conducting their final push into the heart of Germany, the Passover story of the exodus of Jews from slavery in Egypt to the Promised Land felt especially suitable. Milton Feldman, an American Jewish POW who had fought with the 106th Division and was held in Stalag IV-B (Mühlberg) recalled how, at the end of March 1945, he celebrated

---

[106] Ibid., p. 46. See also Lebl, *Jewish Soldiers from Yugoslavia as POWs in Nazi Germany*, p. 31.
[107] See, for example, Asaria-Helfgot, *We Are Witnesses*, pp. 82–3.
[108] Maurice Ofstein, *Diary and Odd Jotting* (unpublished memoirs), p. 16, JMM T2010.353.1.
[109] Rubenstein, *The Invisibly Wounded*, p. 170.
[110] Swiss embassy report on Stalag VIII-B (Lamsdorf), 5 March 1943, p. 7, TNA WO 224/27.
[111] *Prisoners of War Bulletin*, 3:1 (1945), p. 8; Tom Bird, *American POWs of World War II* (Westport, CT and London: Praeger, 1992), p. 90.
[112] Adrian Gilbert, *POW: Allied Prisoners in Europe 1939–1945* (London: Thistle Publishing, 2014), pp. 359–60. See also Elson, *Prisoners of War: An Oral History*, pp. 165–6.

Passover with fifteen other Jewish POWs. He described how 'We went through the whole thing under the nose of the Nazis'.[113] Testimonies from Jewish POWs indicate that similar Passover ceremonies took place that year in other POW camps as well; in Stalag XVIII-C (in Markt Pongau in Austria), although there was no food to celebrate with, several Jewish POWs guarded the doors while another, a son of a Rabbi, said the prayer in a low voice.[114] A Passover ceremony also took place in Stalag VII-A (Moosburg) and even in Stalag IX-B in Bad Orb, where the only remaining Jewish POWs were those who had not identified themselves as Jews to the Germans when the segregation of the Jewish POWs took place in January 1945.[115] Leon Horowitz, an American Jewish POW who was captured in the Battle of the Bulge and was saved from the segregation because of an illness, described the ceremony as 'short and sweet'.[116]

Although it seemed that German commandants were not following a consistent policy when it came to the practice of religion by Jewish POWs, in April 1944 the ICRC explained that they did not receive complaints from Jewish POWs related to religious practice; they seem to have concluded that this was therefore not an issue for them.[117] This is somewhat surprising given what was known by then regarding the German treatment of Jews; it is highly likely that Jewish POWs did not dare to make such complaints in the first place, knowing how futile such action would be and the risks that might be associated with it. The ICRC did, however, confirm that in some camps Jews had full freedom of religion and were able to observe all rituals.[118]

On the other hand, it is interesting to note that in all of the camp visit reports from the Protecting Power and ICRC that have been reviewed in this research, under the section that provides details about the POWs' religious activities, the delegates never made any reference to the religious needs of Jewish POWs. In one instance when Jewish POWs were mentioned in this section it was as part of a census of the different faiths in Stalag XVII-B (in Gneixendorf in Austria); according to the Swiss delegates, Jews consisted of 1.8%, vs. 65.8% Protestants and 31.5% Catholics (as it happens, this figure—1.8%—is quite close to the 1.6% estimate made in this study of the share of American and British Jewish POWs out of the total number of American and British POWs).[119] No reason was given as to the purpose of this census; however, these figures made it clear that the German authorities had monitored the number of Jewish POWs in the camps, although it might have only included those who had declared their Jewish

---

[113] Feldman, *Captured, Frozen, Starved—and Lucky*, ln. 750.
[114] LaCroix, *Journey Out of Darkness*, p. 119.
[115] Memoirs of Aben Caplan, http://memory.loc.gov/diglib/vhp/story/loc.natlib.afc2001001.05190/, accessed 21 August 2020.
[116] Donaldson, *Men of Honor*, p. 31.
[117] De Traz to Laski, 13 April 1944, ACICR BG 25/34.   [118] Ibid.
[119] Swiss embassy report on Stalag XVII-B (Gneixendorf), 24 October 1944, NARA RG 59, box 2224, 250/32/3/1.

identity when captured. It should also be noted that the ICRC did keep track of other minority religions: in one case, when the numbers of Hindu, Muslim, and Sikh Indian POWs in Stalag V-C (Offenburg) kept changing between ICRC visits, the ICRC reported it to the BRC, suggesting that this might be a result of POWs moving between labour detachments.[120] However, with the exception of the report on Stalag XVII-B (Gneixendorf) mentioned above, which gave a breakdown of the POW population by religion, and the reports on the numbers of Palestinian Jewish POWs, which were treated as belonging to a separate British dominion, but not to a religion, a similar count of Jewish POWs in ICRC and Protecting Power visit reports was not found.

As mentioned, most Jews in America and in Britain were not religious; and this was likely reflected in the makeup of the Jewish POW population. But regardless of whether they were religious or not, or the level of their religiosity, religious activities were one way Jewish POWs used to maintain their spirit in captivity. The fact that most Jewish religious celebrations commemorated events from the history of the Jewish people meant that in POW camps, these events served to strengthen the Jewish POWs' connections with their history and heritage, their team spirit, and their links with their families back home, as well as with their religion. Even weekly Sabbath prayers, where they existed, served not only as religious events but also as social ones, similar to the way that Christian POWs who were not necessarily religious chose to attend Sunday mass and hear encouraging words from their pastors. As one American Jewish POW who was segregated at the time in Stalag VII-A (Moosburg) described their Friday night services: 'We formed a nice group, each one proud of his religion as he gave forth in prayer and song.'[121] Given the German treatment of Jews, participation in such events, especially when it was done in secrecy, was also meant as an act of defiance by the Jewish POWs against their captors, and helped them maintain and strengthen all elements of their Jewish identity.

Funerals

The discrepancy between German anti-Semitic policies and the respect that the Wehrmacht paid to non-Soviet Jewish '*Untermenschen*' POWs who died in captivity, would have left external observers of such events greatly confused. At one of these events, the coffin of Sergeant Yitshak Elkind, a Palestinian Jewish POW who had died of cancer in Stalag VIII-B (Lamsdorf), wrapped with the British flag and a flag with the Star of David, was led by two German soldiers who were

---

[120] De Traz to British Red Cross, 2 June 1944, ACICR BG 17 04–09.2.
[121] Memoirs of Aben Caplan, p. 12, http://memory.loc.gov/diglib/vhp/story/loc.natlib.afc2001001.05190/, accessed 21 August 2020.

carrying a wreath with the Swastika sign in its centre; they were followed by a guard of honour, made of nine armed Wehrmacht soldiers, who fired an honour volley after the body was laid in the grave.[122] One of the Jewish POWs then said a prayer in Hebrew.[123] And, although when it came to funerals of non-Soviet Jewish POWs this exact procedure was not always repeated, Jewish religious symbols and the citing of Jewish prayers were always part of such funerals, and the Wehrmacht—sometime grudgingly—was required to show respect for those deceased POWs who the German state considered to be its racial enemies.

The 1929 Geneva Convention was not too specific about the way that funerals for POWs who died in captivity should be held: Article 76 stated that 'The belligerents shall ensure that prisoners of war who have died in captivity are honourably buried, and that the graves bear the necessary indications and are treated with respect and suitably maintained'.[124] The belligerents, for their part, interpreted this to mean that POWs who died in captivity should be given a full military funeral, and this was usually the case for POWs from western armies. There is no clear estimate as for how many American and British Jewish POWs died in German captivity in the Second World War; however, some assumptions can be made based on the overall death rate in captivity of western POWs, which is estimated at 2.35% over five years of captivity.[125] Accounting for the estimated number of American and British Jewish POWs and the number of years each group spent in captivity, the number of American and British Jewish POWs who died in captivity was probably around fifty five.[126] It is also not clear how many of the deceased had revealed their Jewish identity when captured and were therefore entitled to a Jewish funeral; however, from the examples reviewed in this section, which also include cases of French and Yugoslav Jewish POWs, it is clear that the comrades of the deceased, protected by the Geneva Convention, insisted in most cases on providing them with a proper Jewish funeral and on demonstrating the religious aspects of Jewish identity publicly for everyone to see.

On the basis of Article 76 of the 1929 Geneva Convention the OKW issued general guidelines for funerals of POWs in February 1939 in its Camp Commandants Manual; these stated that the funeral should take a 'simple but dignified form' and allow for the participation of camp guards as a military escort

---

[122] Almogi, *With Head Held High*, p. 62.
[123] Oral testimony of Hans Paul Weiner, https://www.iwm.org.uk/collections/item/object/80016806, recorded 20 April 1997, accessed 1 February 2018, IWM catalogue number 17364. See also Aufbau, 4 February 1944, p. 32, https://archive.org/details/aufbau, accessed 30 June 2019.
[124] Article 76 of the 1929 Geneva Convention, https://ihl-databases.icrc.org/ihl/INTRO/305, accessed 4 February 2018.
[125] Overmans, 'Die Kriegsgefangenenpolitik des Deutschen Reichs 1939 bis 1945', p. 799.
[126] Accounting for the cumulative number of Jewish POWs in each year of the war with death rate of (2.4%/5 =) 0.48% per year: 1,500 Palestinian Jewish POWs being held captive for four years; 140 British Jewish POWs captured each year for five years; and 1,250 American Jewish POWs captured in each of the last two years of the war.

and of up to thirty POWs.[127] By 1941, given the number of POWs in German hands and the variety of religions they belonged to, further details were required: a four-page document was issued in July of that year, providing specific guidelines for the funeral process and for the burial of enemy POWs who died in captivity. The guidelines included specifics such as the POWs who were allowed to participate in the funeral (only members of the deceased's nationality who were in the same POW camp with him); the number of honour volleys that should be fired by the German guard of honour (three); and the colour of the bow on the wreath that the German guard of honour would lay on the grave (red). The guidelines also stated that non-Christians should be buried in a simple and dignified manner, and that their graves should be marked with the sign corresponding to their religion. A direct reference to Jewish POWs was made in a paragraph which stated that if a POW-designated cemetery was not available, POWs should be buried in a cemetery in line with their religion; specifically, Jewish POWs should be buried only in a Jewish cemetery.[128] The meaning of this order, which was issued in July 1941 and coincided with the beginning of the mass murder phase of the Holocaust, should not be underestimated: while their Soviet POWs and civilian brethren around Europe were being executed, worked to death, and gassed and their bodies burned or buried in unmarked mass graves, the Wehrmacht was ordered to treat non-Soviet Jewish POWs who died in captivity, while still considered racial enemies of the Reich, as honourable foes who even in their death still deserved its respect.

Several exceptions, which were applied to certain groups of POWs, were also listed in the guidelines. The exceptions included prohibiting a German guard of honour, the honorary salvos, and the laying of the wreath by the Wehrmacht for the following groups of POWs: Polish POWs, Soviet POWs, and German expatriates who were captured while fighting against Germany. While the exclusion of the first two groups was explained by the way they treated German soldiers (and for the Polish also the way the treated *Volksdeutsche*), no reason was given for the exclusion of the German expatriates group; it is possible that, since they were considered to be traitors to Germany, the drafters of the guidelines felt that there was no need to state the obvious.[129]

In this context it is important to reiterate that the group of Palestinian Jewish POWs included a large number of German and Austrian Jews who had immigrated to Palestine before the war and volunteered for the British army; although legally, as discussed in Chapter 1, the Wehrmacht could not prove that they were still German citizens, they did fall under the category of German expatriates and

[127] Dienstanweisung für den Kommandanten eines 'Kriegsgefangenen Mannschafts Stammlagers', p. 26, BA-MA RH 1/612.
[128] Beerdigung gefallender oder verstorbener feindlicher Wehrmachtangehöriger, 29 July 1941, BA R 58/9017.
[129] Ibid.

therefore according to these guidelines they were part of a group that was not entitled to a military funeral. The POW Office issued an order which dealt specifically with funerals of POWs who were German Jewish expatriates only in December of 1944: the order clearly stated that they were part of the excluded group.[130] However, given that this order was issued as part of a set of orders that dealt with the treatment of Jewish POWs in general, and referenced all previous orders related to Jewish POWs, it is likely that it was only meant as a repetition and clarification of the existing July 1941 guidelines mentioned above, which had already been in effect throughout the war.

An extract from the 1941 burial guidelines, which also mentioned the burial of Jewish POWs, was reissued in January 1942 for French POWs.[131] This time the guidelines did not include the exceptions related to Polish, Soviet, and German expatriate POWs, probably because they were not thought to be relevant in the case of the French army. More specific guidelines, this time referring only to Soviet POWs who died in captivity, were issued two months later, in March 1942; these were part of a larger document which was issued by AWA in an attempt to reverse the inhumane treatment of Soviet POWs in order to better utilize them for the benefit of the German economy.[132] The funeral guidelines did not make a specific mention of Jewish POWs, probably because the assumption was that, as per Heydrich's order to his Einsatzgruppen, all Soviet Jewish POWs were murdered upon capture.[133] The guidelines did however state that a Soviet Muslim POW who died in captivity should be buried with his head pointing towards the east and his face towards the south.[134] A separate set of guidelines, issued in the following year, added that Soviet Christian POWs should have a wooden cross to mark their grave, while non-Christian ones should have a wooden plaque.[135] In March 1943, probably in response to issues raised by camp commandants regarding the burial procedures for POWs who were killed during an escape or while committing acts of subordination, the POW Office found it necessary to point out, in its regular command summaries, that '[a]s a matter of principle, every honourably fallen enemy is to be buried with military honours'; this included escapees, 'unless dishonourable acts were committed during [their] flight', and POWs who were killed due to acts of subordination, unless 'violations of the soldier's code of honour have been established without question'.[136]

---

[130] Befehlsammlung 48, order 876, 15 December 1944, BA-MA RW 6/270.
[131] Für die Beerdigung verstorbener französischer Kriegsgefangener (gilt am 30.1.1942), 30 January 1942, PAAA R67004.
[132] Treatment of Soviet prisoners of war, document 695-PS, *IMT, Nazi Conspiracy and Aggression* vol. III (Washington, DC, 1946), pp. 498–509.
[133] Richtlinien für die in die Stalags und Dulags, 17 July 1941, BA R58/9016.
[134] Treatment of Soviet prisoners of war, document 695-PS, *IMT, Nazi Conspiracy and Aggression* vol. III, p. 506.
[135] Müller to SD commanders, 9 January 1943, BA R 58/397.
[136] Befehlsammlung 22, order 278, 9 March 1943, BA-MA RW 6/270.

It can be concluded, therefore, that Jewish POWs in general—with the exception of those who were originally from Germany—were not excluded from the funeral and burial guidelines and, at least in theory, non-Soviet Jewish POWs who died in captivity were supposed to be treated in the same way non-Jewish POWs were treated. In practice, however, the approach of the German authorities to funerals of Jewish POWs was inconsistent: in some cases they allowed for a funeral to be conducted with full military honours, including the guard of honour and the honorary salvos; in others they did so only after protests from the representatives of the POWs and pressure from the ICRC and the Protecting Power; and in some cases, when such protests did not work, funerals took place with partial military honours or with none at all.[137]

In fact, the Germans demonstrated this inconsistency in the funeral of Sergeant Yitshak Elkind, described at the beginning of this section, and initially refused to bury him with full military honours. Elkind, who was born in Russia 1913 but grew up in Danzig in Germany, immigrated to Palestine in 1933.[138] The years he spent in Germany—in all likelihood he held a German citizenship—placed him in the German expatriates group, which was not allowed the standard military funeral. In his memoirs, Sergeant Yosef Karlenboim described how he met, as the representative of the Palestinian Jewish POWs, with the commandant of Stalag VIII-B (Lamsdorf) and insisted that a full military funeral should be conducted. When the commandant responded 'but he was a Jew'; Karlenboim shot back 'so what? for you he was a British Sergeant', saluted and left.[139] Although it is possible that the commandant made his decision based on anti-Semitic reasons, it is also possible that Karlenboim misquoted him and the actual reason he gave was that Elkind was a German expatriate and therefore according to the guidelines was not entitled to a full military funeral. Cyril Rofe, who was held in Stalag VIII-B during the same period, described in his memoirs how the RAF POWs who were about to hold a funeral at the same time for a British POW who had been shot by a German guard, also joined the protest. The issue was escalated to the ICRC, who demanded that a proper funeral be held, and the German authorities eventually relented.[140] In another case, that of Eliahu Krauze, no protest was needed and a funeral with full military honours was held. Krauze, who was born in Poland and immigrated to Palestine in 1939, was (as described in Chapter 1) one of two Palestinian Jewish POWs who were shot in 1944 after being captured following a failed escape attempt. Since he was not part of any of the three excluded groups, he received a proper funeral.[141]

---

[137] See, for example, Sela, *Shackles of Captivity*, pp. 233–4.
[138] Yitzhak Elkind's file, http://en.jabotinsky.org/archive/search-archive/item/?itemId=118589, accessed 1 May 2020, Jabotinsky Institute of Israel.
[139] Almogi, *With Head Held High*, p. 62.
[140] Rofe, *Against the Wind*, p. 31. See also Glantz, *Struggle in Captivity*, pp. 190–1.
[141] Sela, *Shackles of Captivity*, p. 236; Israel War Memorial site, https://www.izkor.gov.il/Eliahu%20Krauze/en_bc2dcfb6d72a8cae22a2d16f72532a92, accessed 1 May 2020.

However, the cases of Krauze and Elkind were the exception rather than the norm. Protests and complaints regarding due process did not always succeed. In another case in Stalag VIII-B (Lamsdorf), the Palestinian Jewish POWs insisted that unless a military funeral, including the customary volley, was given to their dead comrade, they would refuse to attend the funeral. Although the background of the deceased POW in this case is not known, it is likely that the incident occurred because he, too, was a German expatriate. The commandant contacted Berlin and obtained an approval to comply with part of the demands; the funeral took place on the following day, with German soldiers marching behind the coffin and laying a wreath on the grave. They did not, however, stand to attention in front of the grave, nor did they fire the customary honour volley as required, an issue which led to the POWs filing a complaint with the ICRC. The gravestone had the Star of David carved on it, along with the name of the deceased written in Hebrew—all in compliance with the Wehrmacht guidelines.[142]

Jewish clergy—Rabbis—were obviously not part of these ceremonies; this was in fact raised by the Swiss Protecting Power in their visit to Stalag VIII-B (Lamsdorf) in March 1943, reporting that Jewish POWs who died in the labour detachments were buried without funerals since there were no 'rabbins [sic]' available. They probably meant that the funerals were held without a religious ceremony; the commandant accepted the Christian padres' proposal to officiate these funerals in the future.[143] In another case, the SAO in the Center Compound of Stalag Luft III (Sagan), Colonel Delmar Spivey, asked the commandant to arrange for a Rabbi for the Jewish POWs in the camp; interestingly, the commandant did not turn him down on the spot but said that he would look into it. Obviously, nothing came out of this request.[144]

The inconsistency in the approach of the German authorities to funerals of Jewish POWs was also evident in the case of Private Richard Altman, a German Jew who immigrated to Palestine in 1935 and volunteered for the British Army. Altman died in a work accident in Stalag VIII-B's labour detachment E479 in Tarnowitz at the beginning of 1943. The German police officer who came to investigate the accident recognized him as an old school friend of his; it turned out that Altman was born in the town nearby, Gleiwitz, and his parents still lived there. There is no record of the ceremony that took place at his funeral; however, the photos of his grave, taken by the German authorities, clearly show a wreath from his parents, which had an Iron Cross medal, probably awarded to his father in the First World War, attached to it. The photos also show the German army wreath with the Swastika flag on it—which, since Altman would have been

---

[142] Sela, *Shackles of Captivity*, pp. 233–4.
[143] Swiss embassy report on Stalag VIII-B (Lamsdorf), 5 March 1943, p. 7, TNA WO 224/27.
[144] Delmar T. Spivey, *POW Odyssey* (Attleboro, MA: Colonial Lithograph, 1984), p. 77.

considered a German expatriate, was clearly inconsistent with the funeral guidelines for the excluded groups.[145]

These inconsistencies also occurred in the cases of Jewish POWs from other armies, where the caveat related to German expatriate POWs was clearly not relevant. When the first Yugoslav Jewish officer POW in Oflag XIII-B (Nürnberg-Langwasser) died in 1941, his funeral was held in the Jewish cemetery in Nuremberg with ten Jewish officers and ten German officers as an honour guard. One of the Jewish POWs, a Rabbi, said the traditional prayer and a local civilian Jew acted as the cantor. However, a few months later, when another Yugoslav Jewish POW died, there was no longer a German guard of honour. Apparently, the Oflag headquarters decided that Jewish POWs were not entitled to a military funeral anymore.[146] Later, in Oflag VI-C (Osnabrück-Eversheide), for another funeral of a Jewish POW, thirty officer POWs—twelve of them non-Jewish—attended the ceremony, which took place in the Jewish cemetery in Osnabrück; however, no delegates from the Wehrmacht were present.[147] And in a case that turned the captive/captor power struggle on its head, a French Jewish MOC rejected the suggestion of a camp commandant to send a Wehrmacht honour guard to a funeral of a French Jewish POW who was killed while trying to escape. Since the POW was shot without warning, the MOC argued, he did not want German soldiers present at his funeral. The funeral took place without the guard of honour but the MOC was relieved of his role.[148] In a similar case, four French Jewish doctors in Stalag XVII-B (Gneixendorf) were sent to treat Soviet POWs who suffered from typhoid; although the German staff was vaccinated against the disease, the Jewish doctors were not and when one of them, Dr Rosenberg, contracted the disease and died, the POWs refused the offer of the camp commandant to send guard of honour to his funeral.[149]

The case for captured RAF and American airmen was different: in 1943, Hitler issued an order that airmen POWs who died should be buried without a military funeral. Major Gustav Simoleit, the deputy commandant of Stalag Luft III (Sagan), ignored that order when a POW who was injured while trying to escape died of his wounds. Despite finding out that the POW was in fact Jewish, Simoleit, against Hitler's orders, insisted on proceeding with a full military funeral, while concealing the POW's religion even from the Catholic priest who administered last rites.[150] In another case in the same camp, scripture from the Old Testament

---

[145] IDF 12/120/2004. According to Julius Green, a British POW who hid his Jewish identity and was the dental officer of Stalag VIII-B (Lamsdorf), the policeman recognized Altman as his officer from the First World War and saluted the body; however, since Altman was only 12 when the First World War had ended, this was obviously only a rumour (see Green, *From Colditz in Code*, p. 115).

[146] Asaria-Helfgot, *We Are Witnesses*, pp. 37–8.   [147] Ibid., p. 47.

[148] *Le Combattant Volontaire Juif 1939–1945*, p. 61.

[149] Jean Moret-Bailly, 'Le Camp de Base du Stalag XVII B', *Revue d'histoire de la Deuxième Guerre Mondial*, 25 (1957), pp. 7–45, p. 30.

[150] Durand, *Stalag Luft III*, p. 307.

was read as part of the military funeral that was given to an American Jewish POW who died.[151] It seems that military funerals for captured airmen continued in the following years despite Hitler's orders; the only difference was that in order not to attract the attention of the local population, who harboured resentment towards the airmen due to the ongoing bombardments, the customary volley was no longer allowed.[152]

Issues with funerals of non-Jewish POWs existed as well; however, they were not as numerous as those that occurred with regard to the Jewish ones and usually involved minor matters. In one case, when Gunner Henry Crew, a British POW in Stalag VIII-B, was buried on 28 December 1943, the MOC of his labour detachment, E552 (Hindenberg Philipstr), complained that proper procedures were not fully followed—for example, the hearse carried bodies of POWs from other nationalities together with Crew's body. This resulted in an immediate complaint by Stalag VIII-B's MOC to both the ICRC and the Protecting Power and an investigation by the camp's authorities. The commandant at the time of Stalag VIII-B (Lamsdorf), Kapitan zur See Gylek, summarized the outcome of the investigation that followed by issuing a reprimand to the guard company in charge of E552 and emphasized the need for strict adherence to funeral guidelines.[153]

To summarize, when it came to funerals, Jewish POWs expected and insisted that their deceased brethren would be treated in the same manner as members of other religions who died in captivity. After all, the main purpose of the religion designation on a soldier's identification discs was to ensure that if he died his body would be treated in accordance with the customs and rituals of his religion. In some cases, the Wehrmacht, in an act of clear discrimination towards Jewish POWs and in breach of the spirit (although not the letter) of the Geneva Convention, allowed the Jewish rituals to take place but refused to conduct a full military funeral. The religion of the deceased and the personal beliefs of the commandants clearly played a part in the way that funerals of American and British Jewish POWs were conducted; discrimination in funerals, however, stood in contrast with the general overall treatment of American and British Jewish POWs, who usually were not discriminated against or mistreated. Even more surprising is the fact that when cases of discrimination did occur, they were usually the result of an initiative by individual guards or civilians, and not the result of an official policy dictated from above; however, in some of the cases of funerals of Jewish POWs, the order not to conduct them in accordance with military custom was clearly issued by vigilant camp authorities who either decided to follow the OKW's funeral guidelines to the letter (in the case of German expatriates) or to

---

[151] Spivey, *POW Odyssey*, p. 78.
[152] Swiss embassy report on Stalag Luft III (Sagan), 22 February 1944, TNA WO 224/63A.
[153] Beerdigung des Brit. Kgf. Crew, Henry, 19 January 1944, PMA 191/1/44.

follow their own anti-Semitic beliefs. The examples above demonstrate that even when such an order was overturned by the OKW—which on occasion appears to have acted in breach of its own guidelines—camp authorities still did not always issue the necessary orders to conduct the funeral with full military honours. The decentralized structure of the POW organization might provide one explanation for this occurrence: while the POW Office was responsible for issuing camp commandants with regulations related to the treatment of POWs, the commandants themselves reported to the POW commanders in their military districts, and not to the POW Office; this allowed them to have a degree of autonomy in implementing these regulations without suffering any consequences.

OKW guidelines did not forbid funerals of Jewish POWs from having Jewish symbols and ceremonies; in the cases described above, the confrontations with the Jewish POWs were always around the military aspects of the funeral, which the German authorities in some cases refused to allow. For the Jewish POWs, these confrontations were therefore not about the religious aspects of their Jewish identity and the right to demonstrate it in public, but about fighting for equal treatment from the German authorities as Jews—and part of the continuous power struggle between captive and captor.

Conclusion

> When we were captured...we were...very different in terms of our attitude to religion, to Jewish nationalism, to Zionism. We differed from each other in origin [,] social status, and even in the...language we spoke. [But] despite the different categories to which we belonged, the Nazis had their own standard by which we were simply classified: to them we were all Jews.[154]

This is how a Yugoslav Jewish Officer POW described the impact Nazi captivity had on the identity of his fellow Jewish POWs; whatever differences they had among them before they became POWs had now been erased by their captors. Captivity had accentuated their Jewish identity; and for Jewish POWs to be able to maintain and even display aspects of this identity in German POW camps while, in parallel and across Europe, their Detaining Power was executing the 'Final Solution to the Jewish Question', seemed to be a complete contradiction. And yet, due to the Geneva Convention and the Wehrmacht's general adherence to it when it came to POWs from western armies, there were cases where American and British Jewish POWs—in fact, non-Soviet Jewish POWs in

---

[154] Lebl, *Jewish Soldiers from Yugoslavia as POWs in Nazi Germany*, p. 29.

general—were able to do just that. It was not always done in public, and in some cases the Protecting Power and the ICRC had to intervene and force the Wehrmacht to agree to it; nonetheless, in German POW camps during the Second World War, there were cases where Jewish POWs were able to celebrate their Holy days, display their national identity as Palestinian Jews, conduct funerals according to the Jewish rituals, and, in a demonstration of Jewish transnational identity, help their starving European Jewish brethren under the watchful eyes of their SA and SS guards.

The main components of the Jewish identity—ethnicity, culture, religion, and in some cases nationality—were not necessarily aligned. As Harry Levy, a British Jewish RAF Sergeant whose plane was shot down over Belgium in 1942, described it, 'Although an Englishman by birth, by language, by education and culture, I was tied by ancestry to the long, proud history of the Jewish people'.[155] When it came to Jews, religion and ethnicity were usually considered one and the same in this period; however, most Jewish soldiers were not religious, and for them being Jewish had more to do with their Jewish culture and the history of the Jewish people, and less with a religious belief. The Palestinian Jewish POWs were the only group that came close to aligning together these components of the soldier's identity; yet for American and British Jewish soldiers the act of joining the military was in most cases not necessarily driven by their Jewish identity, but demonstrated the strengthening of their national one and of their loyalty to the state.[156] At the time, their Jewish ethnicity and religion were not viewed as the main part of their identity.

The Second World War changed that. What for most of the Jewish soldiers prior to the war was a personal matter that was displayed on the soldier's identification disc and paybook and sometimes celebrated in family gatherings, became, once in POW camps and given the German attitude towards Jews, the overriding element of their identity; whether it was hidden or not, it had become something that, in the POW's mind, might have meant the difference between proper treatment and mistreatment, or even worse—the difference between life and death. Some Jewish soldiers addressed this issue when they joined the army by registering a different religion or changing their names; others removed all mention of their religion when the inevitability of becoming POWs dawned on them. Given the long list of uncertainties which was associated with German captivity, having one less to deal with seemed at the time to be a logical decision. And yet there was a third group who kept their Jewish identity in captivity; in addition to American and British Jewish POWs, this group included the Palestinian Jewish POWs who

---

[155] Harry Levy, *The Dark Side of the Sky* (London: Leo Cooper, 1996), ln. 3501.
[156] For example, for American Jews see Moore, *GI Jews*, pp. 31 and 35. German and Austrian Jewish refugees who fled to Britain, while still seeking revenge on the Nazis, joined the army mainly to 'prove their undivided loyalty to England' (see Kern, *Jewish Refugees from Germany and Austria in the British Army, 1939–45*, p. 89).

volunteered for the British army not necessarily for patriotic reasons but mostly for other ideological—and sometimes economic—ones. Those who hid their Jewish identity were sometimes confronted with that dilemma again when, in several POW camps, the authorities attempted to segregate Jewish POWs from their non-Jewish comrades. Inner struggles regarding self-betrayal, a soldier's dignity and the meaning of Jewish identity, combined with the concern for their ultimate fate, made these dilemmas almost unbearable.

The German approach towards the demonstration of Jewish identity was inconsistent; ironically, this meant that in some cases, Nazi POW camps had become one of the very few spaces in occupied Europe where it was possible for Jews to demonstrate their ethnic and religious identity in public with pride. In some cases they allowed celebrations of Jewish Holy days, and there were even recorded cases of commandants greeting Jewish POWs on the eve of the Jewish New Year.[157] In other cases the POWs had to protest in order to get permission to celebrate their Holy days; but there were also cases where Jewish POWs celebrated these days in secret.[158] When it came to funerals, however, although the display of Jewish religious symbols was not challenged, Jewish POWs in some cases had to protest, not always successfully, in order to receive a full military funeral; some commandants refused to allow it, either relying on a list of exceptions from the POW Office's funeral guidelines or expressing their own anti-Semitic beliefs. These inconsistencies were to some extent similar to those that appeared in the implementation of the segregation order, which, as described in Chapter 3, camp commandants chose to ignore in the majority of cases that involved American and British Jewish POWs. It is possible that had the Jewish POWs insisted on their right to conduct religious activities—in the same way that the Palestinian Jewish POWs had—and with the support of the ICRC and the Protecting Power, they would have been allowed to do so; however, it is more likely that Jewish POWs in most POW camps, without a Rabbi to facilitate such events and well aware of the risks involved, decided to keep a low profile and preferred to celebrate such events in secrecy or not at all. Eventually, however, as the cases described in this chapter show, the Nazi obsession with eradicating all signs of Judaism in their sphere of influence was not total; the walls of the POW camps were able, in some cases, to thwart it.

The act of maintaining a POW's Jewish identity in a German POW camp was first and foremost an act of defiance. Although at that time Jewish POWs might not have known about the fate of the European Jews, they were certainly aware of Germany's anti-Semitic policies and its prejudicial treatment of Jewish civilians.

---

[157] See, for example, Glantz, *Struggle in Captivity*, pp. 111–12; Asaria-Helfgot, *We Are Witnesses*, pp. 82–3.

[158] For POW protests see, for example, test in German captivity, July 1945, p. 67, IDF 182/1867/1998. For celebration in secret see, for example, LaCroix, *Journey Out of Darkness*, p. 119.

A Jewish POW's decision not to hide his Jewish identity when captured, to celebrate Jewish Holy days in secrecy or in public, to appear at the national days of other nations as a representative of a Jewish state that did not yet exist, or to extend help to his suffering Jewish brethren—these were all heroic acts which could have carried serious consequences. But as one of the leaders of the Palestinian Jewish POWs, Sergeant Haim Glovinsky, the MOC of Stalag VIII-B's labour detachment E207 in Ehrenforst, explained after the war: 'we were not scared [to do that] because we had nothing to lose'.[159]

---

[159] Test in German captivity, July 1945, p. 50, IDF 182/1867/1998.

3
Segregation of American and British Jewish POWs

Introduction

'We are all Jews' declared Master Sergeant Roddie Edmonds, the MOC of Stalag IX-A near Ziegenhain in western Germany. He was standing in front of a formation of approximately 1,000 American POWs; the camp commandant was standing in front of him, threatening him with a pistol. It was January 1945 and on the previous day the commandant had issued an order demanding that all Jewish POWs report to him in order to be separated from the rest. In response, Master Sergeant Edmonds instructed the American POWs—Jews and non-Jews alike—to stand outside their barracks, and when the commandant insisted 'they cannot be all Jews', Edmonds repeated, 'We are all Jews...if you shoot me, you'll have to shoot all of us'. The commandant gave up.[1]

Following on from the previous chapters, which dealt with the captivity experience of American and British Jewish POWs and with the behaviour of their immediate captors towards them, this chapter will look into the behaviour of the level above, that of the POW camp commandants and of their superiors, the POW commanders in the military districts; specifically, it will analyse the way that they implemented the order to segregate American and British Jewish POWs. This chapter will show that when it came to Jewish POWs from these armies, segregations were not common, and will offer several explanations for that; one of which, as described above, was that some of the segregations failed due to the strong resistance of fellow POWs and the leadership of the MOCs. For his bravery, Master Sergeant Edmonds was recognized in 2015 by Yad Vashem as Righteous Among the Nations, a commendation given to non-Jews for risking their lives in order to rescue Jews during the Holocaust.[2]

Segregation was the first step in Germany's persecution of Europe's civilian Jews; this was followed by their deportation and eventually, their extermination. Given its obsession with making Europe '*Judenrein*', segregation of Jewish POWs

---

[1] Chris Edmonds and Douglas Century, *No Surrender* (Digital Edition: HarperOne, 2019), pp. 227–30; see also 'We Are All Jews', YVA http://www.yadvashem.org/righteous/stories/edmonds, accessed 15 October 2017.

[2] Ibid.

from their non-Jewish comrades—although in the case of non-Soviet Jewish POWs, this did not lead to their murder—was expected to occur in Second World War Germany. The segregation was also deemed to be acceptable by, among others, the ICRC and the Protecting Power; incredibly, the latter even referred to the placement of British Jewish and non-Jewish POWs together in the same barracks as a breach of the Geneva Convention and as a form of German punishment against the POWs.[3]

The first cases of segregation of Jewish POWs in German POW camps occurred shortly after the beginning of the Polish campaign in 1939, when the first Polish Jewish soldiers had been captured.[4] The Einsatzgruppen, operating behind the advancing troops, were carrying out systematic murder of the Polish intelligentsia, clergy, and political leadership; and the general treatment of Polish POWs by the Wehrmacht was in many cases also brutal.[5] This treatment included the separation of Jewish POWs from their non-Jewish comrades and their abuse by their captors.[6] The POW segregation policy continued after the conclusion of the French and Yugoslavian campaigns, when French and Yugoslav Jewish POWs were in most cases separated from non-Jewish POWs and housed in the 'Judenbaracke'.[7]

The potential consequences of these segregations became apparent during the invasion of the Soviet Union in June 1941, when the Wehrmacht actively helped Heydrich's Einsatzgruppen to identify and execute commissars and Jewish POWs.[8] However, when it came to the first British and American Jewish soldiers who became POWs—during the French campaign in 1940 (the British) and the North Africa and bombing campaigns in 1942 (the Americans)—this chapter will show that the same segregation policy was not fully adhered to. This study has found that throughout the war, there were eleven successful segregation cases of American and British Jewish POWs—a relatively small number compared with the number of POW camps where American and British POWs were held during the Second World War, which varied between 134 (during the early years of the

---

[3] Minutes from the meeting between Melas and Pilloud, 17 October 1941, ACICR BG 17 05/146; Swiss embassy report on Stalag 319 (Cholm), 9 January 1943, p. 5, TNA WO 224/52. For the Geneva Convention's segregation Article see the next section.

[4] Datner, *Crimes against POWs*, pp. 99–107; Krakowski, 'The Fate of Jewish Prisoners of War in the September 1939 Campaign', p. 305. Polish Jewish POWs held by Hungary were segregated in the following year (see testimony of Roman Shtil, YVA O.3-1402).

[5] Alexander Rossino, *Hitler Strikes Poland* (Lawrence, KS: University Press of Kansas, 2003), pp. 10 and 179–85.

[6] JTA, 27 October 1940, https://www.jta.org/archive, accessed 8 May 2019.

[7] ICRC to American Red Cross, 24 April 1941, ACICR BG 25/34, and JTA, 18 November 1941, https://www.jta.org/archive, accessed 8 May 2019; German Foreign Office representative in Belgrade to Berlin, 26 November 1941, PAAA R40960; Durand, *La Captivité*, p. 354; *Le Combattant Volontaire Juif 1939–1945*, pp. 44, 64; Asaria-Helfgot, *We Are Witnesses*, p. 32; testimony of Vladimir Mautner, YVA O.3-6645 p. 19.

[8] Streit, 'The German Army and the Policies of Genocide', p. 4.

war) and fifty-two (in 1945).[9] These cases usually involved placing the Jewish POWs in separate barracks within the camp while continuing to treat them in the same way as the non-Jewish POWs. Other cases, like the one described at the beginning of this chapter, failed due to the strong resistance of fellow POWs and the leadership of the MOCs. The majority of segregation cases occurred towards the end of the war, and were more likely to have been driven by the transfer of the responsibility for the POW Office from the OKW to Himmler's Replacement Army and to SS General Gottlob Berger on 1 October 1944, and to the enforcement of the existing segregation orders, rather than the issuing and implementation of new ones.

This chapter initially describes the Wehrmacht's framework of regulations that was behind the segregation of Jewish POWs, along with the relevant Articles in the 1929 Geneva Convention; it then reviews examples of segregation of American and British Jewish POWs during two phases of the war—at its beginning and during its final months. It also describes the ways in which Jewish POWs were accounted for in POW camps, and the reaction of international bodies—governments, the ICRC, and Jewish organizations—when news about cases of segregation reached them. The following pages demonstrate that when it came to American and British Jewish POWs, the clear orders that were issued by the Wehrmacht from the start of the conflict regarding segregation of Jewish POWs—orders that were repeated during the last stages of the war—were only followed by a relatively small number of camp commandants. This suggests that there was a level of heterogeneity within the POW organization structure when it came to the implementation of Nazi policies which enabled camp commandants to decide whether or not to implement certain policies without suffering any consequences. Potential reasons for disobeying these orders include under-estimation of the number of Jewish POWs, difficulty in identifying them, concern about the reaction of non-Jewish POWs, and, as described in Chapter 4 of this book and especially towards the end of the war, self-preservation and the fear of retribution in the hands of the Allies.

Segregation in the Geneva Convention and OKW Orders

Article 9 of the Geneva Convention allowed—in fact, encouraged—the Detaining Power to 'as far as possible avoid assembling in a single camp prisoners of different races or nationalities'.[10] This racially driven Article was inserted into the

---

[9] The number of POW camps is stated in Vourkoutiotis, *Prisoners of War and the German High Command*, p. 31. According to Neville Wylie, in early 1945 the number of principal POW camps holding American and British POWs was fifty-two (see Wylie, *Barbed Wire Diplomacy*, p. 224).
[10] Article 9 of the 1929 Geneva Convention, https://ihl-databases.icrc.org/ihl/INTRO/305, accessed 14 September 2019. Article 9 is the only place in the Convention where the term 'race' appears.

Convention at the insistence of Britain and the USA in order to avoid the situations that occurred in POW camps in Germany during the First World War: Germany, who saw the participation of troops from the colonies in the war in Europe as an 'affront to civilization', had retaliated by placing European and colonial POWs together in the same camps.[11] The British threatened to do the same to German POWs by housing them together with Ottoman troops, and the German order was quickly reversed. This, together with the typhus outbreak that spread in 1915 in German POW camps, which the Germans blamed on Russian POWs who were housed with French and British POWs, caused Britain and the USA to demand that a specific Article, encouraging national and racial segregation of POWs, be inserted into the 1929 Geneva Convention.[12] The purpose of the Article was to protect POWs from living with people who were alien to them—even if they belonged to the same army—and did not share the same customs, culture, and even hygiene habits.[13] At that time, however, the drafters of the Convention clearly meant for the term 'race' to refer to the POW's skin colour, and not according to the definition of the Nazi racial doctrine; for them, race was a category that, similar to nationality, 'meaningfully subdivided humanity'.[14] As Rüdiger Overmans has noted, 'Exact definitions of previously unquestioned concepts would have been useful'.[15] As it happens, this insistence on segregation by race and nationality had another consequence: since it contradicted the principle of internationalism, it was one of the reasons the Soviet Union refused to ratify the Geneva Convention, a refusal which was later used by Germany as an excuse for removing the Convention's protection from Soviet POWs. This was, however, in breach of Article 82 of the Convention, which stated that a signatory to the Convention had to apply its rules to non-signatory belligerents such as the Soviet Union.[16]

It is interesting to note that towards the end of the war, when the WJC challenged the ICRC to change its non-intervention policy in cases of segregation, the ICRC chose to defend its position based on Article 4 of the Convention, rather than Article 9. Article 4 permitted differences in treatment of POWs based on categories such as rank, health, or gender, however race or nationality were not part of them. The ICRC argued that it did not have the legal justification for

---

[11] Schroer, 'The Emergence and Early Demise of Codified Racial Segregation', pp. 57–8.
[12] Jones, *Violence against Prisoners of War in the First World* War, p. 104; Schroer, 'The Emergence and Early Demise of Codified Racial Segregation', pp. 59, 71.
[13] Ibid., p. 75.
[14] For the use of race to denote skin colour see, for example, AA to OKW, 12 June 1941, PAAA R40717; for the meaning of race in the Geneva Convention see French POW Ministry to the German Foreign Office, 19 October 1944, ACICR BG 25/34; and Santanu Das, *Race, Empire and First World War Writing* (Cambridge: Cambridge University Press, 2011), p. 10. The quote is in Schroer, 'The Emergence and Early Demise of Codified Racial Segregation', p. 76.
[15] Overmans, 'Die Kriegsgefangenenpolitik des Deutschen Reichs 1939 bis 1945', p. 872.
[16] Shneyer, *Pariahs among Pariahs*, p. 25.

intervening since the treatment of the segregated Jewish POWs was the same as non-Jewish ones and therefore it did not breach the Convention.[17]

The nationality and race segregation guidelines issued by the Wehrmacht before the start of the Polish campaign—guidelines that were also in effect during the invasion of the Soviet Union—were clearly driven by the need to comply with the Geneva Convention, as Article 9 was mentioned several times by the OKW and the German Foreign Office as the reason for separating POWs.[18] In a letter to the OKW on 31 December 1940 the German Foreign Office suggested that segregation in general should be implemented not only in order to comply with the Geneva Convention, but also for reasons that 'have been discussed verbally'—which may point to more cynical reasons than the simple adherence to the Convention, and perhaps even to the pre-planning of the Special Treatment of certain groups of POWs.[19] In the West, however, although American and British POWs were kept in separate barracks, and the Germans did segregate French colonial, non-colonial, and French Jewish POWs from each other, there are no records of the Germans segregating American POWs up between African-Americans, Hispanic, and white; nor of British POWs being segregated into Welsh, Scottish, and English.[20] The OKW confirmed as much in a letter to ICRC's delegate in Berlin on 24 March 1942, stating that it did not intend to separate British POWs by ethnicity or nationality; however, it is likely that this statement did not apply to Jewish POWs since the Germans referred to Jews as a 'race', 'Rasse', and not as a separate nationality.[21]

The segregation of Jewish POWs during the Polish campaign followed the guidelines of the 'Commandant Instructions Manual' that was issued by the OKW on 16 February 1939, before the beginning of the war, which required camp commandants to segregate POWs upon arrival according to their nationality, 'race' and gender—again, in line with Article 9 of the Geneva Convention mentioned above.[22] Testimonies given by Polish Jewish POWs who escaped during the war and by others after the war indicate that the segregation order was

---

[17] Burkhardt to WJC, 5 April 1945, USHMM RG-68.045M Acc. 2004.507, reel 54, document 416.
[18] See, for example, OKW to German Foreign Office, 25 August 1942, PAAA R40985; German Foreign Office to OKW, 10 June 1943, PAAA R40720; and Georges Scapini, *Mission sans Gloire* (Paris: Morgan, 1960), p. 191.
[19] German Foreign Office to OKW, 31 December 1940, PAAA R40713.
[20] Scheck, *French Colonial Soldiers in German Captivity*, pp. 53–4.
[21] Marti to ICRC, 19 May 1942, ACICR BG 17 05/11. For OKW references to Jews as race, see, for example, Zusammenfassung aller Bestimmungen über den Arbeitseinsatz wiederergriffener und Arbeitsverweigender Kr. Gef., 2659/42, 10 August 1942, PMA 31/1/6, and 2692/44, 12 June 1944, PMA 744/1/30.
[22] Dienstanweisung für den Kommandanten eines 'Kriegsgefangenen Mannschafts Stammlagers', 16 February 1939, p. 11, BA-MA RH 1/612. Similar guidelines issued to Dulag commandants only required them to segregate POWs by officers, ORs and nationality (see Dienstanweisung für den Kommandanten eines Kriegsgefangenen Durchgangslagers, 22 May 1939, p. 11, BA-MA RH 1/611).

in most case adhered to.²³ The order was also in effect throughout the French campaign in the following year, and was applied to French Jewish, and in some cases British Jewish, POWs as well as to black French colonial troops.²⁴

The OKW confirmed this policy in a meeting with representatives of the ICRC in May 1941, just before the invasion of the Soviet Union, stating that Jewish POWs 'may be placed in special barracks' but insisting that their treatment would be identical to that of non-Jewish POWs.²⁵ As mentioned in Chapter 1, a few weeks later, on 11 June 1941, the German Foreign Office, probably filling a policy gap it had assumed existed regarding the treatment of Jewish POWs, proposed to the POW Office to send the ~1,500 Palestinian Jewish POWs that had been recently captured in Greece to perform military works in the Balkan Peninsula, in a clear breach of the Geneva Convention.²⁶ There is no record of the OKW response to this proposal, but given that most of the Palestinian Jewish POWs ended up in a POW camp in Germany, together with their non-Jewish comrades, it was obviously not accepted. Only a few days later, on 16 June 1941, the POW Office issued order number 7, titled 'Jews in the French Army', which formally clarified this matter by stating that 'there is no intention to place Jewish [POWs] in special camps. However, all French Jewish POWs in Stalags and Oflags should be separated within the POW camps.... Special labelling of Jews is to be foreseen'.²⁷ The last sentence was a reference to an order that would be issued a few months later, on 1 September 1941, by Heydrich; the order instructed all civilian Jews from the age of six in areas directly under German control (such as Germany, Austria, the annexed territories in Poland, and the Protectorate of Bohemia and Moravia) to wear the yellow badge ('*Judenstern*') in public.²⁸ The POW Office's order indicated that the OKW might have been aware of Heydrich's intention to issue the later order and wanted to prepare the camp commandants for it; in at least one case, in Stalag IV-B (Mühlberg), French Jewish POWs were made to wear the *Judenstern* shortly after this order was issued.²⁹

However, the OKW order regarding the identification of Jewish POWs was reversed nine months later, in March 1942: under the title 'Marking of Jews' ('*Kennzeichnen der Juden*'), the new order now referred to all Jewish POWs and stated that unlike civilian Jews, who were marked in order to make them

---

²³ JTA, 17 November 1939 and 27 October 1940, https://www.jta.org/archive, accessed 8 May 2019; Krakowski, 'The Fate of Jewish Prisoners of War in the September 1939 Campaign', p. 305.

²⁴ Intelligence report, 30 June 1943, NARA RG 39, box 942, 270/5/3/1; *Jewish Chronicle* (JC), 14 November 1941, pp. 22–3, https://www.thejc.com/archive, accessed 16 June 2019.

²⁵ Descoeudres to ICRC, 23 May 1941, ACICR BG 25/34. This was confirmed again in December 1941 in a meeting between Scapini, the French ambassador who was responsible for French POWs, and Reinecke (see Scapini, *Mission sans Gloire*, p. 193).

²⁶ Dr Albrecht to Major Stacke of the POW Office, 11 June 1941, PAAA R40741.

²⁷ Sammelmitteilungen 1, order 7, 16 June 1941, BA-MA RW 6/270. For a detailed discussion regarding the POW Office's orders, see Chapter 4 of this book.

²⁸ Polizeiverordnung über die Kennzeichnung der Juden, 1 September 1941, BA R 70-Polen/220.

²⁹ *Le Combattant Volontaire Juif 1939–1945*, p. 71.

identifiable in public, there was no intention to have special labelling for Jewish POWs. However, they 'should, as far as possible, be separated from the other prisoners of war'.[30] Interestingly, the same order summary that included the 'Marking of Jews' order also included a notification to all recipients of these summaries regarding the OKW's intention to distribute a book called 'Law of Land Warfare' ('*Recht der Landkriegsführung*') to all POW camps and labour detachments.[31] The book, written by Dr Alfons Waltzog, a senior Luftwaffe field judge, provided an article by article commentary on three international conventions related to POWs: the 1907 Hague Convention respecting the Laws and Customs of War on Land, the 1929 Geneva Convention relative to the treatment of POWs, and the 1929 Geneva Convention for the Amelioration of the Condition of the Wounded and Sick in Armies in the Field. The book was described by the OKW as 'particularly suitable for the use of prisoner-of-war camps and the other departments dealing with the treatment of prisoners of war' and seems to have been an attempt by the OKW to provide additional clarification to the somewhat dry legal language of the conventions.[32] Specifically, in his comments on Article 9 of the Geneva Convention, Waltzog explained that although 'those who fight together...cannot demand to be separated in captivity', since 'the Jews are a special race, they can be grouped in special camps'; and that 'Separation from other prisoners of war in the same camp and their separate work is also permitted'.[33] Waltzog's interpretation was, in fact, more in compliance with the Convention, which stated that POWs from different races and nationalities should be housed in separate camps—and not, as was the case with mainly Polish, French, and Yugoslav Jewish POWs, in the same camp but in different barracks.

The specific orders to segregate Jewish POWs within the camps might have been an attempt by the POW Office to counter demands by the RSHA to hand them over in order, as the RSHA claimed, to ensure they did not interact with the German population.[34] Although their segregation within the camps did not necessarily solve this issue, it was argued after the war by General Westhoff, the head of the POW Office until October 1944, that his superior, General Reinecke, well aware of the fate of the Soviet Jewish POWs (for which he was partly responsible), might have issued these instructions in order to 'take the wind out of the RSHA's sails'.[35]

At the end of 1944, after SS General Gottlob Berger became the head of the POW Office, another order was issued. Published on 15 December 1944, the order was unambiguously titled 'Treatment of Jewish POWs' and after referencing the previous orders provided additional clarification: specifically, it stated again that there was no intention to concentrate Jewish POWs in special camps; that

---

[30] Befehlssammlung 11, order 5, 11 March 1942, BA-MA RW 6/270.   [31] Order 22, ibid.
[32] Ibid.   [33] Waltzog, *Recht der Landkriegsführung*, pp. 124–5.
[34] Westhoff affidavit, 15 January 1966, BA-MA MSG 2/12655.   [35] Ibid.

Jewish POWs should be housed separately from non-Jewish POWs and as far as possible sent to work outside the camps; and that now there was again an intention to mark Jewish POWs with special labelling. However, two important changes were made to this order: the words 'as far as possible', which were included in the March 1942 order and allowed camp commandants some latitude in implementing the segregation, were removed; and a statement was added, according to which 'Jewish POWs should be treated in the same way non-Jewish POWs of the respective army are treated'—basically, prohibiting discrimination towards Jewish POWs.[36]

POW Camps under the Wehrmacht: Initial Segregation Cases

The first encounters between the Wehrmacht and British Jewish POWs occurred in June 1940, shortly after the start of the French campaign. The OKW's orders regarding segregation were those that had been in effect during the campaign against Poland in the previous year, however unlike the case of Polish and French POWs, their implementation in the case of British Jewish POWs did not seem to have been as strict: towards the end of the introductory speech by Colonel Bornemann, the commandant of Stalag VIII-B (Lamsdorf), to a newly arrived group of British POWs who were captured in France, he ordered all Jewish POWs to step forward. Only one obeyed; and when another Jewish POW, Corporal Alec Jay, tried to join him he was held down by two of his non-Jewish comrades. The Germans did not make any attempt to identify other Jewish POWs and Jay believed that the one who did come forward was interned with the segregated French Jewish POWs.[37] Another British POW, William Harding, described a more determined attempt to identify Jews when he arrived in Stalag VIII-B in June 1940: since the Germans were not satisfied with the number of Jewish POWs who stepped forward, 'we were then ordered to drop our trousers and lift our shirts, were looked at and anyone seen to be circumcised were [sic] taken away'.[38] It is possible that they, too, were placed with the segregated French Jewish POWs, although there is no specific evidence to support that. Although circumcision tests became a standard practice in the East in the following year, this in fact was the only case found where such a test was used in the West as part of the POWs' arrival process.[39] In addition to identifying Jewish POWs and humiliating them

---

[36] Befehlssammlung 48, order 876, 15 December 1944, BA-MA RW 6/270.
[37] Jay, *Facing Fearful Odds*, ln. 2356; ibid., ln. 84.   [38] W. A. Harding, IWM 82/27/1, p. 10.
[39] Interrogation of Reinecke, 23 October 1945, https://www.fold3.com/image/1/231936059, pp. 19–20, accessed 1 October 2019; Pavel Polian, 'First Victims of the Holocaust: Soviet-Jewish Prisoners of War in German Captivity', *Kritika: Explorations in Russian and Eurasian History*, 6:4 (2005), pp. 763–87, p. 786. Circumcision tests for individual soldiers, intended more for humiliation than for identification, were probably more common (*Le Combattant Volontaire Juif 1939–1945*, p. 41).

in public, the German captors saw this, no doubt, as a way of intimidating all POWs and destroying the self-respect and self-confidence of men who only a few days earlier had been proud soldiers fighting for their country. The main reason for using such methods mainly in the East had to do with the Nazi racism, which viewed Slavs, but not the Anglo-Saxons, as an inferior race: the latter were viewed in most cases as honourable foes that should be respected, which might explain the limited number of such incidents in the West.

A segregation that occurred in the following year was recounted in the memoirs of Palestinian Jewish POWs who were captured in Greece. On their way to the permanent POW camps in Germany the POWs were held for several weeks in two POW camps, Stalag XVIII-A (Wolfsberg in Austria) and Stalag XVIII-D (Marburg an der Drau). French Jewish POWs in this military district had already been segregated in the '*Judenbaracke*' since their capture; at the end of 1940 they were sent, together with other non-Aryan POWs, to POW camps in France in order to make the district '*reinrassig*' (racially pure).[40] The Palestinian Jews, arriving several months later, were also segregated from the rest and housed in separate accommodation. Although reports from these camps by the ICRC and the Protecting Power stated that they received the same treatment as the other POWs (the Protecting Power report also mentioned that Red Cross arm bands were taken from, and later returned to, Palestinian Jewish medics), POWs' memoirs indicated differently: their hut in Stalag XVIII-D (Marburg an der Drau) was the one used to house POWs who were not yet deloused and vaccinated; they were forced to sleep on the concrete floor without mattresses; and they were badly treated by the German guards.[41] In addition, at first they were not allowed to go out with the labour detachments (although this changed towards the end of their stay in the camp), and those in Marburg—about 600—were not even allowed contact with other British and Australian POWs. Their concerns were somewhat alleviated when, six weeks after their arrival, representatives of the ICRC visited the camp and registered them.[42] In the meantime, rumours started to circulate that special badges with the word '*Jude*' were being prepared in the camp nearby, and that the prisoners would soon be forced to wear them.[43] In parallel, POWs' complaints to the camp authorities on being called '*Jude*' by the guards went unanswered.[44]

The attempt to mark Jewish POWs—if the rumours were true—did not seem to be the result of an official policy, since the existing OKW order, which was

---

[40] Ibid., p. 59.
[41] ICRC report on Stalag XVIII-D (Marburg an der Drau), 21 July 1941, TNA FO 916/25; Swiss embassy report on Stalag XVIII-A (Wolfsberg), 26 August 1941, TNA WO 224/45; Glantz, *Struggle in Captivity*, pp. 84–6, 89.
[42] Test in German captivity, July 1945, pp. 36–7, IDF 182/1867/1998.
[43] Glantz, *Struggle in Captivity*, p. 88; Haim Glovinsky, 'Four Years', *The Volunteering Book*, pp. 659–63, p. 659.
[44] Sela, *Shackles of Captivity*, p. 79.

issued in the same month, referred only to French Jewish POWs and mentioned only an intention to do so in the future.[45] It is important to note that during the same period, a few cases were recorded of French Jewish POWs being marked by a *Judenstern* or simply an 'X'—in one case it was the non-Jewish POWs who forced the Jewish ones to wear it, and the German camp commandant had to intervene to overrule them.[46] In Oflag XIII-B (Nürnberg-Langwasser), however, where Yugoslavian and French officer POWs were held, in February 1942 only the Yugoslavian Jews, and not the French ones, were required to wear the *Judenstern* (the order was rescinded a few months later after the Jewish POWs were segregated in a special barracks).[47] It is therefore more likely that in the case of the Palestinian Jewish POWs, this was the initiative of local camp commandants, who, faced with an unfamiliar and confused situation, had simply adopted the general behaviour and rules that applied to the Jewish civilian population in German-occupied Poland where such markings were already in force (as mentioned earlier, the decree to mark civilian Jews in the German Reich with the Jewish Star was only issued in September 1941, two months after the incident described above had occurred).[48] This case of segregation did not apply to British Jewish POWs, but only to the Palestinian Jews in the British army, who did not—could not—hide their identity; this might lead to the conclusion that the segregation was based, in this case, on nationality rather than on race, although it is quite obvious that the POWs' ethnicity was the main reason for the discrimination they suffered while in those POW camps.

These incidents, with the exception of being accommodated in the disinfection hut, were only mentioned in the memoirs of the Palestinian Jewish POWs, and not in the ICRC and Protecting Power visiting reports. Since the Protecting Power's visit only took place at the end of August 1941, several weeks after the POWs had been transferred, it is possible that the visiting legation was not even made aware of those incidents.[49] However, the ICRC delegates did meet the POWs prior to their transfer and heard their complaints first hand; it must have decided to omit these complaints from its report, either because it wanted to avoid triggering a cycle of reprisals with Britain, or because it knew that this situation was only temporary. Shortly after their visit, at the end of July 1941, the Palestinian Jewish POWs, along with other British POWs, were put on a train and sent to their final destination—Stalag VIII-B near Lamsdorf in Silesia.[50]

---

[45] Sammelmitteilungen 1, order 7, 16 June 1941, BA-MA RW 6/270.
[46] Examples include Stalags IV-B (Mühlberg) and XII-C (Wiebelsheim) (*Le Combattant Volontaire Juif 1939–1945*, pp. 70–1); Durand, *La Captivité*, pp. 354–5.
[47] Asaria-Helfgot, *We Are Witnesses*, pp. 39–41.
[48] Polizeiverordnung über die Kennzeichnung der Juden, 1 September 1941, Bundesarchive R70 Polen/220.
[49] ICRC visit to Stalag XVIII-D (Marburg an der Drau), 21 July 1941, and Swiss embassy report on Stalag XVIII-D (Marburg an der Drau), 25 August 1941, TNA FO 916/25.
[50] Glantz, *Struggle in Captivity*, p. 90.

Nazi Germany's lukewarm attempts to identify and segregate British Jewish POWs during the early stages of the war might explain the fact that other than the anecdotal evidence of segregation incidents found in POWs' memoirs, only one additional officially recorded case of segregation during that period was found in the sources examined for this research. In August 1941, shortly after the Palestinian Jewish POWs had arrived in Stalag VIII-B (Lamsdorf), they were placed in a separate barracks. Interestingly, the segregation issue was raised in October 1941 by the visiting American embassy delegates in their role as the Protecting Power, and not by the representatives of the POWs.[51] It is also interesting to note that unlike the segregations in Stalags XVIII-A (Wolfsberg) and XVIII-D (Marburg an der Drau), which had occurred only a few weeks earlier, there was no mention in any of the Palestinian Jewish POWs' memoirs that they had felt discriminated against by this event. It seems that, similar to the other nationalities, the Palestinian Jews were content to be housed together and did not consider this to be a discriminatory act (towards the end of the war, however, when they became aware of the risk of this self-segregation—mainly due to the concerns at that stage of the German authorities' ability to protect all POWs—they asked the Jewish Agency in Palestine to intervene and reverse the segregation; it is not known whether the Jewish agency eventually intervened, but even if it did, it was obviously not successful).[52] In any case, the camp commandant explained to the Protecting Power delegates, and RSM Sydney Sherriff, the camp's British MOC, supported him, that despite the segregation, the Palestinian Jewish POWs were being treated in exactly the same manner as the other POWs.[53]

The issue clearly was not resolved because two months later, in December 1941, it was raised again during an ICRC visit. In a meeting between the ICRC representatives and the camp's MOCs, a complaint was made that 'the Jews have been separated from their comrades and placed in special Detachments'.[54] It is not clear from the report who raised this issue and why, and whether the terms 'Jews' referred to the Palestinian or British Jewish POWs (or both). Since there was no record of labour detachments consisting solely of British Jewish POWs, it is more likely that this mention of segregation referred to the Palestinian Jews.

The issue was raised one last time on 12 February 1942. During the meeting of the Protecting Power with the POWs' representatives (the Swiss replaced the USA as the Protecting Power after America's entry into the war in December 1941), Sherriff raised the issue of the Palestinian Jews in the main camp being held in a separate compound and not being allowed to communicate with the other prisoners or to attend entertainment activities—although in all other respects they

---

[51] American embassy report on Stalag VIII-B (Lamsdorf), October 1941, p. 10, TNA WO 224/27.
[52] Pinnes to Golda Meirson (the future Prime Minister of Israel), 6 August 1944, CZA J-10/122.
[53] American embassy report on Stalag VIII-B (Lamsdorf), October 1941, p. 10, TNA WO 224/27.
[54] ICRC report on Stalag VIII-B (Lamsdorf), 13 December 1941, p. 6, ibid.

were treated in the same way as the other POWs. Since, during the previous visit in October 1941, Sherriff did not see an issue with the Palestinian Jews being placed in a separate compound, it seems that this time he viewed their inability to communicate with other POWs or to have access to entertainment as discrimination. In response, the newly appointed commandant, Oberst Ritter von Poschinger, who was described by the inspectors as 'very sympathetic and energetic', said that he was not aware of this and promised to change that.[55] The discrimination indeed ended before the next visit of the delegates, three months later, although the Palestinian Jews continued to share the same barracks and the same labour detachments.[56]

It is interesting to note that during the same period, the RAF POWs who were held in the same camp, Stalag VIII-B, had the same complaint: that they were being kept in a separate compound and were not allowed contact with other prisoners. The commandant admitted that the RAF POWs were being treated in a harsher manner than the rest but explained that this was necessary because they had used every opportunity to escape, and in general caused the majority of the problems in the camp.[57] Most of the RAF prisoners were later transferred to the newly created Stalag Luft III in Sagan, which would become famous for multiple escape attempts—including the Great Escape in March 1944.[58]

Additional cases of segregation of American and British Jewish POWs during the early stages of the war came to light mostly in POWs' memoirs and oral histories and demonstrate that segregation was not limited to Stalags, where non-officer POWs were interned. Yitschak Ben-Aharon, who was mentioned in Chapter 1, was one of three Palestinian Jewish officers captured in Greece in April 1941. Some of the British officers who were interned with him were Jewish, but only four of them declared it when captured. When incarcerated in Oflag V-B (near Biberach) the commandant ordered that all Jewish officers in the camp—the three Palestinian (Ben-Aharon, Hacohen, and Gershoni) and the four declared British Jews—be housed in a separate barracks, despite the protests of the camp's Senior British Officer (SBO). Although the segregation did not result any change in the treatment of the Jewish POWs, it was the first time the Germans intervened in the internal affairs of the British officers in that camp; when the officers were moved to another camp, the segregation was forgotten.[59]

Another case of segregation of Jewish officer POWs was recounted by Edward Chapman, a British RAF officer captured in May 1941, who witnessed an attempt

---

[55] Swiss embassy report on Stalag VIII-B (Lamsdorf), 12 February 1942, pp. 6–7, ibid.
[56] Swiss embassy report on Stalag VIII-B (Lamsdorf), 5 May 1942, p. 1, ibid.
[57] Swiss embassy report on Stalag VIII-B (Lamsdorf), 12 February 1942, p. 7, ibid.; Rofe, *Against the Wind*, p. 27.
[58] Swiss embassy report on Stalag VIII-B (Lamsdorf), 5 May 1942, p. 1, TNA WO 224/27.
[59] ICRC to Red Cross Cairo Office, 31 July 1941, CZA S-25/4851; Ben-Aharon, *Pages from the Calendar*, p. 79; Shimon HaCohen, *From German Captivity* (Tel Aviv: Davar, 1943), pp. 55–6.

to separate British Jewish officer POWs in Oflag VI-B in Dössel near Warburg. According to him, the SBO in the camp, General Victor Fortune, strongly objected to it and the Germans did not go forward with their plan.[60] Patrick Denton, another RAF officer interned in the same camp, remembered that the segregation did in fact take place but was called off after a week when the POWs retaliated by giving their captors the silent treatment—'The impact of 2000 odd bods in total silence… unnerved the Germans completely'. A meeting then took place in which the SBO simply 'pushed a piece of paper across which said "Release all Jewish hostages"'. Twenty-four hours later the Jewish POWs were back in the barracks.[61] In another case, when Second Lieutenant Clifford Cohen, who fought with The Black Watch and was captured in the French campaign, stepped forward when the order for Jews to identify themselves was given in Oflag VII-C in Laufen, all the other officers who were with him on parade stepped forward as well. The Germans decided not to take any further action.[62]

In this context, it should be noted that there was at least one known case where the officer POWs themselves demanded that the Jews among them be segregated: in Oflag IV-C—Colditz—the French officers asked the commandant to house the Jewish officers in a different part of the castle; the Germans were obviously happy to accept their request, although Jewish officer POWs from other nations were not segregated.[63] During the same period, despite the OKW order regarding its intention not to place French Jewish POWs in separate camps, its approach towards their segregation became even stricter.[64] In a letter to the German Foreign Office in September 1941 it argued that the segregation of French Jewish POWs within the same camp is no longer sufficient: not only were the Jewish POWs still rejected by the non-Jewish POWs, but the in-camp segregation did not prevent them from spreading propaganda that impacted 'the good elements' in the camp.[65] The OKW's suggestion was to segregate the French Jewish POWs—or 'at least the officers'—in a separate POW camp, although it stated that their treatment would be identical to that of the non-Jewish French POWs.[66] The German Foreign Office—commenting that the suggestion had its 'complete approval'—passed it on to the Scapini Delegation, which was in charge of the interests of the French POWs.[67] Georges Scapini, a First World War French veteran who lost his eyesight in that war, responded two months later, saying that

---

[60] Oral testimony of Edward Chapman, https://www.iwm.org.uk/collections/item/object/80010951, recorded 12 February 1990, accessed 1 February 2018, IWM catalogue number 11194.
[61] Denton, IWM 81/6/1, p. 38.   [62] Jay, *Facing Fearful Odds*, ln. 2364.
[63] Airey Neave, *They Have Their Exits* (Barnsley: Leo Cooper, 2002), p. 69.
[64] Sammelmitteilungen 1, order 7, 16 June 1941, BA-MA RW 6/270.
[65] OKW to the German Foreign Office, 23 September 1941, PAAA R67004; see also Scapini, *Mission sans Gloire*, pp. 190–1.
[66] OKW to the German Foreign Office, 23 September 1941, PAAA R67004.
[67] German Foreign Office to the OKW, 25 September 1941, and German Foreign Office to the Scapini Delegation, 25 September 1941, ibid.

while he was still waiting for an official response from the French Government, he was of the opinion that Jewish POWs should not be separated from comrades with whom they fought.⁶⁸ Although the French Government's response is not known, the fact that the German Foreign Office thought it necessary to consult it on this issue indicates that it was supposed to have some input into this decision. Regardless, in the following year the Germans began transferring French Jewish Officers to Oflag X-C in Lübeck.⁶⁹

There are several possible reasons for the camp commandants' lacklustre efforts to implement the segregation of American and British Jewish POWs during the early stages of the war. To begin with, it is possible that the Wehrmacht—perhaps due to racial reasons—had greatly underestimated the number of Jewish POWs it was holding, especially after the murder of the Soviet Jewish POWs. Oberstleutnant Theodor Krafft, head of Group 1 in the POW Office's General Department and in charge of POW treatment, wrote after the war that there were about 3,000 Jewish POWs of various nationalities in German POW camps, 'especially Polish and French [Jews]'; and therefore, the number of American and British Jewish POWs among them was probably believed to be negligible.⁷⁰ This, of course, was a much smaller number than the estimated 100,000-plus non-Soviet Jewish POWs actually held in German POW camps.⁷¹ To this point needs to be added the camp commandants' inability to clearly identify Jewish POWs in the first place, combined with the unwillingness of POWs to expose themselves as Jews, which might have made the effort of going through the segregation exercise meaningless.⁷² The commandants, who were constantly reminded of the importance of the POWs to the war economy and of the need to maximize their utilization, must have also been concerned about triggering protests against a step that seemed unjust to most of the POWs, protests that would impact their potential productivity and contribution to the German economy.⁷³ Some of the commandants may also have heard about segregation attempts that failed as a result of such

---

⁶⁸ Scapini Delegation to the German Foreign Office, 25 November 1941, ibid.; see also Yves Durand, *Prisonniers de Guerre, dans les Stalags, les Oflags et les Kommandos, 1939–1945* (Paris: Hachette Littératures, 1994), p. 203.

⁶⁹ ICRC Berlin to ICRC Geneva, 28 July 1942, ACICR BG 17 05/011; see also Durand, *La Captivité*, p. 384.

⁷⁰ Krafft, 10 August 1951, BA-MA MSG 2/12656.

⁷¹ Krakowski, *The Holocaust Encyclopaedia*, pp. 1180–1; Spoerer, 'Die soziale Differenzierung der ausländischen Zivilarbeiter, Kriegsgefangenen und Häftlinge im Deutschen Reich', p. 505. For a discussion on the number of Jewish POWs see the Introduction section of this book.

⁷² In some cases, Jews joining the British army declared themselves as non-Jews; see JTA, 12 November 1939, https://www.jta.org/archive, accessed 8 May 2019; JC, 17 November 1939, p. 8, https://www.thejc.com/archive, accessed 16 June 2019; JTA, 3 January 1940, https://www.jta.org/archive, accessed 8 May 2019. Others threw away their identification tags when captured—see, for examples, Green, *From Colditz in Code*, pp. 47–8 and p. 127; and Moore, *GI Jews*, p. 181. For a discussion regarding declaration of Jewish ethnicity while joining the army see Chapter 2 of this book.

⁷³ See, for example, von Graevenitz letter regarding the handling of POWs, 28 November 1943, BA R 59/48.

protests, which might have deterred them from even attempting to implement the segregation order in the first place. The ICRC and the Protecting Power played a deterrent role as well: such actions—even if they were considered by these organizations to be in line with the Convention—could not have been implemented in secrecy and would have been reported back to the POWs' governments, causing potential reprisals. The German authorities might have felt that while France and Belgium, defeated countries with very limited influence on the way their POWs were being treated, or Poland and Yugoslavia, which no longer existed and had hardly any influence, the USA and Britain, even at such an early stage of the war when the balance of POWs held by both sides was clearly not in their favour, might still retaliate if their own POWs were mistreated.

As discussed in more detail in Chapter 4, it is also possible that in general, camp commandants, most of whom were from an older generation—the vast majority of them had served in the First World War and in 1942 the age of 81% of them was 50 or older—were not fully indoctrinated with Nazi racial policies in a way that the younger generation had been; they might have considered a segregation order to be a political and racially motivated one, and as such, standing against their national conservative values.[74] Only 26% of them were members of the NSDAP vs. 33.7% of Wehrmacht officers who held similar ranks; and the vast majority of those who were members—76%—only joined after Hitler came to power (58% joined in the immediate months that followed the 'Seizure of Power').[75] This indicates that even those who did join the Party, had probably done so not from Nazi convictions but from opportunism.

It seems that the higher ranks in the Party were well aware of this lack of Nazi convictions among camp commandants: when the French General Henri Giraud managed to escape captivity in April 1942, Joseph Goebbels placed the blame directly on the 'false humanitarianism' of the 'old reserve officers' who were in charge.[76] The POW commanders in the military districts, to whom the POW commandants were subordinated and who were in charge of all POW camps in their districts, were of the same character: according to the testimony of one of these commanders, they were, at least at the beginning of the war, 'mostly general staff officers from the old army—men with a strict conception of duty and great talents for organization'.[77] Although the OKW organized regular meetings with them 'in order to explain the ideas of the Führer and of the chief of the OKW

---

[74] See Appendix A for references regarding POW camp commandants.
[75] Of a sample of 250 POW camp commandants, sixty-five were found to be NSDAP members (see BA R/9361-VIII and BA R/9361-IX); the membership rate of similar ranks in the Wehrmacht's front-line officers is based on Bartov's analysis in Omer Bartov, *The Eastern Front, 1941–45, German Troops and the Barbarisation of Warfare* (Basingstoke and New York: Palgrave Macmillan, 2001), p. 52 table 2.10. The assumptions used were that similar ranks were born pre-1900, and that there was an even split between reserve and regular officers.
[76] *Joseph Goebbels Tagebücher 1924–1945* (Munich: Piper, 2003), Band 4, 27 April 1942, p. 1786.
[77] 'Testimony of General Reinhard von Westrem', *IMT, Trials of War Criminals*, vol. XI, p. 49.

concerning the basic decrees', these meetings apparently did not prove to be completely effective.[78]

One example demonstrating this is the case of 63-year-old major Karl Meinel, one of the officers in the POW commander's office in military district VII (which was headquartered in Munich), who complained to the OKW about the treatment of Soviet POWs in his district and refused to hand over to the Einsatzgruppen several hundred of them, who were supposed to be sent to concentration camps. The Gestapo officer who was sent to investigate commented that Major Meinel 'was an old soldier and [could not approve of] such proceedings... from a soldierly point of view'; in his Gestapo file it was mentioned that before the war he had shown 'not only indifference, but "to some extent even aversion" against the National Socialist Creed'.[79] In the same report, the Gestapo officer described the commandant of Stalag VII-A (Moosburg), 65-year-old Oberst Hans Nepf, as 'an old ossified officer who resents any interference in his routine by other authorities'.[80] The Gestapo demanded the OKW to step in; this resulted in Meinel and his superior, the commander of POWs in military district VII, General von Saur, being transferred to other roles, and the Soviet POWs to be sent to Buchenwald where, in all likelihood, they were murdered.[81]

In another case, the commandant of the Vinnitsa POW camp in the Ukraine refused to hand over to the Einsatzkommando 362 Soviet Jewish POWs who were selected for execution. The commandant went even further and initiated court martial proceedings against his deputy and two other officers, who intended to hand over the Jewish POWs.[82] And in a similar case the commandant of Dulag 185 on the Eastern Front, Major Bertold Wittmer—who was not only a member of the Nazi Party, but also of the SS—refused to hand over Soviet Jewish POWs to the Einsatzkommando, arguing that he did not receive a specific order to do so from his superiors in the Wehrmacht. The commander of Einsatzkommando 8, who filed the report, complained to his superiors that Major Wittmer 'not only does not support the solution of the Jewish question... but also applies his own completely absurd viewpoints'.[83] Such cases were not limited to the army: when

---

[78] Ibid., p. 50.

[79] Document R-178, *IMT, Nazi Conspiracy and Aggression Suppl. A* (Washington, DC, 1947), pp. 1250–1.

[80] Ibid., p. 1251. Nepf's interrogation can be found in https://www.fold3.com/image/231923347, accessed 1 December 2020.

[81] Additional description of the Meinel case can be found in Datner, *Crimes against POWs*, pp. 248–57. Meinel and von Saur, however, were still promoted shortly after this incident (see Streim, *Sowjetische Gefangene in Hitlers Vernichtungskrieg*, p. 43 n. 20).

[82] Operational situation report U.S.S.R. no. 128, 3 November 1941, BA R58/218.

[83] Äusserungen des Kommandanten des Dulag 185, Major Witmer, zur Behandlung der Juden-und Partisanenfrage, 3 November 1941, BA R70 Sovjetunion/26 (Wittmer's name in the report was probably misspelled—in other places it appears as Wittmer (see BA-MA RW 59/2130)); Streit, *Keine Kameraden*, pp. 102–3. Interestingly, Wittmer's behaviour did not impact his army career: only six months later, in May 1942, he was promoted to the rank of Oberstleutnant (the equivalent of his SS rank, Obersturmbannführer) and awarded the War Merit Cross 1st class (see report, 9 May 1942, BA

the SD arrived at the Luftwaffe's Stalag Luft II in Lodz (then called Litzmannstadt) on the Eastern Front and demanded that Soviet commissars and Jewish POWs would be handed over to them, the commandant refused.[84]

It is not known what was the outcome of the latter cases and whether the commandants were successful in protecting the Jewish POWs; judging by the Meinel case, they probably were not. These cases, however, might not have been common—a report from Einsatzgruppe C mentioned the commandant of the Borispol Dulag in Ukraine, who requested that the Sonderkommando execute more than 800 Soviet Jewish POWs in his camp; and Streit, in his analysis, estimated them to be the minority and in any case not supported by senior levels in the Wehrmacht.[85] However, they do demonstrate a certain level of opposition to such orders among POW commanders in the military districts and among POW camp commandants, a behaviour that was not found among other rank-holders in the Wehrmacht.

In some cases, other considerations, not necessarily racial ones, might have informed these decisions: even though Jews were considered by the Nazis to be a separate race and at the bottom of the Nazi racial hierarchy, it is possible that the position on that hierarchy of the nationality of the army they belonged to influenced the segregation decision. Slavs, Russians, and Poles were just a level above the Jews; and the French, as part of the Gallic race, were still considered inferior to the Americans and British, who in general received better treatment as POWs.[86] Therefore racial segregation of POWs from the latter armies might simply not have been a priority for the Wehrmacht during the first years of the war compared to the segregation of Jews from those armies whose nationalities were considered more racially inferior. Camp commandants might also have seen the segregation order as intended to satisfy the Wehrmacht's political masters and to stave off pressure from the state's Nazi organs, and as such seemed only to have paid lip service to it by ordering American and British Jews to identify themselves, but did not take any further action to verify whether they had done so.[87] After all, had they wanted, they could have checked the POW's registration card, on which religion was listed, or could even have established circumcision tests as part of the registration process, as was done in the East.[88] However, the commandants knew

---

R 9361-III/564274). The issue of his protection of the Jews was supposed to be dealt with after the war (see memo, 1 June 1942, ibid.) but it probably caused Himmler to block his promotion to the rank of SS-Standartenführer (see Himmler to Spree, 15 February 1943, ibid.).

[84] Marilyn Walton and Michael Eberhardt, *From Commandant to Captive: The Memoirs of Stalag Luft III Commandant* (Kindle Edition: Lulu Publishing, 2015), ln. 1172.

[85] Operational situation report U.S.S.R. no. 132, 12 November 1941, BA R58/219; Streit, *Keine Kameraden*, p. 103.

[86] Ibid., p. 69; MacKenzie, 'The Treatment of Prisoners of War in World War II', p. 504; Pierre Gascar, *Histoire de la captivité des Français en Allemagne, 1939–1945* (Paris: Gallimard, 2016), p. 156.

[87] See, for example, Adolf Westhoff, 15 January 1966, BA-MA MSG 2/12655.

[88] Polian, 'First Victims of the Holocaust', p. 786.

that such a humiliating action would be reported to the ICRC and the Protecting Power, and potentially be met with reprisals. That is probably why only one recorded case of such a test as a means for identifying Jewish POWs during arrival at the POW camp (mentioned above) was found in memoirs; and none were found in the relevant visit reports of the ICRC and the Protecting Power.[89]

The command structure of the Wehrmacht's POW organization, which was described in the Introduction to this book, might also explain the inconsistencies in the implementation of the segregation order. As mentioned earlier, although the POW Office was responsible for issuing orders and general guidelines to the various camps, it had no disciplinary authority over the POW commanders in the military districts and over their subordinates, the POW camp commandants.[90] This meant that the POW Office had only limited influence on the way POW commanders and camp commandants implemented the POW Office's policies.[91] In addition to the inconsistencies described above in the implementation the segregation order, this structure was also the cause of the inconsistency that appeared in the case of Yugoslav Jewish officer POWs: while segregated in Oflag XIII-D in Hammelburg in the Nuremberg military district, they were not segregated in Oflag VI-C (Osnabrück-Eversheide), which was in the Münster military district. Interestingly, the German Foreign Office raised this issue, arguing that the inflammatory activities in Oflag VI-C against the German-supported Nedic government were the result of the Jewish officer POWs not being segregated.[92]

These inconsistencies were further explained by General Reinhard von Westrem, who between 1940–3 served as the POW commander in military district XII in Wiesbaden.[93] In the Nuremberg trials after the war, where he appeared as a witness, he described how camp commandants had some latitude in the way they interpreted the orders they received, and how they were expected to

---

[89] W. A. Harding, p. 10, IWM 82/27/1.

[90] Dienstanweisung für den Kommandanten eines 'Kriegsgefangenen Mannschafts Stammlagers', p. 7, BA-MA RH 1/612; Overmans, 'Die Kriegsgefangenenpolitik des Deutschen Reichs 1939 bis 1945', p. 739. For the disciplinary authority of the POW Office see testimony of Reinhard von Westrem, *IMT, Trials of War Criminals*, vol. XI, p. 48.

[91] This was similar to the situation during the First World War; see Overmans, 'Die Kriegsgefangenenpolitik des Deutschen Reichs 1939 bis 1945', p. 741.

[92] German Foreign Office representative in Belgrade to Berlin, 26 November 1941; OKW to German Foreign Office, 20 April 1942, PAAA R40960. Gerhard Feine, the member of the German legation in Serbia who signed this letter, was involved in the following year in other activities related to Jews: on one hand, as the economic and legal expert in the German legation in Budapest, he pressured the Hungarian authorities to limit bank withdrawals in order to ensure that Jews would not be able to withdraw their money before being deported (see Randolph L. Braham, *The Politics of Genocide: The Holocaust in Hungary* (Detroit: Wayne State University Press, 2000), p. 113, esp. n. 15); on the other, in 1944 he helped rescue, together with Swiss embassy officials and the Swedish diplomat Raoul Wallenberg, some of the remaining Hungarian Jews (see https://www.raoulwallenberg.net/saviors/diplomats/list/gerhart-feine-889/, accessed 1 April 2022, and Conze et al., *Das Amt*, P. 16).

[93] Testimony of Reinhard von Westrem, *IMT, Trials of War Criminals*, vol. XI, p. 48. Interestingly, his Wehrmacht personnel file indicates that he was appointed as POW commander only in April 1942 (see BA-MA PERS 6/71723). Since his testimony was given under oath, it is more likely that his personnel file was not up to date.

demonstrate common sense in doing so.[94] As one of the American Jewish POWs described them, 'the officers in charge of [the POW camp] were different from those elsewhere in the German military. They saw us as soldiers first and as Jews second, if at all.'[95] In any case, from 1942 onwards, and despite increasing pressure from Nazi Gauleiters in their districts and from the RSHA as well, camp commandants could rely, no doubt, on the caveat in the March 1942 updated segregation order that stated that segregation should only be implemented 'as far as possible', to justify their lack of action in implementing it; this might also explain the fact that there were only two testimonies of segregation attempts (both in Stalag II-B in Hammerstein) between 1942 and the beginning of 1945, after SS General Berger took over the POW Office and re-issued a stricter segregation order.[96]

POW Camps under Himmler: Segregations in 1945

The next series of segregations took place at the beginning of 1945, following the change of command at the top of the POW Office. The overall responsibility for the POW camps was given to Himmler in his role as commander of the Replacement Army on 20 July 1944, on the same day as the assassination attempt on Hitler; but it was not until October that the POW Office itself was transferred from the OKW to Himmler and SS General Gottlob Berger was brought in to take it over.[97] The OKW's 1941 and 1942 guidelines regarding the segregation of Jewish POWs that were already in place at that time were quite clear.[98] But the new, stricter order from December 1944 made segregation mandatory by taking away from camp commandants the ability to decide whether or not to implement it by removing the caveat that it should be implemented only 'as far as possible'.[99]

---

[94] Testimony of Reinhard von Westrem, *IMT, Trials of War Criminals*, vol. XI, p. 55.

[95] Martin King, Ken Johnson, and Michael Collins, *Warriors of the 106th* (Philadelphia, PA and Oxford: Casemate, 2017), p. 252.

[96] For pressure on commandants see Testimony of Reinhard von Westrem, *IMT, Trials of War Criminals*, vol. XI, p. 56; Adolf Westhoff, 15 January 1966, BA-MA MSG 2/12655; Krafft, 10 August 1951, BA-MA MSG 2/12656. In May 1943 there was an attempted segregation in Stalag's II-B's (Hammerstein) labour detachment 1; according to Telesfor Lucero, an American POW, when they arrived at the camp the Jews were ordered to step forward. When one did, the majority of the other POWs stepped forward with him and the Germans did not pursue it; it was probably a local initiative of the labour detachment's commandant (see memoirs of Telesfor Lucero, https://wartimememoriesproject.com/ww2/view.php?uid=206841, accessed 4 August 2019). According to another testimony, a few months later there was another unsuccessful segregation attempt in the same stalag (see Elson, *Prisoners of War: an Oral History*, pp. 228–9). For the new order, see Befehlsammlung 48, order 876, 15 December 1944, BA-MA RW 6/270.

[97] Peter Longerich, *Heinrich Himmler* (Oxford: Oxford University Press, 2012), p. 698.

[98] Sammelmitteilungen 1, order 7, 16 May 1941, BA-MA RW 6/270; and Befehlsammlung 11, order 5, 11 March 1942, ibid.

[99] Befehlsammlung 48, order 876, 15 December 1944, ibid.

By that stage of the war, with the Allied armies closing in from the East and the West and the evacuation of most POW camps, the ICRC and the Protecting Power could only perform a limited number of inspections of POW camps; in addition, some of these segregations, either by chance or more likely by deliberate German intention, occurred immediately after such an inspection had taken place.[100] As a result, most of these segregations came to light not through official visiting reports but in POWs' memoirs. The limited number of testimonies regarding these events—which must have been quite traumatic not only for the Jewish POWs but for all POWs in the camp, and thus could be expected to be mentioned in memoirs—demonstrates that the new enforcement drive was not necessarily implemented as rigorously as the new head of the POW Office might have intended.

One such case—one of only three segregation cases that were also recorded by the ICRC and the Protecting Power—was recounted by Captain Irving Lifson, an American Jewish Navigator with the 390th Bomb Group, who was shot down over Germany on 11 December 1943 and sent to Stalag Luft I in Barth.[101] The POWs in the camp had been treated relatively well; the Jews among them held Friday services and on Saturdays they used to replace the cross in the camp's chapel with the Star of David and hold religious services.[102] However, on 17 January 1945 the camp authorities posted two lists: one contained names of POWs the Germans knew to be Jewish, and the other of POWs they suspected of being Jewish.[103] This was a prelude to the segregation of the Jewish POWs: although Lifson had managed to keep his religion off his identification discs, he found himself on the 'suspected' list; another American Jewish POW, Flight Engineer Irving Lerner, who threw away his identification discs before being captured and therefore was not listed as Jewish, was also on the list.[104] One Jewish POW was saved from the segregation by his comrades: when the Germans ordered the Jews in his room to step forward so that they could be taken away, all forty men standing with him stepped forward together; the Germans were forced to leave empty-handed.[105] Interestingly, there were several Cohens left out and a few O'Briens that were included; apparently, the Germans' effort to identify

---

[100] For example, the segregation in Stalag IX-B (Bad Orb) occurred on 25 January 1945, one day after the visit of the Protecting Power in the camp (see Swiss embassy report on Stalag IX-B (Bad Orb), 24 January 1945, NARA RG 389, box 2150, 290/34/19/3).

[101] Swiss embassy report on Stalag Luft I (Barth), 10 April 1945, TNA WO 244/62.

[102] Irving Lifson, 'Loneliest and Happiest Point in One's Life', in Wilbert H. Richarz et al., eds, *The 390th Bomb Group Anthology*, vol. I (Tucson, AZ: 390th Memorial Museum Foundation, 1995), ln. 2560; *Prisoners of War Bulletin*, 3:1 (1945), p. 8; Bird, *American POWs of World War II*, p. 90.

[103] Lifson, 'Loneliest and Happiest Point in One's Life', ln. 2666; oral testimony of Major Milton Stern, an American Jewish POW, https://memory.loc.gov/diglib/vhp-stories/loc.natlib.afc2001001.01348/, accessed 21 August 2020.

[104] Lifson, 'Loneliest and Happiest Point in One's Life', ln. 2575; Donaldson, *Men of Honor*, p. 92.

[105] Fred Weiner, memoirs, https://stalagluft4.org/pdf/weinernew.pdf, accessed 30 April 2018.

Jewish POWs based on Jewish-sounding names was not infallible.[106] The Germans had informed the prisoners that POWs on both lists were about to be sent to an 'all Jewish camp' and Lifson described how 'at that point in time, we didn't know about the extermination camps, but we had a gut feeling that we were going to be killed'.[107] The 250 Jewish POWs were then placed in separate barracks, which at the request of the SAO, Colonel Hubert Zemke, were next to his own; they continued to receive their share of Red Cross parcels, blankets, and clothing.[108] The Jewish POWs did not suffer any harassment there, and were even allowed to conduct religious services; however, they were not allowed out of the compound and could not join the other POWs in their sport games (interestingly, this was in contrast to the report of the Swiss legation, which stated that the Jewish POWs were allowed to mix with their non-Jewish comrades and to take part 'in every kind of entertainment').[109] If there had been a plan to move them to another camp it did not materialize, either due to the protest made by the SAO to the Swiss legation, or simply because the camp they were supposed to be transferred to was overrun by the Red Army.[110] The Jewish POWs believed, however, that it was the unwavering stand taken by the American POW leaders, Colonel Hubert Zemke and Colonel Henry Spicer, who threatened the commandant with an all-out mutiny, that saved them from being sent to a concentration camp.[111]

The same process was repeated a month later, in February 1945, at the morning roll call in Stalag III-A in Luckenwalde, when a list of about thirty names was called. All the names were Jewish-sounding and the POWs that came forward were taken to another part of the compound, behind a separate fence. One Jewish POW remembered the commandant, who knew that he was Jewish, asking him whether there were any Jewish POWs in his barracks. The POW responded that there were none and the commandant moved on.[112] Strangely enough, according to another testimony, the new barracks had much better conditions than the ones the Jewish POWs had just left: the rooms were smaller and instead of stoves, they

---

[106] John Vietor, *Time Out* (Fallbrook, CA: Aero Publishers, 1985), p. 156. See also Wolk, *Jewish Aviators in World War II*, p. 121.
[107] Lifson, 'Loneliest and Happiest Point in One's Life', ln. 2669; LaCroix, *Journey Out of Darkness*, p. 169.
[108] Donaldson, *Men of Honor*, p. 12; see also Bard, *Forgotten Victims*, p. 39; Wolk, *Jewish Aviators in World War II*, pp. 118–19.
[109] Bard, *Forgotten Victims*, p. 40; Donaldson, *Men of Honor*, p. 58. See also Barry Keyter, *From Wings to Jackboots* (London: Janus Publishing, 1995), p. 269. For the Swiss embassy report, see report on Stalag Luft I (Barth), 10 April 1945, TNA WO 224/62.
[110] Swiss report on Stalag Luft I (Barth), 10 April 1945, TNA WO 224/62; Foy, *For You the War Is Over*, p. 30; see also Lifson, 'Loneliest and Happiest Point in One's Life', ln. 2669; and oral testimony of Major Milton Stern, an American Jewish POW, https://memory.loc.gov/diglib/vhp stories/loc.natlib.afc2001001.01348/, accessed 21 August 2020.
[111] Wolk, *American Aviators in World War II*, pp. 118–22. Zemke, however, mentioned the segregation only briefly in his memoirs and did not make any reference to the actions which were attributed to him (see Hubert Zemke, *Zemke's Stalag* (Shrewsbury: Airlife, 1991), p. 28).
[112] Bard, *Forgotten Victims*, p. 41.

were equipped with radiators which the confused POWs initially suspected had been put there in order to poison them. In addition, there were fewer people per room, and each one now had an individual bed instead of the bunk beds in their previous barracks.[113] The fact that the Jewish MOC, Phil Schwartz, was not placed in the segregated compound just added to the confusion.[114] Finally, when the Red Army neared the camp, the Germans marched the POWs to Stalag XI-A in Altengrabow. Private Jacob Blumenfeld, a Jewish POW who fought with the 100th Infantry Division and was also segregated, described how 'along the way [we] managed to merge with the main body of prisoners so that by the time we reached the new camp we were all thoroughly mixed in with the rest of the camp' and the segregation idea was forgotten.[115]

Several cases of segregation attempts failed because of the strong resistance by the POWs' representatives. The SAO in Stalag Luft III's (Sagan) Centre Compound, Colonel Delmar Spivey, was twice ordered by the camp authorities to provide them with a list of Jewish POWs in the camp; he explained to the commandant that all POWs were American and ordered that no such lists should be given.[116] In Stalag Luft VI near Heydekrug, Memelland (today Šilutė in Lithuania), although the guards had regularly distributed anti-Semitic literature to the POWs—which they then collected and burned, in plain sight of the guards—the British Jewish POWs did not suffer any discrimination. However, one day at the beginning of 1945 there was a notice that all of them should assemble the following morning with their belongings in order to be moved to a separate barracks. The notice also stated that going forward, the Jews would have to stand separately during the morning parade. The MOC, Jimmy 'Dixie' Deans, who spoke fluent German, forcefully told the commandant that all POWs were members of the King's Service and according to its rules, all denominations should be respected—'even that of bloody tree-worshippers'.[117] The following day no one showed up and the commandant quietly retracted the order.[118] In a similar case,

---

[113] Oral testimony of Harry Hoare, https://www.iwm.org.uk/collections/item/object/80024614, no recording date, accessed 1 February 2018, IWM catalogue number 27096; Donaldson, *Men of Honor*, p. 110. However, Harry First, another Jewish POW, remembered the conditions in the new barracks to be much worse (ibid., pp. 141–2).

[114] Ibid., p. 111. The Protecting Power report from February 1945 listed another POW—Private RC Wittrup—as the MOC; it is possible that one of them was the MOC, while the other was his deputy (see Swiss embassy visit to Stalag III-A (Luckenwalde), 12 February 1945, TNA WO 227/6).

[115] Donaldson, *Men of Honor*, p. 111. The segregation event was not mentioned in any of the daily orders issued by the commandant during that period (see BA-MA RH 49/36); however, a note asking for a report on the status of the Jewish POWs was sent on 12 February 1945 by the POW commander in military district III to the stalags in the district (see BA-MA 49/28).

[116] Spivey, *POW Odyssey*, pp. 77–8.

[117] Oral testimony of Edgar Hall, https://www.iwm.org.uk/collections/item/object/80005903, recorded 1982, accessed 1 February 2018, IWM catalogue number 6075; testimony of Frank Paules, https://www.b24.net/powStalag6.htm, accessed 4 July 2019; John Dominy, *The Sergeant Escapers* (Reading: Hodder and Stoughton, 1976), p. 126.

[118] Oral testimony of Fred Maltas, https://www.iwm.org.uk/collections/item/object/80033259, no recording date, accessed 1 February 2018, IWM catalogue number 33043.

when during a special rollcall in April 1945 the commandant of Stalag III-B (Fürstenberg an der Oder) ordered all Jewish POWs to take one step forward, nobody moved; however, when the commandant repeated his demand and threatened to shoot the POWs, the whole parade stepped forward together. The commandant left empty-handed.[119]

In Stalag Luft VII near Bankau (today Bąków in Poland) the MOC, an Australian pilot, announced one morning in January 1945 that all Jewish POWs had to report to the German commandant. Some of the Jews tried to hide by digging a chamber under the fireplace but they were found; eventually, nothing came out of it, possibly because of the protests of fellow POWs, and later the whole camp was marched to Luckenwalde near Berlin.[120]

The implementation of the segregation order seemed to have been stricter in military district IV, around Dresden, than elsewhere—existing testimonies point to segregation attempts in three of its POW camps. In Stalag IV-A near Hohnstein Jewish POWs from Britain and other commonwealth countries were sent to a Jewish-only labour detachment. Wilfred Ofstein (whose brother, Maurice, was held in Stalag IV-B (Mühlberg) in the same military district) described how he was sent to the thirty-strong labour detachment 234 near Pirna and 'realized that we were all Jewish in British uniforms...all British Commonwealth—British, Australian and mainly South African and Canadian—we were all Jewish'. According to Ofstein, who described the camp as 'the most comfortable of all' the POW camps he had been in, the Jewish POWs did not have any restrictions and had the same food and rations as the non-Jewish POWs.[121] Sergeant John Gilbert, a British MOC from a nearby labour detachment who visited the labour detachment at the request of the Jewish POWs, confirmed that observation and described the conditions in the factory where the POWs had been employed as quite luxurious in comparison to the POW camp—single beds, lockers and tables, and washing facilities which he described as 'out of this world'.[122] The POWs were even allowed to use the nearby Hitler Youth's football pitch as their exercise grounds.[123] The management of the factory apparently did not assign any importance to the fact that the POWs were Jewish.

The second segregation case in military district IV occurred in Stalag IV-B near Mühlberg. During the morning parade on 18 January 1945, twenty-six Jews were ordered to collect their belongings and to move into a different barracks. According to Henry Watson, a British POW who was also in Stalag IV-B

---

[119] Seymour 'Sy' Lichtenfeld, oral history, https://www.ww2online.org/view/seymour-lichtenfeld #stalag-iii-b, accessed 30 June 2021.

[120] Oral testimony of Leslie Goldwyn, JMM T2014.304; Flight Sergeant Henry Jones, diary of a Prisoner of War, http://www.pegasusarchive.org/pow/henry_jones.htm, accessed 4 July 2019.

[121] Testimony of Wilfred Ofstein, YVA O.3-8111.

[122] John Gilbert, memoirs, http://www.pegasusarchive.org/pow/jack_gilbert.htm, accessed 29 March 2018.

[123] Testimony of Wilfred Ofstein, YVA O.3-8111.

(Mühlberg), some of the POWs avoided the order by gaining access to the camp's office and altering the religion on some of the POWs' forms. Although the Jewish POWs were naturally frightened, the Germans were not strict in enforcing the separation and 'eventually [the Jewish POWs] finished up sleeping in [their] old huts as space occurred'.[124] And in the same month in Stalag IV-C near Wistritz, the MOCs were ordered to draw up lists of Jewish POWs. The explanation given by the commandant to the Protecting Power's delegate—that the lists were for his personal use—did not seem credible to him; however, there was no evidence that a segregation eventually took place, potentially because of his intervention.[125]

In addition to the segregation in Stalag Luft I (Barth) mentioned earlier, there were only two other cases of segregation during the last stages of the war that were found in the visit reports of the ICRC and the Protecting Power. The first was reported by the ICRC after its visit to Stalag VII-A near Moosburg in January 1945. According to the report, thirty-six British Jewish and 110 American Jewish POWs were placed in a separate barracks. They were not moved to a different camp, their treatment was identical to that of the other POWs, and they were even able to hold religious services on Fridays.[126] After one month they were sent back to their original barracks.[127] This might have occurred as a result of the protest that the MOC had lodged with the ICRC when they visited the camp at the end of January 1945.[128] Another 150 French Jewish POWs from the same Stalag were sent to Stalag 383 in Hohenfels, a camp which usually held only NCOs; the ICRC report stated that there was no information regarding their treatment there, however earlier in the war the camp was known to have better conditions than most Stalags.[129]

The second recorded segregation case was reported a month later, in February 1945, after a visit by the Swiss Protecting Power to Stalag II-A (Neubrandenburg): the Swiss delegates, who visited the camp on 19 February 1945, discovered that two out of its fifty-five American labour detachments, in Zachow and Koldenhof, consisted only of Jewish POWs—thirty-two out of the 2,147 American POWs

---

[124] Maurice Ofstein, *Diary and Odd Jottings* (unpublished memoirs), p. 7, JMM T2010.353.1; see also oral testimony of Henry Watson, https://www.iwm.org.uk/collections/item/object/80016749, recorded 7 October 1997, accessed 1 February 2018, IWM catalogue number 17623.

[125] Swiss embassy report on Stalag IV-C (Wistritz), 23–6 January 1945, NARA RG 389, box 2149, 290/34/19/3.

[126] ICRC report on Stalag VII-A (Moosburg), 27 January 1945, p. 4, TNA WO 224/24. See also report on Stalag VII-A (Moosburg), Military Intelligence Service, War Department, 1 November 1945, https://catalog.archives.gov/id/893506, accessed 30 April 2018; and memoirs of Aben Caplan, http://memory.loc.gov/diglib/vhp/story/loc.natlib.afc2001001.05190/, accessed 21 August 2020.

[127] LaCroix, *Journey Out of Darkness*, p. 117; Westheimer, *Sitting It Out*, p. 287.

[128] Ibid. See also Sidney Thomas, Letter, *New York Review*, 12 April 1990, https://www.nybooks.com/articles/1990/04/12/in-stalag-viia/, accessed 15 October 2021.

[129] ICRC report on Stalag VII-A (Moosburg), 27 January 1945, NARA RG 389, box 2149, 290/34/19/3; Almogi, *With Head Held High*, p. 105; MacKenzie, *The Colditz Myth*, p. 103.

held in these fifty-five detachments, approximately 1.5% of the total.[130] The Commandant explained that this was in line with the orders of the German High Command.[131] Upon receiving the report, the American delegation in Geneva asked the Swiss Foreign Office to obtain a copy of the German segregation order, and to make sure that its delegates visited these detachments 'at an early date'.[132] According to the response sent by the Swiss on 22 March 1945, the Germans refused to provide this order, claiming that it was a military document and therefore could not be shared with a foreign power. The Swiss added that due to the current circumstances they had no contact with their delegates in Berlin and therefore they could not instruct them to visit the Jewish labour detachments; however, according to the information they had, the treatment of Jewish POWs was not different to that of the non-Jewish ones.[133]

The segregation of American Jewish POWs in January 1945 in Stalag IX-B in Bad Orb requires a special mention as it was the only recorded event that led, two weeks later, to the segregated Jewish POWs—along with non-Jewish ones who had probably been included in order to meet a workforce quota—being sent as slave labour to the Berga forced labour camp. Out of the 350 POWs who were sent there from Bad Orb only 280 survived; the death rate in that camp and in the evacuation march from it ahead of the advancing Allied armies in April 1945—around 20%—was the highest of all European POW camps where American and British POWs were held in the Second World War.[134]

The segregation of the Jewish POWs in Bad Orb started in mid-January when POWs who had been identified as Jews were sent to a separate barracks.[135] Interestingly, around the same time, the three African-American POWs who were in the camp were also moved to another barracks; however, the move was to the so-called MP (Military Police) barracks, which housed other American POWs whose job was to guard the kitchen against thefts. The reason for this move was not segregation: it was suggested by the camp commandant himself who was

---

[130] This figure—1.5%—is close to the overall estimate of the 1.6% made in this study of the share of American and British Jewish POWs out of the total number of American and British POWs in German captivity.

[131] Swiss embassy report on Stalag II-A (Neubrandenburg), 19–23 February 1945, NARA RG 389, box 2148, 290/34/19/3.

[132] American Interests Geneva Office to State Department, 26 March 1945, NARA RG 389, box 2148, 290/34/19/3.

[133] Berlin was not yet encircled at that stage, however the Swiss legation probably meant that they were not able to establish lines of communication with their Berlin delegate. See American Interests Geneva Office to State Department, 3 May 1945, NARA RG 389, box 2148, 290/34/19/3.

[134] According to a list of names, the total number might have been 344 and not 350—see NARA, RG 389, box 2150, 290/34/19/3; Bard, *Forgotten Victims*, pp. 102–3. On the general situation in Stalag IX-B and Berga see report on Stalag IX-B (Bad Orb), Military Intelligence Service, War Department, 1 November 1945, https://catalog.archives.gov/id/893506, accessed 30 April 2018.

[135] Cohen, *Soldiers and Slaves*, p. 79.

concerned for the African-Americans' safety since according to him, the camp had 'a lot of fanatical idiots'.[136]

A couple of months earlier, in November 1944, about 175 miles away near Berga am Elster, work began on an underground fuel production facility, one in a series of such facilities built in order to address the impact that Allied bombing was having on Germany's fuel situation. The slave labour used to dig these underground facilities was mostly Jewish concentration camp inmates from Buchenwald, who by the end of 1944 were in such a bad physical state they could barely work.[137] The SS was put in charge of building the tunnels, while at the time some of its personnel were also in charge of POW camps in all military districts, and it apparently decided to use the American POWs to speed up the work.[138] It appears that during the second half of January 1945, with most of the Jewish POWs already segregated, an order was received in Stalag IX-B in Bad Orb to send 350 POWs to the camp in Berga, to work side by side with the 1,200 slave labourers, who in addition to the remaining civilian Jews included several hundred Soviet POWs as well as political prisoners from Italy, France, Holland, and Slovakia.[139]

The German in charge of the Americans in Berga, Hauptmann Ludwig Merz, testified after the war that he had heard about the arrival of the American POWs sometime in January, which was around the time that the Germans increased their efforts to identify additional Jewish POWs in Stalag IX-B (Bad Orb). As the original order was not found, it is not clear whether it specifically mentioned Jewish POWs; but the decision to use American POWs was in all likelihood made by the POW commander in military district IX (which was headquartered in Kassel), which also included Stalags IX-A (Ziegenhain) and IX-C (Bad Sulza), who might have seen it as an opportunity to solve both the overcrowding situation in Stalag IX-B, along with the labour shortage in Berga. It is also not clear whether this was in fact a test case for using POWs from western countries as slave labour, in the same way that the Soviet POWs had been used, or a local initiative by the SS to exploit their new dual responsibility for POW labour and for building the Berga fuel plant.[140]

The commandant of Stalag IX-B (Bad Orb), oberst Karl Sieber, who was appointed to this role at the beginning of the January 1945 and was described by his commander as embodying 'the great ideas of National-Socialism', decided to use race as the initial selection criteria for fulfilling the required quota.[141] By doing this he was, in fact, following the POW Office order mentioned earlier,

---

[136] Whitlock, *Given Up for Dead*, p. 118. [137] Cohen, *Soldiers and Slaves*, pp. 9–10.
[138] Westhoff testimony, undated, BA-MA MSG 2/12656; Cohen, *Soldiers and Slaves*, p. 80.
[139] Ibid., pp. 154, 190. [140] Ibid., p. 80.
[141] Sieber evaluation, 21 May 1944, BA-MA PERS 6/10062. As the commandant of Dulag 376 in Kauen he was accused of killing Soviet POWs (see *Encyclopedia of Camps and Ghettos, 1933–1945*, vol. IV, p. 569).

which instructed camp commandants to segregate Jewish POWs and, as far as possible, send them to work outside the camp.[142] Since the number of segregated Jewish POWs at this stage—around eighty—was insufficient, he had a meeting with the MOC, Private Johann Kasten, who spoke fluent German, and demanded that he identify the remaining Jewish POWs.[143] The selection initiative and the meeting itself were in all likelihood timed to occur immediately after the visit of the Protecting Power earlier that day; Sieber probably knew that the outspoken MOC would not hesitate to raise a complaint with the Swiss legation. In any case, Kasten refused the commandant's demand, telling him that the American army '[does] not differentiate by religion', and in response was thrown down the stairs of the administration building.[144] He later assembled all barracks leaders and informed them 'none of the men should admit to being Jewish'.[145]

On the following day, 25 January 1945, the Germans instructed all POWs in the camp to stand outside their barracks and ordered the Jewish POWs to take one step forward. When no one moved, the commandant took a rifle and hit Kasten across the chest; the guards then walked through the formation and pulled out those who, in their opinion, looked Jewish, and those with Jewish-sounding names.[146] To reach their quota they also selected POWs they considered to be troublemakers and even those who were circumcised—including a soldier named O'Reilly, who was clearly not Jewish.[147] Among those selected was Kasten himself, whose defiance the commandant did not like.[148] Some witnesses recalled that the Germans, still not satisfied with the number of POWs selected, called all barracks leaders and warned them of the consequences of not obeying the segregation order; some of them, in turn, informed the Jewish POWs in their barracks that they would have to comply. The commandant then held another formation on the following day, where some of the Jewish POWs did eventually come forward; the resistance of the MOC had limited effect when faced with the insistence of his jailers.[149]

The 350 POWs that were eventually selected—and who, oddly enough, despite Nazi racism, did not include the three African-American POWs, nor POWs from Britain's African colonies who were also held in the camp—were moved to a separate barracks in the camp.[150] Initially they were treated like the other POWs and

---

[142] Befehlsammlung 48, order 876, 15 December 1944, BA-MA RW 6/270.
[143] Cohen, *Soldiers and Slaves*, p. 83.
[144] Swiss embassy report, 24 January 1945, NARA RG 389, box 2150, 290/34/19/3. The segregation of the Jewish POWs was not mentioned in the report. Johan Kasten, unpublished memoirs, https://memory.loc.gov/diglib/vhp-stories/loc.natlib.afc2001001.12002/, accessed 1 August 2021.
[145] Ibid.   [146] Ibid.; Donaldson, *Men of Honor*, p. 44.
[147] Cohen, *Soldiers and Slaves*, p. 32; Donaldson, *Men of Honor*, pp. 70–1.
[148] Cohen, *Soldiers and Slaves*, p. 75.   [149] Whitlock, *Given Up for Dead*, p. 121.
[150] Swiss embassy report on Stalag IX-B (Bad Orb), 24 January 1945, TNA WO 224/30.

some of the Jewish POWs even held Friday services.[151] However, on 8 February 1945 they were marched to the train station and loaded into boxcars. Five days later they arrived at the town of Berga am Elster.[152]

Once in Berga, there was no segregation between Jewish and non-Jewish POWs, and they were all treated in the same brutal manner, working underground and digging tunnels for what was supposed to become the jet fuel factory.[153] The harsh treatment, meagre food rations, and hard work, all typical conditions of German forced labour camps, caused the POWs' health to deteriorate rapidly. Of the seventy POWs who did not survive, some died while in the camp, but the majority of the deaths occurred during the forced march when the camp was evacuated in April 1945.

The Protecting Power again visited Stalag IX-B (Bad Orb), the camp to which the POWs had originally belonged, on 23 March 1945, six weeks after the POWs were sent to Berga. In their previous report from January 1945, the day before the segregation parade was held, the inspectors reported that the camp made 'a rather depressing and poverty-stricken impression'; that was probably the reason for the second visit, which occurred only two months after the previous one and despite the challenging transportation and communication issues that existed at the time.[154] Although the March report mentioned the difficult conditions in the camp, there was no reference to the 350 POWs who had been sent to the labour camp—it is possible that the Swiss legation was told of the situation by POWs in Stalag IX but decided not to mention it in its report.[155]

After the war, American war crimes investigators gathered a substantial amount of evidence related to this case. Although some of the testimonies were based on rumours—for example, that 110 Jewish POWs were shot near the camp in March 1945, or that the Jewish POWs were sent to work in salt mines and all of them died of overwork and starvation—eventually the investigators managed to reconstruct the events and identified some of the individuals responsible for the harsh treatment and the deaths.[156] Interestingly, the court documents did not mention the initial segregation of Jewish POWs in Bad Orb, nor the fact that many of the POWs who were sent to Berga were Jewish.[157] Two of the accused, Sergeant Erwin Metz, who was the commander of the guards in Berga, and his superior, Captain Ludwig Merz, were put on trial and sentenced to death; on appeal, their sentences were commuted to twenty and five years imprisonment,

---

[151] Gerald Daub, oral history, recorded 6 July 2000, archive of the Museum of Jewish Heritage, New York.
[152] Donaldson, *Men of Honor*, p. 71.   [153] Bird, *American POWs of World War II*, p. 108.
[154] Swiss embassy report on Stalag IX-B (Bad Orb), 24 January 1945, NARA RG 389, box 2150, 290/34/19/3.
[155] Swiss embassy report on Stalag IX-B (Bad Orb), 5 April 1945, ACICR BG 17 05/24.
[156] Testimonies of Smith, 23 June 1945, Dollar, 20 September 1945, and Kirby, 24 September 1945, NARA, RG 153, box 35, 270/2/10/1.
[157] NARA, RG 549, box 197, 290/59/9/3.

respectively.¹⁵⁸ Eventually, Merz was freed in 1951 and Metz in 1954.¹⁵⁹ SS Lieutenant Willy Hack, the commandant of the Berga camp, managed to evade capture until 1947, when he was found in East Germany. He was arrested by the Communist authorities and sentenced to death in 1949. The sentence was carried out in Dresden in 1952.¹⁶⁰

It is important to remember that according to the 1929 Geneva Convention, the Detaining Power had the right to use POWs as labour for work that was not directly related to the war effort. There were multiple cases where Allied POWs found themselves working side by side with civilians (especially Polish and French), forced labour, and even concentration camp inmates, in mines and factories. However, in all those cases these POWs were to some extent protected by Article 33 of the Convention, which dealt with labour detachments and made it clear that it was the responsibility of the camp commandant to ensure that the provisions of the Convention, especially those related to food, sanitary conditions, and medical treatment, were applied to them.¹⁶¹ The Berga camp might have been viewed by the commandant of Stalag IX-B (Bad Orb) and his superiors as just another labour detachment; however, once there, the enslaved POWs, now effectively under the control of the SS, did not benefit from the protection of the Convention and were treated in the same way that the SS treated all slave labour under their control during that period.

The fact that despite the severe workforce shortage across Germany and the deteriorating military situation no other cases similar to Berga have been found points to the primacy that the Convention had within the German POW system, even at such a late stage of the war and even after SS personnel were put in charge of POW affairs in the military districts. However, the outcome can also serve as an example as to what the eventual fate of the Jewish POWs, and perhaps POWs in general, might have been had the SS assumed full control over the camps.

The reasons for the limited number of segregations of American and British Jewish POWs in the last months of the war, despite clear orders from an SS General whom camp commandants might have perceived to be stricter, and despite the placement of SS members above the POW commanders in the military districts, are not completely clear. In addition to the reasons mentioned in the previous section, another reason might have been the Germans' inability—or lack of will—to add the burden of creating separate barracks and duplicating logistic processes in an already stretched logistical infrastructure.¹⁶² However, a more plausible explanation—which is discussed in more detail in Chapter 4—is

---

¹⁵⁸ Cohen, *Soldiers and Slaves*, p. 244.   ¹⁵⁹ Ibid., p. 247.   ¹⁶⁰ Ibid., p. 248.
¹⁶¹ Article 33 of the 1929 Geneva Convention, https://ihl-databases.icrc.org/ihl/INTRO/305, accessed 14 September 2019.
¹⁶² As early as August 1942, the OKW complained to the German Foreign Office of the difficulties it encountered in separating POWs and adhering to Article 9 of the Convention (see OKW to the German Foreign Office, 25 August 1942, PAAA R40985).

the fear of commanders at all levels of the personal consequences that they might suffer upon Germany's inevitable defeat as a result of any mistreatment of POWs; this was probably the main reason for the limited number of segregation attempts in the last stages of the war and for the relatively non-discriminatory treatment that Jewish POWs were receiving at that stage.[163]

Identifying Jewish POWs

In the segregation cases described above the Germans had to identify the American and British Jewish POWs before they could segregate them. This was usually done by asking the POWs themselves to declare whether they were Jewish. The reason for this is not completely clear: examples of headcount reports from various POW camps listing numbers of Jewish POWs, along with the requirement to specify a POW's religion when registering him in a camp, meant that the Germans could have identified Jewish POWs, or at least those who declared themselves to be Jewish, based on information already available to them. This was obviously very different to the circumcision tests used by the Wehrmacht to identify Soviet Jewish POWs during the campaign in the East—those found to be circumcised were taken aside and shot.[164]

Throughout the war the POW Office had issued several orders that provided specific guidelines for reporting on various categories of POWs. For example, an order for reporting on the number of medical personnel POWs, which was issued by military district VIII in Breslau on 21 August 1942, stated that going forward Jewish medical personnel should not be listed separately in these reports; it can therefore be assumed that prior to that date, headcount reports did account separately for this category of POWs.[165] Another order, issued on 23 September 1943, instructed POW camps to report on the number of British POWs by dominion—Canadian, South African, etc. The number in each category had next to it, in brackets, another number; since the number of Palestinian Jewish POWs was usually identical to the number in brackets next to it, it is highly likely that the latter indicated the number of Jewish POWs from each dominion. For example, the report on 30 December 1943 from Stalag VIII-B in Teschen (Stalag VIII-B in

---

[163] For a discussion on the fear of retribution as the reason for not mistreating POWs, and about SS General Gottlob Berger's role during the last months of the war, see Chapter 4 of this book.

[164] Polian, 'First Victims of the Holocaust', p. 786. See also interrogation of Reinecke, 23 October 1945, https://www.fold3.com/image/1/231936234, accessed 1 October 2019: at the beginning of the war in the East, Muslim POWs were also thought to be Jews and executed because they were circumcised. This was stopped after Heydrich found out about it (see Heydrich, 'Ergänzung der Richtlinien für die in die Stalags', 17 July 1941, BA R58/9016). Müller, the head of the Sicherheitspolizei, informed his Einsatzkommando commanders in October 1941 that some Jews might not be circumcised at all (Müller, 10 October 1941, BA R58/9016).

[165] Bestandsmeldungen an feindlichem San.-Personal, 21 August 1942, PMA 754/1/132.

Lamsdorf was renamed Stalag 344 earlier that year) listed 6,381 'Insel Briten' (from the British Isles), out of which ten were Jews; and 1,636 'other' POWs, out of which 762 were Jews, 760 of them from Palestine and two from Greece.[166] Although the number of Palestinian Jewish POWs was in all likelihood correct as they were grouped in separate labour detachments and therefore could have been easily accounted for, the accuracy of the other numbers is questionable: the reports issued in later months for the same POW camp listed no Jewish POWs from the British Isles, nor from Greece.[167]

Further evidence that supports the conclusion that Jewish POWs were sometimes accounted for separately in some POW camps appears in a small number of reports by the ICRC and the Protecting Power. In its report on its visit to Oflag VI-B (Dössel) in April 1942, the ICRC listed the breakdown of the camp's POWs' religious denominations: 69% belonged to the Church of England, 19% to the Church of Scotland, 9% were Roman Catholics, and 3% 'Others'—which must have included, in addition to the Hindu POWs who were in the camp, also the Jewish ones. Although the segregation attempt which had occurred in that camp only several months earlier was not mentioned in any of the ICRC reports from that period, the ICRC was no doubt aware of it and probably thought it would be beneficial not to include in its report a detailed breakdown of the 'Others' category.[168]

A similar breakdown, mentioned in Chapter 2, was found in the Protecting Power report on its visit to Stalag XVII-B (Gneixendorf) in October 1944. Under section XII of the report, which described the religious activity of the POWs, a census appeared of the percentage of POWs from each religion: according to the report, 1.8% of the camp's population was Jewish (seventy-seven out of the 4,288 POWs held in the camp), vs. 65.8% Protestants and 31.5% Catholics.[169] No reason was given for the purpose of this census; however, these figures, along with the ones included in the ICRC report mentioned above, might have been compiled by the camp authorities at the request of the delegates. Based on this it can be concluded that the German authorities had monitored the number of Jewish POWs in the camps, probably using the information that appeared on their POW cards.

---

[166] Aufstellung auf im Stalagbereich befindlichen brit. Nach Dominion, 30 December 1943, PMA 121/1/34.

[167] Aufstellung auf im Stalagbereich befindlichen brit. Nach Dominion, 28 February and 29 March 1944, ibid. In this context it should be noted that the cumulative OKW-level POW headcount reports did not have similar breakdowns (see, for example, POW reports from 1 July 1942, BA-MA RW 6/534, and 1 October 1944, BA-MA RW 6/276).

[168] ICRC report on Oflag VI-B (Dössel), 15 April 1942; the ICRC report on Oflag VI-B (Dössel) from 9 December 1941 also did not mention segregation (see TNA WO 224/73). A Protecting Power report from 20 October 1944 on Stalag V-C (Offenburg)—a camp that held only Indians and Arabs— listed clearly on its first page the breakdown of the denominations in the camp: twenty Muslims ('*Mohammedans*'), 150 Hindus, 123 Sikh, and five Christians (see TNA WO 224/19A).

[169] Swiss embassy report on Stalag XVII-B (Gneixendorf), 24 October 1944, NARA RG 59, box 2224, 250/32/3/1.

In this context, it should be noted that section XII of the ICRC and Protecting Power visit reports always dealt with POWs' religious issues; however, Jewish religious issues were rarely mentioned, probably because the delegates visiting the POW camps assumed that doing so would draw unnecessary German attention.

Interestingly, it is possible that the requirement to list the number of Jews in each dominion was not a German initiative but in fact triggered by a request the British government had made two years earlier: in a letter to the German Foreign Office on 29 April 1941, the Protecting Power communicated this request and asked that the dominion or colony to which a British POW belonged be included in the information sent to the British government.[170] When the German Foreign Office passed this request on to the Wehrmacht, citing Article 9 of the Convention as its justification, it added that according to this Article POW lists needed to include not only the POW's nationality but also his race. Interestingly, the Foreign Office gave skin colour as the determining factor for race; without making any reference to Jews, it explained to the OKW that the British request was justified because the 'British Empire contains... different races, such as natives of the most diverse coloured people [*Eingeborene der verschiedensten farbigen Völkerstämme*]'.[171] Apparently, even after years of Nazi rule and indoctrination, there were still inconsistencies in how the term 'race' was used within the different organs of the German state, at least when it came to POWs: the OKW itself during the war issued orders that sometimes referred to Judaism as a race, and sometimes as ethnicity.[172] Even the Reich's Justice Minister, Otto Thierack, contributed to the confusion: guidelines issued by him in January 1943, condemning POWs' relations with German women, made specific reference to relations with members of races which are 'racially more remote' ('*rassisch ferner*') from the German race. The examples listed included Eastern European people, British colonial troops, and native Americans—'*feindliche Ost-Volker, britische und amerikanische hilfsvölker*'—but not Jews.[173]

Despite the various reports described above, the Wehrmacht still faced difficulties in properly identifying all Jewish POWs. Unlike the civilian Jewish population in Europe, most of whom had records going back decades and even centuries identifying them as Jews, or could have been identified as such by their neighbours, it had no alternative means to rely on in order to identify Jewish POWs. As described in Chapter 2, many of them—the numbers are obviously not known—chose to register under a different religion either when they joined the army in

---

[170] American embassy in Berlin to German Foreign Office, 29 April 1941, PAAA R40717.
[171] Lautz to OKW, 12 June 1941, ibid.
[172] For the OKW reference see, for example, Befehlsammlung 33, order 578, 15 January 1944, BA-MA RW 6/270; the order mentioned in the same sentence POWs of Polish ethnicity ('*volkstums*') and those of Jewish race ('*Rasse*'). See also Zusammenfassung aller Bestimmungen über den Arbeitseinsatz wiederergriffener und Arbeitsverweigender Kr. Gef., 2659/42, 10 August 1942, PMA 31/1/6; and 2692/44, 12 June 1944, PMA 744/1/30.
[173] Leaflet signed by Otto Theirack, 14 January 1943, BA R 58/397.

order to have it inscribed on their identification discs or when registering in the POW camp; and many Jewish soldiers who did declare themselves to be Jewish simply threw their identification discs away before being captured.[174] Camp commandants were aware of this and in some cases issued instructions to report on POWs who were suspected of hiding their Jewish origins.[175] In some of the segregation cases described earlier in this chapter camp commandants reverted to selecting Jewish POWs based on their Jewish-sounding names (as was also the case for French Jewish POWs).[176] This difficulty in identifying Jewish POWs must have been one more reason for the lack of effort displayed by the camp commandants in implementing the segregation orders—if they could not be certain that all Jews in the camp had been segregated, then in most cases they decided not to go ahead at all with the implementation of that order.

International Reaction to Segregation

Reports on the segregation and maltreatment of Polish Jewish POWs, who were the first Jewish military combatants to fall into Nazi captivity, appeared in the Jewish press as early as November 1939 and were based on testimonies of escaped Jewish POWs.[177] The ICRC itself was well aware, at least from May 1941 and probably earlier, that Jewish POWs were in some cases being discriminated against: reports and letters from POWs' families indicated that restrictive measures had been taken against French Jewish doctors and medical personnel, who were not allowed to treat other POWs, and at the same time were not designated for repatriation even though their status as Protected Personnel allowed this.[178] Despite that, the ICRC did not raise the issue even when the OKW argued, in a meeting that took place a month later, in June 1941, that Jewish POWs would be treated in the same way that non-Jewish POWs were treated and would face no restrictions due to their race; and in October 1941, during the campaign in North Africa, probably in anticipation of similar treatment, the ICRC asked—but did not challenge—Germany to clarify whether British Jewish soldiers who had recently been captured were being segregated in Italian POW camps.[179]

---

[174] For a discussion regarding Jewish soldiers not declaring their ethnicity when joining the army see Chapter 2.
[175] Sammelheft für den Kommandoführer eines Kgf. Arb. Kdos., Stalag III-A (Luckenwalde), March 1943, p. 39, BA-MA RH 49/33.
[176] Gascar, *Histoire de la captivité des Français en Allemagne, 1939–1945*, p. 51.
[177] JTA, 17 November 1939 and 27 October 1940, https://www.jta.org/archive, accessed 8 May 2019.
[178] Report of Dr Coeudres, 23 May 1941, ACICR BG 25/34.
[179] Notes from a meeting with OKW representatives, 12 June 1941, ACICR BG 17 05/006; minutes from the meeting between Melas and Pilloud, 17 October 1941, ACICR BG 17 05/146.

The ICRC did not raise the issue of segregation with the German authorities because, as it argued later during the war, it did not see it as a breach of the Geneva Convention; in addition, according to the information it had, the American and British Jewish POWs were not, in general, discriminated against and therefore it did not see any immediate reason to intervene.[180] Instead, it addressed any segregation and discrimination issues on a case-by-case basis. Instead of challenging the German policy it decided, in effect, to deal with the outcome rather than with the cause of these issues—an approach that proved to be unsuccessful in solving them.[181] As mentioned earlier in this chapter, the Protecting Power went even further and described a case where Jewish and non-Jewish British POWs shared the same barracks in Stalag 319 (Cholm) as a breach of Article 9 of the Geneva Convention.[182]

The status of the British Jewish POWs was obviously of great concern to the Jewish community in Britain. At the beginning of 1943, Rabbi Dayan Mark Gollop, the Senior Jewish Chaplain in the British Army, asked Major Little of the Directorate of POWs in the War Office to clarify the Jewish POWs' situation. In a letter to Harold Satow of the Foreign Office's POW Department, Little asked whether Jewish POWs had been segregated from their fellow British soldiers in separate camps or labour detachments, in the same way that Palestinian Jewish POWs had been segregated. Little added that segregation of the Palestinian POWs could be justified according to Article 9 of the Geneva Convention; however, he did not have any evidence to suggest that it had been applied to non-Palestinian Jewish POWs.[183] Furthermore, in his opinion the Germans could not identify them even if they wanted to, since some of the Jewish soldiers 'took the precaution of having other religions inscribed on their identity discs'.[184] Little then asked for Satow's advice, not only on whether to ask the Swiss—the Protecting Power—to investigate this issue, but also as to whether it would be in the Jewish POWs' interest to do so at all. Satow responded on 1 March 1943, agreeing that such a question could be put to the Swiss, provided that they acted discretely in the matter and did not ask the Germans directly; although he did not believe that the Germans were segregating Jewish POWs, he did not think it wise to put such an idea into their heads.[185]

The request to the Swiss was made a week later, and the response, which arrived the following month, confirmed that 'generally speaking, it cannot be said that Jews are receiving different treatment from other [POWs]'. The telegram noted,

---

[180] Gallopin to Radziwill, 22 July 1943, ACICR BG 17 05/016; Burkhardt to WJC, 5 April 1945 and meeting between ICRC and WJC, 11 April 1945, USHMM RG-68.045M Acc. 2004.507, reel 54, document 416.
[181] Jean-Clause Favez, *The Red Cross and the Holocaust* (Cambridge: Cambridge University Press, 1999), p. 123.
[182] Swiss embassy report on Stalag 319 (Cholm), 9 January 1943, p. 5, TNA WO 224/52.
[183] Little to Satow, 18 February 1943, TNA FO 916/567.   [184] Ibid.
[185] Satow to Little, 1 March 1943, ibid.

however, that 'they are sometimes housed with Palestinians'.[186] It is interesting to note that the telegram with the English translation of the Swiss response omitted the observation which was included in the original French transcript that 'only in exceptional cases German officers and NCOs abused their authority in treating certain Jewish POWs'; someone—either the translator, or, more likely, the drafter of the letter—had decided to reduce the risk of such a statement triggering a diplomatic incident and simply removed it.[187] Another letter, sent during the same period by Dr Roland Marti, the ICRC delegate in Berlin, to the ICRC headquarters in Geneva, also confirmed that Palestinian Jewish POWs in Jewish-only labour detachments were treated in the same manner as non-Jewish POWs; and in a letter sent on 6 June 1943, the Swiss reiterated that at this stage there was no reason to undertake additional steps regarding this matter.[188] This low-key inquiry by the British War Office was unlikely to alleviate, even temporarily, the concerns of the British Jewish community; however, given that the Swiss findings did not indicate that discrimination against British Jewish POWs had taken place, the approach was probably the correct one for that time.

A similar response was sent by the ICRC to the WJC on 5 May 1943, assuring them that there was no information indicating that the Jewish POWs were treated differently. The ICRC added, however, that such information could only be shared with the authorities of the states of which the POWs were citizens; the WJC, not being such a body, was basically told that it was not entitled to receive it.[189] However, correspondence between the ICRC and the WJC continued to take place in the following years, indicating that the ICRC decided not to be too strict in this matter and accepted the status of the WJC as the de facto representative of Jews.

The segregations of American and British Jewish POWs at the beginning of 1945 and the continued segregation of Polish and French Jewish POWs, which was confirmed again by the ICRC in February 1945, drew the attention of other bodies to this issue.[190] The Scapini delegation, which, despite being French, acted as the de facto Protecting Power for French POWs, raised its own concerns regarding the risk posed to French Jewish POWs from the local population, and in October 1944 asked the German Foreign Office for Jewish-only labour detachments to be dismantled.[191] Sydney Silverman, a member of the British Parliament, raised the issue of segregated British Jewish POWs in the House of Commons on

---

[186] The British Legation in Berne to the Foreign Office in London, 22 April 1943, ibid. Cases of British Jews interned with Palestinian Jews were not found, therefore it is not clear how the Swiss came to that conclusion.
[187] Swiss Foreign Interests Division to the British Legation in Berne, 22 April 1943, ibid.
[188] Marti to ICRC, 17 May 1943, ACICR BG 17 05/017; Swiss Foreign Interests Division to the British Legation in Berne, 8 June 1943, TNA FO 916/567.
[189] ICRC to WJC, 5 May 1943, ACICR BG 25/34.
[190] JTA, 23 February 1945, https://www.jta.org/archive, accessed 8 May 2019.
[191] French POW Ministry to the German Foreign Office, 19 October 1944, ACICR BG 25/34.

28 February 1945 and demanded to know what the British government intended to do 'in view of the obvious sinister intentions of the [segregation] move'.[192] James Griggs, the Secretary of State for War, responded that an inquiry had been made through the Protecting Power; he added that it would take weeks before an answer would be received.[193] A few days later, Ignacy Schwarzbart, a Jewish member of the Polish National Council in London, raised the issue of the segregation of Polish Jewish POWs and asked that they be exchanged for German POWs; in parallel, the British Jewish Congress made a similar appeal to the British Foreign Office, and the American Emergency Committee to Save the Jewish People of Europe asked General Eisenhower to warn Germany of potential retaliation against German POWs in Allied hands for the segregation of Jewish POWs.[194] Eisenhower assured it that 'all feasible steps are being taken'.[195]

On 9 March 1945 the same committee wrote to the ICRC delegate in Washington asking for information regarding the segregation of Polish and French Jewish POWs. The ICRC, which had confirmed on several occasions that such segregation had been taking place for the previous five years, provided a somewhat confusing response: it first argued that it had no information to suggest that such segregation 'has taken, or is taking place'; it then added in the same letter that 'should such a report be true, the [ICRC] is aware of it and has taken whatever action possible to protect these prisoners'.[196] It is not clear why Marc Peter, the ICRC delegate in Washington who signed the ICRC letter, chose to respond in that way; he was either trying to calm Louis Bromfield, the president of the Emergency Committee to Save the Jewish People of Europe, by providing him with false information, or, given that he was in Washington, he simply was not aware that the ICRC itself had only two weeks earlier informed the Polish National Council that segregation of Polish POWs was indeed taking place.[197]

A few days later, however, the ICRC was confronted on this issue head-on by the WJC. By that time, with the Red Army having liberated Auschwitz and the full horrors of the Holocaust slowly being revealed, segregation of Jewish POWs, of which both parties had been aware for a while, must have created a much more sinister interpretation. With the end of the war in sight, the WJC became concerned that the ongoing segregation of Polish and French Jewish POWs and the new cases of segregation of American and British Jewish POWs were a preliminary step in facilitating the expansion of the Final Solution to the last remaining

---

[192] Silverman to Grigg, minutes of the House of Commons, 28 February 1945, https://hansard.parliament.uk/Commons/, accessed 11 July 2019.
[193] Grigg to Silverman, minutes of the House of Commons, 6 March 1945, https://hansard.parliament.uk/Commons/, accessed 11 July 2019.
[194] JTA, 8 March 1945, https://www.jta.org/archive, accessed 8 May 2019.
[195] Congressional Record—Senate, vol. 91 (Washington, DC: U.S. Government Printing Office, 1945), p. 3470 col. 3, 18 April 1945.
[196] Peter to Bromfield, 9 March 1945, ACICR BG 25/34.
[197] JTA, 8 March 1945, https://www.jta.org/archive, accessed 8 May 2019.

group of relatively secure Jews in Europe, which consisted mainly of Polish, American, British, and French Jewish POWs. Given that unlike their civilian brethren the POWs were under the protection of the ICRC, the WJC saw it as the only body that had the power and the legal authority to intervene and protect them. In a telegram sent on 13 March 1945 the WJC did not mince its words: describing the segregation as an 'unprecedented violation of international law' and a 'grave danger', it demanded that immediate action be taken by the ICRC.[198]

At a meeting which took place in Geneva on the same day that the WJC's telegram was sent—clearly organized by phone as a matter of urgency in parallel to sending the telegram, and incidentally, on the same day that Carl Burckhardt, the ICRC's president, met with Ernst Kaltenbrunner, the head of the RSHA, to discuss the situation of Allied POWs—the ICRC refused the WJC's demand for intervention.[199] According to aide-memoir of Gerhart Riegner, the WJC's representative in Geneva who attended the meeting, Professor Beck, the ICRC's legal advisor, went as far as making the incredible argument that the segregation between Jewish and non-Jewish POWs could be compared to the segregation, in Allied POW camps, of Nazi from non-Nazi German POWs, and as such was not a breach of the Geneva Convention. Riegner countered that given the almost complete annihilation of European Jewry, the segregation could only be viewed as a preliminary step before the extermination of the Jewish POWs.[200] At that stage the participants from both organizations assumed that the discussion was only limited to Polish Jewish POWs. However, a few days later the ICRC delegates in Germany reported—erroneously—that, in fact, segregation had been taking place for some time now in all Oflags and Stalags, and had been applied to all Jewish prisoners and not just to Polish Jewish prisoners. The report also stated that there did not seem to be any discrimination in the treatment of Jewish POWs in comparison to non-Jewish ones.[201]

Although the report was soon after confirmed by the ICRC in Geneva to be incorrect, it still raised additional anxiety within the WJC.[202] In a strongly worded letter to Carl Burkhardt the WJC argued that the segregation was in clear violation of Article 4 of the Geneva Convention, which allowed differences in treatment between POWs to be based only on rank, health, profession, or gender, and demanded again immediate action on the part of the ICRC.[203] Burkhardt

---

[198] Riegner to ICRC, 13 March 1945, USHMM RG-68.045M Acc. 2004.507, reel 54, document 416.

[199] Gerald Steinacher, *Humanitarians at War* (Oxford: Oxford University Press, 2017), p. 75. For the ICRC negotiations with Kaltenbrunner regarding the release of POWs see Peter Black, *Ernst Kaltenbrunner—Ideological Soldier of the Third Reich* (Princeton: Princeton University Press, 1984), pp. 240–1.

[200] Meeting between ICRC and WJC, 13 March 1945, USHMM RG-68.045M Acc. 2004.507, reel 54, document 416.

[201] Perrin to Riegner, 23 March 1945, ibid.

[202] Meeting between ICRC and WJC, 11 April 1945, ibid.

[203] Guggenheim and Riegner to Burkhardt, 29 March 1945, meeting between ICRC and WJC, 13 March 1945, ibid.

responded, again conveying the ICRC's legal standpoint regarding the applicability of Article 4—that the ICRC could not intervene because there was no discrimination in the treatment of Jewish POWs, even after segregation. However, a few days later he acknowledged that such segregation was a breach of the spirit, if not the letter, of the Convention.[204]

The exchange, which continued until June 1945, became somewhat theoretical as the war in Europe was approaching its end. Both sides stuck to their original position—the ICRC arguing that legally it had no ground for intervention, and the WJC arguing that not only was the segregation a violation of the Convention, but given what was already known about the extermination of Jews in Europe, there should be no doubt as to the eventual outcome of such action and that the ICRC should act before the situation became irreparable. This seemed to have been a not-so-subtle criticism of the fact that the ICRC did not act when the civilian Jewish population of Europe had been segregated. As the WJC's Aryeh Tartakower put it after the war, the ICRC was asking the Jews 'to wait until the Germans would start killing the Jews' before it could act.[205]

It seems that the WJC was trying to raise the segregation issue with the ICRC using other channels as well: letters from the ICRC in Geneva to the Red Cross societies of France, Czechoslovakia, the USA, Greece, and Poland, probably in response to their earlier inquiries regarding the segregation of Jewish POWs—inquiries that were possibly sent at the request of the WJC—used almost identical language and repeated the same legal argument.[206] A follow-up letter to the American Red Cross (ARC) was a bit more detailed, and suggests that the ICRC was aware of the source of these inquiries: the ICRC asked the ARC to communicate to the American Jewish committees that 'rather than starting a vain legal controversy with the German authorities', it chose to use the means provided by the Geneva Convention to implement 'a particularly careful surveillance policy of the camps' where Jewish POWs had been segregated.[207]

It is not clear why the ICRC chose to defend its non-intervention policy to the WJC by repeatedly using abstract legal arguments. Since the extent of the extermination of the Jews in Europe was known by then, it would have made much more sense to address the sensitivities and anxieties of the WJC by using, for example, the same explanation it had given to the ARC, rather than an argument that served only to increase the suspicion of the WJC that other unknown reasons might be behind the ICRC actions. In any case, even if the ICRC did intend to implement a 'careful surveillance policy', it had a very limited ability to do so

---

[204] Burkhardt to WJC, 5 April 1945, and meeting between ICRC and WJC, 11 April 1945, ibid.

[205] Monty Noam Penkower, 'The World Jewish Congress Confronts the International Red Cross during the Holocaust', *Jewish Social Studies*, 41:3/4 (1979), pp. 229–56, p. 246.

[206] ICRC to the French, Czech, American, Greek, and Polish Red Cross societies (13 April, 17 April, 17 April, 18 April, 3 May 1945), ACICR BG 25/34.

[207] ICRC to ARC (undated, in response to a 16 May 1945 letter), ibid.

during the last months of the war, with tens of thousands of POWs being evacuated from POW camps and with the roads and railroads under constant aerial bombardments. It seems that the only other option the ICRC might have had at this point was to submit an official protest to the German authorities; however, it was probably aware that such a protest was not likely to change anything.

Another reason for the ICRC's refusal to intervene might be found in a more detailed understanding of Carl Burckhardt; the ICRC president 'in all but name' until he was formally appointed to the role at the beginning of 1945 was personally involved in the discussions detailed above.[208] Described by Gerald Steinacher as 'no great admirer of Hitler, but no particular friend of the Jews either', his anti-Semitic beliefs might have played a role in the indifference shown to the fate of the Jewish POWs during these discussions: in 1933 he wrote to a friend that 'there is a certain aspect of Judaism that a healthy Volk has to fight'; and in 1959, fourteen years after the end of the war, his publisher asked him to remove a comment from a draft of his memoir stating that '...it had been the Jews who had wanted the Second World War'.[209] In addition, during the period under discussion he was under immense pressure from both Jewish and non-Jewish organizations, which might explain his refusal to accept the WJC demands—only a month earlier, in February 1945, he complained in a letter to the ICRC delegate in London that the Jews were being ungrateful for everything that the ICRC had done for them.[210]

Available sources show that the segregation of Jewish POWs was never specifically discussed at the level of the American and British governments, which were more concerned with the fate of Allied POWs as a whole. To that end, towards the end of the war those governments had circulated a draft letter which was intended to warn the Wehrmacht against harming POWs in general; however, it was not triggered by, nor did it make any mention of, specific treatment and segregation of Jewish POWs. In any case, by the time the draft letter had received the approval of all relevant bodies and leaflets containing it were dropped over Germany, the war in Europe was almost over; and as Aryeh Kochavi has concluded, 'it is hard to escape the conclusion that when [they] decided against taking any direct and overt action [to protect their POWs] they were taking a calculated risk'.[211]

Conclusion

The act of segregating Jewish POWs held in a German POW camp—regardless of whether it was successful or not—must have been a traumatic event not only for

---

[208] Favez, *The Red Cross and the Holocaust*, p. 284.
[209] Steinacher, *Humanitarians at War*, pp. 29–30.   [210] Ibid., p. 77.
[211] Kochavi, *Confronting Captivity*, pp. 195–202; FRUS, 1945, 3:709, press release issued by the White House, 23 April 1945.

Jewish POWs, but also for their non-Jewish comrades who had witnessed it. As such, when segregations did occur, these events were likely to have been recorded in diaries and letters during the war, reported to the ICRC and the Protecting Power whenever possible, and appear in testimonies and memoirs after the war, especially after the liberated POWs learned about the horrors of the Holocaust and realized what the outcome of such an act might have meant for Jewish POWs.

This study has found nineteen cases of attempts to segregate American and British Jewish POWs in Oflags, Stalags, and Stalag Lufts, six in the early years of the war (two of which failed) and thirteen during its last stages (of which six eventually failed). Only five of these cases were reported by the ICRC or the Protecting Power; and, in total, the successful segregation cases amounted to about 3% of the total number of 134 POW camps where American and British POWs were held during the early years of the war, and 14% of the fifty-two camps they were held in in 1945.[212] Even if the actual number of POW camps where segregation had taken place was twice as high, the fact that more cases have not been found in reports or in memoirs suggests that unlike the segregations of Polish, French, and Yugoslav Jewish POWs, segregation of the American and British Jewish POWs in German POW camps during the Second World War was not common.

There are several potential reasons as to why the majority of camp commandants chose to ignore specific orders from the OKW, issued in 1939 (before the Polish campaign), in 1941 (in relation to French Jewish POWs), in 1942 (in relation to all Jewish POWs), and their reiteration in December 1944—this time removing the caveat that it should only be done on a best-effort basis. As discussed, camp commandants were usually from an older generation and might have preferred the national conservative values of the old German army, which required the chivalrous treatment of an honourable enemy, over Nazism's racialized ones. Even when they did comply with the segregation order, some of them made it clear to the POWs that they were not acting of their own accord, and that despite the segregation they would not forget that POWs were also soldiers and officers and deserved to be treated accordingly.[213] An underestimation of the number of Jewish POWs, together with difficulties in identifying them, and the inability to keep segregations a secret from the ICRC and the Protecting Powers—whose reports might have triggered reprisals—must have played a role as well. In addition, the implementation of segregation during the first years of the war would not only have added unnecessary logistic complications but also might have impacted the productivity of the POWs and their contribution to the German war economy. Commandants therefore appear to have decided in most cases that the effort of going ahead with the implementation of the segregation

---

[212] For the number of POW camps see n. 9 above.
[213] Asaria-Helfgot, *We Are Witnesses*, p. 41.

order was simply not worth it; and, from 1942 until the change of command at the top of the POW Office at the end of 1944, they relied on the wording of the 1942 order, which basically left the final decision in this matter in their hands, as a means for ignoring it. The German High Command and the POW commanders in the military districts, for their part, also do not seem to have insisted on the implementation of this order. And during the last stage of the war it is likely that in addition to the above, self-preservation, both at the camp level and at the senior level, kicked in when the whole chain of command realized that, with defeat being inevitable, there was nothing to gain from the segregation—and mistreatment—of American and British Jewish POWs. This self-preservation appeared to have been a strong enough incentive for the commandants to ignore specific orders issued by a feared SS General and it also helps explain why they did not suffer any repercussions as a result—an indication of the priorities at the time of the individuals in the POW Office chain of command.

From the segregation cases described in this chapter it is obvious that the resistance and support displayed by the non-Jewish POWs, led in most cases by the MOCs, succeeded in some instances in turning the power imbalance on its head and stopped the segregation from taking place. The testimonies of these unsuccessful segregation attempts, with the exception of the one in Stalag VII-A (Moosburg) which was probably reversed due to the ICRC intervention, were found in POWs' memoirs written after the war; and although it is possible that in some cases their writers might have sought to present POWs in a favourable light as staging resistance in support of their Jewish comrades, the number of cases found supports the conclusion that this was more than an anecdotal occurrence. These protests sent a message to the Germans that in extreme cases of injustice they should not expect silent obedience from the POWs and demonstrated that comradeship in the US and British armies was in most cases religion-blind; the military culture of the group fighting to protect its members existed even in POW camps. Although no longer on the battlefield and without any actual weapons, the POWs, and especially their leaders, had done what they could to protect Jewish POWs. This may provide another explanation as to why most POW camp commandants—the exact number is not known but it was, in all likelihood, much higher than 50%—did not even attempt to implement the segregation order; similar to the 1941 Bishop of Munster's sermons against the euthanasia programme, and the 1943 Rosenstrasse protest of non-Jewish German wives against the deportation of their Jewish German husbands, German authorities, in this case POW camp commandants, retreated when they encountered public opposition, in this instance by non-Jewish POWs, to the segregation of Jewish ones.

The segregation of Jewish POWs was obviously driven by Nazi racial doctrine and mirrored the segregation of civilian Jews in Europe, an act that was eventually followed by their deportation and extermination. In view of the ongoing radicalization in Germany's POW policy throughout the war—from the Commissar to

Commando to the Kugel orders, the murder of the Sagan escapers and the lynching of aircrews—a question that remains unanswered is whether the segregation of Jewish POWs was intended to follow the same radicalization process (as the Berga case might suggest); and, if such an outcome was indeed the intention, what was it that protected the non-Soviet Jewish POWs from suffering such a fate. Chapter 4 of this book discusses several explanations for this phenomenon during different stages of the war; however, it is quite possible that had Germany won the war, nothing would have stopped it from ensuring that the fate of Jewish POWs would be identical to that of their civilian brethren.

4
Why Were They Kept Alive? Explaining the Nazi Treatment of Jewish POWs

Introduction

[The German soldiers] were honest in all things except those pertaining to the Fatherland. Anything was excusable if committed in the name of the Third Reich. It made no difference whether it was the breaking of a solemn treaty or the liquidation of the Jews or the starving of a couple of million of Russians [POWs]. [But t]hese same people...delivered Red Cross food and supplies to us [even] when they themselves were hungry [all] because an order said to do it.[1]

This is how the United States Army Airforce's Colonel Delmar Spivey, who was shot down at the end of 1943 over western Germany and became the SAO in Stalag Luft III's (Sagan) Centre Compound, described the contradicting attitudes he had encountered during his time in captivity. The previous chapters dealt with the experience of American and British POWs in German POW camps and analysed the behaviour towards them of their immediate captors and that of their superiors—the POW camp commandants and the POW commanders in the military districts. The purpose of this chapter is to offer an explanation for the attitude adopted by the level above—that of the OKW—towards non-Soviet Jewish POWs, and specifically, towards American and British Jewish POWs: if, as described by the French Jewish philosopher (and POW) Emmanuel Levinas, the Germans' 'systematic desire to exterminate [the Jews] rendered the Geneva Convention nothing more than a piece of paper', why were non-Soviet Jewish POWs treated, in most cases, according to this Convention and spared the fate of their civilian and Soviet POW brethren? This chapter argues that since there was no specific order from Hitler to the contrary, the POW Office was able, throughout the war, to ensure that the Convention was also applied to non-Soviet Jewish POWs; it withstood pressure from other organizations, such as the RSHA and the

---

[1] Spivey, *POW Odyssey*, pp. 50–1.

Nazi Party, to hand these POWs over to their control and to worsen the treatment of POWs in general; and unlike most organizations in the Reich—government, Party, military, and civilian ones—it did not 'work towards the Führer' in anticipating his will and did not implement Nazi racial policies inside POW camps where non-Soviet POWs were held.[2]

In February 1938 Hitler appointed himself as Commander-in-Chief of the Wehrmacht following the removal of the Reich's war minister, Werner von Blomberg, and the Commander-in-Chief of the army (*das Heer*), Werner von Fritsch. In its leading article from 5 February 1938, the Nazi Party paper, the *Völkischer Beobachter*, described how '[t]he natural consequence of the reorganization of the Wehrmacht and the associated personnel changes will be a revitalization of the German army with the spirit of the Party'.[3] In an order issued in December of that year, General Walter von Brauchitsch, who replaced Fritsch as the Commander-in-Chief of the army, described the role of the Nazi worldview in the army's future by declaring that 'The Armed Forces and the National-Socialism are of the same spiritual stem. They will accomplish much for the nation in the future, if they follow the example and teaching of the Führer'.[4] Referring to Adolf Hitler as 'our leader of genius', he made it clear to his officers that they were expected to 'handle any situation in accordance with the views of the Third Reich, even when such views are not laid down in any instruction, regulations, or official orders'.[5] The autonomous status of the Wehrmacht in the tradition of the 'Prusso-German dualism of the military and the political', and its position as an equal to the National Socialist Party, formally came to an end.[6] For the first time in its history, 'The Prusso-German officer corps became...a purely executive agent of the state under political control'; in other words, led by the German High Command, the Wehrmacht was expected to 'work towards the Führer' by anticipating and implementing his will even without receiving specific orders.[7]

In view of these events and declarations, and of the atrocities that took place during the war that was about to be unleashed in the following year, it could have been expected that Jewish POWs, who, like all POWs, came under the jurisdiction—and therefore protection—of the OKW, would not be spared.

---

[2] Levinas, *Carnets de Captivité et Autres Inédits*, p. 210; Kershaw, '"Working towards the Führer": Reflections on the Nature of the Hitler Dictatorship', p. 114.

[3] Quoted in Manfred Messerschmidt, *Die Wehrmacht im NS-Staat, Zeit der Indoktrination* (Hambrug: R. V. Decker's Verlag, 1969), p. 213.

[4] Quoted in O'Neill, *The German Army and the Nazi Party*, p. 103.

[5] Quoted in ibid. Brauchitsch was in fact simply repeating the views which had already been stated by von Fritsch in April 1936 (see Messerschmidt, *Die Wehrmacht im NS-Staat, Zeit der Indoktrination*, p. 82).

[6] Klaus-Jurgen Müller, *The Army, Politics and Society in Germany, 1933–1945: Studies in the Army's Relation to Nazism* (Manchester: Manchester University Press, 1987), p. 30.

[7] Ibid., p. 40.

Policies against Jewish civilians in Europe were going through a radicalization process throughout the war, from segregation to deportation to extermination, and there were multiple examples of Germany going after the smallest Jewish communities in Europe to ensure the continent became completely '*judenrein*'. Himmler tried to persuade the Finnish government—a German ally—to hand over the Finnish Jewish community, 2,000 in total; and the RSHA, which had played a major role in executing Soviet Jewish POWs, had gone through the effort of finding and deporting 770 of Norway's small Jewish community (the rest fled to Sweden).[8]

At the beginning of the war, the treatment of POWs was dictated, in general, by the nature of the war in each front: in the East, where the war was launched as a war of extermination, the Commissar Order (as well as other orders later known as the 'Criminal Orders') had been in place from the start of the campaign and resulted the execution of Soviet commissars and of Soviet Jewish POWs.[9] And although the war in the West was initially launched as a conventional war, it had gone through a brutalization process that resulted, especially during the last year of the war, in atrocities that were previously seen only on the Eastern Front: three noted examples of such atrocities are the massacre of French civilians in the village of Oradour-sur-Glane in southern France, of Canadian POWs during the Normandy landings, and that of American POWs in Malmedy during the Ardennes offensive. It is not a coincidence that these atrocities—as well as others—were committed by Waffen-SS units that had previously fought on the Eastern Front, where such atrocities were common (in the examples above, SS Division Das Reich was responsible for the Oradour-sur-Glane massacre, the 12th SS Panzer Division for the Normandy murders and the 1st SS Panzer Division for the Malmedy one). The Dachau POW trials, which took place in 1947 and dealt only with crimes against American POWs, included more than 200 cases of mainly murder of American POWs during the last year of the war; and the British government estimated the potential number of those involved in murder or mistreatment of POWs to be around 20,000.[10]

At the OKW level, orders and policies dealing with the treatment of POWs from western armies were issued throughout the war and show a clear radicalization trajectory (even though this radicalization never reached the same level of brutality suffered by Soviet POWs): in October 1942 Hitler issued the 'Kommando Befehl', which ordered the execution of captured Allied commando soldiers; the state-sponsored lynching ('Lynchjustiz') of downed American and British

---

[8] Longerich, *Heinrich Himmler*, pp. 618 and 624.
[9] For the Commissar Order see *IMT, Trials of War Criminals*, vol. X, pp. 1055–9.
[10] For the Dachau POW trials see https://www.jewishvirtuallibrary.org/prisoner-of-war-trials-at-dachau, accessed 1 July 2022; for war crimes against British POWs see Priscilla Dale Jones, 'Nazi Atrocities against Allied Airmen: Stalag Luft III (Sagan) and the End of British War Crimes Trials', *Historical Journal*, 41:2 (1998), pp. 543–65, p. 548.

aircrews by German civilians, first proposed by Himmler in August 1943, was publicly endorsed by the regime in March 1944; the 'Kugel [bullet] Erlass' was issued in the same month, ordering the transfer of recaptured officers and non-working NCO POW escapees, with the exception of British and American ones, to the Mauthausen concentration camp, instead of back to a POW camp; and at the end of that month fifty recaptured Allied POWs who escaped from Stalag Luft III (Sagan) were murdered following another direct order by Hitler.[11] This radicalization demonstrates that in the final months of the war, when it came to the treatment of POWs, the differences between the two types of war—war of extermination in the East and a conventional one in the West—were not as distinct as they had been at the beginning of the war: East-Front type atrocities were becoming more and more common in the West.

Since the beginning of the war, Himmler, who at the time was head of the SS, the German police, and the Gestapo, as well as Commissioner for the preservation of the German Volk, kept pressuring to take over more and more responsibilities in the POW organization. He had some success in this: in August 1943 the Wehrmacht was ordered to coordinate searches for escaping POWs with the SS; in July 1944, following the assassination attempt on Hitler, Himmler was appointed commander of the Replacement Army, which put him in charge of the POW commanders in the military districts (and therefore of POW camps); and in September 1944 the process was completed when Hitler ordered the transfer of the POW Office from the OKW to the Replacement Army.[12] On 1 October 1944 Himmler appointed SS General Gottlob Berger as the head of the POW Office, reporting directly to him.[13]

And yet, despite all this, tens of thousands of French and Yugoslavian Jewish POWs—although in most cases segregated in the same POW camp from their non-Jewish comrades—along with thousands of American and British Jewish POWs—most of whom were not segregated—continued to live their lives, with few exceptions, in secure, almost normal conditions, in many cases completely

---

[11] For the Commando Order see *IMT, Trials of War Criminals*, vol. XI, pp. 73–4. For the Lynchjustiz see Kevin Hall, 'Luftgangster over Germany: The Lynching of American Airmen in the Shadow of the Air War', *Historical Social Research*, 43:2 (2018), pp. 277–312, pp. 288–90; 'A Word on the Enemy Air Terror', the *Völkischer Beobachter*, 28–9 May 1944, document 1676-PS, *IMT, Trials of War Criminals*, vol. XI, pp. 166–9; and Treatment of enemy terror flyers, 6 June 1944, document 735-PS, ibid., pp. 169–71. For the Kugel Erlass see *IMT, Nazi Conspiracy and Aggression*, vol. IV (Washington, DC, 1946), pp. 158–60. Testimonies in the Nuremberg trials confirmed that recaptured POWs had been brought to Mauthausen and murdered there; see, for example, the testimony of Jean-Frederic Veith, https://avalon.law.yale.edu/imt/01-28-46.asp, accessed 1 March 2020. For the murder of the Sagan escapees see *IMT, Nazi Conspiracy and Aggression*, vol. IV, p. 158.

[12] For the coordination of searches see Vourkoutiotis, *Prisoners of War and the German High Command*, pp. 104–5. For Himmler's ongoing attempts to gain control over POWs issues see interrogation of Westhoff, 2 November 1945, https://www.fold3.com/image/231908260, accessed 1 October 2019, pp. 30–1. The transfer did not include the POW Office's General Department, which was responsible for the interaction with international bodies.

[13] *IMT, Trials of War Criminals*, vol. XIII, p. 480.

unaware of the events that were taking place just outside their camps. As was shown in the Introduction to this book, the reasons that have been proposed in previous studies for this phenomenon—namely, the different nature of the war in each front, Germany's concern about reprisals against German POWs held by the Allies, and the 'national conservative value system' of the Wehrmacht—are too general in nature, have a few inconsistencies and do not provide a full explanation to this situation. The purpose of this chapter is to offer an alternative explanation: specifically, it will establish that Hitler, who throughout the war did not hesitate to issue orders related to the mistreatment of POWs, probably did not do so in the case of non-Soviet Jewish ones, and assess the reasons for that. And in the absence of such an order, it will argue that, unlike other German state organs such as the RSHA and the NSDAP, the POW Office did not 'work towards the Führer' in anticipating his wishes; the 'national conservative value system' of the POW Office—but not of the Wehrmacht as a whole—was probably the main reason it did not follow General Walter von Brauchitsch's guidance (mentioned above) to implement the views—including racial views—of the Third Reich 'even when such views [were] not laid down in any instruction, regulations, or official orders'.[14]

The chapter begins by demonstrating the level of involvement Hitler had in setting up policies related specifically to the treatment of POWs. It will then establish that the OKW showed an almost blind obedience in following these policies, even when they breached the rights of POWs and posed a clear risk of reprisals against German POWs; and that the conduct of its senior officers was not guided by any 'national conservative value system' that dictated the chivalrous treatment of an honourable enemy, not only when they related to POWs from the Soviet Union, but also to POWs from western armies. The chapter will then analyse the influence that state organs outside the Wehrmacht, such as the RSHA and the Nazi Party, had over the Wehrmacht and the POW Office when it came to setting and implementing POW policies; however, in the absence of a specific order from Hitler to the contrary, it will be shown that when it came to non-Soviet Jewish POWs, these organizations' attempts to force the POW Office to accept the Nazi worldview were in most cases unsuccessful. The chapter will then review the role of the POW Office and the orders it issued that specifically related to non-Soviet Jewish POWs. Finally, it will propose an explanation for the almost non-discriminatory treatment of these POWs.

The Commander-in-Chief: Hitler

The body within the Wehrmacht which was in charge of enemy POWs was the POW Office (*Kriegsgefangenenwesen*). The head of the POW Office reported to

[14] Brauchitsch is quoted in O'Neill, *The German Army and the Nazi Party*, p. 103.

the head of the Wehrmacht's General Office (AWA), a position held throughout the Second World War by Lieutenant General Hermann Reinecke. Reinecke, a committed Nazi who was described as a 'compliant tool of Hitler', reported to the chief of the OKW, Field Marshal Keitel.[15] Called '*Lakeitel*' (Keitel the lackey) behind his back and also described as 'pliable and sycophantic' and 'weak and mediocre', Keitel answered only to the Commander-in-Chief of Germany's armed forces, Adolf Hitler, who from December 1941 until the end of the war was also the Commander-in-Chief of the army (*das Heer*).[16]

Hitler's control of, and involvement in, all aspects of running the German strategy during the Second World War is well documented; as this section will demonstrate, this involvement also included the setting of policies which dealt specifically with the use, treatment, and handling of POWs. Rüdiger Overmans described him as 'the central hub' in these matters and noted how 'in a surprising number of cases, decisions on prisoner-of-war conditions...were decided by Hitler personally' and how he 'interfered deeply with the [POW] system through further orders'.[17] Neville Wylie explained that this led to '[m]any of the decisive policy-decisions...taken in the Führer's headquarters [being taken] with little input from the established bureaucracy [and therefore] the ability of cultural predisposition to influence policy-making was severely limited'.[18] In other words, considerations that might have influenced the behaviour of governments of other countries, such as civil service advice, or long-held values and beliefs and compliance with international treaties, were not necessarily part of Hitler's decision-making process. Surprisingly, his general POW directives included, in addition to setting priorities for the use of POWs in the German economy and instructing the release of POWs from certain countries, also one specific reference to the need to abide by the Geneva Convention—with the exception of Soviet POWs— and to the risk of reprisals against German POWs if Allied POWs were mistreated.[19] Yet, Hitler also issued multiple orders that dealt specifically with the mistreatment of POWs from western armies: The Commando Order, which removed the POW status from Allied commando soldiers captured behind enemy lines, was first announced by Hitler in a radio speech on 7 October 1942; and although there is no documentation showing that the Kugel Erlass was initiated following his (perhaps verbal) direct order, there is no doubt that the OKW issued it in

---

[15] Streit, *Keine Kameraden*, p. 68.
[16] Müller, *Hitler's Wehrmacht*, p. 19; Gaines Post, 'Exploring Political–Military Relations: Nazi Germany', in Daniel Marston and Tamara Leahy, eds, *War, Strategy and History* (Acton, Australia: ANU Press, 2016), p. 10; interrogation of Erwin Lahousen, 23 October 1945, https://www.fold3.com/image/231976506, accessed 1 December 2020.
[17] Overmans, 'Die Kriegsgefangenenpolitik des Deutschen Reichs 1939 bis 1945', pp. 866 and 873.
[18] Wylie, *Barbed Wire Diplomacy*, p. 28.
[19] For examples of directives related to POWs' work see Moll, *Führer-Erlasse 1939–1945*, pp. 210–12, 249–50, and 286; for the directives to release Norwegian and Dutch POWs see ibid., pp. 118–19 and 122. For reference to reprisals and the Convention see ibid., p. 340.

response to Hitler's ongoing accusations that the high command had lost control over POW escapes.[20]

Hitler also issued orders which dealt with specific groups of POWs. These include his order in 1941 to treat Serbian officers 'in the worst possible manner' while providing 'every possible consideration' to the Greek POWs; and his order to execute De Gaulle's Free French soldiers who were captured in the Bir Hakeim battle in 1942 (Erwin Rommel ensured that the order was not carried out).[21] In September 1943, after Italy changed sides, he ordered the execution of captured Italian officers who refused to continue and fight on Germany's side; and at the beginning of 1944, at the same time the Kugel Erlass was issued, he ordered that 103 recaptured Dutch officers should be handed over to the Security Services (*Sicherheitsdienst*—SD), where they faced an almost certain death (the head of the POW Office at the time, General Adolf Westhoff, claimed after the war that he simply ignored that order).[22]

Hitler was also personally involved in the negotiations around the repatriation of wounded POWs: in October 1941 he ordered the last minute cancellation of the first of such exchanges, and in the following year he vetoed, in breach of the Geneva Convention, any POW exchanges that were not based on equal numbers; and in another action that breached the Convention and against objections from the POW Office, he insisted on distributing Nazi propaganda materials in POW camps.[23] And in one of the biggest breaches of the Convention—and of military norms—Hitler ordered to execute fifty of the recaptured POWs who escaped from Stalag Luft III in Sagan in March 1944.

Hitler was the instigator of the longest POW-related incident during the war, the Shackling Crisis. The crisis began with the Germans discovery of British orders to shackle German POWs during the August 1942 Dieppe raid and then escalated in October of that year when British commandos on the German-held Channel island of Sark shot five handcuffed German soldiers they took prisoner when they tried to escape. The year-long reprisals and counter-reprisals which took place after the discovery of their bodies led to the shackling of thousands of

---

[20] For Hitler's announcement of the Commando Order see *IMT, Trials of War Criminals*, vol. XI, pp. 665–6. Hitler's interventions in POW's policies were not always direct; in many cases he did that through General Walter Warlimont, the deputy of the OKW's Operations Department (see Overmans, 'Die Kriegsgefangenenpolitik des Deutschen Reichs 1939 bis 1945', p. 852).

[21] For treatment of Serbian and Greek POWs see *War Journal of Franz Halder*, 9 April 1941, vol. 6, p. 61. For the execution of the French POWs see Overmans, 'Die Kriegsgefangenenpolitik des Deutschen Reichs 1939 bis 1945', pp. 768–9.

[22] For the treatment of Italian officers see treatment of members of the Italian army, 15 September 1943, document NOKW-916, *IMT, Trials of War Criminals*, vol. XI, pp. 1081–3. For the Dutch officers see Westhoff affidavit, 28 November 1947, BA-MA MSG 2/12655. Interestingly, Westhoff, while testifying in Nuremberg, although mentioning the escape of the Dutch officers, did not make any reference to Hitler's order to hand them over to the SD (see *IMT, Nazi Conspiracy and Aggression—Suppl. B* (Washington, DC, 1948), p. 1646).

[23] Wylie, *Barbed Wire Diplomacy*, pp. 88, 131; Westhoff testimony, September 1949, BA-MA MSG 2/12656; see also Overmans, 'Die Kriegsgefangenenpolitik des Deutschen Reichs 1939 bis 1945', p. 854.

POWs on both sides; at one point, the Germans issued a letter—assumed to be on the orders of Hitler—threatening to pull out of the Geneva Convention.[24] Although Hitler's involvement in the Shackling Crisis was driven more by his wish to gain leverage over Britain in other areas and not necessarily by his concern for the treatment of POWs in the battlefield, it serves as another example of his ability to control all aspects of POW policies and to impact the treatment of POWs despite his military commanders, as a whole, objecting to it.[25]

During the last year of the war Hitler became even more involved in POW issues: in 1944 he ordered the mistreatment of POWs, hoping that in return the Allies would do the same to German POWs, which, to his way of thinking, would improve the fighting spirit of the German soldiers and deter them from surrendering (General Westhoff refused to pass on the order); and in January 1945, during a discussion regarding the evacuation of POW camps in the East ahead of the advancing Red Army, he instructed that anyone who tried to escape from the marching columns should be shot.[26] In the following month, February 1945, after the bombing of Dresden and Goebbels's demand to execute tens of thousands of POWs in retaliation, Hitler—who even before the bombing told Goebbels that he was prepared to execute all 250,000 American and British POWs if the Allies initiated gas warfare—pushed for using POWs as human shields by placing them in town centres; he then went as far as suggesting the abandonment of the Geneva Convention altogether, an act that, in his mind, would have strengthened the Wehrmacht's fighting spirit.[27] Grand Admiral Karl Dönitz, Martin Bormann, Jodl, and Himmler managed to convince him that such an act would be detrimental to Germany, and rather than announce such a step in public, it would be better simply to stop observing the Convention.[28] Even as late as March 1945, with the Allies closing in on Germany from both sides and with defeat inevitable, he still insisted on evacuating American and British officer and NCO POWs from the POW camps so that they would not fall into the hands of the advancing armies; and when others in the Nazi leadership suggested that improving the

---

[24] Kochavi, *Confronting Captivity*, p. 47.

[25] Hitler's insistence on continuing with the shackling also caused negotiations for POW exchanges to be halted (see Krafft, 10 August 1951, BA-MA MSG 2/12656).

[26] For the order to mistreat POWs see Westhoff affidavit, 28 November 1947, p. 3, BA-MA MSG 2/12655; Krafft, 10 August 1951, BA-MA MSG 2/12656. For the order to shoot escapees see document 3786-PS, *IMT, Nazi Conspiracy and Aggression*, vol. VI (Washington, DC, 1946), p. 676.

[27] Ian Kershaw, *The End* (Kindle Edition: Penguin, 2011), p. 368 n. 148; Overmans, 'Die Kriegsgefangenenpolitik des Deutschen Reichs 1939 bis 1945', p. 865. Rumours about Hitler's intentions to execute American and British airmen POWs had also reached the Protecting Power and the ICRC (see Spivey, *POW Odyssey*, p. 148).

[28] Note by Dönitz on the conferences with Hitler on the war situation, 19 and 20 February 1945, documents 158-C, *IMT, Trial of the Major War Criminals*, vol. XXXIV (Nuremberg, 1949), pp. 641–2; Wylie, *Barbed Wire Diplomacy*, pp. 255–6; *Joseph Goebbels Tagebücher 1924–1945*, Band 5, 31 March 1945, p. 2181; and Hermann Göring testimony, *IMT, Trial of the Major War Criminals*, vol. IX (Nuremberg, 1947), p. 389. For the OKW analysis of the advantages and disadvantages of repudiating the conventions see document D-606, *IMT, Nazi Conspiracy and Aggression Suppl. A*, pp. 894–905.

conditions of western POWs would assist in building an alliance with the western Allies against the Soviets, he 'vigorously oppose[d]' it.[29]

However, although Wylie rightly observed that Hitler was 'prepared to extend the kind of practices routinely employed in Russia to the western theatre', a policy he undoubtedly had the power to employ regardless of any objections his top lieutenants might have expressed, the fact is that he did not do so.[30] Despite the examples shown above of his involvement in setting POW policies and the eagerness shown by his closest aides to 'translate his Delphic utterances into practical policies', no record was found in this research that indicates that Hitler was involved in setting other policies related specifically to the treatment and handling of non-Soviet Jewish POWs.[31] The lack of such an order (the reasons for which are reviewed later in this chapter)—either in a written or verbal form or even just nuanced—was one reason as to why intervention attempts by state organs such as the RSHA and the NSDAP remained unsuccessful.

It should be noted that the cases described above where Hitler's orders to mistreat and even execute POWs were not carried out were the exception, rather than the rule, and related to specific cases—execution of Free French soldiers after a certain battle and of Dutch escapees; had Hitler issued a general order on American and British Jewish POWs that was aligned with the Nazi racial or political worldview it would have been undoubtedly followed in the same way that the orders that resulted in the murder of the Soviet Jewish POWs and the deportation to concentration camps of the Spanish Republican POWs had been followed. However, despite the public commitment of the Wehrmacht's top commanders to Nazi ideology, the OKW, the head of AWA and of the heads of the POW Office, not receiving any direct guidance from Hitler in relation to non-Soviet Jewish POWs, did not try to anticipate his will by 'working towards the Führer', and were left to decide on their own policies.

The Oberkommando der Wehrmacht (OKW)

In a speech on the first anniversary of the 'Seizure of Power', on 30 January 1934, Hitler confirmed the continuation of the tradition of the 'Prusso-German dualism of the military and the political' by declaring the Wehrmacht as one pillar of Germany's two-pillar state—the other pillar being the NSDAP—and by that, assured the Wehrmacht of its equal status to the Party.[32] However, despite its presumed autonomy and apparently in order to gain favour with the regime, the

---

[29] Berger to Martin, 31 March 1945, HW5/706, TNA; *Joseph Goebbels Tagebücher 1924–1945*, Band 5, 5 March 1945, p. 2136.
[30] Wylie, *Barbed Wire Diplomacy*, p. 152.   [31] Ibid., p. 90.
[32] Müller, *The Army, Politics and Society in Germany, 1933–1945*, p. 30; Klaus-Jurgen Müller, *Das Heer und Hitler* (Stuttgart: Deutsche Verlags-Anstalt, 1969), p. 66.

Wehrmacht began a process of ideological synchronization ('*Gleichschaltung*') with the National Socialist worldview—in effect, it was 'working towards the Führer' from early on.[33] Nazi symbols such as the swastika and the eagle were adopted, and the Wehrmacht did not push back against 'ideological concessions of legally dubious nature', such as the 'Aryan Clause', which was adopted in February 1934 and excluded non-Aryans from serving in the Wehrmacht, or against the instruction prohibiting soldiers from shopping in Jewish-owned shops.[34] In 1938, with the removal of von Blomberg, Hitler took over the roles of war minister and Commander-in-Chief of the Wehrmacht; as described by Omer Bartov, this meant that in effect, 'the army as an institution formed an integral part of rather than a separate entity from the regime'.[35] In fact, from 1943 onwards, an assessment of Wehrmacht officers' attitude towards National-Socialism was incorporated into their six-monthly evaluation (pushing 'Proven conduct against the enemy' to the third place on the list of assessed attributes).[36] This section will demonstrate that as a result of this process, when it came to making decisions related to the treatment of POWs in general, the OKW was no longer an independent body but a committed follower of its Commander-in-Chief, Adolf Hitler; and any national conservative values which might have been held by its members played only a minor part, if any, in its decisions.

There are numerous examples of the Wehrmacht's almost-blind compliance with Hitler's orders and his (sometime vague) guidelines. When Hitler warned his generals in March 1941 that the war in the East would be very different from the war in the West, defining it as a 'war of extermination', urging them to 'forget the concept of comradeship between soldiers' and demanding the '[e]xtermination of the Bolshevist Commissars and of the Communist Intelligentsia', no serious objections were raised.[37] On the contrary—the OKW went ahead and,

---

[33] Bartov, 'Soldiers, Nazis and the War in the Third Reich', p. 54.

[34] Müller, *The Army, Politics and Society in Germany, 1933-1945*, pp. 32-3; O'Neill, *The German Army and the Nazi Party*, p. 115. Interestingly, one dissenting voice to the implementation of the Aryan Clause was that of then-Colonel (later Field Marshal) von Manstein (see Müller, *The Army, Politics and Society in Germany, 1933-1945*, p. 114; and Förster, 'Complicity or Entanglement? Wehrmacht, War and Holocaust', p. 268). The Aryan Clause was extended during the war to also include half- and quarter-Jews (ibid., p. 269).

[35] Bartov, 'Soldiers, Nazis and the War in the Third Reich', p. 60.

[36] See, for example, the evaluations of Oberst Ernst Koß, 13 October 1942 and 17 March 1943, BA-MA PERS 6/6426. A review of several dozen evaluations of POW camp commandants led to the conclusion that they served more as a box-ticking exercise: although 86% of the evaluations commented on the officer's attitude towards National-Socialism, it had always been to praise the officer's dedication to the Nazi cause and the vast majority of the comments seemed to have been chosen from a 'menu' of five to six sentences to describe this attitude (Wehrmacht personnel files can be found in BA-MA, PERS 6).

[37] *War Journal of Franz Halder*, 30 March 1941, vol. 6, pp. 42-3. During the Nuremberg trials some of the generals insisted that they expressed their objections to the orders to their superiors; however, even if that had been true, not even one of them resigned as a result of it (see, for example, von Leeb's testimony in IMT, *Trials of War Criminals*, vol. X, p. 1091). When objections had been raised, they were based on the generals' concern for military discipline, and not due to the morality of the order (see Jacobsen, 'The Kommissarbefehl and Mass Execution of Soviet Russian Prisoners of War', p. 516).

together with the Wehrmacht's legal advisors, meticulously translated Hitler's guidelines into orders that would later result in the mass executions of civilians and Soviet POWs and the death from exhaustion, disease, and starvation of millions of them. These orders, which were later referred to as the Criminal Orders, included the 'Martial Jurisdiction Decree', which was issued on 13 May 1941 and allowed soldiers to execute, without due legal process, anyone they deemed to be resisting them; and the 'Commissar Order', issued on 6 June 1941, which instructed the German army to execute Soviet commissar POWs.[38] In the postwar period it was argued that the Criminal Orders were not passed down the chain of command and therefore were not implemented; however, an analysis of the records of army, corps, and division levels indicated that these orders were issued 'with remarkable bureaucratic routine' and reached at least 60% of all command levels.[39] Executions of captured Soviet commissars were reported by more than 80% of the 150 German divisions who participated in the invasion.[40]

In order to implement the Commissar Order the Wehrmacht had to cooperate with the RSHA and its Einsatzgruppen and hand over to it the commissars as well as other groups of Soviet POWs, including other Communist functionaries and Jews; these groups were not included in the original order but were added later by Heydrich, in his instructions to the Einsatzgruppen, the RSHA units responsible for the execution of the order.[41] The cooperation between the Wehrmacht and the RSHA was formalized on 28 April 1941 in the 'Regulations on the Deployment of the Security Police and the SD in Army Formations' order, which was issued following discussions between the army's quartermaster, General Eduard Wagner, and Heydrich.[42]

Various details related to this cooperation were sent out in a series of orders between June and August 1941; the objections raised by the Wehrmacht did not mention the immorality of murdering defenceless POWs but rather the impact these executions would have on the soldiers' discipline, and resulted in the shifting of the executions from the camp to the 'vicinity of the camp'.[43] One notable exception was Admiral Canaris, the Head of the Abwehr: in response to his written objections to the brutal treatment of Soviet POWs, Keitel himself, true to his nature as an ardent follower of Hitler, noted that '[t]he objections arise from the military concept of chivalrous warfare! This is the destruction of an ideology!

---

[38] For the Wehrmacht's activities to convert Hitler's guidelines into detailed military orders see Förster, 'The German Army and the Ideological War against the Soviet Union', pp. 15–29; and Messerschmidt, *Die Wehrmacht im NS-Staat*, pp. 390–411. On the Criminal Orders see Felix Römer, 'The Wehrmacht in the War of Ideologies: The Army and Hitler's Criminal Orders in the Eastern Front', in Alex J. Kay, Jeff Rutherford, and David Stahel, eds, *Nazi Policy in the Eastern Front, 1941* (Rochester: University of Rochester Press, 2014), pp. 73–100, p. 75.
[39] Ibid., p. 78.   [40] Ibid., p. 88.
[41] 'Richtlinien für die in die Stalags und Dulags', 17 July 1941, BA R58/9016.
[42] Document NOKW-2080, *IMT, Trials of War Criminals*, vol. X, pp. 1240–2.
[43] 'Richtlinien für die in die Stalags und Dulags', 17 July 1941, BA R58/9016.

Therefore, I approve and back the measures.'⁴⁴ And Reinecke, the head of AWA, argued that the necessity of these measures needs to be made clear to the Wehrmacht because apparently some in its officers' corps were 'still entertaining ideas which belonged to the Ice Age and not to the present age of National Socialism'.⁴⁵ Although an order issued by Wagner to the army did specify that Soviet Jewish POWs (along with Asians and German-speaking Russian POWs) should only be segregated, and not liquidated, it was eventually overturned when the various orders were consolidated on 8 September 1941 by Reinecke into one order, which instructed camp commandants to provide full cooperation to the RSHA's Einsatzgruppen.⁴⁶ In any case, Wagner's order was not driven by any national conservative values but was probably a result of the severe labour shortages in the army's operational area.⁴⁷

The amalgamation of Nazi ideology with military execution was also evident in the way these orders were communicated to the lower ranks: Walter von Reichenau, the commander of 6th Army during the first stage of the invasion of the Soviet Union, reminded his soldiers that they 'must have full understanding of the necessity of a severe but just retribution upon the Jewish subhuman elements'; von Manstein, at the time commander of the 11th Army, explained to his soldiers that they came as 'the bearer[s] of a racial concept' and that they 'must appreciate the necessity for the harsh punishment of Jewry, the spiritual bearer of the Bolshevist terror'.⁴⁸

Although the Criminal Orders and the lower-level commands which they triggered were issued to troops fighting in the East, there is no doubt that their spirit filtered into other theatres of war: during the last months of 1941, Wehrmacht commanders in Serbia, who were ordered to execute fifty to one hundred Serbian hostages as reprisals for every German soldier killed by partisans, did not need specific instructions from the OKW nor the help of the RSHA when deciding who to execute; the majority of their victims were Jews, some of which were not

---

⁴⁴ 15 September 1941, document EC-338, *IMT, Nazi Conspiracy and Aggression*, vol. VII (Washington, DC, 1946), p. 414.

⁴⁵ For Reineke's comment see Testimony of Erwin Lahousen, *IMT, Trial of the Major War Criminals*, vol. II, pp. 456–8.

⁴⁶ For Wagner's order see Streit, *Keine Kameraden*, pp. 99–100; for Reinecke's order see regulation for the treatment of Soviet POWs in all prisoner of war camps, 8 September 1941, document 1519-PS, *IMT, Nazi Conspiracy and Aggression*, vol. IV, pp. 58–65. For testimonies of the selection and execution of Soviet Jewish POWs see Shneyer, *Pariahs among Pariahs*, pp. 227–54. Heydrich's guidelines for the selection of certain types of POWs, including Jews, for 'Special Treatment' is found in Heydrich's 'Richtlinien für die in die Stalags und Dulags', 17 July 1941, BA R58/9016.

⁴⁷ See Karsten Linne, '"Die Arbeitskraft sämtlicher Kriegsgefangenen ist rücksichtslos auszunutzen." Die Zwangsarbeit sowjetischer Kriegsgefangener für die Wehrmacht im Osten', *Jahrbücher für Geschichte Osteuropas*, 54:2 (2006), pp. 190–206, p. 194. According to the order, Soviet Jewish POWs were assigned the most dangerous tasks, such as mine clearing.

⁴⁸ The Reichenau order, document NOKW-3411, *IMT, Trials of War Criminals*, vol. X, pp. 1211–14. For Von Manstein's order see document 4064-PS, *IMT, Trial of the Major War Criminals*, vol. XXXIV, pp. 129–32 (translation in *IMT, Trial of the Major War Criminals*, vol. XX (Nuremberg, 1948), p. 642).

even Serbian. As Christopher Browning observed, '[t]his meant that... central European Jewish refugees, mostly Austrians, were shot by troops predominately of Austrian origin in retaliation for casualties inflicted by Serbian partisans on the German army'.[49]

The start of the radicalization of the POW policies in the west can probably be traced to the Commando Order, which specifically targeted British commandos ('and their accomplices') caught behind German lines.[50] The intention not to take them prisoner was announced by Hitler in a radio speech on 7 October 1942; just as the year-long Shackling Crisis was gathering pace, Hitler stated that 'terror and sabotage groups of the British and their accomplices... must be slaughtered ruthlessly in combat'.[51] A few days later this statement was formally issued as the 'Commando Order', which removed the POW status from captured Allied commando soldiers and ordered their transfer to the SD and not to POW camps; in cases where they were believed to have been given this status by mistake, it was withdrawn and the POWs, no longer under the protection of the Convention, were taken from POW camps and executed.[52] The Wehrmacht's operation staff even took the initiative of declining the request of the POW Office to report to the ICRC, as required by the Geneva Convention, enemy deaths resulting from this order, arguing that since this was a decree from Hitler, only the head of AWA or the OKW—Keitel—could make such decisions.[53] And in the following year—1943—in expressing its support for the Luftwaffe's proposal to place POWs as human shields in town centres, the OKW's Operations staff suggested to allow Allies' authorities to learn about this clear violation of the Convention through the death notices that would be sent to them.[54]

The September 1943 armistice between Italy and the Allies created a situation where many Italian units found themselves stationed alongside Wehrmacht units which were, just a few days earlier, their allies. The OKW ensured that Hitler's order to execute all captured Italian officers who refused to join the German side had been implemented; however, it then went even further and in at least one

---

[49] Christopher Browning, 'Wehrmacht Reprisal Policy and the Mass Murder of Jews in Serbia', *Militärgeschichtliche Zeitschrift*, 33:1 (1983), pp. 31–47, p. 39.

[50] The Commando Order, 18 October 1942, document 498-PS, *IMT, Nazi Conspiracy and Aggression*, vol. III, pp. 416–17. The order was later extended to include captured members of Allied military missions with the partisans (see treatment of members of foreign 'military missions', captured together with partisans, 30 July 1944, document 537-PS, *IMT, Nazi Conspiracy and Aggression*, vol. III, p. 439).

[51] *IMT, Trials of War Criminals*, vol. XI, p. 665.

[52] Ibid., pp. 665–6; on the removal of POWs from POW camps see, for example, *IMT, Trials of War Criminals*, vol. X, pp. 116–17.

[53] Reports procedures concerning destruction of sabotage units, 20 May 1943, document NOKW-004, *IMT, Trials of War Criminals*, vol. XI, p. 93. General Warlimont, Jodl's deputy in the OKW's Operations Department, argued in his trial that he did not want the POW Office to send these reports because it would have provided Hitler and other agencies with a way of monitoring such incidents (see ibid., p. 138).

[54] Wylie, *Barbed Wire Diplomacy*, p. 180.

documented case, when the Italian division which was based on Cephalonia island decided to fight the Germans instead of surrendering to them, issued an order that no prisoners should be taken.[55] The order led to the massacre of approximately 5,000 Italian POWs (in addition to 340 Italian officer POWs).[56]

Another example where the OKW demonstrated that it was not guided by any national conservative values is its support for the lynching of downed aircrews, where it did not even require a specific directive signed by Hitler; rather, the OKW was satisfied with 'following the lines of the generally distributed declaration made by... Goebbels' published in the *Völkischer Beobachter* on 28 and 29 May 1944.[57] The OKW was the driving force in the discussions that followed on how to convert these guidelines into an actual order; eventually it was agreed that the Lynch law would be applied to air crews who participated in the strafing of civilians, passenger trains, and hospitals. It then went a step further by suggesting that air crews who were suspected of such actions but have already been transported to POW camps (and hence had already been registered as POWs) should be stripped of their POW status and handed to the SD for 'Special Treatment'— i.e. for execution. Kurt Kaltenbrunner, the head of the RSHA at the time, who also participated in that meeting, 'expressed his complete agreement' with the decisions; and Keitel himself added a hand-written comment to the minutes of that meeting, stating that he was 'against legal procedure' being applied in this case as 'it does not work out'.[58] The German Foreign Office had initially objected to the OKW's suggestion on the grounds that once an air crew member was delivered to a POW camp he was under the protection of the Geneva Convention and could only be executed once the Protecting Power was given a three-month notice; in order to avoid this 'complication', the Foreign Office suggested, and it was agreed, that downed enemy airmen would be considered not as POWs but as criminals, and handed over to the Security Services.[59] At the end of 1944 the OKW went even further and prohibited soldiers from protecting downed airmen from being lynched by civilians, stating that 'No fellow German can understand such an attitude on the part of our armed forces'.[60]

---

[55] For Hitler's order see treatment of members of the Italian army, 15 September 1943, document NOKW-916, *IMT, Trials of War Criminals*, vol. XI, pp. 1081–3; for the OKW order not to take prisoners see Overmans, 'Die Kriegsgefangenenpolitik des Deutschen Reichs 1939 bis 1945', p. 827.

[56] Ibid.; see also Philip Morgan, *The Fall of Mussolini* (Oxford: Oxford University Press, 2007), p. 111.

[57] A word on the enemy air terror, the *Völkischer Beobachter*, 28–9 May 1944, document 1676-PS, *IMT, Trials of War Criminals*, vol. XI, pp. 166–9; and treatment of enemy terror flyers, 6 June 1944, document 735-PS, ibid., pp. 169–71. Hitler mentioned the idea of shooting pilots parachuting from planes as early as September 1942 (see Hugh Trevor-Roper, ed., *Hitler's Table Talk* (New York: Enigma Books, 2000), p. 696).

[58] Treatment of enemy terror flyer, minutes of a meeting, 6 June 1944, document 735-PS, *IMT, Trials of War Criminals*, vol. XI, pp. 169–71.

[59] 20 June 1944, document 728-PS, *IMT, Trials of War Criminals*, vol. XI, pp. 175–7.

[60] Conduct of soldiers in cases where the civilian population takes matters in its own hands with regards to shot-down terror flyers, 11 December 1944, document NOKW-3060, ibid., pp. 179–80.

As was shown above, national conservative values did not play a role in any of the cases described; and therefore, given the Nazification of the German High Command and its willingness to follow Nazi ideology, its approach towards non-Soviet Jewish POWs seems even more incomprehensible. However, there is very little doubt that had Hitler issued a specific order extending the implementation of the Final Solution to non-Soviet Jewish POWs, the OKW would have followed it without hesitation and would have setup the necessary infrastructure for its implementation. The OKW did not need any persuasion to fulfil orders that were in clear breach of the Geneva Convention, regardless of whether they referred to Soviet POWs or those from western armies. The Geneva Convention indeed formed the general framework for the way Germany treated western POWs during the war; however, when orders to breach it were received from above, the OKW implemented them without hesitation or objection and regardless of any risk of reprisal against German POWs held by the Allies.

Interaction between the RSHA and the NSDAP and the Wehrmacht

Before reviewing the next level in the OKW Hierarchy—the POW Office—it is important to analyse the interactions, when it came to POWs, between the OKW and the POW Office and two of the Reich's other state organs—the RSHA and NSDAP. Such analysis can help shed additional light on the roles played by organizations outside the Wehrmacht when it came to the treatment of POWs, and specifically, to that of non-Soviet Jewish POWs.

There are multiple examples of the RSHA's involvement in POW issues. After the completion of the campaign in Poland the RSHA demanded that the POW Office transferred to its control Polish intelligence officer POWs; the POW Office, however, rejected the demand.[61] Two years later, the coordination between the RSHA and the Wehrmacht during the campaign in the East was made clear in the detailed implementation guidelines which were included in Heydrich's 17 July 1941 letter, which stated that '[t]hese directives have been formulated in agreement with the OKW—Prisoners of War department .... The commanders of the Prisoner-of-War and transit camps (Stalags and Dulags) have been informed by the OKW'.[62] Heydrich's deputy, Heinrich Müller, reminded RSHA commanders that '[i]n case difficulties of any kind should occur... refer the competent Armed Forces authorities to the directives laid down in conjunction with the OKW'.[63]

---

[61] Krafft, 10 August 1951, BA-MA MSG 2/12656.
[62] 'Richtlinien für die in die Stalags und Dulags', 17 July 1941, BA R58/9016.
[63] Directives for the Kommandos [sic] of the Chief of the Security Police and the Security Service to be assigned to permanent PW camps and transit PW camps, 26 September 1941, document NO-3417, *IMT, Trials of War Criminals*, vol. XI, pp. 11–15.

In depositions given after the war two members of the POW Office—General Westhoff, who was head of the POW Office from April to October 1944 and then became Inspector of the POW Office, and Oberstleutnant Theodor Krafft, who was in charge of POW treatment in the General Department of the POW Office—testified that throughout the war, the RSHA pressured the POW Office to transfer all Jewish POWs to its control, probably in order to apply to them the same policy it applied to Soviet Jewish POWs.[64] Part of their testimonies can be viewed as attempts to exonerate the Wehrmacht and to present it as a protector of POWs in general and more specifically of Jewish POWs; however, even though they might not reflect the exact circumstances, their testimonies can still be used to demonstrate the general thought process at the time.

According to Westhoff, the RSHA argued that the transfer of Jewish POWs to its control was needed in order to prevent them from coming into contact with the German population; as mentioned in Chapter 3, in response, General Reinecke, who as head of AWA was in charge of the POW Office, 'in order to take the wind out of the RSHA sails', decided to segregate the Jewish POW in separate labour detachments, where contact with the German population was presumably impossible.[65] Since POWs in labour detachments had in fact a greater chance of coming into contact with the German population, the segregation did not necessarily address the RSHA demand. However, in view of the German policy against civilian Jews, it is plausible that the demand—which was backed at a later stage also by Field Marshal Keitel—did indeed occur; and that despite their efforts, even after SS personnel became formally part of the POW organization in October 1944—with SS General Berger as head of the POW Office and the HSSPF being put in charge of the POW commanders in the military districts, who were responsible for the POW camps in their areas—they were not successful in transferring Jewish POWs into RSHA's custody.

Another example demonstrates both Hitler's involvement in POW issues and the RSHA's relentless efforts to implement his orders even during the last months of the war, when German defeat was all but certain: the last Chief of the General Staff of the Luftwaffe, General Karl Koller, testified that at some point during that period, Hitler, in one of his outbursts, ordered that all captured Allied airmen should be turned over to the SD and shot. Koller refused to fulfil the order and even received the backing of the head of the RSHA, Kaltenbrunner; however, Adolf Eichmann, one of the main architects of the Holocaust and Kaltenbrunner's subordinate as the head of Sub-Department IV-B4 of the RSHA, responsible for Jewish affairs, insisted that Hitler's order should be applied at least to the Jewish

---

[64] Westhoff affidavit, 15 January 1966, BA-MA MSG 2/12655; Krafft, 10 August 1951, BA-MA MSG 2/12656.

[65] Westhoff affidavit, 15 January 1966, BA-MA MSG 2/12655.

airmen.[66] Koller testified that he circumvented Eichmann by scattering the pilots among multiple POW camps so that they could not be easily identified.[67]

The RSHA's ability to influence the Wehrmacht when it came to POW policies was also evident when it came to the implementation of the Commando Order. During the Normandy landings, RSHA delegates in France met with the staff of Field Marshal Gerd von Rundstedt, the Commander-in-Chief West, to decide on the treatment of Allied soldiers who landed behind enemy lines in Normandy; if the order was to be strictly applied, as the RSHA demanded, then all captured soldiers would have been either killed on the spot or handed to the SD for 'Special Treatment'.[68] Von Rundstedt, who pushed for a complete suspension of the *Kommandobefehl* in Normandy, eventually had to cave in and reached an agreement with the Paris representatives of the RSHA and the HSSPF, according to which only captured enemy soldiers who landed in the immediate vicinity of the combat area would be excluded from the order; the rest would be handed over to the SD.[69] In addition, the OKW agreed that in 'doubtful cases' the captured soldiers will be turned over to the RSHA, and gave the security services the ultimate authority in deciding the fate of these soldiers; to ensure that the RSHA was fully informed and was able to monitor its implementation, copies of the decision were also sent to the head of the RSHA and to the command staff of Himmler, in his role as head of the SS.[70]

All of these examples demonstrate how the RSHA was able to exert its influence over the highest levels of the Wehrmacht, and show how close was the cooperation between these two organizations. However, attempts to transfer Jewish POWs to the custody of the RSHA were also made at lower levels, with the Gestapo interacting directly with POW Camp commandants. One such attempt was made during the last months of the war, when the Gestapo in Schneidemühl (today Piła in Poland) gave the commandant of Oflag 65 in Berkenbrugge a list of 600 Yugoslavian officer POWs who were either Jewish or suspected of being Communists, and demanded that they be handed over to it for liquidation. According to the POWs in that camp, who were made aware of the plan through

---

[66] IMT, *Trial of the Major War Criminals*, vol. XVIII (Nuremberg, 1948), pp. 586–7.

[67] Testimony of Michael Musmanno, the presiding judge in the Einsatzgruppen Case in Nuremberg, at the trial of Adolf Eichmann in Jerusalem, session 39, 15 May 1961, https://www.nizkor.org/the-trial-of-adolf-eichmann/, accessed 1 February 2021. In the conversation between Koller and Kaltenbrunner that was mentioned in the Nuremberg trials there was no reference to Eichmann; Koller's agreement with Kaltenbrunner, mentioned in the same conversation, was that if they were instructed to implement the order, Koller would delay it by arguing that Allied aviators were spread across multiple POW camps. It is possible that Musmanno misunderstood Koller's comment about actively dispersing the Jewish aviators.

[68] Treatment of commando men, 23 June 1944, document 531-PS, *IMT, Nazi Conspiracy and Aggression*, vol. III, pp. 435–7.

[69] Ibid.; treatment of Kommando [sic] participants, 26 June 1944, document 551-PS, ibid., pp. 440–1.

[70] Treatment of commando men, 23 June 1944, document 531-PS, ibid., pp. 435–7; treatment of Kommando [sic] participants, 26 June 1944, document 551-PS, ibid., pp. 440–1.

a German NCO in the camp's headquarters, the Soviet army's quick advance, together with the camp commandant's delaying actions, saved the lives of the POWs on the list.[71]

The case of Ignaz Hecht, a Polish Jew who was captured in 1940 when fighting with the French army, is another example of the influence the RSHA was able to exert over the lower echelons of the Wehrmacht, this time with a more severe outcome than the example mentioned above. Hecht was part of Stalag X-B's (Sandbostel) Jewish-segregated labour detachment 610 near Bremen. Together with five to six other Jewish POWs he was travelling daily, unguarded, to work in construction sites around Bremen. He apparently used his relative freedom to engage in black market activities and was arrested by the Gestapo on 21 December 1944.[72] After being interrogated, Hecht was 'killed while trying to escape' on 9 February 1945; the Gestapo reported on his death only five weeks later, on 16 March 1945.[73] The archival material related to this case provides a valuable insight into the relations and the power struggle between the Wehrmacht and the RSHA when it came to the question of 'ownership' of POWs, and into their treatment of Jewish POWs from western armies.

According to POW Office regulations, POWs had to be considered as belonging to the army whose uniform they were wearing when captured, and not according to their original citizenship. In fact, in order to demonstrate this requirement, the order issued by the POW Office used as a specific example the case of Polish soldiers who were captured while fighting with the French army; the instruction was that they should be treated as French POWs.[74] Despite that, in the correspondence between the battalion in charge of guarding the labour detachment, Stalag X-B (Sandbostel), military district X (headquartered in Hamburg), and the Gestapo, and in the various reports that were submitted on this case, Hecht was referred to alternatively as either a Jewish POW, a Jewish Polish POW or, in one case, as a Polish POW—and not, as he should have been according to the Wehrmacht's own regulations, as a French POW.[75] There was only one report that mentioned that Hecht was also a French POW; but, based on the wording—'Jewish (Polish French POW)'—this was secondary to the fact that he was Jewish.[76]

---

[71] Josip Presburger, 'Oficiri Jevreji u Zarobljenickim Logorima u Nemackoj (Jewish Officers in Prisoners of War Camps)', 3 *Zbornik, Jevrejski Istorjki Muzej (The Jewish History Museum)*, Belgrade, 1975, pp. 225–82, p. 260.

[72] Gestapo report, 29 December 1944, Service historique de la défense/DAVCC, Caen, 22 P 3000.

[73] Gestapo Bremen to commandant of Stalag X-B (Sandbostel), 16 March 1945, ibid.

[74] Sammelmitteilungen 1, 'Kr. Gef. fremder Volkszugehörigkeit in feindlichen Heeren', 16 June 1941, BA-MA RW6/270.

[75] See, for example, Btn 681 to Stalag XB, 22 February 1945 (Jewish POW); Gestapo to Stalag X-B (Sandbostel), 16 March 1945 (Jewish-Polish); POW commander in military district X to Stalag X-B (Sandbostel), 30 March 1945 (Polish), Service historique de la défense/DAVCC, Caen, 22 P 3000.

[76] Report of Feldwebel Spreen, 8 January 1945, ibid.

Hecht's arrest was reported by his Jewish POW comrades when they returned to the camp after work on 21 December 1944; but when the commandant contacted the Gestapo to confirm that Hecht had indeed been arrested and this was not a case of his comrades trying to cover his escape, the Gestapo denied any knowledge of him.[77] Only when another commandant intervened and used his personal contacts in the Gestapo did they admit that Hecht had been arrested.[78] The Gestapo summarized the initial interrogation report with a recommendation that Hecht should be transferred to the Gestapo's custody and be sent to a 'concentration camp level III', where he would have been executed.[79] The Gestapo interrogator did not make any attempt to hide the reason for this recommendation, concluding that this should be done because 'a Jew is always a danger'.[80] A formal request to transfer Hecht was then submitted by the Gestapo to the commandant of Stalag X-B (Sandbostel).[81] Even though the commandant could have turned down the request on the spot—either on the grounds that Hecht was a French POW, or, even if he was considered a Polish POW and according to the RSHA's own regulations, on the grounds that those could only be handed over to the Gestapo in cases of sabotage or sexual relations with minors—he nonetheless decided to escalate the issue to the OKW instead.[82] Hecht was still alive at that point; however, a response from the OKW, if there had been one, was not found in the files, and it is doubtful whether it would have made a difference to Hecht's eventual fate.

Several conclusions can be drawn from this case. Firstly, the hesitation of the commandant of Stalag X-B (Sandbostel) to reject the Gestapo's demand to transfer Hecht, despite the fact that the Gestapo had no jurisdiction over him, demonstrates that there was a level of fear of the Gestapo within the Wehrmacht. It is possible that the commandant—who was described by his commanders in his periodic evaluations from that period as someone who 'does not stand out', perhaps alluding to indecisiveness—escalated the issue to the OKW in order to provide him with some sort of support in his dealings with the Gestapo (he had done so before the Gestapo reported that Hecht was killed), although he was within his

---

[77] Ibid.   [78] Ibid.
[79] 'Level III' meant a camp from which prisoners were not expected to return. For description of the classification of concentration camps see *IMT, Trial of War Criminals*, vol. V—*The RuSHA Case, The Pohl Case* (Washington, DC, 1950), p. 221.
[80] Rommelmann, 29 December 1944, Service historique de la défense/DAVCC, Caen, 22 P 3000.
[81] Commandant of Stalag X-B (Sandbostel) to POW commander in military district X, 26 January 1945, ibid.
[82] Minutes of the phone call between Werdier and Bock, 23 January 1945, ibid. For RSHA regulations regarding Polish POWs who committed crimes, see punishment of severe offenses, 10 February 1944, document NO-1365, *Trials of War Criminals*, vol. IV, p. 1140. An order issued by the POW commander of military district VI (Westphalia) narrowed the criteria for handing over POWs to the Gestapo only to cases where there were 'demonstrable acts of sabotage' ('*nachweislichen Sabotageakten*'); the decision remained with the POW camp commandant (see document 1514-PS, 27 July 1944, *IMT, Trial of the Major War Criminals*, vol. XX (Nuremberg, 1948), pp. 261–4).

rights to deal with this issue by himself.⁸³ The commandant was clearly not following specific orders which stated that while Soviet POWs could be transferred to the Gestapo without cause, Polish ones could only be handed over if they were accused of very specific offenses and provided that the accusation was proven; furthermore, the decision of whether to remove their POW status was also left in the hands of the camp commandant.⁸⁴ Hecht, even if his status as French POW was not honoured, was not accused of any of those offenses, a fact that was even pointed out by Stalag X-B's staff.⁸⁵

Secondly, the Jewish labour detachment was referred to as a 'western Jewish POW' detachment, which means that there was a clear distinction within the POW organization between POWs from western armies and those from the East; and that this distinction also applied to Jewish POWs.⁸⁶ Within this category, however, the Jewish POWs were referred to as being in a 'closed' detachment, which meant that they were not supposed to work unguarded nor be in contact with German civilians.⁸⁷ These types of definitions were not found in any other source; it is possible that they were more common in the case of French POWs, who had the largest number of Jews among any of the western POWs' nationalities.

Thirdly, it seems that the Geneva Convention and the POW Office rules did not play any role in Hecht's case. Hecht was well aware of the protection he was entitled to due to his status as POW and even made it clear in his statement, saying that 'I would like to note that I am exercising my right under the Geneva regulations'.⁸⁸ This, however did not carry any weight with the Gestapo and a few weeks later, on 9 February 1945, not waiting for a formal response to its demand, Hecht was murdered while 'trying to escape'—a Gestapo code for murdering a prisoner; the Gestapo reported his death—and the cremation of his body, eliminating any possibility of investigation—only five weeks later, on 16 March 1945.⁸⁹ Although it is possible that this murder and potential cover-up were not a standard practice and were enabled by the general chaos that existed during the last weeks of the war, it is clear that had the Wehrmacht insisted on enforcing its

---

⁸³ Wehrmacht personnel file of von Foris, BA-MA PERS 6/2586.

⁸⁴ Delivery of prisoners of war to the secret state police, document 1514-PS, *IMT, Nazi Conspiracy and Aggression*, vol. IV, p. 54. As it happens, the Protecting Power delegate who visited the camp around the same period commented on the performance of the camp's commandant by stating that '[The Stalag's] Authorities are doing nothing to improve the lot of the prisoners' and that the 'Camp Commander and his staff did not bother to ameliorate conditions more than could possibly be helped' (quoted in Vourkoutiotis, *Prisoners of War and the German High Command*, p. 176).

⁸⁵ Minutes of the phone call between Werdier and Bock, 23 January 1945, Service historique de la défense/DAVCC, Caen, 22 P 3000.

⁸⁶ The legal officer of Stalag X-B (Sandbostel), 12 February 1945, ibid.

⁸⁷ Ibid.   ⁸⁸ Hecht's statement, 27 December 1944, ibid.

⁸⁹ Gestapo to the commandant of Stalag X-B (Sandbostel), 16 March 1945, ibid.

own rules, as well as the rules of the Geneva Convention, and demanded that the Gestapo handed Hecht back, this case might have had a different ending.[90]

The case of Ignaz Hecht is unique only because it left a detailed documentation trail that provides an insight into an interaction between bodies which were at the lower levels of the chain of command—in the Wehrmacht's case, the commandants of labour detachment 610 and Stalag X-B (Sandbostel), and in the RSHA case, the Gestapo office in Bremen. It is likely that the outcomes of similar cases were the same: while the POW Office insisted on protecting western POWs through full adherence to the Geneva Convention, the lower echelons of the Wehrmacht, perhaps out of fear, perhaps due to anti-Semitism, gave in to the RSHA demands and did not insist on following its own rules in protecting its POWs.[91] As one POW camp commandant explained—almost apologetically—to the delegate of the Swiss Protecting Power, who complained about the Gestapo's handling of POWs inside the camp, 'the Gestapo has become an integral part of the Wehrmacht since the Reichsführer SS [Himmler] has taken over [in July 1944] the Supreme Command of the Ersatzheer'.[92]

As described in this section, the RSHA was involved not only in discussions related to POW policies, such as the Commando Order, but also in their implementation.[93] After the invasion of the Soviet Union, the RSHA enjoyed almost full cooperation from the Wehrmacht; in cases where officers in the POW organization tried to save 'undesirable' Soviet POWs from execution, the OKW sided with the RSHA and forced these officers to comply with the order.[94] However, based on Westhoff's and Krafft's testimonies after the war, the RSHA was not always able to enforce its will, and the POW Office succeeded in rebuffing the RSHA's demands to extend the cooperation to cases where non-Soviet Jewish POWs were involved. Only an order from senior OKW generals, such as Keitel and Reinecke, could have changed that situation; but, in the absence of a direct instruction from the Commander-in-Chief of the Wehrmacht, Adolf Hitler, such an order was never issued.

---

[90] An example that might support the conclusion that the situation might have ended differently had it occurred earlier in the war is the case, in August 1941, of two escaping Russian POWs who were caught after robbing a German family and murdering the father. The Gestapo in Nuremberg, which reported this case, had proved their guilt by matching their fingerprints and executed them only after it obtained the agreement of the POW Office (see operational situation report U.S.S.R. no. 64, 26 August 1941, BA R58/216).

[91] There were also cases of Polish Jewish POWs, who were captured while fighting with the French Foreign Legion, who were sent to concentration camps (see Favez, *The Red Cross and the Holocaust*, p. 123).

[92] Swiss embassy report on Stalag XVII-B (Gneixendorf), 17 January 1945, TNA WO 224/44.

[93] This conclusion was also reached by Szymon Datner (see Datner, *Crimes against POWs*, pp. xxvii–xxix).

[94] See the case of Major Karl Meinel in military district VII, document R-178, *IMT, Nazi Conspiracy and Aggression Suppl. A*, pp. 1243–69; and additional description in Datner, *Crimes against POWs*, pp. 248–57.

Another organization that was involved in POW affairs was the NSDAP. One aspect of this involvement was its influence on the orders that were issued by the POW Office: as described in the next section, such orders had to be submitted first to various ministries—such as labour, foreign, etc.—but also to the Nazi Party representative who was attached to AWA. These orders were then passed on to Bormann, Hitler's private secretary and the head of the Nazi Party chancellery, and to the Gauleiters, and gave the Party the ability to monitor their implementation.[95] The involvement of the Party representative in the review process of the orders resulted in cases where orders drafted by the POW Office were completely redrafted by the Party chancellery.[96] However, despite that involvement, only a limited number of orders related to Jewish POWs were issued by the POW Office; this might have been a result of the review process, which allowed NSDAP representatives only to make changes to drafts of proposed orders but perhaps not to create new ones.

The approach of the NSDAP to POW issues was demonstrated when representatives from the Party chancellery—Helmuth Friedrichs, Bormann's deputy and the head of the Party Affairs Department, and Hermann Passe, the Wehrmacht liaison in that department—together with representatives from other ministries, attended a meeting with the POW Office to discuss new rules for the treatment of POWs. One of the demands that was raised by the Party chancellery was to limit the number of Red Cross parcels the POWs were receiving; when the head of the General Department in the POW Office at the time, General Westhoff, objected, Friedrichs responded that they could treat POWs as they wanted, and that 'the Geneva Convention was just a piece of paper'.[97]

As in the case of the RSHA, the NSDAP made continuous efforts to get involved and influence the treatment of POWs. Examples of the Party involvement in POW affairs include the attempts by its local Gauleiters to influence POW treatment, which they considered to be too lenient; and the Party's demand to increase POWs' productivity, which resulted in Reinecke issuing orders that, as Streit pointed out, in effect submitted all levels of the POW organization to the Party and made it clear that they were no longer—if they ever were—acting as equals.[98] The involvement of the Party in POW affairs intensified further towards the end of the war, with the OKW issuing an order instructing that '[t]he co-operation of all officers in charge of war prisoners with the functionaries of the Party must be intensified to an even greater extent', and ordering the appointment of liaison

---

[95] Streit, *Keine Kameraden*, p. 261.
[96] Interrogation of Westhoff, 2 November 1945, https://www.fold3.com/image/231908260, accessed 1 October 2019, pp. 19 and 26; see Westhoff's testimony also in *IMT, Trials of War Criminals*, vol. XI, p. 652.
[97] Westhoff Testimony, *IMT, Nazi Conspiracy and Aggression—Suppl. B*, p. 1645.
[98] Testimony of Reinhard von Westrem, *IMT, Trials of War Criminals*, vol. XI, pp. 53 and 56–7; Streit, *Keine Kameraden*, pp. 261–3.

officers between the POW commandants and local Party leaders in order to facilitate the indoctrination of the POW guard units in the National Socialist ideology.[99]

Although, and unlike the case of the RSHA, no evidence was found demonstrating that the Party tried to intervene specifically in the case of Jewish POWs, this cannot be ruled out.[100] Minutes from discussions of the Party's representatives in AWA regarding orders related to Jewish POWs were not found, but given the NSDAP's anti-Semitic policies and its active participation in, and support of, the extermination of civilian Jews, it is likely that its representatives contributed to the text of some of these orders. Specifically, this might have included the references made in POW Office orders (which are described in the next section) to the labelling of Jewish POWs and their segregation from their non-Jewish comrades, and prohibiting POWs' blood donations due to the risk of some of the POWs being Jewish or partly Jewish. Therefore, despite the presumed absence of a direct order from Hitler, it is clear that the NSDAP tried to influence POW policies; judging by the outcome, however, it appears that the POW Office was able in most cases to push back against such influences and maintained its authority in ensuring the protection of POWs, including the non-Soviet Jewish ones, in line with the Geneva Convention.

The Kriegsgefangenenwesen (POW Office)

As described above, the body within the OKW which was in charge of POWs was the POW Office, which was part of the General Office of the OKW. Since, as established earlier in this chapter, no order by Hitler or the levels above the POW Office was found that dealt specifically with the treatment of non-Soviet Jewish POWs, a review of the orders issued by the POW Office should provide an insight into its priorities, and, given the review process each order had to go through, should also reflect the priorities of the OKW and the influence other bodies of the

---

[99] Treatment of prisoners of war—increase in production, 17 August 1944, document 233-PS, IMT, *Trial of the Major War Criminals*, vol. V (Nuremberg, 1947), p. 477. This conclusion was also supported by Szymon Datner (see Datner, *Crimes against POWs*, pp. xxvi–xxvii). Detailed instructions from the OKW regarding cooperation with the NSDAP, and the follow-up orders from the military districts to the POW camp commandants, can be found in OKW letter from 13 May 1943 and POW commander in military district III (which was headquartered in Berlin) letter from 4 June 1943, BA-MA PERS 6/11025. In another example, the head of the Army's personnel office wrote a letter to Himmler in which he (almost apologetically) explained that the commandant of stalag X-C (Nienburg) 'was not disadvantaged in any way in the army because of his membership of the Party' (see head of Army personnel office to Reichsführer SS, 31 October 1944, BA-MA PERS 6/6474).

[100] Joseph Lador-Lederer argues that document NG-4238 of the Nuremberg trials mentioned that the POW Office rejected a demand from the NSDAP to transfer Jewish POWs to the SD; however, this document was not found (Joseph Lador-Lederer, 'Jews as Prisoners-of-War in Germany, with Special Reference to Yugoslav Soldiers', in Yakir Eventov et al., eds, *Yalqut 1948–1978* (Jerusalem: Jerusalem Post, 1978), pp. 171–2).

German state were able to exert on the POW Office. And ultimately, in his role as the Commander-in-Chief of the Wehrmacht and given his involvement in POW issues, such review would reflect the priorities of Hitler himself.

Throughout the war, the POW Office issued multiple orders, guidelines, and policies which dealt with various aspects of the treatment of POWs in German hands. The POW commanders in the military districts were responsible for implementing these policies; however, since the military districts were under the jurisdiction of the Replacement Army, and although the POW Office had the authority to inspect POW camps, it had only limited influence on the way POW commanders in the military districts and their subordinated camp commandants implemented these policies.[101] This only changed in October 1944, when the POW Office was transferred to the responsibility of the Replacement Army and was put directly in charge of the POW commanders in the military districts.

The draft of the orders issued by the POW Office had to be reviewed and approved, depending on the case, by several state bodies; these bodies, which were sometimes also involved in the actual drafting of the orders, included the Reich's Food Ministry, the Foreign Office, the Labour organization, the RSHA, the Propaganda Ministry, and the NSDAP.[102] The latter had their own permanent representative attached to AWA, and therefore was the only body that had received all copies of the orders before they were issued. Only after these bodies had their say was the final draft sent to the head of AWA, General Reinecke, for signature.[103] Reinecke himself was described as 'the key figure in the treatment of prisoners of war' throughout the war.[104] Called 'The Little Keitel' by his opponents, Reinecke was the manifestation of the 'Party General', demonstrating full adherence to the National Socialist worldview as well as unconditional subordination to the objectives and actions of the political leadership.[105] However, he also argued that the treatment of POWs from western armies should be different to that of Soviet POWs; and later in the war, when the RSHA pressured the POW Office to transfer all Jewish POWs to its responsibility, Reinecke successfully rejected this demand.[106]

Six days before the invasion of the Soviet Union, on 16 June 1941, the POW Office began grouping its various orders and guidelines into collections of commands, first named *Sammelmitteilungen* (collection of notices) and later changed

---

[101] Dienstanweisung für den Kommandanten eines 'Kriegsgefangenen Mannschafts Stammlagers', p. 7, BA-MA RH 1/612; and Overmans, 'Die Kriegsgefangenenpolitik des Deutschen Reichs 1939 bis 1945', pp. 739 and 741.

[102] Ibid., p. 853.

[103] Interrogation of Westhoff, 2 November 1945, https://www.fold3.com/image/231908260, accessed 1 October 2019, p. 19.

[104] Streit, *Keine Kamerdan*, p. 68.   [105] Ibid.

[106] Testimony of Erwin Lahousen, *IMT, Trial of the Major War Criminals*, vol. II, p. 459; Westhoff affidavit, 15 January 1966, BA-MA MSG 2/12655. This was later used as an argument in Nuremberg by Reinecke's defence counsel, Dr Hans Surholt (see *IMT, Trials of War Criminals*, vol. X, p. 230).

to *Befehlssammlung* (collection of orders). According to the explanation which was included in the first collection, the intention was to reduce the amount of correspondence between the various departments in the POW Office, the military districts, and the POW camps, and standardize POW policies across the whole POW organization. The POW Office had apparently concluded that the correspondence that was being sent out to the various bodies was too large and fragmented to be viewed as a formal and coherent POW strategy, and decided to re-issue some of these orders, as well as new ones, in a consolidated form. The summaries included notices and instructions covering POW policies, issues raised by individual units that were of interest to the whole POW organization, and other general notices.[107] The summaries also included elaborations and clarifications on previously issued commands which were sent by the various POWs departments only to a small number of military districts and other recipients. It is important to note that these summaries did not include orders which were marked 'secret' or 'top secret', such as the ones related to the treatment of Soviet POWs described earlier.

From collection 11, issued on 11 March 1942, onwards, the commands were given running numbers and by the end of the war a total of 1,162 commands were issued in forty-nine collections.[108] The last collection, issued on 15 January 1945, was numbered 50; one collection, 31, was destroyed by an Allied bombardment before it was sent out and was never distributed.[109] The Collections were distributed to a wide audience: in addition to the military districts where the POW camps resided, they were also sent to multiple departments in the Wehrmacht, as well as to the military governors of Belgium, France, and Serbia. Although the POW Office, as well as the POW commanders in the military districts, issued additional commands throughout the war that were not necessarily included in these command collections, these were not distributed across all areas of the POW organization and were usually intended to provide additional detail and clarification for the high-level orders which were included in the collections.

Judging only by their number, the issue of Jewish POWs was not considered high on the priority list of the POW Office: out of the 1,162 commands which were included in these collections, only eight (less than 0.7%) specifically mentioned Jewish POWs. These eight commands can be divided roughly into four groups: three commands, which have also been mentioned in Chapter 3, dealt with the general treatment of Jewish POWs; two with inquiries of Polish Jewish POWs regarding the fate of their families; and two detailed the treatment of specific categories—including Jews—of French, Belgian, and Dutch POWs.

---

[107] Sammelmitteilungen 1, 16 June 1941, BA-MA RW 6/270.
[108] For an unknown reason the numbers between compilations 48 and 49 and between 49 and 50 were not sequential.
[109] This explanation was given in Befehlsammlung 33, BA-MA RW 6/270.

The fourth category, to which the eighth command belonged, dealt with blood donation by POWs and provides an example of the influence the Nazi racial policy had on the Wehrmacht's POW policies; in all likelihood, it was a result of the involvement that the NSDAP liaison in AWA had on the drafting of these orders. Although it is possible that commands that dealt specifically with Jewish POWs that were marked 'secret' or 'top secret', and therefore were not included in these summaries, existed, none were found in this research. However, given that Jewish POWs were an integral part of all Allied armies and therefore had representation in most, if not all, POW camps, such an order would have had to have been issued to a large number of recipients in POW camps and military districts; had it existed, some form of it was likely to have been found.

The first reference to Jewish POWs in the POW Office's command notices was made on 16 June 1941; as mentioned Chapter 3, it was titled 'Jews in the French Army' and its purpose was to clarify the status of French Jewish POWs. Even though the French POWs formed the majority of POWs at that stage, it is not clear why the order did not include Jewish POWs from other western armies, primarily British Jewish POWs; or why it did not make any reference to Yugoslavian Jewish POWs or to the remaining Polish Jewish POWs (most of them had been released in the previous months). It is also not clear why the order was issued approximately a year after the end of the French campaign; one possibility is that it had been issued earlier only to a sub-set of the military districts, and a decision was made only later to issue it in a wider distribution. It is likely that up to that point camp commandants were treating Jewish POWs according to the guidelines of the 'Commandant Instructions Manual' mentioned above, which required them to segregate POWs upon arrival according to their nationality, 'race' ('*Rasse*'), and gender—in line with Article 9 of the Geneva Convention (for a detailed discussion regarding the segregation of Jewish POWs see Chapter 3).[110] Soviet Jewish POWS fell under a different set of guidelines—the instructions for their 'Special Treatment' were issued by Heydrich on 17 July 1941, a month after the 'Jews in the French Army' order was issued; it is possible that the POW Office knew that Heydrich's order is about to be issued, and since it was also aware of the Commissar Order, which was issued at the beginning of the same month, decided to issue its own order in order to make it clear that French Jewish POWs should be treated under a different set of guidelines.[111]

The order stated that 'there is no intention to place Jewish [POWs] in special camps. However, all French Jewish POWs in Stalags and Oflags should be

---

[110] Dienstanweisung für den Kommandanten eines 'Kriegsgefangenen Mannschafts Stammlagers', 16 February 1939, p. 11, BA-MA RH 1/612. Similar guidelines issued to Dulag commandants only required them to segregate POWs by officers, ORs (Other Ranks), and nationality (see Dienstanweisung für den Kommandanten eines Kriegsgefangenen Durchgangslagers, 22 May 1939, p. 11, BA-MA RH 1/611).

[111] Richtlinien für die in die Stalags und Dulags, 17 July 1941, BA R58/9016.

separated within the POW camps[.] Special labelling of Jews is to be foreseen.'[112] Interestingly, in a meeting with ICRC delegates that took place just a few days before this order was issued, OKW representatives assured the ICRC that Jewish POWs would be treated in the same way that non-Jewish POWs were treated and would face no restrictions due to their race.[113] The ICRC report noted that based on previous reports as well as letters from POWs' families it was already known that this was not the case, and that restrictive measures had already been taken against Jewish POWs: as mentioned earlier, Jewish doctors and medical personnel were not allowed to treat other POWs, and at the same time were not designated for repatriation even though their status as Protected Personnel allowed that.[114]

Nine months later the POW Office issued another order related to Jewish POWs. Although in June 1941 it had informed recipients that the special marking of Jewish POWs was anticipated, on 11 March 1942, in an order titled 'Marking of Jews', the POW Office reversed its previous order and stated that although Jews in the Reich were marked in order to identify them in the streets and in shops, the same did not apply to Jewish POWs. However, and as mentioned in Chapter 3, the order reiterated the instruction to separate Jewish POWs from the rest, adding that this should be implemented 'as far as possible [*soweit wie möglich*]', thereby leaving the final decision regarding segregation in the hands of the camp commandants.[115] The clarification regarding the marking of Jewish POWs might have been in response to several incidents where French and Yugoslavian Jewish POWs had been marked (the latter in February 1942, only a month before the order was issued); in one of those incidents, a French POW had taken the initiative, while the camp commandant was away, and tried to force French Jewish POWs in his camp to wear yellow marks. When the commandant returned, he immediately instructed that the marks should be removed.[116] In any case, while outside the fences of the POW camps the systematic murder of Europe's civilian Jews was continuing unhindered, this command signifies one of the first attempts by the POW Office to keep Nazi ideology from crossing into the camps.

The third order related to the general treatment of Jewish POWs (which was also mentioned in Chapter 3) was issued by the POW Office on 15 December 1944, two and a half months after SS General Berger took over the POW Office. The order was titled 'Treatment of Jewish POWs' and its purpose was to reiterate the previous commands which related to Jewish POWs—those issued on 16 June 1941 and 11 March 1942—and to provide additional clarification. Specifically, it stated again that there was no intention to concentrate Jewish POWs in special

---

[112] Sammelmitteilungen 1, BA-MA RW 6/270.
[113] Notes from a meeting with OKW representatives, 12 June 1941, ACICR BG 17 05/006.
[114] Report of Dr Coeudres, 23 May 1941, ACICR BG 25/34.
[115] Befehlsammlung 11, order 5, 11 March 1942, BA-MA RW 6/270.
[116] For Yugoslavian Jewish POWs, see Asaria-Helfgot, *We Are Witnesses*, pp. 39–40; for marking of French Jewish POWs, see Durand, *La Captivité*, p. 355.

camps; that in the camp Jewish POWs should be housed separately from non-Jewish POWs and as far as possible sent to work outside the camps; and that there was still an intention to mark Jewish POWs at a later stage. However, there were two significant changes from the previous commands: the words 'as far as possible' now only related to sending Jewish POWs to special labour detachments, but not to the segregation itself; by doing that, Berger made segregation mandatory and no longer allowed camp commandants to decide whether to segregate Jewish POWs or not. The second significant change added by Berger forbade camp commandants from discriminating against Jewish POWs by stating that they should be treated in the same way that non-Jewish POWs from the respective army were treated; this, no doubt, was a reference to the fact that POWs from the American and British armies had been treated differently from their Yugoslavian, French, and Belgian comrades; and, of course, the treatment of Soviet and Polish POWs was much worse than the rest. There were also two other minor additions, namely, that contact with the German population should be avoided; and that Jewish POWs whose German citizenship had been revoked and who had died in captivity were not entitled to a military funeral.[117]

The timing of this command, when the Second World War was reaching its final stages, might help explain the rationale behind it: on one hand, Berger, new in his role and wanting to assert his authority, wanted to ensure that previous commands were being adhered to; on the other hand, it is also possible that Berger, well aware that the end of the war and Germany's almost certain capitulation were approaching, was concerned about his eventual fate in the hands of the approaching Allies. His instruction not to discriminate against Jewish POWs, along with his decision not to replace the Wehrmacht staff with SS personnel when he took over the POW Office, could be attributed to his need to present himself to the Allies as the protector of POWs, including the Jewish ones.[118]

The second and third categories of orders related to Jewish POWs were more reactive in nature and provided instructions for dealing with certain situations involving them. The second category included guidelines for dealing with inquiries from Polish Jewish POWs about the fate of their families in Poland. In the first order, issued on 5 April 1943, camp commandants were instructed to forward such inquiries to the headquarters of the German Red Cross in Berlin.[119] Most of the Jewish population in Poland had already been murdered by then and the Germans were about to launch the final operation to clear the Warsaw Ghetto of its remaining inhabitants and send them to the Treblinka extermination camp (the Warsaw Ghetto Uprising took place two weeks after this order had been issued). The timing of this command might have been linked to this; and

---

[117] Befehlsammlung 48, order 876, 15 December 1944, BA-MA RW 6/270.
[118] Feldseber to the British War Office, 16 April 1945, TNA WO 208/4440; Nichol and Rennell, *The Last Escape*, ln. 6054.
[119] Befehlsammlung 23, order 300, 5 April 1943, BA-MA RW 6/270.

referring POWs' inquiries to the German Red Cross, which was in all likelihood aware of the fate of their families, seemed like a delaying tactic.[120] It should be noted that two months earlier, on 2 February 1943, the Jewish Telegraphic Agency (JTA) reported that the German postal service returned letters sent to murdered Polish Jews with the stamp 'Died in the course of the liquidation of the Jewish problem'.[121] Given the secrecy the Germans tried to impose on the extermination of the Jews, it is more likely that this was a result of a decision made by a local German—or perhaps an anti-Semitic Polish—post office clerk rather than of a policy dictated from above.[122] The POW Office order, however, came a few months too late: during the visit of the Swiss embassy delegates to Stalag VIII-B (Lamsdorf) on 28 November 1942, the POWs' representatives raised an issue regarding postcards sent by British Jewish POWs to their relatives in Poland (the reference in the report was probably to the Palestinian Jews, some of whom had immigrated to Palestine from Poland). The cards were returned to the senders marked '*Empfänger Jude*' ('Jewish recipient'). The inspectors indicated that this issue had already been raised by the camp's MOC with the camp's authorities; however, they must have seen it as a major issue since they stated that 'the German High Command will be asked to take position on it'.[123] Since the mass deportation of Jews from the Warsaw Ghetto to the Treblinka extermination camp took place between July and September of 1942, it is likely that the Germans wanted to hide the fact that the POWs' relatives were no longer alive; however, it is not clear why they did not simply destroy these letters, or at least stamp them with a 'Recipient Unknown' notice.

On 1 May 1944, approximately one year after issuing the initial order related to the inquiries of Polish Jewish POWs, the POW Office issued an update to the order, withdrawing it and instead instructing camp commandants to reject any requests from Polish Jewish POWs for information about their families.[124] It is not clear why the Germans had decided on that specific date to stop the charade of forwarding these inquiries to the German Red Cross; one possibility is that they realized by then that the murder of the Jewish population in Europe was no longer a secret.

The third area where the POW Office had felt that a general policy order should be issued was the handling of a specific category of French and Belgian POWs: those who were either Jewish, or of Polish nationality, or belonged to the Polish

---

[120] As early as August 1941, the ICRC was asked to stop sending requests for information to the German Red Cross regarding missing people (see Favez, *The Red Cross and the Holocaust*, pp. 56–7). This decision was reversed later but only for non-Jews (see ibid., p. 60).

[121] 'Nazis Return Letters with Stamp "Died during Liquidation of Jewish Problem"', JTA, 2 February 1943, https://www.jta.org/archive, accessed 8 May 2019.

[122] Letters sent from POW camps by Yugoslavian Jewish POWs to their families after they were sent to the concentration camps were returned with 'Recipient Unknown' or 'Left' (see Keynan, *Memories from a Life I Have Not Lived*, p. 875).

[123] Swiss embassy report on Stalag VIII-B (Lamsdorf), 28 November 1942, p. 5, TNA WO 224/27.

[124] Befehlsammlung 35, order 645, 1 May 1944, BA-MA RW 6/270.

Legion; and who either refused to work, or who had been recaptured after an escape. Various orders, which were issued by the POW Office in 1942, stated that unlike their French and Belgian comrades, who were sent to the General Gouvernement as a deterrent against escaping back to their home countries, these POWs were sent to Stalag 303 in Norway (this was later changed to Stalag II-D in Stargard in Pomerania).[125] These orders were updated in 1943, probably due to the acute manpower shortage in the Reich: from June 1943 onwards, recaptured and work-refusing French and Belgian POWs were no longer sent to POW camps in the General Gouvernement but remained in the military district where they were captured and were forced to work in tougher conditions. French and Belgian Jewish POWs (as well as non-Jewish POWs of Polish nationality and those who belonged to the Polish Legion) continued to be sent to Stalag II-D (Stargard).[126] Given the numerous orders which dealt with this topic the POW Office probably felt a clarification was required and, as part of its order compilation, issued another order on 15 January 1944, re-iterating the 1943 instructions related to this specific category of POWs and reminding the recipients that French and Belgian Jewish POWs still had to be sent to Stalag II-D (Stargard) (in the next order compilation, issued on the same date, this was changed to Stalag II-E in Schwerin).[127]

The fact that French and Belgian (and later Dutch as well) Jewish POWs were included in the same category as French and Belgian POWs who had Polish nationality, and both were sent together to a special POW camp, may indicate that there was an intention, perhaps once the war was over, to treat them differently to the non-Jewish and non-Polish French and Belgian POWs.[128] The fact that at a later stage, despite the critical manpower shortages in the Reich, they were still being sent to the special camp supports this conclusion.[129]

The fourth category referencing Jewish POWs had an impact on all POWs, Jews and non-Jews alike. Issued on 10 August 1942, it was a direct manifestation of the Nazi racial policy; more specifically, it dealt with the racial purity aspect of blood donations and clarified the POW Office policy in cases where POWs were used as blood donors, an activity that was not specifically forbidden in the 1929

---

[125] Sicherungsmaßnahmen dated 6 May, 11 July, and 7 November 1942 in PMA 189/1/43 and 10 August 1942 in PMA 33/1/6.
[126] Sicherungsmaßnahmen dated 26 June and 10 July 1943 in PMA 190/1/43, and 12 August 1943 in PMA 202/1/47.
[127] Befehlsammlung 32, order 541, and Befehlsammlung 33, order 578, both on 15 January 1944, BA-MA RW 6/270.
[128] Abtransport wiederergriffener oder die Arbeit verweigernder Kriegsgefangener in Sonderlager, 7 February 1944, PMA 191/1/44 and BA-MA RH 49/35.
[129] In June 1944 a new order related to recaptured and work-refusing POWs was issued. The order replaced all previous ones and stated that from now on 'security considerations take precedence over labour requirements'; the approach towards French, Belgian, Dutch, and Polish Jewish POWs remained the same (see Zusammenfassung aller Bestimmungen Über den Arbeitseinsatz wiederergriffener und Arbeitsverweigernder Kr. Gef., 12 June 1944, PMA 744/1/30).

Geneva Convention. The order prohibited blood donations from POWs since 'it cannot be ruled out with certainty that even part-Jews [*jüdische Mischlinge*] among the prisoners of war will be used as blood donors'.[130] Since the Nuremberg laws, which dealt with the definition of a Jew, had been in place since 1935, it is surprising that the blood donation order was not issued at a much earlier stage; it is possible that the NSDAP or even the RSHA, in its role as protector of the racial purity of the German Volk, had noticed this omission and applied pressure to close this 'loophole'. It is also possible that the reference to POWs who were part-Jewish supports the conclusion, mentioned in Chapter 3, that the POW Office already had lists of POWs who were fully Jewish; this is not surprising given that religion was part of the information that every POW was required to provide when captured (although not all Jewish POWs declared their religion when captured).[131] Although the Germans could have argued that they were required to track these numbers in order to adhere to the Geneva Convention's Article 16, which guaranteed the freedom to practice religion, the fact that these reports did not mention any other religion points towards an intention to use this information in a more sinister way at some point in the future.

The command summaries described above, by their definition, were those that detailed the main POW policies of the OKW; inclusion in the command summaries meant that these policies were distributed across the POW organization and were expected to be implemented in all parts of it. The summaries, however, did not include all of the commands issued throughout the war by the various departments of the POW Office, nor all those that were issued by the POW commanders in the military districts. These commands, which did not deal with general policy issues, were usually of lesser importance and were distributed to a smaller number of recipients; they were only included in the summaries if they were deemed to be relevant to the whole of the POW organization. Judging by the reference numbers identifying them it can be assumed that throughout the war several thousand such commands, meeting summaries and regulations were issued, sometimes providing low-level details regarding the implementation of the policies mentioned in the command summaries—including reporting templates, details of the reporting cycles, the number of copies that should be made of each report, and the list of their recipients. Some of these commands and guidelines included direct and indirect references to Jewish POWs but perhaps were not deemed important enough, were too detailed, or were not relevant to the whole of the POW organization to be included in the command summaries.

One example of an indirect reference was the religion practices guidelines, which referenced non-Christian religions (but not making specific mention of any of them), allowing worshippers to practice them only in cases where

---

[130] Befehlsammlung 15, order 111, 10 August 1942, BA-MA RW 6/270.
[131] For more details see the Identifying Jewish POWs section in Chapter 3.

clergymen of that religion were among the POWs (which was in breach of the Convention, which guaranteed complete freedom of practice). Examples of direct reference include the funeral guidelines, which specifically instructed camp commandants to bury Jewish POWs in the Jewish cemetery of the nearest town if the POW camp did not have a cemetery.[132] The meaning of the funeral guidelines (which are discussed in detail in Chapter 2) should be put in the right context, as they clearly demonstrate the difference in the treatment between Soviet and non-Soviet Jewish POWs: issued in July 1941, less than two weeks after Heydrich issued his instructions to the Einsatzgruppen for the liquidation of Soviet Jewish POWs, the OKW issued a formal order that instructed camp commandants to provide non-Soviet Jewish POWs who died in captivity with a full military funeral. In another example of an order that made specific reference to Jewish POWs, the POW Office issued an instruction on 30 October 1941 that in exceptional cases hospitals were allowed to use French and British doctors and medical orderlies—even if they were Jewish ('*auch wenn sie Juden sind*')—to treat POWs from other nationalities.[133] This seemed to be a reflection of the shortage in medical staff, which required the Germans to use British and French doctors in treating POWs from other nationalities.

In addition to commands which referred to Jewish POWs there were other commands issued by the POW Office that are also worth noting for what was not mentioned in them. For example, an order from 10 October 1941 stated that Algerian, Tunisian, and Malagasy POWs—who were all part of the French army—should not be kept in POW camps inside Germany.[134] This was similar to the order to remove French Black African colonial POWs from German soil; in both cases, Jewish POWs were not mentioned.[135] A more detailed command, issued on 7 August 1942 and not included in the POW Office's commands collection, instructed camp commandants to list the names of the remaining non-European French POWs in three separate groups: Blacks, white North Africans, and the rest (including Moroccans, Tunisians, Algerians, Indo-Chinese, and POWs from France's American colonies who were part French).[136] Again, there was no mention of Jewish POWs.

Another order that made specific reference to the nationality of the POW dealt with reporting procedures in case of death of a POW. The OKW was very specific about the type of information and documents, including letters from comrades of

---

[132] For practice of non-Christian religions, see Religionsausübung der Kriegsgefangene, 12 May 1941, PMA 202/1/47, pp. 2–3; for funeral guidelines, see Beerdigung gefallender oder verstorbener feindlicher Wehrmachtangehöriger, 29 July 1941, BA R 58/9017. See also the Religious and Cultural Activity section in Chapter 2.
[133] Heranziehung von franz. und englischen Artzen u. Sanitätsunterpersonal, 2108/41, 30 October 1941, PMA 188/1/42.
[134] Sammelmitteilungen 5, order 6, 10 October 1941, BA-MA RW 6/270.
[135] Scheck, *French Colonial Soldiers in German Captivity*, p. 54.
[136] Abtransport von franz. Kr. Gef. Negern, Marokkanern, Tunesiern usw. sowie weissen Nordafrikanern, 7 August 1942, PMA 189/1/43.

the deceased, that should be sent to the German Red Cross in such cases. It also made it clear that if the deceased POW was Russian, no such report was necessary. There was no specific mention of Jewish POWs in this order and it can therefore be assumed that they were included in the regular reports.[137] In another example, an order listed release procedures for several groups of POWs, including French, Belgians, and minorities in the Yugoslavian and Soviet armies (such as Romanian, Croatian, and Ukrainian).[138] Unlike the case of the Polish POWs, Jewish POWs were not mentioned as a separate group that should be excluded from the order; it can therefore be concluded that they were viewed as part of the armies they fought with and treated in the same manner as their comrades—an outcome that was not in their favour since as civilians, their fate was sealed.

In summary, out of the eight commands which referenced Jewish POWs that were issued by the POW Office as part of its periodical collection of commands, two referred to inquiries by Polish Jewish POWs regarding their families; two to the treatment of French and Belgian Jewish POWs who either refused to work or escaped and were recaptured; and one prohibited blood donations from POWs as their Jewishness could not have been ruled out. Only three commands gave instructions regarding the general treatment of Jewish POWs—and high-level instructions at that. While their civilian brethren around Europe were being loaded onto trains headed to concentration and extermination camps, POW camp commandants were ordered simply to house Jewish POWs in separate barracks—an order that, when it came to American and British Jewish POWs, was not followed until the last stages of the war, and even then only in a relatively small number of cases.[139] This set of commands indicates that even though the German state had specific laws dealing with every aspect of Jewish life within German society and within German-occupied Europe, these rules were not transferred to the military sphere; unlike Soviet Jewish POWs, the OKW did not receive specific instructions for the treatment of non-Soviet Jewish ones, and the orders issued by the POW Office seemed to have been in reaction to events, rather than driving a policy aligned with the German State's escalating anti-Jewish actions.

Explaining the Fate of Non-Soviet Jewish POWs

As demonstrated in this chapter, the OKW was for most of the period Hitler was in power fully aligned with the National Socialist worldview and demonstrated almost blind obedience to him as its Commander-in-Chief. This obedience

---

[137] Sammelmitteilungen 3, order 14, 23 July 1941, BA/MA RW6/270. For some reason the order made specific reference to Russian, but not to Soviet POWs.
[138] Sammelmitteilungen 6, order 18, 11 November 1941, BA/MA RW6/270.
[139] Additional details can be found in Chapter 3.

included the implementation of the Criminal Orders in the East, which led to the murder of tens of thousands of Soviet commissars, Jewish POWs, and civilians; the implementation of the Commando Order and the Kugel Erlass; and allowing the RSHA access to POW camps to identify Spanish Republican POWs, who despite being protected by the Geneva Convention, were then transferred to concentration camps where the majority of them perished.

Given this, the protection provided to non-Soviet Jewish POWs raises two questions. The first is why did the POW Office continue to protect non-Soviet Jewish POWs, despite the fact that in parallel, policies against civilian Jews on one hand and against western POWs in general on the other were going through a radicalization process, and state bodies were attempting to extend National Socialist ideologies to Jewish POWs inside POW camps. The second and more fundamental question is why did Hitler, despite his obsession with implementing the 'Final Solution to the Jewish Question', not issue an order to apply the Final Solution to non-Soviet Jewish POWs, an order that would have undoubtedly been followed to the letter by an obedient and compliant OKW. As it happens, and despite his direct involvement in multiple POW matters that breached the Geneva Convention, such an order was never issued.

The Role of the POW Office

The role played by the POW Office in the protection of non-Soviet POWs is analysed based on two stages of the war: from the beginning of the war until October 1944, when the POW Office was part of the OKW; and from October 1944 until the end of the war, when the POW Office—and POW camps—were under the control of SS General Gottlob Berger. The explanations relate primarily to the approach taken by the OKW and the POW Office; the behaviour of the levels below, including POW camp commandants, camp guards, and German citizens towards Jewish POWs was addressed in the previous chapters of this book.

One potential explanation for the POW Office's behaviour is its commitment to treating enemy POWs according to the 1929 Geneva Convention. Germany ratified the Geneva Convention in 1934, when Hitler was already in power; Overmans argued that despite the fact that the ratification was mostly a propagandistic step and part of Hitler's attempt to demonstrate 'a spirit of reconciliation and of understanding', the OKW's pre-war plans for dealing with POWs were eventually based on the Convention 'both because of the impression on neutral foreign countries as well as in the interest of the German prisoners of war who are subject to retaliatory measures'.[140] The POW Office made the prominence of the

---

[140] Both quotes are in Overmans, 'Die Kriegsgefangenenpolitik des Deutschen Reichs 1939 bis 1945', pp. 730 and 738.

Convention clear in the POW commandants' manuals that were issued before the war broke out and in the various orders that were issued throughout the war.[141] The manuals stated that anyone involved in the 'treatment, monitoring and employment' of POWs should be made familiar with the Convention; and that violations of it might result serious consequences to German POWs in enemy hands.[142] Interestingly, even when it came to Soviet POWs, the manual for labour detachments' commandants stated that, while the Geneva Convention did not apply to them, it should still 'generally be the basis for [their] treatment'.[143]

Overmans explains further that during the last stages of the war, when the vast numbers of Allied POWs could have been used as the last mean of pressure against the advancing Allies, the commitment to preserve the Convention kept Germany's hands tied.[144] Neville Wylie adds that the resilience of the Convention stemmed from its 'capacity to persist in the face of changing circumstances'; Germany and the western Allies complied with the Convention because they expected to have relative gains from it and shared, even at the height of the war, common concerns about the treatment of their own POWs.[145]

However, the role played by the POW Office as the guardian of the Convention did not guarantee full compliance with it. As General Westhoff made it clear in his testimony in Nuremberg, '[without] specific orders from the Fuehrer [sic] that the Geneva Convention can be disregarded, it [was] my duty to abide by the rules and act so that the rules of the Geneva Convention will be observed'.[146] But when such orders did arrive, they were executed: the most obvious example is, of course, the fate of the Soviet POWs. Although Germany argued that Soviet POWs

---

[141] The Convention was also repeatedly referred to in the orders issued by the POW Office: for example, in 1941 it reminded camp commandant that Article 36 of the Convention 'prohibits the stoppage or confiscation of incoming or outgoing mail of POWs' (see Sammelmitteilungen 1, 16 June 1941, BA-MA RW6/270). This did not apply, however, to everyone: in January 1945, Polish POWs were prohibited from sending letters to their next of kin in Belgium, France, or Holland. In the same order compilation in 1945, camp commandants were instructed to avoid using the term 'penal commandos' to describe labour detachment where convicted POWs were interned because the term suggested double punishment, which was in violation of Article 52 of the 1929 Geneva Convention (see Befehlsammlung 50, orders 900 and 908, 15 January 1944, NARA RG 389, box 695, 290/33/33/6).

[142] Dienstanweisung für den Kommandanten eines 'Kriegsgefangenen Mannschafts Stammlagers', 16 February 1939, pp. 7–8, BA-MA RH 1/612. Later in the war, the POW Office issued additional orders related to reprisals, reminding commandants 'not be guided by [their] personal attitude when dealing with English [POWs], as there are concerns of repercussions for German POWs' (see Besprechungsnotizen 7488/41, 21 October 1941, PMA 31/1/5).

[143] Handbuch für Arbeitskommandoführer, Wehrkreis XIII, 1 June 1943, BA-MA RH 49/24, p. 42.

[144] Overmans, 'Die Kriegsgefangenenpolitik des Deutschen Reichs 1939 bis 1945', p. 730.

[145] Wylie, Barbed Wire Diplomacy, pp. 17–18. Hitler's senior lieutenants were apparently well aware of the importance of preserving, at least outwardly, Germany's compliance with the Convention. When Himmler, in January 1943, separately asked Keitel and Ribbentrop to consider the removal of POW status from Polish Officer POWs he was quite careful in choosing his words: to Field Marshal Keitel he wrote 'I understand very well that certain considerations must be made here regarding the Geneva Convention'; and to Ribbentrop 'I know that my wish to no longer treat Polish officers as prisoners of war certainly raises serious concerns' (see Himmler to Keitel and Himmler to Ribbentrop, 18 January 1943, BA NS 19/1694).

[146] Westhoff Testimony, IMT, Nazi Conspiracy and Aggression—Suppl. B, p. 1644.

were not protected by the Convention because the Soviet Union did not ratify it, this claim ignored the fact—which was even highlighted by the POW Office itself—that Article 82 of the Convention clearly stated that 'if one of the belligerents is not a party to the Convention, its provisions shall, nevertheless, remain binding as between the belligerents who are parties thereto'.[147] Germany also ignored the ratification by both countries of the Fourth Hague Convention on War on Land of 1907 which specifically prohibited the killing or wounding of soldiers who surrendered.[148] The well-known result of this was the death, according to several estimates, of more than 3 million Soviet POWs—more than 55% of the total number of Soviet POWs captured by Germany.[149]

When it came to western POWs, some of the breaches for which the POW Office was directly responsible, while not leading to the same catastrophic outcomes, included reduction in the food rations of POWs, which resulted in hunger and poor health, especially in cases when Red Cross food parcels became unavailable; and cases of shooting and serious harassment by guards and civilian employers.[150] It can be argued that the major breaches of the Geneva Convention which concerned western POWs—the Commando Order, the Kugel Erlass, the lynching of downed airmen, the murder of Italian officers who, after Italy's surrender to the Allies, refused to continue to fight on Germany's side, and the murder of the fifty escapees from Stalag Luft III (Sagan)—all resulted from policies dictated from above and referred to POWs who were captured outside the camps, and therefore the POW Office could have done very little in order to stop them from being implemented. The POW Office's resistance to the demands from the RSHA to hand over non-Soviet Jewish POWs might suggest that it could hold its ground when it came to treatment of POWs who were already in POW camps; however, the cases of commando soldiers and downed airmen who were stripped of their POW status even after they were brought to POW camps, and the cases described below of the French West African troops and the Spanish Republican POWs,

---

[147] POW Office to the OKW's Foreign Relations Department, 24 June 1941 (copy in *Das Stalag X B Sandbostel* (Hamburg: Dölling und Galitz Verlag), p. 36); Article 82 of the 1929 Geneva Convention, https://ihl-databases.icrc.org/ihl/INTRO/305, accessed 14 September 2019. The defence in the Nuremberg trials argued that for various reasons, Article 82 did not apply to Soviet POWs (see legal opinion by Professor Reinhart Maurach, *IMT, Trials of War Criminals*, vol. XI, pp. 44–8).

[148] Kochavi, *Confronting Captivity*, p. 2; Article 23 of the 1907 Hague Convention respecting the Laws and Customs of War on Land, https://ihl-databases.icrc.org/ihl/INTRO/195, accessed 20 December 2020.

[149] For the estimated number of Soviet POWs who died in German captivity see n. 16 in the Introduction to this book.

[150] Satow and See, when referring to food provisions in their report after the war on the activities of the POW Department of the British Foreign Office, stated that '[i]t can be said without fear of contradiction that the rations issued...to British prisoners of war were never...equivalent to the rations [as defined by the Convention]' (see Harold Satow and M. J. See, *The Work of the Prisoners of War Department during the Second World War* (London: British Foreign Office, 1950), p. 18). For the cases of shooting and serious harassment of American and British POWs see Vourkoutiotis, *Prisoners of War and the German High Command*, p. 180 n. 28 and pp. 180–2.

minority groups who fought as part of the French army, refute this argument: when receiving orders from above which forced it to breach the Geneva Convention, the POW Office was in no position to object to them, whether they related to POWs inside or outside the POW camps.

The French West African troops were subjected to a German propaganda campaign even before war broke out in the West.[151] The campaign, combined with situational factors such as the strong resistance shown by some of the West African units and rumours of mutilation of German POWs, were behind the massacres, upon capture, of approximately 3,000 West African soldiers, mostly by SS units.[152] After the armistice, 20,000 West African troops ended up in German POW camps; during the first months they were segregated from their white comrades, housed in makeshift camps, and were not allowed visits by delegates of the Protecting Power at the time, the USA.[153] According to some estimates, the harsh treatment, poor sanitation, and meagre food rations led to a death rate of up to 20% among them.[154] A few examples suggest that even though cases of their mistreatment after the first few months of captivity were not common, there were cases where these POWs were the subject of 'scientific' racial studies and life-threatening medical experiments.[155]

The second group, the Spanish Republican soldiers who fought with the French army, consisted of refugees from the Spanish Civil War who escaped to France after Franco's army defeated their Republican side. Most of these soldiers became POWs after the conclusion of the French campaign; they were taken to POW camps in Germany and, like the French Jewish POWs, segregated within the same POW camp from their French comrades.[156] However, that was where the parallels ended: not long after their capture, the POW Office allowed Gestapo agents, who apparently had detailed information regarding the identity of the Spanish POWs, into the POW camps in order to interrogate them.[157] Eventually, all Spanish POWs, despite their POW status as members of the French army, were sent to concentration camps such as Dachau, Mauthausen, and Buchenwald. The ICRC tried to intervene, unsuccessfully, on their behalf, but they received no support from either the Vichy government or the Spanish one.[158] It is estimated

---

[151] Scheck, *Hitler's African Victims*, pp. 102, 105, and 107–9. One German radio announcement warned that a French regiment, composed of 'foreign thugs and Jews', had arrived at the front (*Le Combattant Volontaire Juif 1939–1945*, p. 41).

[152] Scheck, *Hitler's African Victims*, p. 142. For cases of massacre of French Colonial troops see ibid., pp. 21–41 and 58.

[153] Scheck, *French Colonial Soldiers in German Captivity*, p. 59.

[154] Scheck, *Hitler's African Victims*, pp. 44 and 58–9. According to David Killingray the number was even higher—50% (see Killingray, 'Africans and African Americans in Enemy Hands', p. 181).

[155] Scheck, *French Colonial Soldiers in German Captivity*, pp. 113, 209–10.

[156] Testimony of Francois Boix, *IMT, Trial of the Major War Criminals*, vol. VI, p. 267.

[157] Fabréguet, 'Un Groupe de Réfugiés Politiques', p. 34.

[158] Favez, *The Red Cross and the Holocaust*, p. 57.

that out of the 8,000–9,000 Spanish Republican POWs who were sent to the concentration camps, only about 1,500 survived.[159]

The massacres of the French colonial troops during the last stages of the French campaign can be attributed to decisions of local commanders, who were clearly driven by racial attitudes and German propaganda—although it should be noted that these attitudes did not lead to cases of mass massacres of captured Jewish soldiers in the Western Front. However, the segregation of the colonial troops, the prevention of Protecting Power visits, and their poor treatment were not decisions of local commanders, but most likely of the levels above the POW Office.[160] Likewise, when the POW Office allowed the RSHA into POW camps to identify Spanish Republicans, following the same process that was applied to Soviet commissars and Soviet Jewish POWs and with almost identical outcomes, it clearly demonstrated that, when instructed, it did not hesitate to apply Eastern Front policies to non-Soviet POWs who were protected by the Geneva Convention. While the POW Office used the Convention as a benchmark for the day-to-day treatment of western POWs in categories such as food, shelter, clothing, and sending letters, the Convention did not play any substantial part in the German leadership's decision-making process when higher-priority considerations—such as ideological ones—were involved. As Westhoff testified, had an order come directly from Hitler overruling the Geneva Convention and ordering the transfer of non-Soviet Jewish POWs to concentration camps, it is highly unlikely that the POW Office, despite being entrusted with their protection, would have been in a position to subvert it, and their fate would have been the same as that of the Spanish Republican POWs.

However, such an order was never received; and without one, the POW Office, prior to October 1944, did not take any initiative to implement Nazi policies on its own. While doing so, it was guided by its concern for reprisals against German POWs in enemy hands as well as by the supremacy of the Geneva Convention. But it is highly likely that the third and main reason for this behaviour was that despite the unconditional subordination of senior officers in the OKW to the National Socialist worldview—Keitel and Reinecke are just two examples—the 'national conservative value system' of the staff in the POW organization, which required them to treat their enemies in an honourable manner, was the reason Nazi policies were not actively implemented in POW camps where non-Soviet Jewish POWs were held.

Several examples regarding the character of the staff in the POW organization—some of which were mentioned in the previous chapter—demonstrate this point.

---

[159] Fabréguet, 'Un Groupe de Réfugiés Politiques', pp. 34–7; Testimony of Francois Boix, *IMT, Trial of the Major War Criminals*, vol. VI, p. 267. For analysis of the number of Spanish POWs in Mauthausen also see David W. Pike, *In the Service of Stalin, The Spanish Communists in Exile 1939–1945* (Oxford: Clarendon Press, 1993), p. 60.

[160] On the responsibility for the massacres see Scheck, *Hitler's African Victims*, p. 62.

In his testimony during the Nuremberg trials, General Reinhard von Westrem, who was the POW commander in military district XII—himself a member of the Nazi Party since 1931 who was 60 years old when the Second World War broke—explained that the POW commanders in the military districts were, at least at the beginning of the war, 'mostly general staff officers from the old army'.[161] The British Joint Intelligence Sub Committee (JISC) described POW camp commandants as ' "dug-out" officers of the old German Army'; and Heydrich himself complained to Himmler that some POW camp commandants in the East were not as forthcoming when it came to handing over Soviet Jewish POWs for execution.[162] As mentioned earlier, when French General Henri Giraud managed to escape captivity in April 1942, Joseph Goebbels blamed the 'false humanitarianism' of the 'old reserve officers' who were in charge.[163] Colonel Friedrich Von Lindeiner, the commandant of Stalag Luft III in Sagan at the time of the March 1944 escape, can serve as an example of the type of officers Goebbels had in mind: 61 years old when he was appointed to his role, he was described as an 'officer of the old school of German soldiers'.[164] He insisted that for him, a Jew was just another POW, and in his speech to his officers after taking command of the camp he emphasized that '[t]he Geneva Convention is the basis for our behaviour' and that 'it is against the tradition of the German soldier to violate the precept of law, humaneness, and chivalry even against the enemy'.[165] Another example is that of the commandant of Oflag XIII-B (Nürnberg-Langwasser), Oberstleutnant Freiherr (Baron) Christoph von Imhoff: When informing the Yugoslav Jewish officer POWs in the camp that they were about to be segregated from their non-Jewish comrades, he insisted that the order was not his own but the OKW's; he then stated that he would do his utmost to make their life tolerable and that he would never forget that they were also soldiers and officers.[166]

Major Hans-Joachim Breyer, who served as the head of the POW Department of the OKW from the beginning of the war until January 1942, can be used to demonstrate the type of people that held roles in the higher levels of the POW organization. Breyer fought in the First World War, was injured in a gas attack, and spent time in British captivity.[167] In January 1942, when the department

---

[161] Testimony of General Reinhard von Westrem, *IMT, Trials of War Criminals*, vol. XI, p. 49. His Party membership was listed in his Wehrmacht personnel file, BA-MA PERS 6/71723.

[162] For the JISC report see report on prisoners of war in Germany, 29 July 1944, TNA CAB 79/79/1; for Heydrich see operational situation report U.S.S.R. no. 128, 3 November 1941, document NO-3157, *IMT, Trials of War Criminals*, vol. IV, p. 152.

[163] *Joseph Goebbels Tagebücher 1924–1945*, Band 4, 27 April 1942, p. 1786.

[164] Walton and Eberhardt, *From Commandant to Captive*, ln. 333.

[165] Delmar Spivey, oral history, AFRHA, irisnum 01015417, reel 31923; Walton and Eberhardt, *From Commandant to Captive*, ln. 1477. This testimony was given by Von Lindeiner himself after the war, and therefore should not be taken at face value; however, it does provide insight into his general thought process.

[166] Asaria-Helfgot, *We Are Witnesses*, p. 41.

[167] Breyer to POW commander of military district III, 10 October 1944, BA-MA PERS 6/11025.

became the POW Office, he was appointed as head of its General Department under General von Graevenitz, responsible mainly for the treatment of western POWs, a position he held until the beginning of 1943.[168] Fifty years old when the war broke and described as 'reasonable and approachable', he was well versed in the details of the Geneva Convention.[169] Two days after the invasion of the Soviet Union he even wrote to the OKW's Foreign Relations Department and pointed out that based on Article 82 of the Convention, Germany would have to apply it to Soviet POWs even though the Soviet Union did not ratify the Convention (his opinion was of course rejected).[170]

Although Breyer was responsible for initiating—apparently without an approval from his superiors—the reprisal against British POWs for the housing, by the Canadian authorities, of German POWs in inadequate conditions in Fort Henry, Canada, other actions demonstrated that he might have perceived his role quite differently: in meetings held with the commanders of POWs in the military districts Breyer always emphasized the importance of compliance with the Geneva Convention and reminded participants that German POWs would suffer for any violation of the Convention.[171] His approach towards Soviet POWs, however, clearly demonstrates that he was not driven only by a concern over reprisals, a concept that did not exist in the campaign in the East: in 1941, when 25,000 Soviet POWs were transferred to work in SS-controlled factories, Breyer insisted that they remained under the responsibility of the Wehrmacht in order to ensure that they would be treated properly.[172] A year later he warned the Krupp company, which employed thousands of mostly Soviet POWs, that through an anonymous letter from a member of the German public he became aware of 'very substantial complaints' related to their treatment of POWs; and he also allowed, against German policy, a representative of the ICRC to visit a Soviet POW camp.[173] It is possible that his actions eventually led to his demotion: at the beginning of 1943 he was transferred to a new position as a the commandant of Stalag III-D in Berlin.[174] Although in his six-month appraisal in April 1944 he was rated as 'above average' and as having an 'impeccable National Socialist convictions', it is possible that, at least until October 1944, his behaviour represented the general attitude within the POW Office.[175]

---

[168] Streit, *Keine Kamerdan*, p. 68.
[169] Ibid., pp. 67–8 and n. 4. Marcel Junod, *Warrior without Weapons* (London, 1951), p. 170.
[170] POW Office to the OKW's Foreign Relations Department, 24 June 1941 (copy in *Das Stalag X B Sandbostel*, p. 36).
[171] For the meetings with POW commanders see the testimony of General Reinhard von Westrem, IMT, *Trials of War Criminals*, vol. XI, p. 50. For the Fort Henry incident see Wylie, 'Captured by the Nazis: "Reciprocity" and "National Conservatism" in German Policy towards British POWs', ln. 2463.
[172] Streit, *Keine Kameraden*, p. 251.
[173] For the Krupp letter see Streit, *Keine Kameraden*, pp. 221–2. For the Soviet POW camp visit see Junod, *Warrior without Weapons*, pp. 227–9.
[174] Evaluation of Breyer, 28 February 1944, BA-MA PERS 6/11025.
[175] Ibid.

Another case, that of Oberstleutnant Hermann Hagen, might also support the conclusion regarding the general attitude within the POW Office, and even imply that the POW organization served as some sort of a safe haven within the Wehrmacht for individuals who refused to conform: Hagen got into repeated arguments, presumably on ideological grounds, with NSDAP representatives in military district VII (in the Munich area), and since his commanders decided that any future interaction between him and the Party was 'out of the question', in 1942 he was transferred to the POW organization and sent to Oflag X-B (Sandbostel) as commandant.[176] Interestingly, his new commander, who in Hagen's 1943 evaluation still commended his 'perfect National Socialist attitude', was apparently made to retract his feedback and the evaluation had to be reissued without those comments.[177]

To summarize, until the last year of the war, unless overridden by direct orders from their superiors, the staff of the POW Office, responsible for the well-being of enemy POWs as well as for that of German POWs in enemy hands and driven by national conservative values that required the honourable treatment of their enemies, did not 'work towards the Führer' but followed the rules of the Convention and ensured they were applied to all POWs—including the Jews among them.

This approach should have changed in 1944. In July of that year, following the assassination attempt on Hitler, Himmler was made commander of the Replacement Army, which included responsibility for the military districts and for the POW camps which resided in these districts. In October of that year Himmler completed his long-term goal of taking over the POW organization when the POW Office, which was until then under the responsibility of the OKW, was also transferred to him. As described in the Introduction to this book, SS personnel were then appointed to various roles in the POW Office chain of command (although the POW organization was not made formally part of the SS). During this period, in the closing stages of the Second World War and with the final capitulation of Germany all but inevitable, it appears that Nazi leaders—including Himmler, who went as far as ordering, in mid-March 1945, to stop the killing of Jewish inmates in concentration camps (although he reversed this order a few weeks later), and even Ernst Kaltenbrunner, the feared head of the RSHA—had become more concerned with their personal fate than with the implementation of Nazi ideology.[178] The possibility of being personally held accountable and

---

[176] Military district VII to OKH, 17 June 1942, and an undated memo, Wehrmacht personnel file of Oberstleutnant Dr Hermann Hagen, BA-MA PERS 6/9169.

[177] Hagen evaluations from 3 September 1943 and 3 March 1944, ibid.

[178] For Himmler's negotiations during the last months of the war and his order to stop the murder of Jewish inmates see Longerich, *Heinrich Himmler*, pp. 707–9 and 724–30. For his decision to reverse this order and to ensure that no concentration camp inmate would fall alive into enemy hands, see Kershaw, *The End*, p. 330. For Kaltenbrunner's negotiations with the ICRC see Black, *Ernst Kaltenbrunner—Ideological Soldier of the Third Reich*, pp. 240–1.

punished by the victors for involvement in atrocities committed by Germany during the war, including the mistreatment of POWs—Jewish and non-Jewish—became real.

On this point it would be useful to point to a report by the British JISC, which was concerned at the time with the fate of POWs in general had Hitler decided to take drastic actions against them before Germany's final capitulation. Submitted on 29 July 1944 to the British War Cabinet, the analysis of the potential risk to POWs described two scenarios: the first assumed that Germany's military leaders would be in control during the last days of the war, and the second assumed a chaotic breakdown of the German state. Interestingly, the conclusion from both scenarios was similar: the risk to POWs would be very low, either because a state of relative order would be maintained during that period by the leaders of the Wehrmacht; or, in the second scenario, because local camp commandants, most of whom were assumed to still be carrying on the traditions of the old German Army and who were at that stage more concerned with their own self-preservation, would still be the ones in charge of the POWs and would like to 'curry favour' with the expected victors. In addition, the report stated that 'camp guards would have everything to lose and nothing to gain by ill-treating Allied prisoners of war'.[179]

Judging by the outcome, the JISC analysis was correct; self-preservation and the fear of retribution were probably the main reasons for the relatively non-discriminatory treatment that Jewish POWs received during the last stages of the war and for the general improvement—with the exception of the forced marches at the end of the war—in the conditions of POWs in general.[180] It can also be assumed that most of the objections of the Nazi and Wehrmacht leadership to Hitler's insistence to withdraw from the Geneva Convention three months before the end of the war were driven by their concern about retribution—their personal fate took precedence over fanatical implementation of National Socialist ideology.

The man in charge of the POW system and therefore responsible for the fate of all POWs in German hands during that chaotic period provides an interesting example for the contradiction between the fanatical commitment of individuals to National Socialist ideology on one hand and their practical considerations—such as self-preservation and the fear of retribution—on the other. SS General Gottlob Berger was a committed Nazi who joined the Party as early as 1922 and had held several roles prior to becoming head of the POW Office: in 1938 he was appointed by Himmler as head of the SS Recruitment Office, a role for which he

---

[179] Report on prisoners of war in Germany, 29 July 1944, TNA CAB 79/79/1.

[180] For the improvement in the conditions of the POWs see Overmans, 'Die Kriegsgefangenenpolitik des Deutschen Reichs 1939 bis 1945', p. 864. Colonel Hubert Zemke, an American POW held in Stalag Luft I (Barth), described in his memoirs the change in the behaviour of the POW camp guards during the final weeks of the war, when the realization that their fate was at the hands of their captives had dawned on them (see Zemke, *Zemke's Stalag*, pp. 68–9).

was described as 'the unsung and despised creator of the SS recruiting system and the real founder of the Waffen-SS'; and in 1940 he was appointed as the head of the SS Main Office, which was responsible, among other things, for personnel administration, recruitment, and education and care of the Waffen-SS.[181] Among his responsibilities was the distribution of guidance pamphlets to all SS members, some of which contained extreme anti-Semitic propaganda.[182] He was also present in 1943 when Himmler delivered his Poznan speech where he talked about the extermination of the Jews, and therefore was fully aware of the fate of the Jews in Europe—although given his senior role, he must have known about these plans much earlier.[183] After he was appointed to the role of Head of the POW Office, Berger, who was known as one of Himmler's Twelve Apostles, wasted no time in creating a new command level between the POW Office and the POW commanders in the military districts, appointing the HSSPF in the military districts as 'Higher Commanders of Prisoners of War'.[184] Berger decided to adhere to international regulations, which prohibited police personnel from participating in POW guard duties, and gave his new appointees ranks of Generals in the Waffen SS, even though some of them only held low military ranks.[185] This meant in effect the subordination to SS personnel of both the commanders of POWs in the military districts—and hence the POW camps—and the guard battalions, who were deployed in guard duties in the POW camps and the labour detachments.[186]

Once in charge of the POW Office, Berger—whose son and son-in-law were both killed in the war—became less fanatical and more practical: aware of the fate that might await him at the hands of the Allies after the war, he claimed in his post-war interrogations that he disobeyed specific orders from Hitler to shoot and punish POWs, to destroy Red Cross parcels already stored in the camps, and to place American and British POWs in the centre of large cities to act as human shields (testimonies from officers in the POW Office claimed, however, that in fact it was POW Office personnel who watered down the orders).[187] At one point he went as far as organizing a POWs' medical conference in Berlin and used the opportunity to persuade several senior officer POWs to travel on his behalf to

---

[181] For Berger as head of the Recruitment Office see Gerhard Rempel, 'Gottlob Berger and Waffen-SS Recruitment: 1939-1945', *Militärgeschichtliche Mitteilungen*, 27:1 (1980), 107-22, p. 107. For Berger as head of the Main Office see *IMT, Nazi Conspiracy and Aggression*, vol. VIII, p. 772.

[182] *IMT, Trials of War Criminals*, vol. XIV—*The Ministries Case* (Washington, DC, 1952), pp. 529-30.

[183] Ibid., p. 537.

[184] *IMT, Trials of War Criminals*, vol. XIII, p. 480; Overmans, 'Die Kriegsgefangenenpolitik des Deutschen Reichs 1939 bis 1945', p. 863.

[185] Westhoff testimony, undated, p. 3, BA-MA MSG 2/12656. See also testimony of SS General Friedrich von Eberstein, *IMT, Trial of the Major War Criminals*, vol. XX, p. 306.

[186] Overmans, 'Die Kriegsgefangenenpolitik des Deutschen Reichs 1939 bis 1945', p. 863.

[187] Nichol and Rennell, *The Last Escape*, ln. 6057; Krafft, 10 August 1951, BA-MA MSG 2/12656. On the deaths of Berger's son and son-in-law see Delmar Spivey, oral history, AFRHA, irisnum 01015417, reel 31923.

Switzerland and enter into negotiations with the Allies.[188] His actions were not limited to western POWs: he also increased the food rations of Soviet POWs and allowed the ICRC to supply them during the forced marches in the last months of the war (although given the mayhem that existed during that period it is doubtful that the ICRC was able to do so).[189] And an Ultra intercept from the last days of the war may also support his claim to be the protector of the POWs: on 19 April 1945 he accused the commander of POWs in military district IV of 'complete forgetfulness of [his] duty' after he abandoned 30,000 POWs who were marching northward; he ordered the commander to find appropriate billets for them and to ensure they were supplied with Red Cross parcels.[190]

Given the situation in the German leadership during the last months of the war, with Himmler and Joachim von Ribbentrop, the minister for Foreign Affairs, holding their own negotiations with the West, Berger, despite the way he tried to portray himself after the war, had probably been operating in an environment which was quite accommodating towards his actions and the personal risks he had taken were probably minimal. In any case, although some, if not all, of his claims were self-serving and were difficult to corroborate, judging by the outcome it is plausible that driven by the fear of retribution, his actions, or rather lack of them, and especially his decision not to appoint SS personnel to the lower levels of the POW organization and to keep them outside of the POW camps, helped to secure the fate of the POWs, including the Jewish ones, in the last months of the war. It is possible that had a more fanatical senior SS person been appointed to this role, he would have displayed a more ruthless commitment to Nazi ideology in running the POW camps.[191] Berger's inaction probably helped in sparing him the death penalty: in the Nuremberg trials he was charged as part of the Ministries Case and was found guilty on four counts, including war crimes and crimes against humanity. He was sentenced in 1949 to twenty-five years in prison but this was later reduced to ten years with the judges citing his involvement in the protection of POWs as their main reason for leniency.[192] Berger was eventually released in 1951, spending a total of six years in prison.[193]

Judging by his history as a committed member of the SS, a highly likely explanation for Berger's actions is the fear of retribution.[194] As a senior and trusted member of the SS he was given almost free reign by Himmler and Hitler and used it to position himself as the benefactor of the POWs, in order to use them to

---

[188] Durand, *Stalag Luft III*, pp. 340–1; Spivey, *POW Odyssey*, pp. 146–7 and 153.
[189] Overmans, 'Die Kriegsgefangenenpolitik des Deutschen Reichs 1939 bis 1945', p. 864.
[190] Berger to POW Commander Wehrkreis IV, 19 April 1945, TNA HW 5-706.
[191] Nichol and Rennell, *The Last Escape*, ln. 6234.
[192] IMT, *Trials of War Criminals*, vol. XIV, p. 1004.
[193] Nichol and Rennell, *The Last Escape*, ln. 6208.
[194] This conclusion is also supported by Overmans; see Overmans, 'Die Kriegsgefangenenpolitik des Deutschen Reichs 1939 bis 1945', p. 864.

testify in his favour after the war.[195] Berger was not able to prevent the forced marches during the last months of the war, from locations which were evacuated as the Red Army advanced, of hundreds of thousands of POWs, in severe weather conditions and with minimal supplies of food and in poor sanitary conditions, which may have resulted the deaths of 2,500–3,500 American and British POWs; the evacuations, although in line with the Geneva Convention which required belligerents to transfer POWs away from war zones, were probably ordered by Hitler who wanted to prevent the POWs from joining their liberators in the fight against Germany.[196] However, despite their hardships, the fate of these POWs still stands in stark contrast to the murders, during the same period, of hundreds of thousands of other prisoners of the Reich, including concentration camp inmates and those incarcerated in Gestapo prisons, at the hands of their mostly SS guards; unlike the POWs, they were not protected by the Geneva Convention.[197]

To summarize, the POW Office played a crucial role throughout the war in the protection of non-Soviet Jewish POWs and is the main reason they were treated, in most cases, according to the 1929 Geneva Convention. It did not adopt the proactive approach of other organizations who implemented Nazi policies even when they were not 'laid down in any instruction, regulations, or official orders'.[198] Before October 1944 the POW Office and its personnel, most of whom were committed to treating non-Soviet POWs as honourable enemies and responsible for the fate of German POWs and the enforcement of the Geneva Convention, used their position to shield these POWs inside POW camps—including the Jewish ones—from the effect of policies, orders, and the influence of external bodies that were in breach of the Convention. After October 1944, with an SS General as head of the POW Office and the POW camps and despite the chaos of the last months of the war, non-Soviet Jewish POWs continued to remain protected; concerns about retribution in the hands of the Allies and about personal fate took precedence over any commitment to the Nazis' racial ideology.

The Absence of a Führer Order

Finding an answer to the second question—why did Hitler not issue a direct order to apply the Final Solution to non-Soviet Jewish POWs—is challenging. As most sources only discuss the question of whether such an order existed at all,

---

[195] Wylie, *Barbed Wire Diplomacy*, p. 253.
[196] On the forced marches see Kochavi, *Confronting Captivity*, pp. 203–22; on the estimated number of deaths see Nichol and Rennell, *The Last Escape*, ln. 7542. Hitler's order to prepare for the evacuation of the POW camps was issued on 19 July 1944 (see Hugh Trevor-Roper, *Hitler's War Directives 1939–1945* (Edinburgh: Birlinn, 2004), p. 250).
[197] Kochavi, *Confronting Captivity*, p. 221; Kershaw, *The End*, pp. 328–36.
[198] Quoted in O'Neill, *The German Army and the Nazi Party*, p. 103.

this question was not addressed; and due to the lack of any written sources on this matter, there could be several explanations for it. A discussion around the reasons for the absence of such order should be divided into two periods, separated roughly by the bombing of Dresden in February 1945, when Hitler—at the encouragement of Goebbels—demonstrated how far he was willing to go by raising the idea of abandoning the Geneva Convention for western POWs.

The possibility that Hitler was not aware of the existence of non-Soviet Jewish POWs, or, perhaps for racial reasons, dismissed their numbers as insignificant, is highly unlikely. As mentioned earlier, the POW Office issued its first command that referenced Jewish POWs, titled 'Jews in the French Army', on 16 June 1941; given that these orders all passed at one point through the desk of Bormann, it is likely that their existence was at least mentioned in discussions with Hitler. Hitler's request in 1942 for a breakdown by origin of the British POWs should also have made him aware, if he was not already, of the large contingent of Palestinian Jewish POWs who were held in POW camps in Germany.[199] News about their capture had appeared in the German press in the previous year, describing how 'not less than 1,000 Palestinian Jews, among them many formerly from Germany' were captured in Greece.[200] The existence of these Jewish POWs had also been discussed at the highest level of the Wehrmacht: General Franz Halder, the army's chief-of-staff, noted in his diary on 2 May 1941 the capture in Greece of '1,350 Jews and Arabs'.[201] Hitler, who at one point ordered the execution of a 74-year-old German Jew after reading in a newspaper that he was sentenced 'only' to 2.5 years in prison for black market activities, was unlikely to be unaware of that.[202] And if he had not heard about their existence earlier, then the first exchange of seriously wounded POWs, which included sixty of the Palestinian Jewish POWs, could not have gone unnoticed since Hitler was heavily involved in all aspects of that exchange.[203]

The exchange that included the Palestinian Jewish POWs might point towards one explanation for Hitler's approach—pragmatism. It demonstrated that in certain circumstances, Hitler could bend his ideological fanaticism to practical requirements: after multiple delays, the exchange finally took place in October 1943, and Germany, which was keen on getting back as many POWs as possible following its defeats in Africa, did not even let the Allies' bombing campaign that was taking place at the time to halt it. Supporting the pragmatism argument, although unrelated specifically to Jewish POWs, was the deployment of Soviet POWs in Germany: in 1942, when faced with the inevitability of labour shortages as a result of the extended war in the East, Hitler, who had initially opposed Soviet

---

[199] Wylie, *Barbed Wire Diplomacy*, p. 137.   [200] Der Führer, Karlsruhe, 21 May 1941.
[201] *War Journal of Franz Halder*, 2 May 1941, vol. 6, p. 95.
[202] Document NNG-287, 25 October 1941, *IMT, Trials of War Criminals*, vol. III—*The Justice Case* (Washington, DC, 1951), pp. 429–31.
[203] Kochavi, *Confronting Captivity*, p. 125.

POWs being brought into Germany, changed his position.²⁰⁴ In both cases, practical needs took priority over any racial dogmas.

Another potential explanation is that Hitler was planning to apply the Final Solution to all Jewish POWs—and not only the Soviet ones—once Germany had won the war. This would explain the POW Office's orders early on to segregate Jewish POWs; it would also explain the different treatment of French and Belgian Jewish POWs who were either recaptured after escaping or refused to work, since unlike their non-Jewish comrades they were sent to different POW camps; and the recording of the number of Jewish POWs in some POW camps (but not in all of them).²⁰⁵ It is possible that the treatment of Jewish POWs would have followed the same steps as those that were applied to Europe's civilian Jewish population—segregation, deportation, and eventually extermination. However, as suggested by MacKenzie, sending non-Soviet Jewish POWs to concentration camps before the war was over could not have been kept a secret and would have meant a public breach of the Geneva Convention, resulting in heavy reprisals—and it is possible that, unlike in February 1945, Hitler was not yet willing to go that far at that stage of the war.²⁰⁶

Most discussions regarding Hitler's approach to POWs after the bombing of Dresden focus on the risks posed to western POWs in general, and not necessarily to the Jewish ones, should he decide, in a last act of vengeance, to murder them. In March 1945, after learning that his Lynchjustiz order was not being adhered to, Hitler did order that all captured Allied airmen should be handed over to the SD for liquidation; however, this verbal order encountered strong objections and was never converted into a formal, written one.²⁰⁷ Although there are no records of similar orders, it is possible that other such verbal orders during the last stages of the war were simply ignored; Goebbels himself wrote in his diary that month that 'orders issued in Berlin practically never reach lower levels'.²⁰⁸ A review of the large number of testimonies from POWs who heard rumours indicating that a formal order to murder POWs was in fact issued concluded that these rumours were baseless and if anything, they were spread by guards and other camp personnel who wanted to gain favour with the POWs just before they themselves surrendered by demonstrating the risks they were taking by ignoring such orders.²⁰⁹ An order of similar magnitude and consequences, known as the 'Nero Order', was in fact issued by Hitler on 19 March 1945 and instructed the

---

²⁰⁴ Overmans, 'Die Kriegsgefangenenpolitik des Deutschen Reichs 1939 bis 1945', p. 870.
²⁰⁵ Befehlsammlung 32, order 541, and Befehlsammlung 33, order 578, both on 15 January 1944, BA-MA RW 6/270.
²⁰⁶ MacKenzie, 'The Treatment of Prisoners of War in World War II', p. 504. Segregation as the first step towards extermination was also mentioned by Datner, *Crimes against POWs*, p. 107.
²⁰⁷ IMT, *Trial of the Major War Criminals*, vol. XVIII, pp. 586–7.
²⁰⁸ *Joseph Goebbels Tagebücher 1924–1945*, Band 5, 27 March 1945, p. 2171.
²⁰⁹ For a discussion regarding the existence of such order see Nichol and Rennell, *The Last Escape*, lns 5936–99.

destruction of anything that could assist the advancing Allied armies, such as 'military traffic, communications, industrial and supply facilities'.[210] However, the order—which was in general ignored—did not make any reference to POWs, who, in theory, could have also been considered as a means of assisting the Allies. It is highly likely, however, that at that late stage of the war such an order would have been ignored as well, although a similar order—which was in all probability a verbal one—to murder concentration camp inmates before destroying the camps was followed in some cases.[211]

Since Hitler never hesitated to use POWs to achieve objectives unrelated to POW matters—as he had done with the Shackling Crisis, which was intended to limit the activities of British commando units—it is possible that he intended to use non-Soviet Jewish POWs as cards of last resort to force the Allies to change other policies. The idea of using Jews as hostages to blackmail the West was not new and was used by the Nazis as early as Kristallnacht in November 1938.[212] It is possible—as Churchill suggested to Roosevelt—that Hitler either intended to murder all Allies' POWs or to use them as a bargaining chip to force the Allies' hand in preventing the unconditional surrender of Germany or for creating a wedge between the Soviet Union and its western Allies.[213] Given the chaos that existed during the last months of the war it is possible that Hitler, deep in his bunker and with limited connection to reality, ordering the movement of imaginary divisions from one front to the other, was more focused on exacting revenge on those closer to him whom he felt had betrayed him; POWs, and specifically Jewish POWs, simply were not part of his priorities at that late stage, and in the end, an order to murder them was never issued.

Conclusion

Several conclusions have been reached in this chapter. The first one relates to Hitler: although, as has been established, he was heavily involved in setting POW policies and in issuing orders and instructions that dealt with the treatment of POWs, none of them related to the treatment of non-Soviet Jewish POWs; and although it is possible that such an order was issued during the last months of the war, if this did occur, like many other orders he issued during that time, it was

---

[210] Moll, *Führer-Erlasse 1939–1945*, pp. 486–7.
[211] Kershaw, *The End*, p. 228 and especially n. 86. According to Gottlob Berger, a few days before Hitler's suicide he ordered him to kill the POW group known as the '*Prominenten*'—the well-connected American and British POWs who were held as hostages. Hugh Trevor-Roper, who recorded Berger's testimony, noted that from Berger's 'incoherent narrative' it was not clear whether Hitler was in fact referring to the POWs or to another group (see Hugh Trevor-Roper, *The Last Days of Hitler* (London: Pan Books, 2012) ln. 2442).
[212] Longerich, *Heinrich Himmler*, pp. 705–6.
[213] Churchill to Roosevelt, 22 March 1945, CHAR 20/213A/23-24.

simply ignored. The second conclusion relates to the OKW and to the Wehrmacht as a whole, which proved to be an obedient follower of Hitler and of the National Socialist worldview; when instructed, they implemented orders even when they were in breach of the Geneva Convention and against any national conservative values the Wehrmacht might have held. These included the Commissar Order, which stripped the POW status from certain groups of Soviet POWs and handed them over for execution to the RSHA; the Commando Order, which did the same to certain categories of POWs from western armies; the order, following Italy's capitulation, to execute all captured Italian officers; and the Kugel Erlass, which sent recaptured POWs (with the exception of American and British ones) to concentration camps where they were executed. These orders did not include specific references to Jewish POWs (as mentioned, Heydrich only added them later to his list of 'undesirables' who should be executed as part of the Commissar Order); however, it is clear from the way that they were implemented by the OKW and the POW Office, and by the cooperation of these bodies with the RSHA, that had an order been issued to hand over non-Soviet Jewish POWs to the RSHA or to send them to concentration camps, it would have been followed without hesitation. Cases where Hitler's orders to mistreat or execute POWs were ignored—such as his instructions to murder the Free French troops or the Dutch officer escapees—were the exception rather than the rule, as the Spanish Republicans POWs' case can attest: although they fought for a country which was a signatory to the Geneva Convention, and despite the fact that POW Office guidelines required that they be treated, according to their uniform, as French soldiers, they were sent to concentration camps where the vast majority of them perished.

The third conclusion relates to the role played by the RSHA and the NSDAP. Both organizations were involved in multiple aspects of setting POW policies, drafting orders, and implementing them; however, in the absence of a specific order from its superiors, the POW Office was able to stand its ground and although it did require camp commandants and other personnel in the POW organization to interact with the NSDAP, it refused the demands of the RSHA (and probably of the NSDAP as well) to hand over Jewish POWs to its custody. As the case of the Polish-French-Jewish POW Hecht demonstrated, this did not mean that the POW Office policies were always adhered to; but in general, non-Soviet Jewish POWs inside the POW camps were protected from the radicalization of both POW and anti-Jewish policies that were taking place outside the camps' fences.

The fourth conclusion from this study is that Germany did not have any specific policy for dealing with non-Soviet Jewish POWs.[214] The POW Office's command collections included only eight orders—0.7% of the total number of

---

[214] This conclusion is also supported by Overmans; see Overmans, 'Die Kriegsgefangenenpolitik des Deutschen Reichs 1939 bis 1945', p. 872.

orders that were included in these collections—that mentioned Jewish POWs. Out of these eight orders, only three related to their general treatment, instructing camp commandants to segregate them in the same camp from their non-Jewish comrades (which Germany argued was in line with Article 9 of the Geneva Convention). The segregation orders were in general only implemented with French, Polish, and Yugoslavian Jewish POWs, whereas American and British Jewish POWs were in most cases not segregated. The possibility that specific orders referencing Jewish POWs were marked as 'Secret' and therefore not included in the widely distributed command collections is highly unlikely since, unlike other orders marked 'Secret', such orders or correspondence referring to them were not found in any of the archives reviewed in this study. It is possible that the order to segregate the Jewish POWs was only the first step in applying the 'Final Solution' to non-Soviet Jewish POWs, and the next steps that were applied to Europe's civilian Jewish population—deportation and extermination—were to follow had Germany won the war. Fortunately, the possibility of such an outcome will never be known.

The POW Office's ability to protect non-Soviet POWs inside the camps, Jews and non-Jews alike—in view of the Commando and Kugel Orders, their authority outside camps was limited—stemmed from one reason: POW Office personnel followed orders. As long as they did not receive an order to the contrary they were able to abide by the Geneva Convention and objected to any attempt to treat POWs in a manner that breached it. And, in the absence of such order, it was the national conservative values of many in the POW organization, which dictated the honourable treatment of foes, that stopped them from implementing Nazi racial policies inside POW camps despite the radicalization in POW and anti-Jewish policies that was taking place outside. However, it should be emphasized that neither the concern over reprisals, the need to adhere to the Geneva Convention, nor the personal values held by members of the POW organization would have meant anything had a specific order been issued before October 1944 to hand over Jewish POWs to the RSHA. The POW Office would have followed it without hesitation, as it followed all other orders that breached the Geneva Convention and condemned western POWs to death.

In theory, following such an order—or even issuing a similar one of its own accord—should have been less of an issue for the POW Office after October 1944, when the POW organization was headed by an SS General known as 'The Almighty Gottlob' Berger. However, with the war drawing to an end, personal considerations and the fear of personal retribution in the hands of the Allies took precedence over any ideological dogmas and over the personal oath to the Führer. Although Berger issued one final order regarding the segregation of Jewish POWs, he also reminded camp commandants that they should not be discriminated against; eventually, under his leadership and with the exception of the forced marches during the winter of 1945, the treatment of POWs in general improved during the last months of the war. Unlike his predecessors in the POW Office, it is quite possible that had Berger received an order from Hitler to execute Jewish POWs, he would have disobeyed it.

And therefore the last, and most important, question of this chapter remains: given the Nazi obsession with the extermination of Europe's civilian Jewish population, and the murder of the Soviet Jewish POWs, what kept Hitler from issuing an order similar to the Commissar Order and applying it to all Jewish POWs in German hands? The answer to this question can only be a hypothetical one. It is quite possible that Hitler planned all along to murder non-Soviet Jewish POWs; the segregation orders might have been the first step in that process. However, for pragmatic reasons, he might have also wanted to wait until Germany won the war, when he could have done it without interference and without risking reprisals against German POWs. By the time the war was reaching its final stages and Hitler was ready to abandon the Geneva Convention, it became too late; most of the Nazi leadership was busy looking for ways to save themselves and, even if such an order had been issued, it is highly likely that, as was the case with the Nero Order, it would not have been followed. To that end, it is worth quoting Hugh Trevor-Roper, who described Hitler in those last days as:

> [S]ome cannibal god, rejoicing in the ruin of his own temples. Almost his last orders were for execution: prisoners were to be slaughtered, his old surgeon was to be murdered, his own brother-in-law was executed, all traitors, without further specification, were to die. Like an ancient hero, Hitler wished to be sent with human sacrifices to his grave.[215]

However, none of these orders made a specific reference to Jewish POWs; and even if they did, by then there was no one left to carry them out.

---

[215] Trevor-Roper, *The Last Days of Hitler*, ln. 1730.

Conclusion

'[B]ecause I was Jewish I assumed I'd be killed.'[1] This was how Wilfred Ofstein, a British Jewish soldier, assessed his situation when he was taken prisoner in North Africa in June 1942. This was, most likely, the thought that went through the minds of most Jewish soldiers who were captured by the Wehrmacht during the Second World War; and on the face of it, their story—the story of the non-Soviet Jewish POWs who were held in German POW camps—is inexplicable. Germany's murderous obsession with the extermination of the Jews in Europe resulted in the biggest genocide in history; however, the relentless hunt for each and every Jew in Nazi-controlled Europe stopped at the gates of the POW camps where non-Soviet POWs were incarcerated. Furthermore, inside the camps, they were not, in general, mistreated or discriminated against and were treated, in most cases, in the same way their non-Jewish comrades were treated.

This research draws on individual stories of POWs, both Jewish and non-Jewish, and various primary and secondary sources, to build a comprehensive picture of the experience of American and British Jewish POWs in German captivity. To complete this picture, the approaches of German state organs towards these POWs—the OKW, the POW organization, the RSHA, and the NSDAP—have also been studied. The four main research questions posed in this study—how were American and British Jewish POWs treated by their immediate captors (camp and labour detachment commandants, guards, etc.) and why; how were they able to maintain their Jewish identity in captivity; why was the instruction to segregate them rarely followed; and why were they treated, in most cases, according to the Geneva Convention—have all been addressed in the previous chapters. And although this research has focused on the experience of American and British Jewish POWs, the discussions around the research questions led to several observations which apply to most, if not all, non-Soviet Jewish POWs—with the exception of the Polish Jewish POWs, who were badly treated (although not condemned to death like their Soviet Jewish POW brethren).

According to Goffman, POW camps, along with jails and concentration camps, are included in the category of Total Institutions that are meant to 'protect the community against what are felt to be intentional dangers to it, with the welfare of the persons thus sequestered not the immediate issue'.[2] While the second part of

---

[1] Testimony of Wilfred Ofstein, YVA O.3–8111.   [2] Goffman, *Asylums*, pp. 4–5.

this definition, when applied to POWs in general, is largely correct, this study showed that protection of the community which is mentioned in its first part worked in both directions: the fences of the POW camps protected non-Soviet Jewish POWs from the genocide that was taking place across Europe. Therefore, during the Second World War, German POW camps did not fully adhere to the accepted definition of a Total Institution as an establishment intended to protect the communities around it from the supposed dangers resulting from the establishment's inhabitants. The POW camp system did provide such protection to the outside population; however, its inadvertent function ended up being to protect the communities inside—not only non-Soviet Jews, but non-Soviet POWs in general—from the radicalization, throughout the war, of Germany's POWs policies, policies that in general impacted upon POWs who were caught outside the camps and therefore were not protected by the camps' fences.

When it came to Jewish POWs, there were, of course, exceptions, and some of the Nazi racial policies did manage to infiltrate into the POW camps, as demonstrated by the segregation order, which mostly impacted Polish, French, and Yugoslavian Jewish POWs, or the order that prohibited blood donations from POWs for fear that the donor might be Jewish (or partly Jewish).[3] But the approach towards Jewish rituals that took place inside the camp clearly demonstrates the contradiction between the German racial policies outside the POW camps, and especially Germany's 'furious onslaught aimed at eliminating any trace of "Jewishness"', and the treatment of non-Soviet Jewish POWs: there were camps where Jewish POWs were allowed to practice their religion in the open; cases of funerals of Jewish POWs who died in captivity which were conducted with full military honours, including a Wehrmacht honour guard placing wreaths on graves which were marked with the Star of David; and Palestinian Jewish POWs who were able to celebrate Jewish Holy days and display their national identity in the open.[4] And although cases of mistreatment and discrimination against non-Soviet Jewish POWs did exist, they were usually a result of the anti-Semitism of individual commandants (mostly in labour detachments), guards, and civilians who interacted with the Jewish POWs, and not of a formal policy dictated from above. The military discipline which was instilled in the Wehrmacht's soldiers was, in most cases, strong enough to overcome any personal anti-Semitic beliefs and ensured that when it came to Jewish POWs, orders were followed and the Geneva Convention was in most cases adhered to.

The role played by the POW organization's chain of command—the POW Office, the POW commanders in the military districts, and the POW camp commandants—in the protection of non-Soviet Jewish POWs is the first important

---

[3] Befehlssammlung 15, order 111, 10 August 1942, BA-MA RW 6/270.
[4] Saul Friedländer, *Nazi Germany and the Jews: The Years of Extermination: 1939–1945* (London: Phoenix, 2008), p. xiv.

finding of this study. Despite the constant pressure on the POW Office by the RSHA to hand Jewish POWs over to it, and despite the fact that the POW Office was subordinated to an officer known as a '[Nazi] Party General', it was able to withstand this pressure.[5] Unlike other bodies of the Nazi state, who competed among themselves in interpreting and executing Hitler's wishes and intentions, the POW Organization remained the exception: the concept of 'working towards the Führer'—Raul Hilberg called it 'a matter of spirit, of shared comprehension'— which meant that no specific orders were required in order to execute Nazi policies, did not filter into its ranks.[6] Having said that, it is important to note that the POW Office, as part of a hierarchical military organization, had to follow orders; however, in the case of non-Soviet Jewish POWs, in the absence of such orders, the personnel of the POW Organization, most of whom were still carrying on the traditions of the old German Army that required the chivalrous treatment of its enemies, did not take any initiative to implement Nazi policies.

It is possible that one of the ways the POW Office chose to protect the non-Soviet Jewish POWs was by keeping any reference to them to a minimum. This can be seen by the fact that before December 1944 there was no mention of any general policy for the treatment of non-Soviet Jewish POWs; as Overmans pointed out, unlike policies that dealt with POWs from specific countries and even though Germany had a clear policy when it came to dealing with the civilian Jewish population in occupied Europe, the Wehrmacht did not have a 'Jewish POWs policy'.[7] In fact, it did not have a formal policy even when it came to Soviet Jewish POWs, most of whom were murdered shortly after they had been captured. While it willingly cooperated with the Einsatzgruppen and handed Soviet Jewish POWs over to them for execution, there was no mention of Jews in the Commissar Order; they were only added later by Heydrich when he issued the Einsatzgruppen with detailed instructions related to the implementation of the order.[8]

The POW Office seemed to have issued orders and guidelines that dealt with the treatment of non-Soviet Jewish POWs only in response to external events: on 16 June 1941, six days before the invasion of the Soviet Union and five days after the German Foreign Office suggested sending the recently captured Palestinian Jewish POWs to perform military works in the Balkan Peninsula, it issued an order reminding camp commandants that Jewish POWs—the order referred to French Jewish POWs—should only be segregated within the POW camps. The

---

[5] For the 'Party General' reference see Streit, *Keine Kameraden*, p. 68.
[6] Hilberg, *The Destruction of the European Jews*, vol. I, p. 52.
[7] Overmans, 'Die Kriegsgefangenenpolitik des Deutschen Reichs 1939 bis 1945', p. 872.
[8] Regulations on the deployment of the security police and the SD in army formations, 28 April 1941, document NOKW-2080, *IMT, Trials of War Criminals*, vol. X, pp. 1240–2. A later attempt by Wagner, the Army's quartermaster, to reverse Heydrich's order from 17 July 1941 to liquidate Soviet Jewish POWs was not implemented (see Streit, *Keine Kameraden*, pp. 99–100).

order was issued, in all likelihood, in order to distinguish between the treatment of the Jewish POWs that were already in captivity and the treatment of the Soviet Jewish soldiers the Wehrmacht expected to take prisoner. Its burial guidelines, which made a specific reference to the burial of Jewish POWs—albeit only the non-Soviet ones—were issued in July 1941, in the same month that Heydrich's infamous order, which included Jewish POWs in the list of 'undesirables' that should be executed, was issued. Eight months later, in March 1942, the POW Office issued another order, titled 'Marking of the Jews', this time referring to all Jewish POWs; in addition to reminding POW camp commandants that Jewish POWs should be segregated, it also instructed them not to mark Jewish POWs. The order was probably meant to address the confusion that existed at the time regarding the need to mark Jewish POWs in the same way civilian Jews were marked outside POW camps. And the last order that made a reference to the treatment of Jewish POWs was only issued almost three years later, in December 1944: this was the first order that set a clear policy—albeit still a high-level one— for the treatment of Jewish POWs. Appropriately titled 'Treatment of Jewish POWs', the order repeated the segregation requirement but its uniqueness was in that it formally instructed camp commandants to treat Jewish POWs in the same way that non-Jewish POWs from the respective army were treated—in essence, forbidding the commandants from discriminating against Jewish POWs.[9] Again, it is possible that at this late stage of the war and concerned about his eventual fate, Berger, the head of the POW Office, had added the 'no discrimination' part in anticipation of the possible defeat of the Germany, which might have led to acts of vengeance against the Jewish POWs.

It can be argued that unlike the treatment of Soviet Jewish POWs, which was governed by the Commissar Order and by Heydrich's instructions to the Einsatzgruppen, when it came to non-Soviet Jewish POWs, the lack of a clear Jewish POW Policy occurred simply because there was no need for one. Jewish soldiers were fully integrated into their national armies; even the easily identifiable Palestinian Jews who fought in separate units in the British army were treated as British soldiers, in the same way that the captured Indian soldiers were treated. But as this stands in clear contrast to what was going on outside the POW camps, where Germany was stripping Jews all over Europe of their basic human rights and implementing clear and unambivalent anti-Jewish policies, it is possible that the POW Office decided to minimize references to Jewish POWs in an attempt not to draw attention to them. That is why the three orders mentioned above, out of the 1,162 orders issued by the POW Office throughout the war in its 'Collection of Orders' publications, were the only ones that made any reference to the treatment of Jewish POWs. This was, in all probability, not done solely on moral

---

[9] Befehlsammlung 48, order 876, 15 December 1944, BA-MA RW 6/270.

grounds but also because, as suggested by Aryeh Kochavi, Rüdiger Overmans, Christian Streit, Aron Shneyer, and David Killingray, the POW Office was also responsible for German POWs held by the Allies and did not want to create any situation that would lead to reprisals against them.[10]

The level of independence that existed within the POW organization, and specifically, at the levels of POW commanders in the military districts and camp commandants, had also contributed to the relatively fair treatment of the non-Soviet Jewish POWs—as was evident with the implementation of the segregation orders. The POW Organization, while still an organization with a military hierarchy, was not necessarily a homogenous one; and while in most cases officers were careful not to express opinions which were against the official policy, there were also cases where, perhaps feeling that there would be limited consequences, they decided they could ignore certain orders. This was possible partly due to the structure of the POW organization—POW camps came under the jurisdiction of the military districts, which were subordinated to the Replacement Army, and not under the POW Office which was part of the OKW—and partly because, as mentioned, these officers were in most cases of an older generation and held a traditional set of military values which included the chivalric treatment of their enemies. As can be seen from the case of the segregation order, POW commanders and camp commandants were not concerned, apparently, with the consequences of their actions and when it came to American and British Jewish POWs, rarely implemented it—even after the order was re-issued by the SS General in charge of the POW organization.

Since the first cases of segregation—those of Polish, French, and Yugoslavian Jewish POWs—occurred before the issuing of the Commissar Order and the invasion of the Soviet Union and before the beginning of the mass murder phase of the Holocaust, it is possible that camp commandants became aware of the potential deadly outcome of segregating Jewish POWs and this influenced their reluctance to implement this order; after all, the murder of Soviet commissars (if they were not murdered upon capture), of Soviet Jewish POWs, and of Europe's civilian Jewish population also began with their segregation, which was then followed by their deportation and eventually extermination. This may explain why camp commandants, especially in the case of American and British Jewish POWs, did their utmost to ignore the order; and it may also explain cases on the Eastern Front—albeit rare—where they refused to hand Soviet Jewish POWs over to the RSHA. Objections by MOCs and non-Jewish POWs who stood by their Jewish comrades, and the impact that such actions might have had on the economic output of the POWs, also contributed to the camp commandants' reluctance to

---

[10] Kochavi, *Confronting Captivity*, p. 195; Overmans, 'German Treatment of Jewish Prisoners of War in the Second World War', lns 1240–60; Streit, *Keine Kameraden*, p. 70; Shneyer, *Pariahs among Pariahs*, p. 82; and Killingray, 'Africans and African Americans in Enemy Hands', p. 199.

implement the order; and, towards the end of the war, the fear of Allied retribution became an additional consideration.

The discussion regarding the reasons for the behaviour of the POW Organization during the Second World War should not, however, detract from comprehending the significance of this behaviour. Taking a step back and looking at the bigger picture, this behaviour raises a few fundamental questions: how was this organization, which operated within a larger, hierarchical, Nazified organization—the Wehrmacht—able to not 'work towards the Führer'? How was it possible, when most German state and private organizations toed the Party line even without being given direct orders, for this one organization to decide that it would not do so? Was there a formal, albeit secret and most likely verbal, decision to do so? And if the POW Office's behaviour and that of the POW commanders in the military districts and of the camp commandants carried no consequences, no repercussions, does that mean that other organizations could have acted in the same way—but chose not to? Was their decision to act the way they did driven by fear of repercussions, by opportunism, or out of true belief in the Nazi ideology? Answering these questions may shed additional light on the decisions made by German organizations in the Third Reich when it came to understanding their level of willingness to cooperate with the regime and adopt its ideology.

The behaviour of the POW Organization leads to the second important finding of this research: non-Soviet Jewish POWs were generally not discriminated against, and camp commandants were able, in the case of American and British Jewish POWs, to usually ignore specific orders to segregate them simply because, unlike Soviet Jewish POWs, whose murder was one of the outcomes of the Commissar Order, an order to murder or discriminate against non-Soviet Jewish POWs was never issued. Hitler, in his role as the Commander-in-Chief of the Wehrmacht, was the only authority who could have issued such an order; without it, the RSHA, the NSDAP, and the SS, all powerful organs of the Nazi state who were 'working towards the Führer', were not able to enforce their will on the OKW and especially on the POW Office.

As was shown in this research, the two main arguments found in the literature that explain the treatment of non-Soviet Jewish POWs—the concern over reprisals against German POWs held by the Allies, and the 'national conservative value system' of the Wehrmacht—played a major role in the decision-making process of the POW Office, but not in that of the OKW.[11] Another argument—that the treatment of POWs in each front was dictated by the nature of the war in that front, an extermination war in the East vs. a conventional one in the West—does not address the fact that multiple Eastern-Front type atrocities took place in the West during the last year of the war, nor the continuous radicalization in

---

[11] For a review of the literature regarding the reprisal and national conservative arguments, see the Introduction to this book.

Germany's policies towards POWs from western armies. Nevertheless, the POW organization personnel did not adopt the proactive approach of other organizations in the Reich, and that of their superiors in the OKW, who were eager to implement Nazi policies even without specific orders; they ensured that the Geneva Convention was in most cases adhered to and were able to resist the pressure exerted on them to hand over non-Soviet Jewish POW to the control of the RSHA.

As was demonstrated with the Commissar Order, the Commando Order, and the Kugel Erlass, and with the treatment of the Spanish Republicans, the POW Office did follow orders that were in clear breach of the Geneva Convention, or were against its 'national conservative value system', or that could have triggered reprisals against German POWs in the hands of the Allies. Therefore, it is highly likely that had an order been issued by Hitler before 1945 to liquidate all non-Soviet Jewish POWs it would have been implemented as well. In 1945, however, with the Second World War reaching its final stages and Germany's leaders fearing retribution at the hands of the Allies, it is possible that had such an order been issued, it would have been ignored, in the same way that other orders issued by Hitler during that period were.

Whether such an order existed during the last stages of the war can be assessed by drawing parallels with the discussion around the existence of an order from Hitler to implement the 'Final Solution to the Jewish Question'. Although no written 'Final Solution' order signed by the upper echelons of the Nazi regime has ever been found, most studies—as well as the eventual outcome of genocide—point towards the existence of such an order, most probably in a verbal form but perhaps even just implied.[12] As Christopher Browning noted, Hitler's top lieutenants 'needed little more than a nod from [him] to perceive that the time had come to extend the killing process to the European Jews'.[13] In the case of the non-Soviet Jewish POWs, none was given—otherwise the fate of all non-Soviet POWs (their number towards the end of the war is estimated at around 60,000) would have been the same as that of their civilian, and Soviet POW, brethren.[14]

The absence of such an order enabled the POW Office—and the POW organization as a whole—to continue to follow the existing regulations, which required, when it came to non-Soviet Jewish POWs, adherence to the Geneva Convention. The result was that day-to-day lives in a POW camp for these POWs were not much different from the lives of tens of thousands of non-Jewish POWs who were

---

[12] Martin Broszat, 'Hitler und die Genesis der "Endlösung". Aus Anlaß der Thesen von David Irving', *Vierteljahrshefte für Zeitgeschichte*, 25:4 (1977), pp. 739–75, p. 747.

[13] Christopher R. Browning, 'A Reply to Martin Broszat Regarding the Origins of the Final Solution', *Simon Wiesenthal Center Annual*, 1 (1984), pp. 113–32, p. 124.

[14] For a discussion on the number of Jewish POWs see the Introduction section of this book. Since most Polish Jewish POWs were released in the months following the end of the campaign in Poland, the 60,000 number consists mainly of French, American, and British Jewish POWs.

incarcerated with them; yes, for these men being a Jewish POW imprisoned by a regime determined to exterminate their people added a dimension of constant fear to an already difficult situation. However, the Geneva Convention did, eventually, achieve its purpose and protected them. At a time when millions of their brethren were being slaughtered, sometimes just miles away from their camp, there were Jewish POWs who were able to work side by side with German civilians, to visit their shops, to receive medical treatment from German doctors, and to celebrate their Holy days, just like their non-Jewish comrades. The POW camp was indeed a separate universe for most of the non-Soviet Jewish POWs, its fences providing protection from the unprecedented genocide that was taking place outside.

The significance of this finding is that it raises a question regarding the accepted view of the Holocaust as a German attempt to make Europe *Judenrein* by indiscriminately murdering, as Christopher Browning described it, 'every last Jew in Europe upon whom they could lay their hands'.[15] The perception of the Holocaust being an indiscriminate attempt to completely eradicate a specific ethnic group by using all means available to the state and regardless of the state's dire situation is rooted not only in the actual events of which the Holocaust consisted, but also in the rhetoric used by the Nazis, and especially by Hitler. One of his more famous references to the annihilation of the Jews was made in his speech on 30 January 1939, where he declared that in case of another world war, its outcome would be 'the annihilation of the Jewish race in Europe'. Hitler repeated this statement several times in the coming years; and although some scholars argue that it was mainly for propaganda purposes, these statements, together with the events that were taking place in parallel, were paramount in establishing this long-held perception.[16]

The survival of approximately 60,000 non-Soviet Jewish POWs shows that there were cases where parts of the Nazi system could phase the implementation of the Holocaust and even pause it altogether. Although there are recorded cases of groups of civilian Jews who survived due to an ad hoc agreement with the German authorities or due to a temporary change in policy, these cases were the exception, rather than the rule. They include the intermarried German Jews who were arrested in Berlin in 1943 and were only released after Hitler and Goebbels decided, for tactical reasons, that the Rosenstrasse protests organized by their non-Jewish wives were risking the population's support for Goebbels's

---

[15] Christopher Browning, 'The Nazi Decision to Commit Mass Murder: Three Interpretations', p. 473.
[16] For Hitler's Jewish annihilation speech and its repetitions see Hans Mommsen, 'Hitler's Reichstag Speech of 30 January 1939', *History and Memory*, 9:1/2 (1997), pp. 147–61, p. 156. Mommsen argued that at the time, this statement was perceived as propaganda (see ibid., p. 152). Kershaw explains that although 'annihilation' ('*Vernichtung*'), being one of Hitler's favourite words, was often used by him to emphasize his threats to his audience, it was not a meaningless term (see Ian Kershaw, *Hitler 1936–1945: Nemesis* (London: Penguin Books, 2001), pp. 151–3).

announcement of 'total war'; and the approximately 1,700 Hungarian Jews who were saved from extermination following the negotiations between Dr Rudolf Kastner, one of the leaders of Hungarian Jewry, and Adolf Eichmann that resulted in a large ransom being paid to guarantee their release.[17] To put this number in context: the survivors accounted for about 0.4% of the total number of Hungarian Jews who perished in the Holocaust.[18]

However, the conclusions of the January 1942 Wannsee conference made it clear that the Nazis intended to apply the 'Final Solution' to all Jews in Europe, including those in countries that at the time were not part of the Reich, such as England and the unoccupied parts of France and the Soviet Union; those in countries which were allied with Germany, such as Finland, Italy, and Hungary; and even to Jews in neutral countries such as Sweden and Switzerland. The breakdown of the number of Jews per country which was listed in the conference's minutes even included the small Jewish community of Albania, 200 in total.[19] And although there were plans to delay the extermination process in some countries for tactical reasons, the speed at which it was implemented in Hungary in 1944—approximately 437,000 Jews were deported to Auschwitz in less than two months—can only be explained by Germany's obsession with making Europe *Judenrein* even when it was facing an imminent defeat.[20] These actions stood in stark contrast to the eventual survival of the non-Soviet Jewish POWs; unlike the Hungarian Jews, Germany did not rush to murder them and they remained untouched even during the last stages of the war, when Germany's ultimate collapse could no longer be denied by its top leaders. The specific reasons for this phenomenon have all been discussed in detail; however, when one looks at the

---

[17] For the Rosenstrasse protests see Nathan Stoltzfus, 'Historical Evidence and Plausible History: Interpreting the Berlin Gestapo's Attempted "Final Roundup" of Jews', *Central European History*, 38:3 (2005), pp. 450–9, p. 450. For the Kastner-Eichmann negotiations see Hilberg, *The Destruction of the European Jews*, vol. II, p. 903.

[18] The US Holocaust Memorial Museum, https://encyclopedia.ushmm.org/content/en/article/jewish-losses-during-the-holocaust-by-country, accessed 1 May 2021.

[19] The minutes of the Wannsee conference, 20 January 1942, document NG-2586-G, *IMT, Trials of War Criminals*, vol. XIII, pp. 212–13.

[20] For the proposed delays in Scandinavia see ibid. For the number of Hungarian Jews who were deported to Auschwitz see Michael Berenbaum, 'Forward', in Randolph L. Braham and Scott Miller, eds, *The Nazis' Last Victims* (Detroit: Wayne State University Press, 2002), ln. 71. For an explanation of the speed of the extermination in Hungary see Hilberg, *The Destruction of the European Jews*, vol. II, p. 854; Braham, *The Politics of Genocide*, p. 78. Although the Jews of Tunisia, 90,000 in total, were under German occupation between November 1942 and May 1943, they did not suffer the same fate as the Hungarian Jews due to several reasons, including the short duration of the occupation and the stage of the war in which the country was occupied. Had the occupation of Tunisia lasted longer it is possible that they, too, would have been sent to extermination camps in Europe (for more details see Dan Michman, 'Were the Jews of North Africa Included in the Practical Planning for the "Final Solution of the Jewish Question"?', in Alex J. Kay and David Stahel, eds, *Mass Violence in Nazi-Occupied Europe* (Bloomington: Indiana University Press, 2018), pp. 59–78, pp. 69–70; and Eli Bar-Chen, 'Tunisian Jews' Fate under Nazi Occupation and the Possibility of Reviewing the Holocaust', *Zmanim: A Historical Quarterly*, 67 (1999), pp. 34–47).

bigger picture, this outcome—60,000 Jews living in relative safety at the heart of Nazi Germany—is simply incomprehensible.

The survival of the non-Soviet Jewish POWs, which stands in contrast to the perceived indiscriminate nature of the Holocaust that led to the extermination of millions of their civilian and Soviet POW brethren, was a result of the unofficial yet largely consistent approach—albeit one that was only formalized in the last months of the war—of the POW Office. The approach was followed throughout the war and withstood the pressure of the radicalization of Germany's POW and anti-Jewish policies, and the pressure of the RSHA that demanded that these Jewish POWs be transferred to its control. A unique set of circumstances—the absence of an order from Hitler to murder, or to discriminate against, non-Soviet Jewish POWs; the unique character of the POW organization, which was not 'working towards the Führer', and its insistence on the enforcement of the Geneva Convention; the ability of officers lower in its hierarchy to delay or even ignore the implementation of orders without suffering any consequences; the protection provided by the fences of the POW camps, which broke the mould of a 'Total Institution'; the Wehrmacht's discipline, that ensured that its soldiers in most cases followed the Geneva Convention rules rather than the anti-Semitic beliefs they might have held; and, towards the end of the war, the fear of retribution in the hands of the Allies—combined together to make non-Soviet Jewish POWs, and especially the American and British ones, the most protected Jews in Nazi-occupied Europe.

APPENDIX A

Sample of POW Commanders and Camp Commandants

* Only year of birth is known

#	Last name	First name	DOB	BA MA file
1	Aichholz	Hans	27/07/1884	RW 59/2130
2	Albrecht	Otto	02/11/1887	RW 59/2130
3	Anderten	William von	14/12/1887	PERS 6/10236
4	Arendt	Egon	18/08/1889	PERS 6/10224
5	Asmus	Leopold	13/08/1893	PERS 6/10696
6	Auer	Artur	23/09/1890	RW 59/2130
7	Auffhammer	Ludwig	10/06/1887	PERS 6/10718
8	Ballas	Richard	04/04/1886	PERS 6/10840
9	Becker	Otto	11/05/1885	PERS 6/5427
10	Beckow	Werner von	21/10/1891	RW 59/2130
11	Behrends	Robert	04/07/1887	PERS 6/10983
12	Behrens	Ernst	26/09/1888	PERS 6/10974
13	Bernardi	Bernhard	27/06/1885	PERS 6/12385
14	Berndt	Erich	16/05/1892	PERS 6/12382
15	Bernuth	Fritz von	29/09/1885	RW 59/2130
16	Bertram	Werner	22/01/1893	PERS 6/10477
17	Bessinger	Carl	29/01/1889	PERS 6/10494
18	Beutler	Karl	03/04/1894	PERS 6/10516
19	Bielas	Alois	11/06/1884	PERS 6/70506
20	Bielfeld	Peter	23/04/1888	PERS 6/451
21	Bier	Rudolph	03/11/1886	PERS 6/10510
22	Biess	Paul	26/12/1872	PERS 6/26904
23	Bilfinger	Hans von	08/05/1886	PERS 6/10502
24	Bischoff	Ernst	18/04/1885	RW 59/2130
25	Blau	Albrecht	06/11/1885	PERS 6/9865
26	Block	Lothar von	21/05/1889	PERS 6/1104
27	Blümel*		01/01/1883	RW 59/2130
28	Bode	Georg	15/08/1882	RW 59/2130
29	Bodecker	Eduard von	04/12/1888	PERS 6/10739
30	Boehm	Wilhelm	16/07/1886	PERS 6/10730
31	Boetticher	Heinrich	02/01/1887	PERS 6/111963
32	Bombach	Aribert	27/01/1897	PERS 6/12131
33	Bornemann	Rudolf	04/04/1873	PERS 6/251976
34	Bosse	Siegfried von	26/08/1888	PERS 6/12613
35	Botzheim	Erich Freiherr von	10/01/1871	PERS 6/2527

244   APPENDIX A

#	Last name	First name	DOB	BA MA file
36	Braune	Werner	09/12/1887	PERS 6/2776
37	Braxator	Georg	29/03/1888	PERS 6/11052
38	Breyer	Hans Joachim	04/07/1889	PERS 6/11025
39	Bülow	Ernst von	14/08/1887	PERS 6/12636
40	Burger	Otto	20/10/1888	PERS 6/11185
41	Burkhardt	Johannes	14/05/1887	PERS 6/11190
42	Büttner	Arthur	03/03/1872	PERS 6/76768
43	Canitz	Gotthold	20/04/1894	PERS 6/12430
44	Capesius*	Max	01/01/1886	RW 59/2130
45	Chalons	Werner	13/04/1890	PERS 6/12292
46	Clüver	August	24/12/1881	PERS 6/11147
47	Crede	Leopold	04/06/1891	PERS 6/10961
48	Däublin	Walter	16/12/1897	PERS 6/10943
49	Deichmann	Paul	14/10/1890	PERS 6/9779
50	Detmering	Rolf	19/02/1889	PERS 6/517
51	Dietz	Hermann	07/06/1894	PERS 6/10657
52	Dillmann	Johann	18/12/1887	PERS 6/10660
53	Döhren	Georg von	23/05/1884	PERS 6/1182
54	Drobnig	Walter	22/07/1888	PERS 6/1195
55	Duday	Bruno	14/03/1880	RW 59/2130
56	Ebke	August	01/08/1890	PERS 6/10241
57	Ehrenberg	Hans	18/09/1888	PERS 6/1203
58	Ehrhardt*	Bernhard	01/01/1888	RW 59/2130
59	Engeström	Richard von	17/02/1887	PERS 6/10003
60	Ergert	Karl	22/05/1887	PERS 6/9979
61	Estlinger*	Otto	01/01/1886	RW 59/2130
62	Euler	Ludwig	22/04/1885	PERS 6/76910
63	Euler*	Friedrich	01/01/1883	RW 59/2130
64	Flotow	Alfred von	01/01/1888	PERS 6/10531
65	Folkert	Ralph	20/07/1895	PERS 6/10544
66	Foris	Bernhard von	01/03/1892	PERS 6/2586
67	Frank	Engelbert	17/09/1886	PERS 6/2602
68	Franke	Albrecht	19/05/1893	PERS 6/2608
69	Franzen	Dr. Karl	02/01/1891	PERS 6/110632
70	Friedl*	Ludwig	01/01/1883	RW 59/2130
71	Friese	Friedrich	13/08/1893	PERS 6/8831
72	Frölich	Felix	03/05/1881	RW 59/2130
73	Fürst	Friedrich	26/05/1889	PERS 6/566
74	Gall	Ernst	28/10/1888	PERS 6/7283
75	Geiger	Felix	06/07/1896	PERS 6/10341
76	Georgi	Richard	31/03/1884	PERS 6/1276
77	Geyer*	Rudolf	01/01/1881	RW 59/2130
78	Giese	Arthur	27/10/1887	PERS 6/9542
79	Gläsche	Edgar	14/04/1889	PERS 6/9562
80	Gluth	Friedrich	26/09/1887	RW 59/2130
81	Goeckel	Günther von	12/04/1889	PERS 6/1294
82	Grabinger	Gotthold	20/04/1889	PERS 6/9907

#	Last name	First name	DOB	BA MA file
83	Groest*	Arthur	01/01/1885	RW 59/2130
84	Grunert	Gerd	08/04/1897	PERS 6/10258
85	Gunzelmann	Emil	17/07/1887	PERS 6/591
86	Guth	Josef Franz	03/04/1888	PERS 6/10184
87	Gutschmidt*	Johannes	01/01/1876	RW 59/2130
88	Gylek*		01/01/1880	RW 59/2130
89	Haendler	Kurt	15/02/1897	PERS 6/8930
90	Hagen	Hermann	28/08/1892	PERS 6/9169
91	Harsdorf*	von	01/01/1887	RW 59/2130
92	Henne		27/03/1897	RW 59/2130
93	Hermann	Eduard	08/05/1886	RW 59/2130
94	Hesselmann	Martin	02/08/1896	RW 59/2130
95	Hildebrandt	Johannes	01/05/1890	PERS 6/9186
96	Hindenburg	Oskar von	31/01/1883	PERS 6/299388
97	Hölzinger	Fritz	08/04/1895	RW 59/2130
98	Hönig	Heinrich	12/04/1891	RW 59/2130
99	Hörbach	Hans von	18/03/1882	PERS 6/9251
100	Hossenfelder	Werner	13/11/1888	RW 59/2130
101	Idel	Gerhard	23/11/1896	RW 59/2130
102	Ihssen	Hugo	16/11/1887	PERS 6/1421
103	Jäger	Emil	31/10/1892	PERS 6/6490
104	Jarzebecki*		01/01/1887	RW 59/2130
105	Jauch	Hans	20/07/1883	PERS 6/110944
106	Jouin	Gerald	13/12/1899	RW 59/2130
107	Junker	Theodor	19/09/1886	RW 59/2130
108	Kadelke	Otto	05/04/1885	PERS 6/8497
109	Kahlen	Friedrich	29/03/1891	PERS 6/7912
110	Kaiser*	Emil	01/01/1888	RW 59/2130
111	Karge	Franz	05/08/1889	RW 59/2130
112	Karkowski	Oskar	03/05/1884	RW 59/2130
113	Kastel	Theodor	12/07/1888	PERS 6/9438
114	Keller	Georg	12/01/1886	PERS 6/8155
115	Kemminger	Anton	17/12/1887	PERS 6/7306
116	Kettler	Maximilian von	02/06/1890	RW 59/2130
117	Keyser	Max	02/10/1891	PERS 6/8205
118	Klein	Erich	02/12/1898	PERS 6/8320
119	Klein	Johannes	28/11/1887	RW 59/2130
120	Klemm	Kuno	05/03/1888	PERS 6/1469
121	Kling	Hans	25/03/1884	RW 59/2130
122	Kniebe*		01/01/1883	RW 59/2130
123	Knoll	Franz Karl	03/10/1892	PERS 6/7955
124	Kokail	Bernhard	24/10/1886	PERS 6/7827
125	Körpert*		01/01/1883	RW 59/2130
126	Koss	Ernst von	04/03/1893	PERS 6/6426
127	Kothmüller	Eugen	10/07/1888	PERS 6/6429
128	Krane*	von	01/01/1885	RW 59/2130
129	Kratz	Adalbert	18/07/1894	PERS 6/8374

246 APPENDIX A

#	Last name	First name	DOB	BA MA file
130	Krützfeldt		01/10/1884	RW 59/2130
131	Küchler*		01/01/1881	RW 59/2130
132	Kuehn*	Walter	01/01/1885	RW 59/2130
133	Kühn	Heinrich	09/04/1891	RW 59/2130
134	Kühne	Hermann	29/09/1886	PERS 6/8156
135	Laepple*	Victor	01/01/1882	RW 59/2130
136	Lap	Engelbert	19/10/1886	PERS 6/8689
137	Viseur	Paul le	14/12/1892	RW 59/2130
138	Lefevre*		01/01/1886	RW 59/2130
139	Lengnick	Heinz	18/11/1888	RW 59/2130
140	Lieckfeld*	Albert	01/01/1884	RW 59/2130
141	Lincke	Wilhelm	12/02/1874	PERS 6/13269
142	Linde	Siegfried von der	12/07/1893	PERS 6/1571
143	Lindeiner-Wildau	Friedrich von	12/12/1880	PERS 6/153948
144	Lindenau*	Wilhelm	01/01/1881	RW 59/2130
145	Linhart	Heinrich	07/04/1895	RW 59/2130
146	Lippmann*		01/01/1889	RW 59/2130
147	Lobinger	Karl, Dr	31/12/1893	PERS 6/44301
148	Lorentzen	Theodor	08/08/1894	PERS 6/8724
149	Lorenz	Curt	22/06/1891	RW 59/2130
150	Lucius	Kurt	04/12/1884	PERS 6/22284
151	Lüders	Willibald	03/10/1886	PERS 6/12863
152	Lühe	Ernst	16/04/1895	PERS 6/9414
153	Lührsen	Otto	27/09/1886	PERS 6/9374
154	Lutter	Alfred	20/04/1894	PERS 6/9686
155	Macholz	Hans	24/06/1891	PERS 6/9675
156	Malischek	Hans	23/09/1888	RW 59/2130
157	Mangelsdorf	Hermann	04/07/1890	PERS 6/11753
158	Marquard	Hugo	27/02/1886	RW 59/2130
159	Marwitz	Hugo der	16/02/1886	RW 59/2130
160	Meiser	Hans	20/09/1886	RW 59/2130
161	Meley	Ernst	04/07/1891	RW 59/2130
162	Mensing	Franz	02/12/1890	PERS 6/8809
163	Menz*		01/01/1887	RW 59/2130
164	Messner	Josef	26/08/1894	PERS 6/69590
165	Metternich*	Wolff	01/01/1877	RW 59/2130
166	Meurer	Fritz	30/11/1896	PERS 6/12232
167	Meyer*	Rudolf	01/01/1894	RW 59/2130
168	Minsinger	Alfred	05/02/1882	RW 59/2130
169	Möller	Fritz	15/03/1889	RW 59/2130
170	Müller*	Friedrich	01/01/1888	RW 59/2130
171	Nau*	Wilhelm	01/01/1873	RW 59/2130
172	Nehls	Ernst	07/03/1887	RW 59/2130
173	Neugebauer	Erich	02/03/1884	PERS 6/9490
174	Neureiter	Camillo	05/11/1894	PERS 6/9537
175	Nickisch-Rosenegk	Karl von	02/10/1886	PERS 6/6245
176	Nieter	Rudolf	09/08/1892	PERS 6/6203

#	Last name	First name	DOB	BA MA file
177	Obenauer*	Georg	01/01/1891	RW 59/2130
178	Obendorf*	Richard	01/01/1893	RW 59/2130
179	Ochernal	Theodor	05/11/1891	PERS 6/11966
180	Ossmann	Friedrich	11/10/1888	PERS 6/6945
181	Oster	Hugo	01/10/1882	PERS 6/6952
182	Oven	Walter von	26/11/1889	RW 59/2130
183	Pabst*	Ernst	01/01/1891	RW 59/2130
184	Pamperl	Franz	15/01/1888	PERS 6/6124
185	Pawliska	Ernst	18/06/1885	RW 59/2130
186	Pellet	Alfred	05/02/1883	RW 59/2130
187	Peter	Franz	25/08/1888	RW 59/2130
188	Petersen	Wilhelm	04/04/1887	PERS 6/11369
189	Petroschky	Kurt	24/01/1887	RW 59/2130
190	Petry	Alfred	15/09/1894	PERS 6/1724
191	Petters*	Kurt	01/01/1883	RW 59/2130
192	Pfeiffer	Ernst	20/11/1884	RW 59/2130
193	Pfeiffer	Werner	10/09/1894	PERS 6/7786
194	Pirch	Carl von	21/11/1881	RW 59/2130
195	Pitzschke*	Erich	01/01/1887	RW 59/2130
196	Plammer	Adolf	28/11/1884	PERS 6/300359
197	Pönicke	Maximilian	11/05/1891	PERS 6/6719
198	Pösche*	Hermann	01/01/1890	RW 59/2130
199	Pottiez*		01/01/1884	RW 59/2130
200	Prätorius	Hugo	26/02/1889	RW 59/2130
201	Prawitt	Gerhard	25/10/1899	PERS 6/7237
202	Puttkamer	Jesco von	26/08/1876	PERS 6/5775
203	Quandt	Paul	09/03/1880	PERS 6/298292
204	Queckbörner	Ludwig	08/05/1886	PERS 6/9279
205	Rampacher	Hermann	10/07/1884	PERS 6/6474
206	Recke	Hilmar von der	28/09/1885	PERS 6/9347
207	Reckow	Werner von	21/10/1891	PERS 6/8915
208	Reim	Erich	18/07/1890	PERS 6/5892
209	Reinkober*	Fritz	01/01/1891	RW 59/2130
210	Rengert*	Adolf	01/01/1882	RW 59/2130
211	Reymann	Achim	16/12/1886	PERS 6/6043
212	Richter	Martin	12/02/1884	PERS 6/5908
213	Ried	Hadrian	14/01/1887	PERS 6/5983
214	Riess	Friedrich	28/09/1885	PERS 6/7248
215	Rievers	Max	28/09/1878	PERS 6/44508
216	Roeder-Diersburg	Egenolf Freiherr von	16/04/1890	PERS 6/6104
217	Rüling	Alfred	02/12/1894	PERS 6/6087
218	Ründe	Herbert	19/08/1886	RW 59/2130
219	Saenger	Wolfgang	07/08/1884	PERS 6/12038
220	Sauer	Otto	24/07/1887	PERS 6/12268
221	Saur	Otto von	01/03/1876	PERS 6/11866
222	Schaal	Wilhelm	16/08/1884	PERS 6/12169
223	Scheffler	Johannes	16/07/1887	RW 59/2130

APPENDIX A

#	Last name	First name	DOB	BA MA file
224	Schemmel	Nikolaus	25/12/1873	PERS 6/11865
225	Scherer	Willibald	13/07/1892	PERS 6/4541
226	Schierbrandt	Oswald von	10/03/1883	PERS 6/22448
227	Schilling	Hans	11/04/1889	PERS 6/11668
228	Schirmbacher*	Karl	01/01/1890	RW 59/2130
229	Schlich	Rudolf	19/11/1893	RW 59/2130
230	Schmidt-Vogelsang	Ernst	21/01/1894	PERS 6/7710
231	Schmitt	Lorenz	14/01/1890	PERS 6/7725
232	Schneider	Fritz	11/07/1885	PERS 6/12565
233	Schrader	Kurt	30/12/1884	PERS 6/12108
234	Schröder	Carl	21/06/1888	RW 59/2130
235	Schroeter	Max	19/02/1892	RW 59/2130
236	Schwabe*		01/01/1886	RW 59/2130
237	Schweisfurth	Emil	25/05/1891	PERS 6/5814
238	Schwenzer	Erich	26/05/1886	PERS 6/5691
239	Seelmann-Eggebert	Kurt	22/08/1889	RW 59/2130
240	Sieber	Karl	11/10/1895	PERS 6/10062
241	Siggel	Helmut	27/05/1885	RW 59/2130
242	Simoleit	Gustav	24/08/1895	PERS 6/216867
243	Simon	Bruno	23/12/1886	PERS 6/9393
244	Simon	Gerhard	25/12/1893	PERS 6/9403
245	Skala*		01/01/1886	RW 59/2130
246	Stahmer	Johannes	10/05/1894	RW 59/2130
247	Starke	Gottfried	31/07/1887	PERS 6/11695
248	Starzinski	Josef	12/09/1894	PERS 6/11693
249	Steimann	Siegfried	24/02/1890	PERS 6/11688
250	Steinäcker	Hans-Joachim von	30/12/1887	RW 59/2130
251	Steinbrecht	Walter	08/02/1888	PERS 6/7198
252	Steiniger	Erich	19/07/1889	PERS 6/11687
253	Stenzel	Willy Karl	08/01/1892	PERS 6/12344
254	Stern*	Walther von Monbary	01/01/1886	RW 59/2130
255	Stietencron	von	20/08/1887	RW 59/2130
256	Stockhausen	Hunold	30/01/1891	PERS 6/943
257	Stossier	Josef	19/08/1897	RW 59/2130
258	Strandes	Günther von	13/05/1887	PERS 6/9089
259	Strehle	Josef	26/04/1896	PERS 6/9052
260	Strohbach*	Willy	01/01/1883	RW 59/2130
261	Sturm	Carl	03/05/1879	PERS 6/1961
262	Szekely de Doba	Gustav	03/08/1888	RW 59/2130
263	Tafel	Theodor	21/05/1878	PERS 6/12761
264	Teichmann	Rudolf	17/10/1885	PERS 6/7318
265	Teuber	Johannes	10/06/1881	RW 59/2130
266	Teufelhart	Leopold	27/02/1888	RW 59/2130
267	Theissen		19/02/1894	PERS 6/7514
268	Thielebein	Albert	19/11/1890	PERS 6/7544
269	Topf	Erwin	22/12/1898	PERS 6/6283
270	Trefz	Ernst	25/04/1896	PERS 6/12198

#	Last name	First name	DOB	BA MA file
271	Treiter	Gregor	05/09/1895	PERS 6/12200
272	Tscherny	Maximilian	15/04/1881	PERS 6/6296
273	Uechtritz	Helmuth von	07/07/1890	RW 59/2130
274	Vick*	Hans	01/01/1893	RW 59/2130
275	Viehof	Karl	03/05/1898	PERS 6/8578
276	Vilmar	Kurt	17/03/1882	PERS 6/36784
277	Voigtel	Martin	27/04/1898	PERS 6/110774
278	Volkmann	von	30/03/1889	RW 59/2130
279	Voss	Erich	13/07/1891	PERS 6/2017
280	Wanke	Franz	11/05/1887	RW 59/2130
281	Warder-Gunning	Adolf	19/09/1886	RW 59/2130
282	Warnstedt	Gustav	04/02/1898	PERS 6/5664
283	Weber*	Anton	01/01/1883	RW 59/2130
284	Wegner	Wilhelm	20/08/1885	RW 59/2130
285	Weiss	Martin	12/10/1890	RW 59/2130
286	Wellhausen	Paul	26/04/1889	PERS 6/7604
287	Westmann	Heinrich	26/07/1896	PERS 6/7372
288	Westphal	Heinrich	15/03/1895	PERS 6/7375
289	Westrem-Gutacker	Reinhard von zum	29/04/1879	PERS 6/71723
290	Wilcke*	Oskar	01/01/1879	RW 59/2130
291	Winckler	Hartwig von	19/01/1888	PERS 6/5552
292	Winiwarter	Franz	01/06/1887	PERS 6/7492
293	Wittas	Paul	10/01/1886	PERS 6/301373
294	Wittmer	Berthold	05/03/1879	RW 59/2130
295	Wolf	Julius	01/09/1889	PERS 6/6136
296	Wuffge	Erich	25/09/1885	RW 59/2130
297	Wülcknitz	Joachim von	18/11/1893	PERS 6/8851
298	Wussow	Theodor von	05/08/1886	RW 59/2130
299	Zantner	Alfred	30/01/1890	PERS 6/9690
300	Zemsch	Ludwig	29/02/1884	PERS 6/9704
301	Zerboni di Sposetti	Artur von	01/04/1882	PERS 6/13283
302	Zimmermann	Curt von	05/02/1876	PERS 6/70350

Bibliography

Primary Sources

Archives

Bundesarchiv (BA), Berlin: NS19, R58, R59, R70, R9361.
Bundesarchiv-Militärarchiv (BA-MA), Freiburg: MSG 2, PERS 6, RH 1, RH 20, RH 26, RH 49, RW 59, RW 6.
Central Zionist Archive (CZA), Jerusalem: J-10, S-25.
The Churchill Archive (CHAR), online: 20.
Imperial War Museum Archive (IWM), London: 81, 82, 99; Memoirs of Badcock, James; Denton, Patrick; Harding, William; oral histories of Camplin, Leonard; Chapman, Edward; Hall, Edgar; Hoare, Harry; Lyon, Jack; Maltas, Fred; Saunders, George; Watson, Henry; Weiner, Hans Paul.
International Committee of the Red Cross Archive (ACICR), Geneva: BG 17, BG 25.
Israel Defence Force Archive (IDF), Tel Aviv: 12, 182.
Israel State Archives, Jerusalem: M 109.
Jewish Military Museum Archive (JMM), London: T2010, T2014; memoirs of Ofstein, Maurice, *Diary and Odd Jottings*; Weiner, Hans Paul, unpublished memoirs; oral history of Goldwyn, Leslie.
London Metropolitan Museum (LMA), London: ACC/3121.
Museum of Jewish Heritage, New York: oral history of Daub, Gerald.
National Archives and Record Administration (NARA), College Park, Maryland: RG 39, RG 59, RG 153, RG 389, RG 549.
The National Archives (TNA), London: CAB 66, CAB 79, CAB 80, CO 323, FO 916, HW 5, WO 208, WO 224, WO 309.
Politisches Archiv des Auswärtigen Amts (PAAA), Berlin: R40713, R40717, R40718, R40720, R40741, R40954, R40960, R40999, R40985, R67004.
Prague Military Archive (PMA), Prague: 31, 33, 121, 129, 188, 189, 190, 191, 194, 195, 202, 744, 754.
Service Historique de la Défense/DAVCC, Caen: 22 P 3000.
Swiss Federal Archives (AFS), Bern: E2001.
US Holocaust Memorial Museum Archive (USHMM), Washington, DC: RG 68.045M.
Yad Vashem Archive (YVA), Jerusalem: O.3; Memoirs of Grüner, Mosche; Mautner, Vladimir; Ofstein, Wilfred; Rozentzweig, Menachem; Shtil, Roman; Weinstein, Tibor; Zigelbaum, Moshe.

Published Primary Sources

Adler, Murray, oral history, https://stalagluft4.org/naratives.html.
Almogi, Yosef, *Berosh Mooram* [With Head Held High] (Tel Aviv: Ministry of Defence Publishing, 1989).
Asaria-Helfgot, Zvi, *Edim Anachnu* [We Are Witnesses] (Tel Aviv: Yavne, 1970).
Ben-Aharon, Yitschak, 'BaShevi HaNazi [in Nazi Captivity]', in Zeev Shefer and Yitshak Lamdan, eds, *Sefer Hahitnadvut* [The Volunteering Book] (Jerusalem: Mosad Bialik, 1949), pp. 648–58.

Ben-Aharon, Yitschak, *Dapim Min Haluach 1906-1993* [Pages from the Calendar] (Tel Aviv: HaKibutz HaMe'uchad, 1994).
Bird, Tom, *American POWs of World War II* (Westport, CT and London: Praeger, 1992).
Caplan, Aben, Memoirs, http://memory.loc.gov/diglib/vhp/story/loc.natlib.afc2001001.05190/.
Donaldson, Jeff, *Men of Honor: American GIs in the Jewish Holocaust* (Central Point, OR: Hellgate Press, 2005).
Elson, Aaron, *Prisoners of War: An Oral History* (New Britain, CT: Chi Chi Press, 2023).
Elworthy, Jack, memoirs, http://www.pegasusarchive.org/pow/jack_elworthy.htm.
Feldman, Milton and Bauer, Seth, *Captured, Frozen, Starved—and Lucky: How One Jewish American GI Survived a Nazi Stalag* (Kindle Edition: CreateSpace Independent Publishing Platform, 2018).
Foreign Relations of the United States (FRUS), 1945, vol. III.
Fox, Sonny, *But You Made the Front Page!* (Kindle Edition: Argos Navis Author Services, 2012).
Gilbert, John, memoirs, http://www.pegasusarchive.org/pow/jack_gilbert.htm.
Glantz, Alexander, *Hamaavak Becavlei Hashevi* [Struggle in Captivity] (Tel Aviv: Eshel, 1966).
Glovinsky, Haim, 'Arba Shanim [Four Years]', in Zeev Shefer and Yitshak Lamdan, eds, *Sefer Hahitnadvut* [The Volunteering Book] (Jerusalem: Mosad Bialik, 1949), pp. 659–63.
Goebbels, Joseph, *Tagebücher 1924–1945* (Munich: Piper, 2003).
Green, Julius, *From Colditz in Code* (London: Robert Hale & Company, 1971).
Guttridge, Tom, *Behind the Wire, Everyday Life as a POW* (Stroud: Amberley, 2017).
HaCohen, Shimon, *Mehashevi HaGermani* [from German Captivity] (Tel Aviv: Davar, 1943).
Halder, Franz, *War Journal (English Edition)*, Archives of Fort Leavenworth, Kansas.
Harvey, Arthur, memoirs, http://www.pegasusarchive.org/pow/alan_harvey.htm.
IMT, *Nazi Conspiracy and Aggression*, vols III, IV, V, VI, VII, VIII (Washington, DC: U.S. Government Printing Office, 1946).
IMT, *Nazi Conspiracy and Aggression Suppl. A* (Washington, DC: U.S. Government Printing Office, 1947).
IMT, *Nazi Conspiracy and Aggression Suppl. B* (Washington, DC: U.S. Government Printing Office, 1948).
IMT, *Trial of the Major War Criminals*, vols II, V, VI, IX (Nuremberg: Secretariat of the Tribunal, 1947).
IMT, *Trial of the Major War Criminals*, vols XVIII, XV, XX (Nuremberg: Secretariat of the Tribunal, 1948).
IMT, *Trial of the Major War Criminals*, vol. XXXIV (Nuremberg: Secretariat of the Tribunal, 1949).
IMT, *Trials of War Criminals*, vol. III—*The Justice Case* (Washington, DC: U.S. Government Printing Office, 1951).
IMT, *Trials of War Criminals*, vol. IV—*The Einsatzgruppen Case, The RuSHA Case* (Washington, DC: U.S. Government Printing Office, 1950).
IMT, *Trial of War Criminals*, vol. V—*The RuSHA Case, The Pohl Case* (Washington, DC: U.S. Government Printing Office, 1950).
IMT, *Trials of War Criminals*, vol. X—*The High Command Case* (Washington, DC: U.S. Government Printing Office, 1950).
IMT, *Trials of War Criminals*, vol. XI—*The High Command Case, The Hostage Case* (Washington, DC: U.S. Government Printing Office, 1950).
IMT, *Trials of War Criminals*, vol. XIII—*The Ministries Case* (Washington, DC: U.S. Government Printing Office, 1952).
IMT, *Trials of War Criminals*, vol. XIV—*The Ministries Case* (Washington, DC: U.S. Government Printing Office, 1952).

Jones, Henry, diary of a prisoner of war, http://www.pegasusarchive.org/pow/henry_jones.htm.
Junod, Marcel, *Warrior without Weapons* (London: International Committee of the Red Cross, 1951).
Karlenboim, Yosef, 'HaShevi [The Captivity]', in Zeev Shefer and Yitshak Lamdan, eds, *Sefer Hahitnadvut* [The Volunteering Book] (Jerusalem: Mosad Bialik, 1949), pp. 628–41.
Karp, Julius, 'The Julius Karp Story', unpublished memoir, https://stalagluft4.org/pdf/JuliusKarp.pdf.
Kasten, Johann, https://memory.loc.gov/diglib/vhp-stories/loc.natlib.afc2001001.12002/.
Keyter, Barry, *From Wings to Jackboots* (London: Janus Publishing, 1995).
Kimbarow, Sam, http://www.jewishsightseeing.com/usa/california/san_diego/veterans_administration/19990423-world_war_ii_pows.htm.
King, Martin, Johnson, Ken, and Collins, Michael, *Warriors of the 106th* (Philadelphia, PA and Oxford: Casemate, 2017).
Krebs, William, https://www.b24.net/powStalag6.htm.
Kuptsow, Aaron, http://www.merkki.com/kuptsowaaron.htm#ak.
LaCroix, Hal, *Journey Out of Darkness* (Westport, CT and London: Praeger, 2007).
Le Combattant Volontaire Juif 1939–1945 (Paris: Imprimerie Abexpress, 1971).
Levinas, Emmanuel, *Carnets de Captivité et Autres Inédits* (Paris: Bernard Grasset, 2017).
Levy, Harry, *The Dark Side of the Sky* (London: Leo Cooper, 1996).
Lichtenfeld, Seymour 'Sy', oral history, https://www.ww2online.org/view/seymour-lichtenfeld#stalag-iii-b.
Lifson, Irving, 'Loneliest and Happiest Point in One's Life', in Wilbert H. Richarz et al., eds, *The 390th Bomb Group Anthology*, vol. I (Tucson, AZ: 390th Memorial Museum Foundation, 1995).
Loevsky, Louis, http://www.americanairmuseum.com/person/150458.
Lucero, Telesfor, https://wartimememoriesproject.com/ww2/view.php?uid=206841.
Moll, Martin, *Führer-Erlasse 1939–1945* (Hamburg: Nikol Verlag, 2011).
Neave, Airey, *They Have Their Exits* (Barnsley: Leo Cooper, 2002).
Paules, Frank, https://www.b24.net/powStalag6.htm.
Pringle, Jack, *Colditz Last Stop* (London: William Kimber, 1988).
Read, Fredrick, *A War Fought Behind the Wire* (Kindle Edition: F. C. Read, 2013).
Rofe, Cyril, *Against the Wind* (London: Hodder and Stoughton, 1956).
Rubenstein, Norman, *The Invisibly Wounded* (Hull: The Glenvil Group, 1989).
Satow, Harold and See, M. J., *The Work of the Prisoners of War Department during the Second World War* (London: The British Foreign Office, 1950).
Sela (Slodash), Shlomo, *BeCavlei HeShevi* [Shackles of Captivity] (Tel Aviv: Mif'alei Tarbut ve-Chinuch, 1986).
Spiller, Harry, *Prisoners of Nazis: Accounts by American POWs in World War II* (Jefferson, NC and London: McFarland and Company, 1998).
Spivey, Delmar T., oral history, Airforce Historical Research Agency, Irisnum 01015418, Reel 31923.
Spivey, Delmar T., *POW Odyssey* (Attleboro, MA: Colonial Lithograph, 1984).
Stern, Milton, oral history, https://memory.loc.gov/diglib/vhp-stories/loc.natlib.afc2001001.01348/.
Stovroff, Irwin, https://www.vetshelpingheroes.org/about-irwin-stovroff/.
Trevor-Roper, Hugh, ed., *Hitler's Table Talk* (New York: Enigma Books, 2000).
Trevor-Roper, Hugh, ed., *Hitler's War Directives 1939–1945* (Edinburgh: Birlinn, 2004).
United States Congressional Record—Senate, vol. 91 (Washington, DC: U.S. Government Printing Office, 1945).

Vietor, John, *Time Out* (Fallbrook, CA: Aero Publishers, 1985).
Waltzog, Alfons, *Recht der Landkriegsführung* (Berlin: Franz Vahlen, 1942).
Watchman, Alan, oral history, https://www.iwm.org.uk/collections/item/object/80010966.
Weiner, Fred, memoirs, https://stalagluft4.org/pdf/weinernew.pdf.
Westheimer, David, *Sitting It Out* (Houston: Rice University Press, 1992).
Winograd, Leonard, 'Double Jeopardy: What an American Army Officer, a Jew, Remembers of Prison Life in Germany', *American Jewish Archives Journal*, 1 (1976).
Wolk, Bruce, *Jewish Aviators in World War II* (Jefferson, NC: McFarland & Company, 2016).
Yerushalmi, Aharon, *Shlosha Sheh-Barchoo* [Three Who Escaped] (Tel Aviv: Ayanot, 1957).
Yordan, Fritz, *Brichati me Hashevi* [My Escape from Captivity] (Ain Harod: HaKibutz HaMe'uchad, 1945).
Zemke, Hubert, *Zemke's Stalag* (Shrewsbury: Airlife, 1991).

Newspapers, News Agencies, and Bulletins

Aufbau.
The Checkerboard (99th Infantry Division Association).
Der Führer.
Jewish Chronicle (JC).
Jewish Telegraphic Agency (JTA).
New York Times.
Prisoners of War Bulletin.
Sunday Post (Scotland).

Online Resources

https://aad.archives.gov/aad/series-description.jsp?s=644&cat=GP24&bc=,sl—World War II Prisoners of War Data File, NARA.
https://avalon.law.yale.edu/imt—Nuremberg Trial Proceedings.
http://www.axpow.org/roster.html#—The American Ex-Prisoners of War Organization.
https://b24.net/powStalag4.htm—Testimonies of POWs.
https://catalog.archives.gov—US military intelligence service reports.
https://www.fold3.com/—NARA, WWII Nuremberg Interrogation Records.
https://hansard.parliament.uk/—British Parliament proceedings.
https://ihl-databases.icrc.org—The International Red Cross Organization online database.
https://www.izkor.gov.il—Israel war memorial site.
http://en.jabotinsky.org/archive—Files of fallen Palestinian Jewish POWs.
https://www.jewishpioneers.com—The Palestinian Jewish POWs information website.
https://www.nizkor.org/the-trial-of-adolf-eichmann/—Transcripts of the trial of Adolf Eichmann.
https://www.jewishvirtuallibrary.org—Einsatzgruppen operational situaton reports.
http://www.pegasusarchive.org/pow/—Experiences of POWs during the Second World War.
https://www.va.gov/opa/publications/factsheets/fs_americas_wars.pdf—US Department of Veteran Affairs.
https://wartimememoriesproject.com/ww2/—The Wartime Memories Project—The Second World War.
https://www.ww2online.org/—The Digital Collections of the National WWII Museum.

Secondary Literature

Anderson, Benedict, *Imagined Communities* (London and New York: Verso, 2016).

Angress, Werner T., 'Dokumentation. Das deutsche Militär und die Juden im Ersten Weltkrieg', *Militärgeschichtliche Mitteilungen*, 19:1 (1976), pp. 77–88.

Bar-Chen, Eli, 'Tunisian Jews' Fate under Nazi Occupation and the Possibility of Reviewing the Holocaust', *Zmanim: A Historical Quarterly*, 67 (1999), pp. 34–47.

Bard, Mitchell, *Forgotten Victims: The Abandonment of Americans in Hitler's Camps* (Boulder and Oxford: Westview Press, 1994).

Bartov, Omer, 'Soldiers, Nazis and the War in the Third Reich', *Journal of Modern History*, 63 (1991), pp. 44–60.

Bartov, Omer, *Hitler's Army* (New York: Oxford University Press, 1992).

Bartov, Omer, 'The Conduct of War: Soldiers and the Barbarization of Warfare', *Journal of Modern History*, Supplement: Resistance against the Third Reich, 64 (1992), pp. S32–S45.

Bartov, Omer, *The Eastern Front, 1941–45, German Troops and the Barbarisation of Warfare* (Basingstoke and New York: Palgrave Macmillan, 2001).

Bentwich, Norman, 'Palestine Nationality and the Mandate', *Journal of Comparative Legislation and International Law*, 21:4 (1939), pp. 230–2.

Binner, Jens, 'Aspekte jüdischer Geschichte in Niedersachsen. Lager—Zwangsarbeit—Deportation 1938 bis 1945', Conceference presentation, 1 November 2012, Hannover.

Black, Peter, *Ernst Kaltenbrunner—Ideological Soldier of the Third Reich* (Princeton: Princeton University Press, 1984).

Braham, Randolph L., *The Politics of Genocide: The Holocaust in Hungary* (Detroit: Wayne State University Press, 2000).

Braham, Randolph L. and Miller, Scott, eds, *The Nazis' Last Victims* (Detroit: Wayne State University Press, 2002).

Broszat, Martin, 'Hitler und die Genesis der "Endlösung". Aus Anlaß der Thesen von David Irving', *Vierteljahrshefte für Zeitgeschichte*, 25:4 (1977), pp. 739–75.

Browning, Christopher, 'A Reply to Martin Broszat Regarding the Origins of the Final Solution', *Simon Wiesenthal Center Annual*, 1 (1984), pp. 113–32.

Browning, Christopher, *Fateful Months* (New York and London: Holmes & Meier, 1991).

Browning, Christopher, 'The Nazi Decision to Commit Mass Murder: Three Interpretations', *German Studies Review*, 17:3 (1994), pp. 473–81.

Browning, Christopher, *Ordinary Men: Reserve Police Battalion 101 and the Final Solution in Poland* (New York and London: Harper Perennial, 2017).

Campbell, Bruce, 'The SA after the Rohm Purge', *Journal of Contemporary History*, 28:4 (1993), pp. 659–74.

Caplan, Laura, 'The Captain Leslie Caplan Story', https://stalagluft4.org/pdf/CaptainCaplan.pdf.

Cohen, Roger, *Soldiers and Slaves* (New York: Anchor Books, 2005).

Conze, Eckart, Frei, Norbert, Hayes, Peter, and Zimmermann, Moshe, *Das Amt und die Vergangenheit—Deutsche Diplomaten im Dritten Reich und in der Bundesrepublik* (Munich: Pantheon, 2010).

Das, Santanu, *Race, Empire and First World War Writing* (Cambridge: Cambridge University Press, 2011).

Dashefsky, Arnold, 'Being Jewish: An Approach to Conceptualization and Operationalization', in Isidore D. Passow and Samuel T. Lachs, eds, *Gratz College Anniversary Volume, 1895–1970* (Philadelphia, PA: Gratz College, 1971), pp. 35–46.

Datner, Szymon, *Crimes against POWs: Responsibility of the Wehrmacht* (Warsaw: Zachodnia Agencja Prasowa, 1964).

Dominy, John, *The Sergeant Escapers* (Reading: Hodder and Stoughton, 1976).

Döscher, Hans Jürgen, *Das Auswärtige Amt in Dritten Reich* (Berlin: Siedler, 1987).

Dublin, Louis and Kohs, Samuel, *American Jews in World War II*, vol. 2 (New York: The Dial Press, 1947).
Durand, Arthur, *Stalag Luft III* (London: Simon and Schuster, 1989).
Durand, Yves, *La Captivité* (Paris: Fédération Nationale des Combattants Prisonniers de Guerre et Combattants d'Algérie, Tunisie, Maroc, 1980).
Durand, Yves, *Prisonniers de Guerre, dans les Stalags, les Oflags et les Kommandos, 1939–1945* (Paris: Hachette Littératures, 1994).
Edmonds, Chris and Century, Douglas, *No Surrender* (Digital Edition: HarperOne, 2019).
Fabréguet, Michel, 'Un Groupe de Réfugiés Politiques: les Républicains Espagnols des Camps d'internement Français aux Camps de Concentration Nationaux-Socialistes (1939–1941)', *Revue d'histoire de la Deuxième Guerre mondiale et des conflits contemporains*, 36:144 (1986), pp. 19–38.
Favez, Jean-Clause, *The Red Cross and the Holocaust* (Cambridge: Cambridge University Press, 1999).
Förster, Jürgen, 'Complicity or Entanglement? Wehrmacht, War and Holocaust', in Michael Berenbaum and Abraham Peck, eds, *The Holocaust and History* (Bloomington: Indiana University Press, 2002).
Förster, Jürgen, 'The German Army and the Ideological War against the Soviet Union', in Gerhard Hirschfeld, ed., *The Policies of Genocide, Jews and Soviet Prisoners of War in Nazi Germany* (New York and Abingdon: Routledge, 2015), pp. 15–29.
Foy, David, *For You the War Is Over* (New York: Stein and Day, 1984).
Fredrickson, George M., *Racism: A Short History* (Princeton and Oxford: Princeton University Press, 2015).
Friedländer, Saul, *Nazi Germany and the Jews: The Years of Extermination: 1939–1945* (London: Phoenix, 2008).
Fritz, Stephen G., '"We Are Trying...to Change the Face of the World"—Ideology and Motivation in the Wehrmacht on the Eastern Front: The View from Below', *Journal of Military History*, 60:4 (1996), pp. 683–710.
Fulbruk, Mary and Rublack, Ulinka, 'In Relation: The "Social Self" and Ego-Documents', *German History* 28:3 (2010), pp. 263–72.
Garner, James Wilford, 'Recent Conventions for the Regulations of War', *American Journal of International Law*, 26:4 (1932), pp. 807–11.
Gascar, Pierre, *Histoire de la captivité des français en Allemagne, 1939–1945* (Paris: Gallimard, 2016).
Geck, Stefan, *Das deutsche Kriegsgefangenenwesen 1939–1945*, unpublished PhD thesis, Mainz University (1998).
Gelber, Yoav, *Toldot Hahitnadvut*, vol. 1 [The History of Volunteering] (Jerusalem: Yad Ben Tzvi, 1979).
Gelber, Yoav, 'Palestinian POWs in German Captivity', *Yad Vashem Studies*, 14 (1981), pp. 89–137.
Gelber, Yoav, *Toldot Hahitnadvut*, vol. 4 [The History of Volunteering] (Jerusalem: Yad Ben Tzvi, 1984).
Gerwarth, Robert, *Hitler's Hangman, The Life of Heydrich* (New Haven, CT and London: Yale University Press, 2012).
Gilbert, Adrian, *POW: Allied Prisoners in Europe 1939–1945* (London: Thistle Publishing, 2014).
Goffman, Erving, *Asylums* (New York and London: Taylor & Francis, 2017).
Gurock, Jeffrey, 'Twentieth-Century American Orthodoxy's Era of Non-Observance, 1900–1960', *Torah U-Madda Journal*, 9 (2000), pp. 87–107.

Hall, Kevin, 'Luftgangster over Germany: The Lynching of American Airmen in the Shadow of the Air War', *Historical Social Research*, 43:2 (2018), Special Issue: Visualities—Sports, Bodies, and Visual Sources, pp. 277–312.
Hartmann, Christian, *Wehrmacht im Ostkrieg* (Munich: R. Oldenbourg Verlag, 2009).
Hasselbring, Andrew, *American Prisoners of War in the Third Reich*, unpublished PhD thesis, Temple University (1991).
Hilberg, Raul, *The Destruction of the European Jews* (New Haven, CT and London: Yale University Press, 2003).
Hirschman, Charles, 'The Origins and Demise of the Concept of Race', *Population and Development Review*, 30:3 (2004), pp. 385–415.
Jacobsen, Hans-Adolf, 'The Kommissarbefehl and Mass Execution of Soviet Russian Prisoners of War', in Martin Broszat, Hans Buchheim, Hans-Adolf Jacobsen, and Helmut Krausnick, eds, *Anatomy of the SS State* (Cambridge: Walker and Company, 1968), pp. 505–35.
Jacques, Johanna, 'A "Most Astonishing" Circumstance: The Survival of Jewish POWs in German War Captivity during the Second World War', *Social & Legal Studies*, 30:3 (2021), pp. 362–83.
Jay, John, *Facing Fearful Odds* (Barnsley: Pen and Sword, 2014).
Jones, Heather, *Violence against Prisoners of War in the First World War: Britain, France and Germany 1914–1920* (Cambridge: Cambridge University Press, 2011).
Jones, Priscilla Dale, 'Nazi Atrocities against Allied Airmen: Stalag Luft III and the End of British War Crimes Trials', *Historical Journal*, 41:2 (1998), pp. 543–65.
Kay, Alex J. and Stahel, David, 'Crimes of the Wehrmacht: A Re-evaluation', *Journal of Perpetrator Research*, 3.1 (2020), pp. 95–127.
Kern, Steven, *Jewish Refugees from Germany and Austria in the British Army, 1939–45*, unpublished PhD thesis, University of Nottingham (2004).
Kershaw, Ian, '"Working towards the Führer." Reflections on the Nature of the Hitler Dictatorship', *Contemporary European History*, 2:2 (1993), pp. 103–18.
Kershaw, Ian, *Hitler 1936–1945: Nemesis* (London: Penguin Books, 2001).
Kershaw, Ian, *The End* (Penguin Kindle Edition, 2011).
Keynan, Irit, *Memories from a Life I Have Not Lived* (Tel Aviv: Pardes, 2020).
Killingray, David, 'Africans and African Americans in Enemy Hands', in Bob Moore and Kent Fedorowich, eds, *Prisoners of War and Their Captors in World War II* (Oxford: Berg, 1996), pp. 181–204.
Kitchen, Martin, *The German Officer Corps 1890–1914* (Oxford: Clarendon Press, 1968).
Kochavi, Arieh, *Confronting Captivity* (Chapel Hill, NC and London: University of North Carolina Press, 2005).
Krakowski, Shmuel, 'The Fate of Jewish Prisoners of War in the September 1939 Campaign', *Yad Vashem Studies*, 12 (1977), pp. 297–333.
Krakowski, Shmuel, 'Jewish Prisoners of War', in Israel Gutman, ed., *Encyclopedia of the Holocaust* (Tel Aviv: Hakibutz HaMe'uchad, 1990), pp. 1180–1.
Lador-Lederer, Joseph, 'Jews as Prisoners-of-War in Germany, with Special Reference to Yugoslav Soldiers', in Yakir Eventov et al., eds, *Yalqut 1948–1978* (Jerusalem: Jerusalem Post, 1978).
Lebl, Ženi, *Jewish Soldiers from Yugoslavia as POWs in Nazi Germany* (Tel Aviv: The Association of WWII Veterans in Israel—the Yugoslav section, 1995).
Linne, Karsten, '"Die Arbeitskraft sämtlicher Kriegsgefangenen ist rücksichtslos auszunutzen." Die Zwangsarbeit sowjetischer Kriegsgefangener für die Wehrmacht im Osten', *Jahrbücher für Geschichte Osteuropas*, 54:2 (2006), pp. 190–206.

Lipman, Vivian, *Social History of the Jews in England, 1850–1950* (London: Watts & Co, 1954).
Lipstadt, Deborah, *Beyond Belief* (New York: The Free Press, 1986).
Longerich, Peter, *Heinrich Himmler* (Oxford: Oxford University Press, 2012).
MacKenzie, Simon, 'The Treatment of Prisoners of War in World War II', *Journal of Modern History*, 66 (1994), pp. 487–520.
MacKenzie, Simon, *The Colditz Myth* (New York: Oxford University Press, 2004).
Makepeace, Clare, *Captives of War* (Cambridge: Cambridge University Press, 2017).
McGill, Nettie, 'Some Characteristics of Jewish Youth in New York City', *Jewish Social Service Quarterly*, 14 (1937), pp. 251–72.
Megargee, Geoffrey P., ed., *The United States Holocaust Memorial Museum Encyclopedia of Camps and Ghettos, 1933–1945*, vol. IV (Bloomington: Indiana University Press, 2022).
Messerschmidt, Manfred, *Die Wehrmacht im NS-Staat, Zeit der Indoktrination* (Hambrug: R. V. Decker's Verlag, 1969).
Michman, Dan, 'Were the Jews of North Africa Included in the Practical Planning for the "Final Solution of the Jewish Question"?', in Alex J. Kay and David Stahel, eds, *Mass Violence in Nazi-Occupied Europe* (Bloomington: Indiana University Press, 2018), pp. 59–78.
Mommsen, Hans, 'Hitler's Reichstag Speech of 30 January 1939', *History and Memory*, 9:1/2 (1997), pp. 147–61.
Moore, Bob, *Prisoners of War—Europe: 1939–1956* (Oxford: Oxford University Press, 2022).
Moore, Deborah, *GI Jews* (Cambridge, MA: The Belknap Press, 2006).
Moret-Bailly, Jean, 'Le Camp de Base du Stalag XVII B', *Revue d'histoire de la Deuxième Guerre Mondial*, 25 (1957), pp. 7–45.
Morgan, Philip, *The Fall of Mussolini* (Oxford: Oxford University Press, 2007).
Moriss, Henry and Sugarman, Martin, *We Will Remember Them* (Portland, OR and London: Vallentine Mitchell, 2011).
Müller, Klaus-Jurgen, *Das Heer und Hitler* (Stuttgart: Deutsche Verlags-Anstalt, 1969).
Müller, Klaus-Jurgen, *The Army, Politics and Society in Germany, 1933–1945: Studies in the Army's Relation to Nazism* (Manchester: Manchester University Press, 1987).
Müller, Rolf-Dieter, *Hitler's Wehrmacht* (Lexington, KY: University Press of Kentucky, 2016).
Neitzel, Sönke and Welzer, Harald, *Soldaten* (London: Simon and Schuster, 2012).
Nichol, John, and Rennell, Tony, *The Last Escape: The Untold Story of Allied Prisoners of War in Germany 1944–1945* (New York and London: Penguin Books, 2003).
Noakes, Jeremy and Pridham, Geoffrey, *Nazism 1939–1945*, Vol. 3: *Foreign Policy, War and Racial Extermination* (Liverpool: Liverpool University Press, 2014).
O'Neill, Robert, *The German Army and the Nazi Party* (London: Corgi Books, 1968).
Overmans, Rüdiger, 'Die Kriegsgefangenenpolitik des Deutschs Reichs 1939 bis 1945', in Jörg Echternkamp, ed., *Das Deutsche Reich und der Zweite Weltkrieg*, Band 9/2 (Munich: Deutsche Verlags-Anstalt, 2005), 729–875.
Overmans, Rüdiger, 'German Treatment of Jewish Prisoners of War in the Second World War', in Anne-Marie Pathé and Fabien Théofilakis, eds, *Wartime Captivity in the 20th Century* (New York and Oxford: Berghahn, 2016), lns 1133–1301.
Penkower, Monty Noam, 'The World Jewish Congress Confronts the International Red Cross during the Holocaust', *Jewish Social Studies*, 41:3/4 (1979), pp. 229–56.
Penslar, Derek, *Shylock's Children: Economics and Jewish Identity in Modern Europe* (London: University of California Press, 2001).
Pike, David W., *In the Service of Stalin, The Spanish Communists in Exile 1939–1945* (Oxford: Clarendon Press, 1993).
Polian, Pavel, 'First Victims of the Holocaust: Soviet-Jewish Prisoners of War in German Captivity', *Kritika: Explorations in Russian and Eurasian History*, 6:4 (2005), pp. 763–87.

Post, Gaines, 'Exploring Political–Military Relations: Nazi Germany', in Daniel Marston and Tamara Leahy, eds, *War, Strategy and History* (Acton, Australia: ANU Press, 2016).

Presburger, Josip, 'Oficiri Jevreji u Zarobljenickim Logorima u Nemackoj [Jewish Officers in Prisoners of War Camps]', *3 Zbornik, Jevrejski Istorjki Muzej* [The Jewish History Museum] (Belgrade, 1975), pp. 225–82.

Quinnett, Robert, *Hitler's Political Officers: The National Socialist Leadership Officers*, unpublished PhD thesis, University of Oklahoma (1973).

Rempel, Gerhard, 'Gottlob Berger and Waffen-SS Recruitment: 1939–1945', *Militärgeschichtliche Mitteilungen*, 27:1 (1980), pp. 107–22.

Richard, Delphine, 'La captivité en Allemagne des soldats juifs de France pendant la Seconde Guerre mondiale: l'ébauche d'un phénomène diasporique éphémère?', *Diasporas*, 31 (2018), pp. 65–81.

Rieber, Alfred, 'Nationalizing Imperial Armies: A Comparative and Transnational Study of Three Empires', in Stefan Berger and Alexei Miller, eds, *Nationalising Empires* (New York and Budapest: CEU Press, 2005), pp. 593–628.

Römer, Felix, 'The Wehrmacht in the War of Ideologies: The Army and Hitler's Criminal Orders in the Eastern Front', in Alex J. Kay, Jeff Rutherford, and David Stahel, eds, *Nazi Policy in the Eastern Front, 1941* (Rochester: University of Rochester Press, 2014), pp. 73–100.

Römer, Felix, *Comrades, The Wehrmacht from Within* (Oxford: Oxford University Press, 2019).

Rossino Alexander, *Hitler Strikes Poland* (Lawrence, KS: University Press of Kansas, 2003).

Sait, Bryce, *The Indoctrination of the Wehrmacht* (New York and Oxford: Berghahn, 2019).

Sarna, Jonathan, *American Judaism* (New Haven, CT and London: Yale University Press, 2019).

Scapini, Georges, *Mission sans Gloire* (Paris: Morgan, 1960).

Scheck, Raffael, *Hitler's African Victims* (Cambridge: Cambridge University Press, 2008).

Scheck, Rafael, *French Colonial Soldiers in German Captivity during World War II* (Cambridge: Cambridge University Press, 2014).

Schenderlein, Anne, *Germany on Their Mind* (New York: Berghahn, 2020).

Schroer, Timothy L., 'The Emergence and Early Demise of Codified Racial Segregation of Prisoners of War under the Geneva Conventions of 1929 and 1949', *Journal of the History of International Law*, 15:1 (2013), pp. 53–76.

Sebag-Montefiore, Hugh, *Dunkirk, Fight to the Last Man* (London: Penguin, 2007).

Shils, Edward A. and Janowitz, Morris, 'Cohesion and Disintegration in the Wehrmacht in World War II', *Public Opinion Quarterly*, 12:2 (1948), pp. 280–315.

Shneyer, Aron, *Pariahs among Pariahs* (Jerusalem: Yad Vashem, 2016).

Sklare, Marshall and Greenblum, Joseph, *Jewish Identity on the Suburban Frontier* (Chicago: The University of Chicago Press, 1979).

Smith, Elaine, 'Class, Ethnicity and Politics in the Jewish East End, 1918–1939', *Jewish Historical Studies*, 32 (1990–2), pp. 355–69.

Spoerer, Mark, 'Die soziale Differenzierung der ausländischen Zivilarbeiter, Kriegsgefangenen und Häftlinge im Deutschen Reich', in Jörg Echternkamp, ed., *Das Deutsche Reich und der Zweite Weltkrieg*, Band 9/2 (Munich: Deutsche Verlags-Anstalt, 2005), pp. 485–576.

Stahel, David, 'The Wehrmacht and National Socialist Military Thinking', *War in History*, 24:3 (2017), pp. 336–61.

Das Stalag X B Sandbostel: Geschichte und Nachgeschichte eines Kriegsgefangenenlagers (Hamburg: Dölling und Galitz Verlag, 2015).

Stargardt, Nicolas, *The German War* (New York: Penguin, 2015).

Steinacher, Gerald, *Humanitarians at War* (Oxford: Oxford University Press, 2017).

Steinberg, Milton, *A Partisan Guide to the Jewish Problem* (Indianapolis and New York: Charter Books, 1963).
Stoltzfus, Nathan, 'Historical Evidence and Plausible History: Interpreting the Berlin Gestapo's Attempted "Final Roundup" of Jews', *Central European History*, 38:3 (2005), pp. 450–9.
Streim, Alfred, *Sowjetische Gefangene in Hitlers Vernichtungskrieg* (Heidelberg: C. F. Müller Juristische Verlag, 1982).
Streit, Christian, *Keine Kameraden* (Stuttgart: Deutsche Verlags-Anstalt, 1978).
Streit, Christian, 'The German Army and the Policies of Genocide', in Gerhard Hirschfeld, ed., *The Policies of Genocide, Jews and Soviet Prisoners of War in Nazi Germany* (New York and Abingdon: Routledge, 2015), pp. 1–14.
Sugarman, Martin, 'Two Notes on Jews on Active Service', *Jewish Historical Studies*, 39 (2004), pp. 177–82.
Szajkowski, Zosa, 'Private and Organized American Jewish Overseas Relief (1914–1938)', *American Jewish Historical Quarterly*, 57:1 (1967), pp. 52–3, 55–106.
Trevor-Roper, Hugh, *The Last Days of Hitler* (London: Pan Books, 2012).
Vourkoutiotis, Vasilis, *Prisoners of War and the German High Command* (New York: Palgrave Macmillan, 2003).
Wallis, Russell, *British POWs and the Holocaust: Witnessing the Nazi Atrocities* (New York and London: I. B. Tauris, 2017).
Walton, Marilyn and Eberhardt, Michael, *From Commandant to Captive, the Memoirs of Stalag Luft III Commandant* (Kindle Edition: Lulu Publishing, 2015).
Weitkamp, Sebastian, 'Kooperativtäter—die Beteiligung des Auswärtigen Amts an der NS-Gewaltpolitik jenseits der "Endlösung"', in Johannes Hurter and Thomas Raithel, eds, *Das Auswärtige Amt in der NS-Diktatur* (Berlin: De Gruyter Oldenbourg, 2014), pp. 197–218.
Wette, Wolfram, *The Wehrmacht: History, Myth and Reality* (Cambridge, MA and London: Harvard University Press, 2007).
Whitlock, Flint, *Given Up for Dead: American GIs in the Nazi Concentration Camp at Berga* (New York: Basic Books, 2006).
Wickiewicz, Anna, *Captivity in British Uniform* (Opole: Centralne Muzeum Jeńców Wojennych, 2018).
Wilkinson, Oliver, *British Prisoners of War in First World War Germany* (Cambridge: Cambridge University Press, 2017).
Winter, Jay and Sivan, Emmanuel, *War and Remembrance in the Twentieth Century* (New York: Cambridge University Press, 2005).
Wylie, Neville, 'Captured by the Nazis: "Reciprocity" and "National Conservatism" in German Policy towards British POWs', in Claus-Christian W. Szejnmann, ed., *Rethinking History, Dictatorship and War* (London: Continuum, 2009).
Wylie, Neville, *Barbed Wire Diplomacy* (Oxford: Oxford University Press, 2010).
Wylie, Neville, 'The 1929 Prisoner of War Convention and the Building of the Inter-War Prisoner of War Regime', in Sibylle Scheipers, ed., *Prisoners in War* (New York: Oxford University Press, 2010), pp. 91–110.
Wynn, Stephen, *Stalag 383 Bavaria* (Barnsley: Pen & Sword, 2021).
Yaacovi, Yohanan, *The Road to Captivity*, unpublished MA thesis, Tel Aviv University (1976).

Index

For references to individual POW camps and their locations (the modern place name is added in brackets if different) see 'POW camps (specific camps)'. For references to accounts of individual POWs' experiences see 'POW testimonies (British and Commonwealth)' and 'POW testimonies (American)'.

For the benefit of digital users, indexed terms that span two pages (e.g., 52–53) may, on occasion, appear on only one of those pages.

African American soldiers *see* black POWs
Albrecht, Erich 54–6
Allgemeines Wehrmachtsamt (AWA) *see* OKW General Office
Allied POWs
   historiography 7–17
   Jewish POWs 5
   minority and political groups, from 15–16
   numbers of 3–7
   reciprocal protection of Allied and German POWs 5, 9, 13–14, 17–19, 56, 186–7
Allman, John 80–1
Altman, Richard, Private 132–3
American armed forces, Jewish soldiers in 6
American Jewish POWs *see* POWs
American POWs (Jewish and non-Jewish)
   African American soldiers *see* black POWs
   numbers of 5
armed forces, German *see* German soldiers; Wehrmacht
Armed Forces High Command *see* OKW
Australian POWs 5

Barlow, David 116–17
Belgian POWs 3–4, 5
Ben-Aharon, Yitschak 84, 150
Berg, Roger 102
Berga slave labour camp 11, 45, 116–17, 163–7, 179–80
Berger, Gottlob, Lieutenant General SS 7, 33–5, 40, 57, 96, 141, 145–6, 157, 184, 196, 207–8, 214, 222–5, 230–1, 234–5
black POWs 15–16, 55–6
Blomberg, Werner von, Field Marshall 182, 189–90
blood donation order 210–11
Blumenfeld, Jacob, Private 159–60

Bombach, Aribert, Lieutenant Colonel 59–60
Bormann, Martin 188–9, 202
Brauchitsch, Walter von, Field Marshall 11–12, 182, 184–5
Breyer, Hans-Joachim, Major 32, 219–20
British armed forces
   Jewish soldiers in 6
   Palestinian Jews in 6
British Jewish POWs *see* Palestinian Jews; POWs
British POWs (Jewish and non-Jewish) 3–4, 5
Bromfield, Louis 174
Burckhardt, Carl 43–4, 175–7
burials *see* funerals

camps *see* POW camps
Canadian POWs 5
Canaris, Admiral Wilhelm 23, 191–2
capital punishment in the German army 41
Caplan, Aben, Technical Sergeant 109–10, 122
capture and transit
   arrival at POW camp 56–8
   capture experience of British and American soldiers 43–8
   capture experience of Palestinian Jewish soldiers 48–56
   initial processing after capture 39–42
   Jewish identity, and 105–11
Chapman, Edward 150–1
Charlton, Michael, Captain Father 125
Cheneviere, Jacques 50–1
Churchill, Winston 228
Cohen, Clifford, Second Lieutenant 150–1
colonial soldiers *see* French POWs
commissar order *see* Führer Orders
Cornell, Edwin 116–17
court cases as to Jewish POWs 86–9
Crew, Henry, Gunner 134

current explanations for German treatment of Jewish POWs
  absence of Führer Order 225–8
  author's approach in current book 37–8
  behaviour of POW camp personnel 12–13
  German compliance with Geneva Convention *see* Geneva Convention (1929)
  German fears of Allied retribution 61
  historiography 17–22
  Hitler's role 185–9, 225–8
  interaction between RSHA, Nazi Party and Wehrmacht 195–203
  introduction to 181–5
  OKW's role 189–95
  POW Office's role 203–25
  reciprocal protection of Allied and German POWs 5, 17–19

Daub, Gerald 109–10
Deans, Jimmy 'Dixie' 160–1
Death Squads *see* Einsatzgruppen
Denton, Patrick 150–1
Dönitz, Karl, Grand Admiral 188–9
Dutch POWs
  number of 3–4
  number of Jewish POWs 5
  Sweden as Protecting Power 55n.88

Eden, Anthony 50
Edmonds, Roddie, Master Sergeant 139
Eichmann, Adolf 196–7, 239–40
Einsatzgruppen ('Action Groups' i.e. Death Squads) 1–2, 8–9, 11–12, 54, 61–2, 130, 140–1, 154, 191–2, 211–12, 234–6
Eisenberg, Dov 82–3
Eisenhower, Dwight, General 173–4
Elkind, Yitshak 127–8
escaped POWs 91–4, 184
evacuation of POW camps, Geneva Convention, and 15
exchanges of POWs *see* POW organization, policy and regime

Fahnert, Reinhard, Sergeant 59–60
Feldman, Milton 1–2, 125–6
Final Solution *see* Holocaust
Fine, Hyman, Second Lieutenant 45
First World War *see* World War I
Fortune, Victor, Major General 150–1
Fox, Sonny 45, 102
Franco, Francisco 217–18
French POWs
  colonial soldiers 15–16
  historiography 13–14
  mistreatment of Jewish POWs 1–2
  number of 3–4
  number of Jewish POWs 5
  reciprocal protection with German POWs 13–14
  Spanish Republicans *see* Spanish Republican POWs
  see also POW testimonies (French)
Friedrichs, Helmuth 202
Fritsch, Werner von, Colonel General 182
Fromm, Friedrich, Colonel-General 32 (33), 33–5
Führer Orders
  absence of 225–8
  black POWs 15–16, 55–6
  burial of airmen POWs 107
  commissar order 228–9
  execution of captured Allied airmen 196–7
  execution of captured Allied commando soldiers ('Kommando Befehl') 21–2, 40, 100, 183–4, 186–7, 193, 197, 201, 213–14, 216–17, 228–9, 238
  execution of captured Italian officers 193–4
  Geneva Convention, as to 218
  German soldiers' disobedience of 223–4, 228–31
  Holocaust 195, 214
  Kugel (bullet) Erlass 22, 40, 86, 93, 100, 179–80, 183–4, 186–7, 213–14, 216–17, 228–30, 238
  lynching of shot-down Allied aircrews, as to 194
  mistreatment of POWs, as to 184–5
  non-Soviet Jewish POWs, as to 181–2, 203–4, 214, 230–1
  POWs in German economy 17–18
  transfer of POW Office 184
  transfer of POWs to prevent liberation 224–5
  see also POW Office
funerals
  black POWs 15–16
  compliance/non-compliance with Geneva Convention 15–16
  expression of Jewish identity 127–35
  Führer Order as to burial of airmen POWs 133–4
  inconsistencies in German approach 137
  see also Jewish identity

Galen, Clemens Count von, Bishop of Münster 179
Galler, Harry, Private 63
Gattung, Harold, Corporal 46

INDEX   263

Geneva Convention (1929)
  blood donation by POWs 210–11
  Detaining Powers' duty disclose legal documents to Protecting Power 89
  Detaining Powers' responsibilities for POWs 42–3
  entitlement to legal representation 88
  escaped POWs 91–4
  evacuation of POW camps 15, 224–5
  funerals 127–35
  general description of 35–6
  German compliance 2–3, 5–7, 12–14, 35–41, 57–8, 61–2, 64, 85, 94–101, 186–7, 201, 203, 214–16, 218–20, 225, 230, 232–3, 237–8, 241
  German non-compliance 4–5, 7, 10–11, 15–16, 35–6, 76, 181–2, 187, 193, 195, 200–2, 216–17, 228–9, 238
  German POW policy, and 7
  German racial policy, and 49–50
  Hitler's repudiation of 17, 18–19, 187–9, 214–16, 218, 222, 224–7, 231
  'Italian Military Internees' (IMIs) 5
  Jewish POWs in concentration/extermination camps 10–11
  medical treatment 89–91
  POW camp personnel compliance 17–18, 37, 39–40, 45–6, 57–61, 66–8, 70, 78–9, 82
  POWs' uniforms 52–3
  POWs' work for Detaining Power 29–32, 55–6, 63, 167
  Protecting Power provisions 23–4, 36, 88
  Protecting Powers' rights of access to POW camps 23–4
  protection of POWs 2–3, 37–8, 57–8, 87–8, 117–18, 121, 194, 200–1, 218, 238–9
  reciprocal protection of Allied and German POWs 5, 13–14, 17–19, 56, 186–7, 225
  religious and cultural activity 121–7, 210–11
  scope of protection 53–4
  segregation in 141–6
  segregation of Jewish POWs 140–1, 172, 175–6, 141–6, 206, 229–30
  supremacy of military law of Detaining Power 86
  time limit for POW status of escaped POWs 88–9
  see also current explanations for German treatment of Jewish POWs; International Committee of the Red Cross
German armed forces see German soldiers; Wehrmacht
German POWs, reciprocal protection of Allied and German POWs 5, 9, 13–14, 17–19, 56, 186–7, 225

German soldiers
  adherence to military discipline and values 41
  anti-Semitic behaviour and motivations 40–1
  behaviour of 96–7
  capital punishment in the German army 41
  cohesion and discipline 96–7
  ideology 96–7
  interactions with Jewish POWs 40–2
  military value system 97
  non-fighting troops 97–8
  see also POW camp personnel
Giraud, Henri, General 153–4, 218–19
Glantz, Alexander 88, 92–3
Glesner, Jack 87
Glovinsky, Haim 137–8
Goebbels, Joseph 153–4, 188–9, 194, 218–19, 225–8, 239–40
Goldenberg, Martin 103
Gollop, Dayan Mark, Rabbi 172
Graevenitz, Hans von, Lieutenant General 32 (34), 219–20
Greek POWs 4
Green, Julius, Captain 108–9, 121
Griggs, James 173–4
Grüner, Mosche 90–1, 118

Hagen, Hermann, Lieutenant General 221
Halder, Franz, Colonel-General 48–9
Hecht, Ignaz 198–201, 229
Heydrich, Reinhard 9, 140–1, 144, 191, 195, 206, 228–9, 234–6
Higher SS and Police Leaders (Höherer SS- und Polizeiführer - HSSPF) see SS
Himmler, Heinrich 33–5, 57, 157–68, 182–4, 188–9, 197, 201, 218–19, 221–5
historiography
  author's approach in current book 3, 36–8
  current explanations for German treatment of Jewish POWs 17–22, 36–7
  German POW organization 27–36
  literature review 7–17
  numbers of Jewish POWs 3–7
  POW organization, policy and regime 7–16
  shortcomings of previous studies and research 36–7
  see also current explanations for German treatment of Jewish POWs
Hitler, Adolf
  ascension to power 54–5, 89, 97–8, 153, 214–15
  assassination attempt on (July 1944 'Bomb Plot') 33–5, 157, 184, 221–2
  Gottlob, and General SS 224–5, 230–1

264 INDEX

Hitler, Adolf (*cont.*)
  black POWs, and 15–16
  British concerns about possible actions against POWs 222
  Burckhardt, and 177
  Commander-in-Chief of the Wehrmacht 21–2, 32, 37–8, 182, 201, 185–9
  Führer Orders *see* Führer Orders
  Geneva Convention, and 17, 18–19, 35–6, 54–5, 89, 214–15, 218
  Holocaust, and 64–5
  Bormann, and 202
  OKW's loyalty to 213–14
  OKW's status under 9
  POW policy involvement 15, 18–19, 55–6, 183–9, 228–31
  POWs' defiance of 88
  Brauchitsch, and Field Marshall 182
  'War of Extermination' in the East 11–12, 17
  Wehrmacht's loyalty to 97, 190–1
  Keitel, and Field Marshall 191–2
  see also Führer Orders
Höherer SS- und Polizeiführer (Higher SS and Police Leaders) *see* SS
Holocaust
  absence of Führer Order to extend to Jewish POWs 195, 214, 225–8, 238, 240–1
  historiography 7–13, 25–6, 38
  mass murder phase 61–2, 109, 128–9, 236–7
  origins of 196–7
  POWs and 2–3, 39–40, 46–7, 78–9, 110–11, 135–6
  progression of 57
  reports in Allied press 39
  revealing of 174–5, 177–8
  segregation of Jewish POWs, and 174–5, 229–30
  survival of Jewish POWs as challenge to accepted view of 239–41
Holocaust victims
  interactions with Jewish POWs 105, 117–21
  non-Jewish POWs' rescue efforts 139
  shared identity with Jewish POWs 117–21
Horowitz, Leon 125–6
HSSPF *see* SS

ICRC *see* International Committee of the Red Cross
identification *see* segregation
Imhoff, Freiherr Christoph von, Lieutenant Colonel 218–19
IMIs *see* Italian POWs
International Committee of the Red Cross (ICRC)
  archive sources 23–4, 82
  categorisation of POW groups 43–4, 51
  communication with Jewish organizations 25, 37, 49–50, 174–7
  communication with national governments 43–4, 49–51, 58–9, 81, 131, 135, 174, 217–18
  communication with OKW POW Office 33–5, 193, 206–7
  communication with POW MOCs 81
  communication with POWs 81–2, 112, 124–6, 132, 134, 137, 223–4
  coverage of POW camp incidents by reports of 99
  delegations 24–5, 42–3, 82, 121, 143, 148, 172–5, 177, 206–7
  headquarters 121, 172–3
  president 43–4, 175, 177
  records of POWs 50–1
  Reich Security Main Office (RSHA) and 175
  reports 24, 58–9, 63, 65, 68–9, 73–4, 94–5, 126–7, 147, 162, 169–70
  segregation of Jewish POWs 139–44, 147–9, 152–3, 155–6, 158–9, 162, 169, 171–9
  visits to POW camps 23–5, 32, 49–51, 64–5, 69–70, 76, 83–4, 99, 126–7, 147, 149, 158, 220
International Reaction to Segregation of Jewish POWs 171–7
Italian POW camps 5
Italian POWs ('Italian Military Internees' or IMIs)
  Führer Order for execution of captured Italian officers 193–4
  protection by Geneva Convention 5

Jay, Alec 60–1
Jewish identity
  alignment of components of 136
  author's approach in current book 3, 37, 102, 105
  capture and transit 105–11
  concealment of 136–7
  cultural activity 121–7
  cultural expression 121–7
  differences within 135–6
  experience in World War I and World War II contrasted 103
  funerals 127–35
  history, in 102–3
  Holocaust victims, shared identity with 117–21
  impact of captivity on 135–6
  impact of World War II on 136–7
  importance for soldiers' self-identity 103

inconsistencies in German approach 137
interactions between Jewish POWs and
  Holocaust victims 117–21
keeping of 136–8
maintenance of 105
maintenance of as act of defiance 137–8
Palestinian Jews 103–4
Palestinian POWs 111–15, 136
POW camps, in 111–15
POW testimony 135
religion as private matter 104
religious activity 121–7
segregation 115–17
Jewish organisations, communication with ICRC
  see International Committee of the Red
  Cross; World Jewish Congress
Jewish POWs (Allied)
  concentration/extermination camps,
    in 10–11
  equal treatment of Jewish and non-Jewish
    POWs according to nationality 7
  escapes 91–4
  historiography 9–11
  interactions with people outside POW
    camps 100
  judicial proceedings as to 86–9
  medical treatment 89–91
  numbers of 5
  overview of POW experience 94–101
  reactions to discrimination and
    mistreatment 99
  see also current explanations for German
    treatment of Jewish POWs
Jewish POWs (British and American)
  author's approach in current book 3, 36–8
  capture and transit 42–56, 105–11
  (non-)existence of official policy to treat
    Jewish POWs differently 96
  experience of captivity see POW camps
  experience of discrimination 58–61
  extent of discrimination and mistreatment 95
  Final Solution (Holocaust), and 2–3
  focus of current book on 5, 6
  Geneva Convention protection see Geneva
    Convention (1929)
  historiography 7–17
  interactions with camp guards 40–2
  interactions with Holocaust victims 117–21
  Jewish identity see Jewish identity
  number of American POWs 6
  number of British POWs 6
  overview of POW experience 94–101
  protection by Wehrmacht see POW Office;
    Wehrmacht

reactions to discrimination and
  mistreatment 99
RSHA 'Special Treatment' policy 1–2
survival 38
see also American POWs (Jewish and
  non-Jewish)
Jewish soldiers
  American armed forces, in 6
  British armed forces, in 6
Jodl, Alfred, Colonel General 18–19, 188–9
Judaism see religion
judicial proceedings as to Jewish POWs 86–9

Kaltenbrunner, Ernst 175, 194, 196–7, 221–2
Kaplan, Simon, Sergeant 77–8
Karlenboim, Yosef, Sergeant 78–80, 83, 90, 99,
  120–3, 131
Kasten, Johann, Private 164–5
Kastner, Rudolf 239–40
Keitel, Wilhelm, Field Marshal 32, 33–5 (35),
  185–6, 191–3, 196, 201, 218
Kinoy, Ernst 116–17
Koller, Karl, General 196–7
Krafft, Theodor, Lieutenant Colonel 152–3,
  196, 201
Krauze, Eliahu 131
Krauze, Eliyahu 82–3
Kriegsgefangenenwesen see POW Office
  (OKW)
Kuptsow, Aaron, Second Lieutenant 110

Lange, Walter 52–3
Lerner, Irving, Flight Engineer 158–9
Levinas, Emmanuel 181–2
Levine, Bernie, Lieutenant 108–9
Lifson, Irving, Captain 158–9
Lindeiner, Friedrich Von, Colonel 218–19
literature review see historiography
Loevsky, Louis, Second Lieutenant 105–6
Lorbeerbaum, Samuel 87

MacMichael, Harold, Sir 50
Manstein, Ernst von, Field Marshal 192
Margesson, David 50
Marti, Roland 172–3
Meinel, Karl, Major 154–5
Merz, Ludwig, Captain 164, 166–7
Metz, Erwin, Sergeant 166–7
minority and political groups see black POWs;
  Spanish Republican POWs
Morris, John 106
Morrison, Herbert 53–4
Moyne, Walter Guinness, 1st Baron 50
Müller, Heinrich 195

Namier, Lewis 51–2
National Socialist Leadership Officers programme (Nationalsozialistischer Führungsoffizier – NSFO) *see* Nazi Party
Nazi Party (Nationalsozialistische Deutsche Arbeiterpartei – NSDAP)
  archive sources 23
  attempts to control POW-related matters 189
  author's approach in current book 37–8, 232
  blood donation order 210–11
  membership 153
  National Socialist Leadership Officers programme (Nationalsozialistischer Führungsoffizier - NSFO) 98–9
  OKW and 35–6, 195–203
  POW Office and 184–5, 195–206, 221, 229, 232
  Wehrmacht and 189–90
  see also Nazi Party
Netherlands *see* Dutch POWs
New Zealand POWs 5
Norwegian POWs 3–4
NSDAP (Nationalsozialistische Deutsche Arbeiterpartei) *see* Nazi Party
NSFO (Nationalsozialistischer Führungsoffizier - National Socialist Leadership Officers programme) *see* Nazi Party

Oberkommando der Wehrmacht *see* OKW
Ofstein, Maurice 161
Ofstein, Wilfred 61, 118, 161, 232
OKW (Oberkommando der Wehrmacht - Armed Forces High Command)
  archive sources 23
  author's approach in current book 232
  Camp Commandants Manual 128–9
  conservative values 21–2, 237–8
  co-operation with Nazi orders and policies 21–2, 185, 228–9, 238
  current explanations for treatment of Jewish POWs 181–7, 189–95, 213–14, 228–9
  funeral guidelines 134–5
  guidelines and instructions to POW camps 17–18, 63, 121–3, 128–9, 157, 178–9
  jurisdiction over POW camps 28–9, 32–5, 57, 63, 140–1, 184, 236
  meetings with camp commanders 153–4
  Nazi Party and 35–6, 195–203
  Nazification 21–2, 213–14, 228–9
  non-cooperation with Nazi orders and policies 2–3, 237
  POW Office *see* POW Office (OKW)
  segregation, and 115, 141–6, 151–4, 157, 170–1, 178–9
  support for Geneva Convention 18–19, 57–8
  see also Wehrmacht
OKW General Office (Allgemeines Wehrmachtsamt - AWA) 9, 19, 32–5, 185–6, 203–6

Palestinian Jewish POWs
  author's approach in current book 42
  Jewish identity 103–4, 111–15, 136
  maintenance of Jewish identity 137
  overview of POW experience 94–101
  Palestinian Jews' recruitment in British armed forces 6
  reactions to discrimination and mistreatment 99
  religious expression 137
  Stalag VIII-B (Lamsdorf), in 61–85
Palter, Sam 118
Pantke, Fritz, Sergeant 82–4
Parkinson, Cosmo, Sir 51–2
Peter, Marc 174
Polish POWs
  historiography 8–9
  mistreatment of Jewish POWs 1–2
  number of 3–4, 8–9
  number of Jewish POWs 5, 8–9
political minority groups *see* Spanish Republican POWs
POW camp commanders *see* POW camp personnel
POW camp personnel
  behaviour of 12–13, 96–9
  Camp Commandants Manual 128–9
  compliance with Geneva Convention 17–18, 37, 39–40, 45–6, 57–61, 66–8, 70, 78–9, 82
  ideology 96–9
  numbers of 97–8
  OKW guidelines and instructions 17–18, 63, 121–3, 128–9, 157, 178–9
  Protecting Power communication with POW commanders 74–5, 132, 161–2, 201
POW camps
  activities outside the camps 85–94
  author's approach in current book 42
  escapes 91–4
  evacuation *see* evacuation of POW camps
  experience of captivity, author's approach in current book 37, 39–40
  ICRC and *see* International Committee of the Red Cross

interactions between POWs and guards 40–2
interactions between POWs and people outside camps 100
Italian POW camps 5
Jewish identity in *see* Jewish identity
life inside the camps 56–85
OKW jurisdiction 28–9, 32–5, 57, 63, 140–1, 184, 236
POWs' descriptions of captivity *see* POW testimonies (American); POW testimonies (British and Commonwealth); POW testimonies (French)
Protecting Powers' rights of access 23–4
protection of POWs from radicalization of POW policies 40, 100
segregation of Jewish POWs *see* segregation
specific camps *see* POW camps (specific camps)
'Total Institution,' as 40
transfer to SS control 40
transit of POWs to the camps 42–56, 105–11
see also POWs
POW camps (specific camps)
  Dulag 185 (Thessaloniki) 154–5
  locations (map) 29–32 (30)
  Oflag 65 (Berkenbrugge) 197–8
  Oflag IV-C (Colditz Castle) 10–11, 151–2
  Oflag V-B (Biberach) 150
  Oflag VI-B (Dössel) 150–1, 169
  Oflag VI-C (Osnabrück-Eversheide) 124–5, 133, 156
  Oflag VII-C (Laufen) 150–1
  Oflag X-B (Sandbostel) 221
  Oflag X-C (Lübeck) 151–2
  Oflag XIII-B (Nürnberg-Langwasser) 124–5, 133, 147–8, 218–19
  Oflag XIII-D (Hammelburg) 156
  Stalag 303 (Lillehammer) 209–10
  Stalag 319 (Cholm) 69, 172
  Stalag 344 (Lamsdorf) 67
  Stalag 383 (Hohenfels) 69, 114, 162
  Stalag I-B (Hohenstein) 29
  Stalag II-A (Neubrandenburg) 162–3
  Stalag II-B (Hammerstein) 63, 156–7
  Stalag II-D (Stargard) 209–10
  Stalag II-E (Schwerin) 209–10
  Stalag III-A (Luckenwalde) 159–60
  Stalag III-B (Fürstenberg an der Oder) 160–1
  Stalag III-D (Berlin) 220
  Stalag IV-A (Hohnstein) 61, 161
  Stalag IV-B (Mühlberg) 1–2, 124–6, 144, 161–2
  Stalag IV-C (Wistritz) 161–2
  Stalag IV-F (Hartmannsdorf) 57–8
  Stalag IX-A (Ziegenhain) 139, 164
  Stalag IX-B (Bad Orb) 11, 45, 102, 116–17, 125–6, 163–7
  Stalag IX-C (Bad Sulza) 87, 164
  Stalag Luft I (Barth) 45, 116, 125, 158–9, 162
  Stalag Luft II (Litzmannstadt (Lodz)) 154–5
  Stalag Luft III (Sagan) 19, 59, 133–4, 150, 160–1, 181–4, 187, 216–19
  Stalag Luft IV, (Gross Tychow (Tychowo)) 59–60, 65
  Stalag Luft VI (Heydekrug, (Šilutė)) 160–1
  Stalag Luft VII (Bankau (Bąków)) 161
  Stalag V-C (Offenburg) 126–7
  Stalag VII-A (Moosburg) 58–9, 118, 122, 125–7, 154, 162, 179
  Stalag VIII-B (Lamsdorf) 23–5, 29, 41, 56, 58–87, 90–4, 113–14, 118–21, 123–5, 127–8, 131–4, 137–8, 146–50, 168–9, 208–9
  Stalag VIII-B (Teschen) 168–9
  Stalag X-B (Sandbostel) 198–201
  Stalag XI-A (Altengrabow) 159–60
  Stalag XIII-C (Hammelburg) 46
  Stalag XVII-B (Gneixendorf) 126–7, 133, 169–70
  Stalag XVIII-A (Wolfsberg) 56, 58–9, 90–1, 147, 149
  Stalag XVIII-C (Markt Pongau) 102, 125–6
  Stalag XVIII-D (Marburg an der Drau (Maribur)) 56, 147
  Stalag XXI-B (Thure (Tur)) 63
  typical layout (diagram) 29–32 (31)
POW exchanges *see* POW policy and regime
POW Office (OKW) (Kriegsgefangenenwesen)
  author's approach in current book 37–8
  communication with ICRC 33–5, 193, 206–7
  current explanations for German treatment of Jewish POWs 203–13
  historiography 15
  jurisdiction over POW camps 28–9, 32–5, 57, 63, 140–1, 184, 236
  Nazi Party and 184–5, 195–206, 221, 229, 232
  non-cooperation with Nazi racial policy 2–3
  protection of POWs 37–8
  role of 214–25
POW organization, policy and regime
  author's approach in current book 37, 232
  equal treatment of Jewish and non-Jewish POWs according to nationality 7
  (non-)existence of official policy to treat Jewish POWs differently 96

POW organization, policy and regime (*cont.*)
  Geneva Convention, and *see* Geneva Convention (1929)
  historiography 7–17, 27–36
  locations of POW camps (map) 29–32 (30)
  organization structures (diagrams) 32 (33–5)
  POW exchanges 14–15
  POWs from minority and political groups 15–16
  protection of Jewish POWs *see* POW Office; Wehrmacht
  protection within POW camps from radicalization of policies 40
  reciprocal protection of Allied and German POWs 5, 9, 13–14
  segregation of Jewish POWs *see* segregation
  treatment of POWs according to uniform worn at capture 52–3
  typical layout of POW camps (diagram) 29–32 (31)
  wartime radicalization of 1–2, 40
  Wehrmacht's approach and role in 37–8
  see also OKW; POW camps; POW camps (specific camps); POW Office; SS
POW testimonies (American)
  Barlow, David 116–17
  Caplan, Aben, Technical Sergeant 109–10, 122
  Cornell, Edwin 116–17
  Daub, Gerald 109–10
  Edmonds, Roddie, Master Sergeant 139
  Feldman, Milton 1–2, 125–6
  Fine, Hyman, Second Lieutenant 45
  Fox, Sonny 45, 102
  Gattung, Harold, Corporal 46
  Horowitz, Leon 125–6
  Kinoy, Ernst 116–17
  Kuptsow, Aaron, Second Lieutenant 110
  Lerner, Irving, Flight Engineer 158–9
  Levine, Bernie, Lieutenant 108–9
  Lifson, Irving, Captain 158–9
  Loevsky, Louis, Second Lieutenant 105–6
  Palter, Sam 118
  Radish, Harold 109–10
  Schenk, David 109–10
  Shapiro, William 104
  Spivey, Delmar, Colonel 59, 132, 160–1, 181–2
  Stovroff, Irwin, Second Lieutenant 45
  Weiner, Fred, Staff Sergeant 116
  Westheimer, David 118
  Whiteway, Curtis 46
  Winograd, Leonard 39, 44–5, 110
POW testimonies (British and Commonwealth)
  Altman, Richard, Private 132–3
  Ben-Aharon, Yitschak 84, 150
  Blumenfeld, Jacob, Private 159–60
  Chapman, Edward 150–1
  Cohen, Clifford, Second Lieutenant 150–1
  Crew, Henry, Gunner 134
  Denton, Patrick 150–1
  Elkind, Yitshak 127–8
  Galler, Harry, Private 63
  Glantz, Alexander 88, 92–3
  Glesner, Jack 87
  Goldenberg, Martin 103
  Green, Julius, Captain 108–9, 121
  Grüner, Mosche 118
  Jay, Alec 60–1
  Karlenboim, Yosef 90, 120–3, 131
  Krauze, Eliahu 131
  Ofstein, Wilfred 61, 118, 161, 232
  Rofe, Cyril 61, 64, 90, 131
  Rubenstein, Norman 43, 45–6, 63, 93, 103
  Sakol, Bernard 108–9
  Saunders, George 90
  Schustermann, Assir, Sergeant Major 63
  Sela, Shlomo 62, 68
  Weiner, Paul 49, 84–5, 119
  Weinstein, Tibor 64, 88–9, 92
  Yerushalmi, Aharon 92
  Zigelbaum, Moshe 92, 118
  Zmudziak, Isac 66
POW testimonies (French)
  Berg, Roger 102
  Hecht, Ignaz 198–201, 229
primary sources 22–7, 36–7
prisoners of war *see* POWs
Protecting Power
  communication with Allied governments 172
  communication with German authorities 33, 69, 72, 87, 131, 135–6, 170
  communication with POW commanders 74–5, 132, 161–2, 201
  communication with POWs 24–5, 32, 68, 99, 112, 134, 137, 149–50, 155–6, 177–8
  definition of 14n.42
  deterrent role 152–3, 178–9, 218
  execution of captured Allied airmen, and 194
  Geneva Convention, and 23–4, 36, 88
  legal representation by 88, 89
  reports 24, 58–60, 63, 67–8, 71–2, 82, 94–5, 126–7, 147–8, 155–6, 158–9, 162, 169–70, 178–9
  rights of access to POW camps 23–4
  role of 49–50
  Scapini delegation as 173–4
  segregation, and 139–40, 147–8, 172
  Sweden as 55n.88
  Switzerland as 82, 132, 149–50, 162–3, 172, 201

USA as 23–4, 49–50, 63, 65, 149–50
visits to POW camps 23–4, 78, 83–4, 99, 125, 132, 148–9, 155–6, 158, 161–6, 217–18

racial policy
   author's approach in current book 37–8
   extermination of Soviet POWs 5
   historiography 11–12
   OKW non-cooperation with 2–3
   wartime radicalization of 1–2, 37–8
   see also Holocaust
Radish, Harold 109–10
Read, Fredrick, Regimental Sergeant Major 86–7
Red Cross Organization see International Committee of the Red Cross
Reich Security Main Office (Reichssicherheitshauptamt – RSHA)
   archive sources 23
   attempts to control POW camps 17, 57, 145, 156–7
   attempts to control POW-related matters 2–3, 17, 204, 216–18, 228–30, 233–4, 237–8, 241
   author's approach in current book 37–8, 232
   commissar order, and 228–9
   current explanations for German treatment of Jewish POWs 181–5, 189, 191–204, 210–11, 213–14, 221–2, 229
   head of 9, 194, 221–2
   ICRC and 175
   murder squads see Einsatzgruppen
   non-cooperation from POW camp commanders 236–7
   'Special Treatment' ('Sonderbehandlung') of Soviet Jewish POWs 1–2
Reichenau, Walter von, Field Marshal 192
Reichssicherheitshauptamt (RSHA) see Reich Security Main Office
Reinecke, Hermann, General 9, 32 (34), 32, 33–5 (35), 145, 185–6, 189, 191–3, 196, 201, 204, 218
religion
   expression of Jewish identity 137, 121–7
   Jewish identity, and 104, 121–7
   private matter for Jews, as 104
   see also Jewish identity
Renton, Colonel Alexander 48
Ribbentrop, Joachim von 224
Riegner, Gerhart 175
Rofe, Cyril 61, 64, 90, 131
Rommel, Erwin, Field Marshal 187
Roosevelt, Franklin 228
RSHA (Reichssicherheitshauptamt) see Reich Security Main Office
Rubenstein, Norman 43, 45–6, 63, 93, 103

Rubli, Jean-Maurice 64–5
Rundstedt, Gerd von, Field Marshal 197

SA (Sturmabteilung – Storm Detachment) 65, 67, 81–2, 94, 100, 120–1, 135–6
Sakol, Bernard 108–9
Saunders, George 90
Saur, Karl-Otto von, Lieutenant-General 154
Scapini, Georges 151–2, 173–4
Scapini delegation as Protecting Power 173–4
Schenk, David 109–10
Schienkiewicz, Erwin, Sergeant-Major SS 46
Schustermann, Assir, Sergeant Major 63
Schutzstaffeln see SS
Schwartz, Phil 159–60
Schwarzbart, Ignacy 173–4
Schweiger, Otto 87
SD see Sicherheitsdienst
Second World War see World War II
segregation
   author's approach in current book 37, 139
   first stage of German persecution of Jews, as 139–40
   Geneva Convention, and 141–6
   ICRC acceptance of 139–40
   identification of Jewish POWs 168–71
   inconsistencies in German approach 137
   initial cases under OKW 146–57
   international reaction to 171–7
   Jewish identity, and 115–17
   late cases under Himmler 157–68
   OKW orders as to 141–6
   POW camps, in 115–17
   POW testimony 139
Sela, Shlomo 62, 68
Shapiro, William 104
Sherriff, Sydney, Regimental Sergeant Major 62
Sicherheitsdienst (SD) (SS Security Service) 154–5, 187, 191, 193–4, 196–7, 227–8
Sieber, Karl, Colonel 164–5
Silverman, Sydney 173–4
Simoleit, Gustav, Major 133–4
Smoira, Moshe 52–3
sources of information see historiography
South African POWs 5
Soviet POWs
   Einsatzgruppen executions 1–2
   German non-compliance with Geneva Convention 4
   historiography 8–9
   Jewish POWs 5
   Nazi racial policy 5
   number of 1–2, 4
   number of deaths of 4
   'Special Treatment' 1–2

Spanish Republican POWs 15–16, 213–14
'Special Treatment' 1–2
Spicer, Henry, Colonel 158–9
Spivey, Delmar, Colonel 59, 132, 160–1, 181–2
SS (Schutzstaffeln - Protection Squads)
   archive sources 23
   current explanations for treatment of
      Jewish POWs 17
   escaped POWs, and 91–2, 184
   Higher SS and Police Leaders (Höherer
      SS- und Polizeiführer - HSSPF) 33–5,
      196–7, 222–3
   individuals' alignment with Nazi ideology 45–7
   jurisdiction over POW camps 11, 33–5,
      40, 57, 156–7, 164, 167–8, 178–9, 184,
      196–7, 201, 207–8, 214, 221–5,
      230–1, 236–7
   murder squads *see* Einsatzgruppen
   treatment of Jewish POWs 60–1, 88–90, 93,
      94, 121, 124–5, 135–6, 154–5, 166–7, 183,
      217, 220, 224–5
Storm Detachment (Sturmabteilung) *see* SA
Stovroff, Irwin, Second Lieutenant 45
Sturmabteilung *see* SA
Sweden as Protecting Power 55n.88
Switzerland as Protecting Power 82, 132,
   149–50, 162–3, 172, 201

Thierack, Otto 170
transit of POWs *see* capture and transit

United States (USA), Protecting Power, as 23–4,
   49–50, 63, 65, 149–50

Wagner, Eduard, General 191–2
Waltzog, Alfons 52–3, 144–5
'War of Extermination' in the East 11–12, 17,
   101, 228–31
Warner, Sydney Jeannetta 50–1
Warrender, Victor 106
Wehrmacht
   author's approach in current book 37–8
   capital punishment in the German
      army 41
   cooperation with Einsatzgruppen 1–2
   cooperation with Nazi racial policies 11–12
   High Command *see* OKW
   historiography 11–12

Nazification 11–13, 97–9, 101
POW organization *see* POW Office; POW
   organization, policy and regime
protection of POWs 37–8
Supreme Commander *see* Hitler, Adolf
'War of Extermination' in the East,
   and 101
see also German soldiers; OKW
Weiner, Fred, Staff Sergeant 116
Weiner, Paul 49, 84–5, 119
Weinstein, Tibor 64, 88–9, 92
Westheimer, David 118
Westhoff, Adolf, General 32 (34), 145, 187–9,
   196, 201, 215–16
Westrem, Reinhard von, Lieutenant General 23,
   156–7, 218–19
Whiteway, Curtis, Staff Sergeant 46
Winant, John 50
Winograd, Leonard 39, 44–5, 110
Wittmer, Bertold, Major SS 154–5
WJC *see* World Jewish Congress
World Jewish Congress (WJC)
   archive sources 25
   communication with ICRC 49–50, 173–7
   segregation, and 142–3, 173–7
World War I
   capital punishment in the German army 41
   Jewish identity in 103
World War II
   Allied victories 1942–45 5
   capital punishment in the German army 41
   German victories 1939–42 3–4
   Jewish identity in 103, 136–7
   'War of Extermination' in the East 11–12, 17,
      101, 190–1

Yerushalmi, Aharon 92
Yugoslavian POWs
   historiography 13–14
   mistreatment of Jewish POWs 1–2
   number of 4
   number of Jewish POWs 5
   reciprocal protection with German
      POWs 13–14

Zemke, Hubert, Colonel 158–9
Zigelbaum, Moshe 92, 118
Zmudziak, Isac 66